Understanding Law for Public Administration

Charles Szypszak, JD

Professor of Public Law and Government
University of North Carolina at Chapel Hill
School of Government
Chapel Hill, North Carolina

JONES AND BARTLETT PUBLISHERS

Sudbury, Massachusetts

BOSTON   TORONTO   LONDON   SINGAPORE

World Headquarters

Jones and Bartlett Publishers
40 Tall Pine Drive
Sudbury, MA 01776
978-443-5000
info@jbpub.com
www.jbpub.com

Jones and Bartlett Publishers
Canada
6339 Ormindale Way
Mississauga, Ontario L5V 1J2
Canada

Jones and Bartlett Publishers
International
Barb House, Barb Mews
London W6 7PA
United Kingdom

Jones and Bartlett's books and products are available through most bookstores and online booksellers. To contact Jones and Bartlett Publishers directly, call 800-832-0034, fax 978-443-8000, or visit our website at www.jbpub.com.

Substantial discounts on bulk quantities of Jones and Bartlett's publications are available to corporations, professional associations, and other qualified organizations. For details and specific discount information, contact the special sales department at Jones and Bartlett via the above contact information or send an email to specialsales@jbpub.com.

This publication is designed to provide accurate and authoritative information in regard to the Subject Matter covered. It is sold with the understanding that the publisher is not engaged in rendering legal, accounting, or other professional service. If legal advice or other expert assistance is required, the service of a competent professional person should be sought.

Production Credits
Publisher: Michael Brown
Editorial Assistant: Catie Heverling
Editorial Assistant: Teresa Reilly
Senior Production Editor: Tracey Chapman
Associate Production Editor: Kate Stein
Senior Marketing Manager: Sophie Fleck
Manufacturing and Inventory Control Supervisor: Amy Bacus
Composition: Achorn International
Art: DiacriTech
Cover Design: Scott Moden
Cover Image: © Sebastian Kaulitzki/ShutterStock, Inc.
Printing and Binding: Malloy, Inc.
Cover Printing: Malloy, Inc.

Library of Congress Cataloging-in-Publication Data
Szypszak, Charles.
    Understanding law for public administration / Charles Szypszak.
      p. cm.
    Includes bibliographical references and index.
    ISBN-13: 978-0-7637-8011-1 (pbk.)
    ISBN-10: 0-7637-8011-1 (pbk.)
    1. Administrative law—United States. I. Title.
KF5402.S99 2009
  342.73—dc22

                                                    2009029077
6048

Printed in the United States of America
15 14   10 9 8 7 6 5 4 3

Contents

Preface

In our time cynicism about the law abounds. The legislative process often seems aimless and individuals regularly seem to suffer injustice in the court system. Despite even the best intentions, the law will be flawed—it is a human endeavor subject to human limitations and differences. But history proves that there is no form of governance better suited to the pursuit of happiness than a rule of law. Studying the law in principle and in practice enables us to honor it when it works and to reform it when it does not.

This book is for students and practitioners of public administration and policy and for anyone else who wants to better understand how law relates to the public good. It combines an introduction to basic legal principles, an analysis of instructive cases, and consideration of practicalities. Material is arranged sequentially to build a cohesive analytical framework. The first five chapters consider the notion of a rule of law and fundamental constitutional law principles. The next eight chapters introduce basic law subjects regularly encountered in government affairs but not traditionally covered in public administration classrooms. The material includes opinions from 24 cases, abridged to enable readers to focus on the points relevant to the discussion. Some of the opinions are from landmark U.S. Supreme Court opinions, others are especially informative and illustrative cases from other federal and state courts. All were chosen for the insight they give into how judges interpret the law and define fundamental rights. The final two chapters discuss the nature of working with lawyers and researching the law for self-education—information that could be helpful for making sound decisions.

This book is realistic, but no cynicism is intended. Its perspective was formed not only from law study and teaching but also from more than 20 years of direct experience giving legal advice, representing adversaries in disputes, and working with public officials on legal problems and law reform. This experience has revealed serious shortcomings with the legal system. It also has illuminated the importance of taking personal responsibility for doing better. Making the right choices should matter to us all, whether from religious belief in an eternal soul, philosophical conclusion about a moral life, or scientific knowledge that even the flap of a butterfly's wings is part of atmospheric change. No one alone can change the world, but our fate depends on the cumulative effect of individual choices. As Plato said, "The penalty good men pay for indifference to public affairs is to be ruled by evil men." Understanding the law helps us to find the best path. And as Anne Frank said in the most dire of situations, "How wonderful it is that nobody need wait a single moment before starting to improve the world."

Charles Szypszak

About the Author

Charles Szypszak is Professor of Public Law and Government at the School of Government at the University of North Carolina at Chapel Hill. He provides counsel to state, national, and international institutions, organizations, and public officials on real property registration and conveyance laws and other public law subjects. He also teaches Law for Public Administration in the School's graduate program in public administration. Prior to 2005 he was a director of a general practice firm in New Hampshire and an adjunct professor of law at Franklin Pierce Law Center. He is the author of several books and many articles on real property and other law topics. He earned a BA from the University of Southern California, an MA from San Diego State University, and a JD from the University of Virginia School of Law, and he was a Captain in the U.S. Marine Corps.

About Using This Book

This book provides an introduction to all aspects of law and the legal system that someone in public administration is likely to encounter. It is not a comprehensive encyclopedic resource or complete or necessarily current statement of the law. Anyone considering a legal issue should do current research and seek legal counsel as appropriate. But the basics covered in this book should provide a starting point and context for further research of most legal issues encountered in public affairs.

To understand law's unifying themes, all 15 chapters are best read in the order in which they are presented. The final chapter on legal research provides tools for continuing self-education. Instructors who want to supplement readings and discussion with research and writing assignments should consider assigning the final chapter soon after the first. One approach to research assignments that has proved successful involves three projects. The first requires students to find specific sources in response to prompts similar to the examples at the end of the final chapter. This introduces students first hand to the major resources and familiarizes them with challenges peculiar to legal research. The second assignment involves supplying students with a statute and a couple of relevant cases and requires them to describe how this authority sheds light on a policy question also supplied to them. The third assignment requires researching and describing the law governing an assigned problem likely to arise in public administration. The overall sequence builds some confidence in doing basic legal research and provides a better sense of its inherent limitations especially for someone without a law school education and legal experience.

Within the book, reference notes are provided only when specific attribution is necessary. The 24 opinion excerpts are abridged to present the material essential to the discussion within which they appear. Omissions from the opinions are shown only if they are part of a sentence.

Chapter 1

What Is Law?

We are firmly convinced, and we act on that conviction, that with nations as with individuals,
our interests soundly calculated will ever be found inseparable from our moral duties.

Thomas Jefferson

CHAPTER OBJECTIVES

After studying this chapter you should better understand:

- What is commonly meant by a rule of law
- The nature of formal law and its limits for governing behavior
- The interrelationship of norms, moral codes, and formal laws
- The fundamental characteristics of the U.S. constitutional system
- The basic sources of formal law in the U.S. legal system

The law is our constant companion. As with most companions, our relationship is complex; sometimes supportive and other times maddening. Abortion, the death penalty, prayer in schools, government takings, and affirmative action are only a few examples of current issues that are the subject of much public attention and serious disagreement. Courthouses and law offices are crowded with individuals immersed in the legal process as parties or witnesses in criminal proceedings and civil lawsuits. The system is conspicuous in American culture: it is a recurrent setting for film and television, in popular novels, and in casual conversation. Jokes about lawyers are commonplace, as are expressions of frustration with lawyers' influence. Yet becoming a lawyer still attracts many of the nation's most gifted and ambitious individuals. There are more than 750 thousand lawyers in the country,[1] and hundreds of law schools produce a steady stream of new graduates. To what extent do the perceptions we have about the law and about the legal process reflect their true nature?

This book examines the nature of the law and of the legal process. It also describes the general nature of the laws, cases, and legal principles that public administrators are most likely to encounter. A grasp of these subjects can be valuable to anyone. But more than passing familiarity with basic law subjects is necessary for public administrators to be able to make wise decisions about issues and problems involving the law. Decision makers should also appreciate the nature of sources of law and what makes laws matter or not matter.

The question considered in this chapter, "What is law?" is not just an academic exercise. Law is much more than the words of legislators or judges that can be found in published statutes and court decisions. Law does involve such rules, but decision makers should not assume that these rules explain what governs the behavior of others. Law involves more amorphous but equally important considerations. Everyone knows that there are formal laws that are routinely ignored and that there are sources of constraints on behavior other than formal law. Public administrators therefore should consider formal laws and what makes them legitimate as well as other factors that govern behavior.

This chapter considers the sources of rules that govern our behavior, including what we mean when we say a society is governed by a "rule of law," and the nature of natural and formal legal constraints. It also provides an introduction to the formal sources of law in the U.S. legal system, including legislation, court decisions, agency regulations, and international laws. Together these subjects build a framework for exploration in the remainder of this book of the substance of modern law and the operation of the legal process.

Rules and Their Legitimacy

Common notions about law involve rules that govern behavior and relationships. The terms "positive law" and "formal law" are used to refer to a set of rules that a government proclaims and enforces. Humans are not necessarily ruled by formal law; a society can be imagined in which there is none. "Anarchy" refers to a condition in which society is not effectively governed by any government or formal laws. As James Madison, the primary architect of the U.S. Constitution, said, "If men were angels, no government would be necessary."[2] But humans are not angels, and the experience of civilization shows that anarchic conditions are likely to result in violence and destruction. As William Golding put it in his classic novel *Lord of the Flies*, humans seem to face a choice: "Which is better—to have laws and agree, or to hunt and kill?"[3]

It is easy to see that it is better to be ruled by laws to which we agree than by primitive force, but throughout history civilizations have struggled with the essential question of how those laws are determined. The philosopher Plato, in *The Republic*, described the possibility of ideal rules emanating from benevolent "philosopher kings" who would use their power and superior intellect in society's best interest. But history has not given us much reason to expect such philosophic or benevolent tendencies from those with power. Autocratic rule has tended to entail flagrant abuses. In 1933, Hitler used the "The Law for Removing the Distress of People and Reich" to give himself the unfettered power he needed for fascist rule.[4] The Soviets, who also presided over a brutally repressive regime, were expert at adopting formal rules. Their constitution cynically proclaimed that "citizens of the USSR have the right to protection by the courts against encroachments on their honor and reputation, life and health, and personal freedom and property."[5] But encroachment upon life, liberty, and property occurred at the pleasure of those who controlled the state and the party apparatus. These and many other experiences confirm economist Frederic Bastiat's observation that "the law has been applied to annihilating the justice that it was supposed to maintain; to limiting and destroying rights which its real purpose was to respect. The law has placed the collective force at the disposal of the unscrupulous who wish, without risk, to exploit the person, liberty, and property of others. It has converted plunder into a right, in order to protect plunder."[6]

Rule of Law

The founders of the U.S. legal system were well aware of the lessons of history about human tendencies toward seizing power and oppressing others. When they declared independence from England they listed the king's "abuses and usurpations" against them, and they declared a right to oppose such oppression by instituting a new government that would better protect rights they said were "unalienable." They sought to create a country governed by a "rule of law." As Chief Justice John Marshall famously said in one of the earliest cases decided by the U.S. Supreme Court, "The government of the United States has been emphatically termed a government of laws, and not of men."[7] Since then, government leaders and scholars have continued to refer to an ideal as a rule of law, usually as a contrast to the extremes of anarchy and authoritarianism. What does it really mean to be governed by a rule of law?

Powerful concepts embedded within the notion of a government of laws include a conviction that the law should be adopted in an open and democratic process. In a republic, elected representatives enact the formal laws through a legislative process. The legitimacy of these formal laws stems from the notion of the consent of the governed. As explained by philosopher John Locke, whose ideas were expressed in the Declaration of Independence, although we are born into a state of natural law and no one has inherent power over others, "every man that hath any possession or enjoyment of any part of the dominions of any government doth thereby give his tacit consent, and is as far forth obliged to obedience to the laws of government during such enjoyment as anyone under it."[8] According to this view of government's legitimacy, the people empower their representatives to make and enforce rules for the common good, which are applied to everyone.[9]

The U.S. Agency for International Development invokes broader concepts when it says:

> *The term 'rule of law' embodies the basic principles of equal treatment of all people before the law, fairness, and both constitutional and actual guarantees of basic human rights. A predictable legal system with fair, transparent, and effective judicial institutions is essential to the protection of citizens against the arbitrary use of state authority and lawless acts of both organizations and individuals.*[10]

This well-reasoned definition of a rule of law refers to other conditions that must exist together with rules. Legitimacy comes not only from the process by which the rules are adopted and enforced, but also the extent to which the rules reflect society's customs and notions of proper human conduct.

Natural Law

The existence of formal laws alone does not equate to a rule of law. We know from history that lofty constitutional principles and comprehensive legislative schemes cannot by themselves guarantee rights and freedom. Formal law does not constrain harmful tendencies or protect individual liberties unless it coexists with mutual respect for individual rights within society. Thomas Jefferson warned about confusing observance of formal law with liberty. He said that "rightful liberty is unobstructed action according to our will within the limits drawn around us by the equal rights of others. I do not add 'within the limits of the law' because law is often but the tyrant's will, and always so when it violates the rights of an individual."[11] Jefferson thereby reminded us that law can be something worse than an empty or cynical exercise, and time has proved him right.

We also know that even when formal laws are the product of a representative enactment process they do not always govern public behavior. Some laws are entirely unknown to the public or even though known they are routinely ignored. For example, there are state laws that still proscribe sexual conduct in which adults routinely privately engage. We also hear of inane laws, such as those prohibiting sleeping while wearing shoes or playing dominoes on a Sunday. Laws are not seen as legitimate unless they reflect community notions of right and wrong. Law philosopher Ronald Dworkin put it this way: the legal rule "represents the community's effort to capture moral rights."[12] When a formal law fails to capture those rights, or loses touch with them, the law is likely not to be followed or enforced.

Formal rules also fail to result in a rule of law when they become too distant or unwieldy. The power of formal law and legal process cannot possibly reach all aspects of interactions among members of a society. Economist Frederick Hayek noted this natural limitation when he said that a rule of law "means, not that everything is regulated by law, but, on the contrary, that the coercive power of the state can be used only in cases defined in advance by the law and in such a way that it can be foreseen how it will be used."[13] Even the American Bar Association's Model Rules of Professional Conduct acknowledge the limitations of rule formalization. The description of the rules' scope includes the following comment:

> *Compliance with the Rules, as with all law in an open society, depends primarily upon understanding and voluntary compliance, secondarily upon reinforcement by peer and public opinion and finally, when necessary, upon enforcement through disciplinary proceedings. The Rules do not, however, exhaust the moral and ethical considerations that should inform a lawyer, for no worthwhile human activity can be completely defined by legal rules. The Rules simply provide a framework for the ethical practice of law.*[14]

To understand what does constrain human activity we must consider the extra-legal bonds that exist as a matter of common understanding and custom.

Laws are an accurate measure of behavior when they reflect basic notions of right The concept of natural law is a foundation of the American legal system. Natu been defined as "a system of rules and principles for the guidance of human conc independently of enacted law or of the systems particular to any one people, might be discovered by the rational intelligence of man, and would be found to grow out of and conform to his *nature*, meaning by that word his whole mental, moral, and physical constitution."[15] Many eminent philosophers, including Aristotle, Thomas Aquinas, Thomas Hobbes, John Locke, and Thomas Jefferson have described the importance of natural law to human society. Jefferson wrote of this concept in the Declaration of Independence when he referred to the unalienable rights of life, liberty, and the pursuit of happiness.

Obviously, notions of custom and morality guide those who enact and interpret the law. Legislatures sometimes expressly incorporate such concepts into their enacted laws. For example, unfair trade practice laws prohibit deception and authorize multiple damage awards and attorneys' fees compensation to those harmed by such behavior. Businesses have been struck with substantial verdicts based on violations of these standards of decency even in the harsh commercial realm. The law governing common sales also adopts boundaries of good faith. The Uniform Commercial Code declares that "[e]very contract or duty [governed by the Code] imposes an obligation of good faith in its performance or enforcement," which means "honesty in fact in the conduct or transaction concerned."[16] The Code also authorizes courts not to enforce a contract that is "unconscionable,"[17] which courts have used to invalidate contractual agreements based on perceived unreasonableness.[18]

Judges also sometime explicitly refer to natural law in their analysis. For example, North Carolina's constitution does not state that the government must pay compensation for property taken from citizens through exercise of the power of eminent domain, but the state's supreme court said that a right to compensation is "so grounded in natural law and justice that it is part of the fundamental law of this State."[19] Courts also regularly defer to a sense of community standards in defining other important constraints. For example, the U.S. Supreme Court invoked such standards for determining whether laws against obscenity violate constitutional guaranties of free expression. In the 1964 case *Jacobellis v. Ohio*,[20] involving an obscenity prosecution for a movie depicting an adulterous love scene, Justice Potter Stewart famously said, "I shall not today attempt further to define the kinds of material I understand to be embraced within that shorthand description; and perhaps I could never succeed in intelligibly doing so. But I know it when I see it, and the motion picture involved in this case is not that."[21] He believed that communities share unarticulated notions of unacceptable depictions of sexual material and that such notions could be the basis for deciding cases.

Even in the criminal context, our legal system acknowledges that the formal laws must sometimes defer to behavioral norms. This can be seen with "jury nullification," by which a jury decides a case based on the jury's sense of what is right without regard to the court's instructions. As one court put it, "The pages of history shine on instances of the jury's exercise of its prerogative to disregard uncontradicted evidence and instructions of the judge."[22] Judge Learned Hand described the jury as "introduc[ing] a slack into the enforcement of law, tempering its rigor by the mollifying influence of current ethical conventions."[23]

Community norms also underlie everyday exchanges. The innumerable social and business interactions in which individuals engage depend on trusting relationships and predominant norms of behavior by which individuals keep their word and act in good faith. Participants in a market economy rely on each other's willingness to do business, which can be diminished by a reputation for bad behavior. Reasonable business people prefer to expend their energies in a mutually cooperative way rather than focus on disagreements.[24] The limited reach of formal law means we must rely to a great extent on other constraints to govern our actions in our relationships. As Nobel Prize-winning economist Amartya Sen has explained, "Successful operation of an exchange economy depends on mutual trust and the use of norms—explicit and implicit. When these behavioral modes are plentiful, it is easy to overlook their role."[25] We depend on behavioral norms to facilitate our commercial and private interactions and constrain harmful tendencies, and these norms deserve attention as much when they are present as when they are absent.

Despite the inseparability of law and moral standards in core legal building blocks, much modern legal theory has strived to isolate morality from formal law analysis. Oliver Wendell Holmes, Jr., was the pathfinder in this movement. In his 1897 article "The Path of the Law," he launched a quest for "legal realism" based on what has been called "moral skepticism."[26] Although acknowledging that a community would resist laws that violated basic moral senses, Holmes said that confusing legal and moral ideas will render the law useless in its essential role of providing predictable rules. He argued that the law should be seen scientifically as "the prediction of the incidence of the public force through the instrumentality of the courts."[27] Whatever the merits of social realism in the development and application of coherent formal rules, it necessarily falls short of providing a complete picture of how a society is governed. The result, as legal scholar Lon L. Fuller said, is that "the legal mind generally exhausts itself in thinking about law and is content to leave unexamined the thing to which law is being related and from which it is being distinguished."[28] Analytically separating morality from formal law causes us to fail to appreciate the extent to which morality legitimates law and governs our extralegal behavior.

Sources of Norms

What is the nature of the norms and moral codes that legitimize laws and guide behavior? They have spiritual, philosophical, and social origins, and many bright minds and devout souls have searched for clarity about what is right. Aristotle's philosophy is a solid enough foundation for understanding the basic nature of behavioral norms, for several reasons. It is consistent with our predominant moral concepts. It profoundly influences the development of democratic government. It also puts virtue in the context of relationships, which is the sense in which morality results in constraints on behavior.

Aristotle saw moral virtues as habits that moderate between extremes. He said virtues are not instinctive—they must be learned and practiced within a culture.[29] Philosopher Leszek Kołakowski explained this notion of virtue as the "moral skills essential for life in a human community, [that] in one important respect resemble other, non-moral skills. . . . We learn virtues by being brought up in a community where they are practised, in the same way as we learn to swim, or to use a knife and fork."[30] Those who achieve these virtues aim their actions, in Aristotle's terms, "to the right person, to the right extent, at the right time, with the right motive, and in the right way."[31] Of the virtues identified by Aristotle, two in particular are at the heart of shared concepts of social norms of interactive behavior: truthfulness and justice. The person who loves truth, Aristotle said, will be "truthful where nothing is at stake, will still more be truthful where something is at stake; he will avoid falsehood as something base, seeing that he avoided it even for its own sake."[32] Justice is a closely related concept, which requires, among other things, keeping faith in one's agreements.[33]

Fundamentally, these virtues put our behavioral choices in the context of our relationships with others. Even those who have never considered philosophical definitions tend to share this conviction, as expressed in the "Golden Rule," by which we know it is right to treat others as we would want to be treated ourselves, a profound imperative on which the world's cultures generally have agreed. As philosopher Immanuel Kant said, "There is . . . only a single categorical imperative and it is this: Act only on that maxim through which you can at the same time will that it should become a universal law."[34] Religious tenets worldwide express the same notion. For example:

Buddhist Udana-Varga: "Hurt not others in ways that you yourself would find hurtful."

Christian New Testament: "Therefore all things whatsoever ye would that men should do to you, do ye even so to them: for this is the law and the prophets."

Confucian Avalects: "What you do not want done to yourself, do not do to others."

Hindu Mahabharata: "This is the sum of duty: do naught to others which if done to thee would cause thee pain."

Islamic Sunnah: "None of you truly believes until he wishes for his brother what he wishes for himself."

Jewish Talmud: "What is hateful to you, do not do to your fellowman. This is the entire Law; all the rest is commentary."

Of course behavior does not always reflect philosophical or religious principles, and many aspects of community standards of expected and acceptable behavior vary among societies and over time. What one society abhors may be condoned by another; what was once forbidden may become commonplace. Nevertheless, the commonality of the Golden Rule in philosophical and sacred commandments reflects that at least as a matter of principle humans tend to ascribe to the same fundamental notions of right and wrong. These fundamental notions are at risk if we lose touch with their importance. To avoid disintegration of the essential governing norms we must abide by Shakespeare's advice, "This above all—to thine ownself be true; And it must follow, as the night the day, thou canst not then be false to any man."[35] Or as Kołakowski put it, "[W]e should always be on guard against self-deception and self-satisfaction, and scrupulous in examining the true motives of our actions."[36] Those who formulate the law and administer the legal process need to heed this advice and must strive to align their motives and actions with society's moral principles.

Public administrators may not be the kind of philosophers that Plato imagined could benevolently govern for the public good. Public administrators are humans with practical responsibilities, and they cannot reasonably be expected to act in all ways as if they are enlightened philosophers. But one need not be a philosopher to guide behavior according to thoughtful principles. As the Stoic philosopher Epictetus said, "Never call yourself a philosopher and do not talk a great deal among non-philosophers about philosophical propositions, but do what follows from them."[37]

Evolution of Formal Law

As notions of fairness and justice have continued to evolve throughout history, civilizations have developed formal legal systems to reflect those notions and to organize a functioning society with increasingly complicated interrelationships. Although the founders of the United States declared independence from English rule, many fundamental aspects of the government, civil and criminal laws, and judicial procedures that governed the colonies were continued in the federal and state systems. Formal law is a product of thousands of years of evolution in legal traditions. These shared concepts about law and legal process continue to bind Western political and legal systems.

Scholars trace the Western legal tradition at least as far back as the Babylonians. In 1901 a stone monument was found in the Persian mountains on which were engraved hundreds of laws. These laws have become known as "Hammurabi's Code" named after the Babylonian ruler believed to have proclaimed a code during his reign in 1795–1750 B.C. Jewish law incorporated many aspects of Babylonian law, as expressed in the Ten Commandments, the Torah, and the Talmud.[38] These laws were believed to have emanated from God, and they were interrelated with religious practices. Many of the proscriptions, such as the commandments against murdering and stealing, are embedded in modern law.

The Greeks are known for laws not necessarily issued by a deity and for the emergence of laws, especially criminal laws, that focused on individual rather than family or collective responsibility.[39] The writings of Ancient Greek philosophers such as Aristotle, about individual liberties, property ownership, and criminal procedure, were influential in the development of modern Western legal systems and remain sources of enlightenment for legal scholars.

Similarly, the period of Roman dominance made important contributions to development of modern legal systems in the Mediterranean region and beyond. The Romans were governed by published imperial edicts and judicial opinions. In the sixth century Roman Emperor Justinian published the first comprehensive set of formal legal rules in the *Corpus Juris Civilis*, or Justinian Code, from which Western legal systems draw inspiration.[40] Justinian collected all of the imperial edicts into one source and collected judicial opinions into a digest. The word "Code," which is now used to describe the collection of statutes currently in force, is derived from the word "codex" that the Romans used to describe their compilation.[41] The Romans are also known for the emergence of a professional class of lawyers who valued legal reasoning and argument,[42] although religious leaders continued to play a major role in the development of formal law.

While Mesopotamian, Greek, and Roman innovations built a framework for a comprehensive system of formal laws, many core aspects of the U.S. legal system are derived from innovations in English law. One of the most important developments is the idea of a constitution as the ultimate source of formal law. Western constitutional law customarily is traced to the Magna Carta of 1215, a charter to which English church leaders and nobles compelled King John to agree. The Magna Carta challenged the notion that monarchs are divinely chosen rulers subject to no earthly authority. King John agreed that certain rights were inviolable, such as the right that no "freeman" may be deprived of property or liberty except by process of the law. The king acknowledged that even he was bound by law,[43] principles later expressed in the U.S. Declaration of Independence and in the Bill of Rights.

England is also important for development of a system of common law. The English Parliament, and other legislatures, enact statutes as rules to address many matters involving government and individual relationships. The common law emerged to address matters not covered by such enactments. It is the body of judicial decisions resolving disputes according to judges' sense of custom and justice. Once a common law principle is established, by tradition the courts later abide by it as a matter of *stare decisis*, by which prior decisions on the same issue within the same jurisdiction are considered to be binding precedent in the same or substantially same circumstances in later cases. Over time the common law is adapted to new circumstances, and new common law principles evolve to deal with previously unaddressed situations. This English common law tradition survived the American Revolution in the United States. The newly established federal and state courts relied on English judicial opinions and law scholars as authorities in deciding cases. Most areas of the law remain heavily influenced by these English common law principles. For example, courts rely on common law to resolve property ownership disputes or claims for damages as a result of personal injuries and to define some crimes such as fraud.

This brief introduction to the evolution of formal law in Western Civilization is intended to give some perspective about the philosophical and cultural traditions that underlie modern law. Legislatures and courts do not often speak of such traditions when they pass laws or decide cases. But history unquestionably influences their initiatives and decisions. An understanding of this framework can lead to greater understanding of the nature of law and legal process.

Sources of Formal Law

Formal law is a complex puzzle with pieces that do not fit neatly together and with no discernable perimeter. Answers to legal questions can be found in any of a myriad of constitutions, statutes, ordinances, regulations, judicial opinions, and other sources. Moreover, the nature of formal law cannot be understood without also understanding the manner in which law makers are allocated power within the legal system. The following sections discuss each of the major sources of law, beginning with a discussion of the constitutional system and the main features of the manner in which legal authority is allocated, then continuing with a discussion of the principal sources of formal law.

Constitutional System

Formal laws begin with a constitution—a compact authorizing a government to exercise entrusted powers and forbidding government from infringing on certain rights. With the U.S. Constitution the states established a federalist government, granting certain powers to a central government but continuing their own self-government over other matters. The states' constitutions in turn address their forms of government and limitations on their powers, which are in large degree modeled on the federal structure.

Recognizing the truth of Baron Acton's famous statement, "Power tends to corrupt, and absolute power corrupts absolutely," the framers of the U.S. legal system intentionally installed counterweights to the concentration of power. The states ratifying the U.S. Constitution agreed to surrender some of their power to the federal government to facilitate interstate commerce and self-defense and to promote prosperity and growth. But the states retained power over other matters. The founders also created separate branches of government—legislative, executive, and judicial—at both the federal and state levels, which were intended to have the tendency to check each other's natural inclination to assume ever greater authority. James Madison, who said no government would have been necessary if humans were angels, also observed that "If angels were to govern men, neither external nor internal controls on government would be necessary."[44] The framers understood that humans were not angels and built controls into the legal system.

Federalist System

When the states joined the federal union, their citizens became subject to federal laws enacted pursuant to the powers that the U.S. Constitution gave to the federal government. Article VI of Constitution provides, "This constitution, and the laws of the United States which shall be made in pursuance thereof, and all treaties made, or which shall be made, under the authority of the United States, shall be the supreme law of the land; and the judges in every state shall be bound thereby, anything in the constitutions or laws of any State to the contrary notwithstanding." With this Supremacy Clause the states conceded state law to matters assigned to the federal government in the Constitution. The states' authority to enact laws in conflict with federal law is said to be "preempted." A federal law preempts any state law or regulation if the federal law expressly does so or if preemption is implicit in the structure and purpose of the federal law. A state may be preempted from legislating in an entire field of law if the federal law is so expansive as to indicate that it was intended to occupy the field.[45]

Separation of Powers

The federal and each state constitution established three branches of government: the legislative branch to make law, the executive branch to enforce the law, and the judicial branch to resolve disputes. As discussed in other chapters in this book, the U.S. Constitution was not always entirely clear about which branch had a particular power or about how to resolve conflicts when more than one branch assumed the same power. A very important question not expressly addressed in the Constitution was how to resolve questions about whether a branch exceeded its constitutional authority. As discussed in Chapter 2, in the 1803 case of *Marbury v. Madison* the U.S. Supreme Court said that it was its role to declare what the law was and to determine whether a legislative or executive act was unconstitutional. Although at the time not all leading political figures thought the Court had such an implied role—some thought each branch determined the extent of its power and that the states ultimately could nullify actions not constitutionally authorized—the view expressed in *Marbury v. Madison* was accepted as establishing the Court's ultimate arbitral authority.

The framers intended for there to be tension among the branches of government in the exercise of power. A separation of powers intentionally put the branches at odds to prevent any one branch from becoming tyrannical. In addition to dividing power among each of the branches, the Constitution gave each branch some involvement in the others' activities. One example of this interrelatedness is the process for enacting law. The Constitution gave the power to make law only to Congress, but the president was enabled to block legislation with a veto. The framers left the final say with Congress, however, which may override a veto with a two-thirds vote of both chambers. As another example of the checks built into the system, the Constitution gave the president the power to appoint federal judges, but those appointments are subject to the Senate's approval. Also, Congress was given control over the judiciary's budget, may impeach federal judges, may initiate amendments to the Constitution if it disagrees with the judiciary's interpretation, and may change laws or enact new laws in response to court decisions. Conflicts among the branches are inevitable, but the framers saw tension as essential for preventing the power consolidation that history showed would otherwise occur.

Many important legal issues involve the tensions among branches of government. Some U.S. Supreme Court justices have seen their roles as protectors, ready to declare legislative acts invalid if they infringe on the justices' understanding of what rights should be. Other justices have tended to defer to elected legislators as those who are constitutionally empowered to express the will of the people. Some justices seem to express both views over time, depending on the nature of the issue. Differing views about the proper role of the branches of government is a recurring theme in the discussion of substantive law in later chapters in this book.

Legislation

The federal and state legislatures enact statutes governing matters over which they have constitutional authority. Article I of the U.S. Constitution establishes Congress to enact federal laws. Provisions in state constitutions similarly establish state legislatures.

Legislative Enactment Process

Statutes become law through a legislative process. In the U.S., Congress members initiate legislation by introducing a bill. The president may propose legislation with an executive communication, which is referred to a congressional committee with responsibility for the subject matter of the proposal, and a member of the committee may then introduce the bill. A similar process is followed in the state legislatures.

Bills can be public or private. In essence a public bill is supposed to affect everyone within a jurisdiction generally, and a private bill is supposed to affect only a specific individual, entity, or area within the jurisdiction. Bills usually are numbered in chronological order according to when they are introduced and are preceded with an abbreviation for the chamber in which they are introduced—for example "H." for the House of Representatives and "S." for the Senate in the federal system. In the U.S. Congress, and in some state legislatures, a proposal can also take the form of a resolution. In Congress a joint resolution is effectively the same as a bill but usually begins with a statement of intent. A simple resolution is a statement by a legislative body about a procedural or similar matter and is not submitted to the president. A concurrent resolution is an expression by both chambers that does not become a statute.

Legislative chambers have procedures for referring bills to committees for study and debate. Usually the chamber's presiding officer—a speaker of the house or senate majority leader—assigns the bill to a committee. Committees consider bills within their areas of responsibility and may use subcommittees to further delegate and allocate responsibility. Committees may hold public hearings to receive testimony and comments about the advisability of the proposed legislation. The committee may endorse the legislation as proposed and report it to the legislative chamber for a vote, table it so it is not to be considered, or amend the bill to propose a variation. If the bill is passed in one chamber, it is sent to the other for its consideration, which may refer the bill to its own committee for consideration and hearings. If there is disagreement, a conference committee of both chambers may attempt to reconcile differences.

Bills passed by both chambers are presented to the executive—president or governor—who may choose to sign it into law or to veto it, in which case the legislature will need a supermajority to override the veto. The bill may also become law if there is neither approval nor a veto within a designated time. The rules for such disposition vary within jurisdictions. In the federal system, if Congress is not in session, the bill fails by a "pocket veto" if it is not signed within 10 days excluding Sundays; if Congress is in session, the bill becomes law after 10 days.

Voter Legislation   Allows citizens to vote

About half of the states have a process that enables citizens to introduce a proposed law through a process called an initiative. The process might entail placing matters directly on a ballot for voter approval, or legislative endorsement may be required before the matter is submitted to the voters. A famous initiative is California's Proposition 13, approved by the voters in 1978, which amended Article 13A of the California Constitution to cap the state's property tax. About half of the states have referendum provisions for citizens to reject, approve, or repeal legislation that the legislature enacted or is proposing. This is begun with a citizen petition, or a proposal by the legislature or a state commission or department, which is presented to the voters. The initiative and referendum procedures are seen by some as empowering citizens to change the law directly, and by others as enabling special interest groups to secure legislation that would not survive the legislative deliberative process.

Federal Legislation

Congress has the constitutional authority to enact legislation concerning the powers entrusted to it in Article I of the U.S. Constitution. Section 8 of Article 1 gives Congress power over 17 specific subjects, such as "[t]o promote the progress of science and useful arts, by securing for limited times to authors and inventors the exclusive right to their respective writings and discoveries" through patents, trademarks, and copyrights; "[t]o constitute tribunals inferior to the supreme court" such as the federal district courts and courts of appeals; and to raise and maintain armed forces. Congress also is empowered to "lay and collect taxes." In addition, Article I contains two clauses that over time have been interpreted as giving Congress very broad powers to extend its authority to pass laws affecting many details of private economic and social activity. One such broad clause gives Congress the power "[t]o regulate commerce . . . among the several states," which is known as the Commerce Clause. The second clause grants the power "[t]o make all laws which shall be necessary and proper for carrying into execution" the powers expressly enumerated, which is known as the Necessary and Proper Clause. The meaning of these two clauses was the subject of serious disagreement among the leaders who were first responsible for creating an operational federal government, and the issue remains a fundamental constitutional question that affects the balance of power in the country.

The extent of implied federal power to legislate arose in the Washington administration in connection with establishing a national bank. Secretary of State Thomas Jefferson maintained that an overly strong federal government was a threat to individual liberty. He said that Congress did not have power to create a national bank on the theory that a bank was "necessary and proper" because though perhaps convenient it was not necessary.[46] Attorney General Edmund Randolph and constitutional framer James Madison agreed with Jefferson.[47] Secretary of the Treasury Alexander Hamilton, who envisioned a strong federal government and powerful national economy, argued that a bank was essential to a functioning federal government and therefore necessary; he also argued that it was sufficiently related to the enumerated power to collect taxes.[48] The disagreement was eventually decided in favor of Hamilton's expansive view. In 1819 in *McCulloch v. Maryland,*[49] the U.S. Supreme Court held that Congress had the constitutional power to establish the bank. Chief Justice John Marshall said, "Let the end be legitimate, let it be within the scope of the constitution, and all means which are appropriate, which are plainly adapted to that end, which are not prohibited, but consist with the letter and spirit of the constitution, are constitutional."[50] Chief Justice Marshall similarly interpreted the Commerce Clause expansively in *Gibbons v. Ogden,*[51] holding that the powers of Congress applied not only to commercial traffic between states but also more broadly to commerce connected to interstate trade.

The early U.S. Supreme Court cases set the groundwork for later expansion of the federal government's powers. Over the decades federal law has steadily grown in its breadth and detail. Federal statutes now address virtually every sphere of economic and social activity. The following are some of the major subjects addressed in the 50 titles of the current federal statutes:

- Air transportation
- Bankruptcy
- Banking
- Contracts with the federal government
- Copyrights, patents, and trademarks
- Customs
- Emergency management
- Environmental protection
- Federal courts and federal court procedure
- Federal lands
- Firearms
- Food and drug preparation and sale
- Foreign relations
- Health care
- Homeland security
- Income and estate taxes
- Indian affairs
- Interstate highways
- Labor conditions and labor unions
- Military and veteran affairs
- Postal service
- Power generation
- Railroads
- Retirement plans
- Stock markets and securities
- Telephone, radio, and television lines and broadcasts

State Legislation

The U.S. Constitution expressly reserved powers to the states in several ways. The ultimate power of self-governance was reserved in Article V, which enables two thirds of the states to propose an amendment to the Constitution. A proposed amendment becomes effective by approval of three quarters of the state legislatures or constitutional conventions. In addition, the Tenth Amendment, added to the Constitution in the Bill of Rights, provides as follows: "The powers not delegated to the United States by the Constitution, nor prohibited by it to the States, are reserved to the States respectively, or to the people." The federal government has tended to assume for itself increasing authority to govern, which the courts have only occasionally resisted. Nonetheless, state law continues to govern many aspects of individual and commercial affairs.

A state's basic governance is prescribed in its constitution. Each state has a constitution establishing state and local governments and declaring rights of its citizens. Many states' current state constitutions are different versions than the state first adopted, and state constitutions tend to have been amended much more often than the U.S. Constitution. As law scholar G. Alan Tarr observed, "Most state constitutions have been amended more than once for every year that they have been in operation, a proliferation of amendments that shows that there is no reluctance to tinker with the handiwork of the founders of state constitutions."[52]

The typical state constitution is three times longer than the U.S. Constitution.[53] State constitutions have declarations of individual rights similar to the federal Bill of Rights. They tend to be more specific and to identify rights not expressly enumerated in the U.S. Constitution. For example, Florida's constitution declares a right of privacy: "Every natural person has the right to be let alone and free from governmental intrusion into the person's private life except as otherwise provided herein."[54] The U.S. Constitution does not contain a similar declaration. As discussed in the next chapter, however, the U.S. Supreme Court has held that such a right was implied in the Constitution within the "penumbra" of other explicit rights. State constitutions may differently address many other important individual rights.

State constitutions establish the same basic kind of three-branch governmental structure as the federal system. The details of the legislative, executive, and judicial branches, and their reciprocal checks and balances, vary among the states. For example, a number of states have more than one elected executive officer, providing for such other elected officials as a deputy governor, attorney general, secretary of state, and treasurer. These officers need not be of the same party as the governor, which can create something of a balance of power even within the executive branch.

A state's constitution is the source of its legislature's authority to pass laws on particular subjects. The U.S. Constitution is seen as granting specific powers to a federal government but not requiring them to be exercised. State constitutions, however, often impose affirmative obligations on the state government. For instance, the North Carolina Constitution declares that "[t]he people have a right to the privilege of education, and it is the duty of the State to guard and maintain that right."[55] Declarations of such rights can have an impact on many aspects of state government. For example, in some states, including North Carolina, the legislature and judiciary battle over the nature of the legislature's obligation to fund public education. Other state constitutional provisions may similarly reflect issues deemed important to the particular state in which they exist. For example, Idaho requires its legislature "to pass all necessary laws to provide for the protection of livestock" against certain infectious diseases.[56]

The process for enacting legislation in the states is fundamentally the same as the federal process. State legislators tend to meet less often than Congress, sometimes only a few months every other year. Much of their legislative effort will be concentrated on the budget and sources of revenue. Many states adopt uniform state legislation recommended by such bodies as the National Conference of Commissioners on Uniform State Laws, a group of legal scholars and experts who propose laws for state adoption. For example, the Uniform Commercial Code, now in effect in nearly all jurisdictions, unified laws governing many aspects of lending and commercial transactions. Even with such uniform laws states often have variations. State approaches vary considerably as result of tradition, political inclinations, or happenstance.

The length and organization of state statutes vary widely. Some state statutory compilations occupy a few feet of shelf space, others take up a wall of shelves. The following are some of the major areas of law typically addressed by state statutes:

- Agriculture
- Alcoholic beverage sales
- Archives, museums, and public libraries
- Commercial sales
- Criminal offenses and procedure
- Corporations, limited liability companies, partnerships, and other businesses
- Electricity, cable, and other utilities
- Estates, inheritances, wills, and trusts
- Jails and prisons
- Hospitals
- Leases and evictions
- Local government powers and organization
- Motor vehicle licensing and registration
- Personal property security interests
- Professional licenses
- Public records
- Real estate conveyances, mortgages, and taxes
- Schools and universities
- State courts and state court procedure
- State income and sales taxes
- State personnel law
- State roads and highways
- State social services
- Worker compensation
- Zoning, land use planning, and environmental protection

The U.S. Constitution does not address local governments within the states. There are differing views about the source of local government power. The prevailing view is called "Dillon's Rule," named after judge and law scholar John F. Dillon, who in the late 1800s said that local governments could have only those powers that are expressly granted in state constitutions or statutes, or those that are necessarily or fairly implied in those express grants.[57] The other approach is called "home rule," by which local governments are deemed to have broad power to govern within their jurisdictions, and they need not have specific authority in the state constitution or statute over a particular matter.

The allocation of local government authority also varies among the states. There are more than 89,000 local governments in the country, including more than 3,000 counties and almost 40,000 general purpose cities, municipalities, towns, townships, or boroughs. Georgia alone has 154 counties; Hawaii and Delaware only 3. Only Connecticut, the District of Columbia, and Rhode Island do not have counties; Louisiana has similar governmental regions called parishes. Illinois has 1,299 municipalities; Nevada has 19. In addition, there are more than 13,000 school districts and more than 14,000 special purpose districts with authority to govern specific local public functions.[58] School districts can be independently established together with the power to tax, or they can be aligned with other local government units and dependent on those units' power to tax.

The nature of local government management also varies. The most common form is a council-manager approach in which an elected city council appoints a manager to act as chief administrative officer responsible for most day-to-day functions, and an elected mayor presides over council meetings. Another common organizational form, typically found in smaller communities, is the mayor-council approach, in which the mayor is the functional administrator. The specific allocation of powers and duties is prescribed by statute, or in charters that typically are approved by the state legislature.

Local governments provide many essential services. They or enterprises to which they grant franchises provide police, fire, emergency rescue, schools, libraries, and public utilities such as electric, water, and sewer. They build and maintain many roads, bridges, and other elements of infrastructure. Local governments also are the primary source of land-use regulations, and they regulate traffic and prohibit nuisances. Local government enactments usually are called ordinances, but those that apply to land use are often called regulations.

The coverage of local ordinances varies widely from state to state and within states. The following are some of the main areas typically addressed in a local code of ordinances:

- Animal control
- Building and housing code
- Business operation and vending licenses
- Cemeteries
- Garbage disposal
- Land use and subdivision
- Libraries
- Municipal contracts
- Municipal personnel
- Noise and nuisances

- Police and fire administration
- Public transportation
- Signs and advertising
- Streets, sidewalks, and parking
- Traffic laws
- Water, sewer, and septic

Judicial Decisions

The federal and state constitutions establish courts with judicial power to resolve controversies between individuals and between individuals and their government. Constitutions authorize a judiciary and its basic jurisdiction and authorize the legislature to determine the other details of court organization and procedure. When a matter can be heard only in one court, that court is said to have exclusive jurisdiction. When matters can be heard in more than court, those courts are said to have concurrent jurisdiction. The federal system and each state system have trial courts of general jurisdiction to resolve two kinds of matters: criminal and civil. Criminal matters involve prosecutions by the government for violations of a criminal statute. Because someone's liberty or life is at stake, courts typically give priority on their calendars to criminal matters. Civil cases involve claims among individuals or legal entities. Some are decided by judges and others by juries. A right to have a dispute decided by a jury is sometimes constitutionally guaranteed, as in a criminal prosecution; for some kinds of disputes a right to a jury trial is afforded by legislation. Questions of law are decided by judges, and fact questions are decided either by juries if a right to a jury trial for the particular issue exists, or otherwise by judges.

A party who is dissatisfied with the way the law has been applied in a trial may have the matter reviewed by an appellate court. Appeals courts do not hear new testimony or receive new evidence. They examine legal issues and reverse decisions in which the law was incorrectly applied. Appeals can be "discretionary" or "as of right." If the appeal is discretionary, the appellate court may simply decline to consider it. Even when an appeal is "as of right," the court does not necessarily hear the argument or issue an opinion. The court may simply affirm the decision without an opinion or explanation.

Judges and the Law

Judges decide whether statutes enacted by legislators are constitutional, and they interpret how statutes apply. Judges also develop common law rules. Judges' influence on law therefore is considerable and their views about justice and fairness have a lot to do with the fabric of formal law.

Appointed judges are nominated by the executive and are therefore likely to reflect the views of the elected administration at the time of appointment. But they remain in office despite changes in administration. Life tenure reflects a notion that judges are more likely to make decisions without being swayed by changing political influences. In states that have elected judges, some effort is made through laws or ethical canons to prevent judicial candidates from being elected based on predisposed political views.[59]

Judges usually are not typical citizens. They tend to be very well educated and prominent figures and usually had extensive legal experience before becoming judges. They are in a sense expected to be undemocratic and to decide cases in an enlightened way that does not necessarily reflect popular opinion. Of course judges are humans with their own political and philosophical perspectives. Still, judges are products of the communities in which they serve. They should not be assumed to be oblivious to the norms of the society or to the impact of their decisions. As former President and U.S. Supreme Court Chief Justice William Howard Taft said, "Nothing tends more to render judges careful in their decisions and anxiously solicitous to do exact justice than the consciousness that every act of theirs is to be subjected to the intelligent scrutiny of their fellow-men, and to their candid criticism. . . . In the case of judges having a life tenure, indeed, their very independence makes the right freely to comment on their decisions of greater importance, because it is the only practical and available instrument in the hands of a free people to keep such judges alive to the reasonable demands of those they serve."[60]

The evolution of formal law in the United States therefore necessarily has had much to do with the capabilities and inclinations of influential judges. No judge had more of an impact than U.S. Supreme Court Chief Justice John Marshall. As described in the next chapter, his 1803 opinion in *Marbury v. Madison* established the principle of judicial review of legislation for constitutionality. Later in *Gibbons v. Ogden*,[61] he broadly interpreted federal power over interstate commerce to pave the way for expansion of the federal government. The law might have evolved very differently without Marshall's influence.

Other prominent judges also have been agents of fundamental changes in the law. For example, Justice Roger Traynor's opinions while on the California Supreme Court became a framework for holding manufacturers liable for defectively manufactured products.[62] During the period when Earl Warren was Chief Justice of the U.S. Supreme Court, the Court issued opinions involving issues that previous courts had left to the legislatures. In the 1954 case *Brown v. Board of Education*,[63] Warren led the Court to declare that segregated public schools violated the Equal Protection Clause of the Fourteenth Amendment, reversing prior cases that held "separate but equal" schools were permissible. The nature of criminal procedure underwent a similar significant change in 1966 with *Miranda v. Arizona*,[64] in which Warren, writing for a bare minority of justices on the Court, held that a criminal suspect must "be clearly informed" of certain constitutional rights before being interrogated. The Court said such warnings had to be mandated to address coercive police practices, and the warnings continue to be a routine feature of arrests. Many other significant constitutional interpretations were transformed during the Warren years.

The law evolves according to prevailing judges' views about justice and the courts' proper role. The propriety of change through judicial decision making is the subject of considerable debate involving widely divergent views. Some see judges as safeguards against the tendencies of majorities to use legislative power to their own advantage. Others see judges as undemocratic elitists who should not presume to know better than those who pursue change through the legislative process. The path of the law is a product of tension between often-competing impulses, which may not be very smooth or efficient, but it has resulted in fundamental changes peacefully achieved.

Federal Courts

Article III, Section 1 of the U.S. Constitution states, "The judicial Power of the United States, shall be vested in one supreme Court, and in such inferior Courts as Congress may from time to time ordain and establish." Article III, Section 2 states the following with respect to federal jurisdiction:

> *The judicial Power shall extend to all Cases, in Law and Equity, arising under this Constitution, the Laws of the United States, and Treaties made, or which shall be made, under their Authority;—to all Cases affecting Ambassadors, other public ministers and Consuls;—to all Cases of admiralty and maritime Jurisdiction;—to Controversies to which the United States shall be a Party;—to Controversies between two or more States;—between a State and Citizens of another State;—between Citizens of different States;—between Citizens of the same State claiming Lands under Grants of different States, and between a State, or the Citizens thereof, and foreign States, Citizens or Subjects.*

This constitutional provision gives federal courts jurisdiction over several kinds of cases that were considered to be appropriate for the unified federal system rather than individual state systems, including cases arising under the U.S. Constitution and federal laws, sometimes referred to as "federal questions." The Constitution also empowers federal courts to consider disputes between citizens of different states, which is called diversity jurisdiction. Congress sets minimum requirements for diversity cases, such as a minimum dollar amount in dispute. The wisdom of allowing state diversity jurisdiction cases in the federal courts has been the subject of considerable debate. Supporters argue that it affords aggrieved citizens an opportunity to avoid local prejudices that might be encountered in state courts. They also argue that federal courts have more resources than state courts and may be better equipped to hear difficult or controversial cases. Opponents argue that diversity jurisdiction unduly shifts a burden to federal courts. They note that juries and judges in federal courts come from the same local populations as in state courts, and that modern state courts are not as provincial or lacking in resources as was once feared.

The federal court system consists of trial and appellate courts. District courts are the federal trial courts with general jurisdiction over civil and criminal matters. There are 94 districts including at least one in each state, the District of Columbia, and Puerto Rico. As described above, they have jurisdiction over federal questions and diversity cases. Under current law, diversity cases must involve at least $75,000 not including interest and costs.

Although most cases in the federal system are filed in district courts, there are other specialized courts that also conduct trials. Federal courts have exclusive jurisdiction over bankruptcies filed under federal law. Each federal judicial district handles bankruptcy matters, and in almost all districts these cases are heard in a bankruptcy court. The Court of International Trade has nationwide jurisdiction over international trade and customs issues. The Court of Federal Claims has jurisdiction over most claims for damages involving federal contracts, federal eminent domain, and many other kinds of claims against the federal government. Congress has also created legislative courts that do not have full judicial power. These include the Court of Military Appeals, the Tax Court, and the Court of Veterans' Appeals.

U.S. courts of appeals hear cases from the federal district courts located within their regions. There are eleven regional circuits and a District of Columbia circuit. For example, the first Circuit hears appeals from district courts in Maine, Massachusetts, New Hampshire, Rhode Island, and Puerto Rico, and the Ninth Circuit hears appeals from district courts in Alaska, Arizona, California, Guam, Hawaii, Idaho, Montana, Nevada, the Northern Mariana Islands, and Oregon. The Federal Circuit has nationwide jurisdiction over appeals involving specific kinds of matters, including certain claims against the U.S. government, government contracts, international trade, patents, trademarks, federal personnel, and veterans' benefits.

The U.S. Supreme Court hears appeals involving federal constitutional rights or federal law from the courts of appeals, state supreme courts, and in rare circumstances from other courts. (Note the legal convention, followed in this book, that the capitalized phrase "Supreme Court" or word "Court" means the U.S. Supreme Court.) Congress sets the number of justices—there is a chief justice and eight associate justices, whom the president appoints for life subject to Senate confirmation. Although the Court receives thousands of requests for review it agrees to hear and issues opinions for fewer than 100 annually. Therefore, although the phrase "I'll take this all the way to the United States Supreme Court!" may often be uttered in response to an unwelcome trial outcome, the odds of being heard at the Court are very long. Most cases involve disagreements among the courts of appeals or an important and unsettled question of law.

State Courts

Although each state establishes its own courts, the systems tend to be similar in basic features. States have a system of trial courts with regional courts of general jurisdiction, and local or specialized courts for certain kinds of matters. They also will have at least one appellate court. Increasingly, the state courts follow rules of procedure and evidence modeled on the federal rules, but all states have their own procedural variations and may retain peculiar procedures that have been fundamentally unchanged for many decades.

A typical state trial court system has local courts that hear minor criminal offenses, landlord tenant cases, and civil disputes up to a certain amount, and county courts that hear more serious criminal matters and civil disputes that exceed the relatively small jurisdictional limits of the local courts. The local courts often are called district courts, and the county courts often are called superior courts. Specialized courts hear other matters. For example, county probate courts may have jurisdiction over matters involving a deceased's estate, and states may have family courts to handle divorces and child custody matters.

All states have at least one appellate court, and the highest state court usually is called the supreme court. Sometimes it goes by another name, which can be confusing. For example, in New York the highest appeals court is called the court of appeals. New York's supreme court is primarily a trial court, with civil and criminal branches, but it also has an appellate branch that is an intermediate court of appeals. Many courts, especially in the larger states, have intermediate appellate courts. The rules vary about which cases may be brought in which appellate courts within a state that has more than one, and about a party's right to be heard in the highest court. States that have intermediate appeals courts often require appeals to be brought in those courts in the first instance, and the highest court has discretion to review the decisions.

Agency Regulations

As discussed in much more detail in Chapter 11 of this book, administrative agencies issue and enforce regulations pursuant to authority delegated to them by legislatures. Federal and state agencies have been authorized to issue regulations affecting a vast array of government activities, commerce, social services, and other details of modern life. In recent decades administrative agencies and their regulations have grown explosively. There are now more than 500 federal agencies, and each state has dozens of its own agencies. The reach of administrative regulations is very broad. For example, there are extensive federal regulations on aeronautics, armed forces, environmental protection, federal highways, federal lands, food and drug preparation and distribution, immigration, labor standards, occupational health and safety, railroads, social security, and worker's compensation. State administrative regulations also govern many areas of public and private activities. For example, detailed state regulations are likely in the areas of farm production and distribution, fisheries and harbors, public utilities, state contracts, state highways and roads, and state taxes, among other things. Sometimes state and federal regulations are interrelated with many details addressed by a federal agency and others addressed at the state level. This is so, for example, for many environmental, employment, health, and safety regulations.

International Law

International law is a complex and highly specialized field of the law. Individuals and organizations involved in international law matters engage experts in the field. This book can provide only a very brief overview sufficient to give some sense of the laws likely to be encountered.

"International law" refers to treaties, agreements, and rules affecting nations or individuals of different nations. "Public international law" is a term used to refer to multilateral agreements affecting many nations, such as the Geneva Conventions and the Universal Declaration of Human Rights. It is also used to refer to agreements between two nations or among nations within a region, such as the North American Free Trade Agreement. International dispute resolution also involves international law custom based on recognized principles not addressed with express agreements. "Private international law" is a term used to describe rules for determining which jurisdiction's laws apply to a dispute between individuals or entities from more than one nation, and rules for determining the forum in which a dispute between such parties must be heard. The term "foreign law" usually is employed when referring to the law of another nation that applies to matters within that other nation's jurisdiction.

A number of international organizations are involved in implementing international conventions, such as the United Nations Commission on International Trade Law and the Hague Conference on Private International Law. Under Article II, Section 2 of the U.S. Constitution, the president has the power to bind the United States to treaties with two-thirds consent of the U.S. Senate.

The very notion of an international law can be challenged because throughout history, nations and individuals have tended to abide by international agreements when to do so suits their present interests, and to discount or disregard prior commitments when circumstances change. Nevertheless, both national and international tribunals often apply rules of international agreements to restrict commerce, resolve disputes, and prosecute violators of international principles. International rules may affect any activity involving a government, entity, or individual in another nation. For example, international agreements may affect the extent to which goods or services may be sold to someone in another nation, or whether cultural items may be exported. They govern the payment of tariffs for exported or imported goods. International rules also may be important for determining whether an agreement or judgment can be enforced in another country. For example, although a party seeking recovery for breach of contract from a foreign company may be able to obtain a judgment in the United States, both international law and the law of the breaching party's nation may affect the party's ability to recover the judgment.

Modern international agreements add layers of complexity to the usual considerations about sources of applicable law. For example, the members of the European Union have agreed to abide by European Union laws governing a wide range of commercial and private affairs, to be bound by the enactments of the Union's political institutions, and to resolve certain kinds of disputes through a unified court system. The system facilitates the movement of individuals and capital among the nations involved, and in many ways simplifies an understanding of the law. Similar issues arise with arrangements into which other countries have entered, such as the North American Free Trade Agreement to which the United States, Canada, and Mexico have agreed.

Review Questions

1. What is commonly meant by a rule of law?
2. What is commonly meant by formal law?
3. What is the nature of the norms and moral codes that legitimize laws and guide behavior?
4. What is the basic nature of the federalist system in the United States?
5. In what fundamental way does the U.S. Constitution separate powers and why does it do so?

6. Give some examples of important subjects likely to be governed by federal, state, and local legislation.

7. What is the general nature of federal court jurisdiction?

8. How is a typical state court system structured?

9. Who issues statutes, cases, and regulations, and how does each fit within the modern system of U.S. formal law?

10. How do judges' views about justice and the courts' proper role affect the evolution of the law?

Notes

1. Lawyers' Occupational Outlook Handbook, U.S. Department of Labor, Bureau of Labor Statistics, *available at* http://www.bls.gov/oco/ocos053.htm.

2. The Federalist No. 51, at 262 (James Madison) (Bantam Books ed. 1982).

3. William Golding, Lord of the Flies 222 (Farber & Farber Ltd. 1961).

4. *See* William L. Shirer, The Rise and Fall of the Third Reich 198 (1960).

5. Constitution of the Soviet Union, art. 57(1) (1977).

6. Frederic Bastiat, The Law 9 (1848).

7. Marbury v. Madison, 5 U.S. (1 Cranch) 137, 163 (1803).

8. John Locke, Of Civil Government, Second Treatise § 119 (Gateway ed. 1955).

9. *Id.* §§ 134–138.

10. USAID, Strengthening the Rule of Law & Respect for Human Rights *(available at* http://www.usaid.gov/our_work/democracy_and_governance/technical_areas/rule_of_law (last visited May 9, 2008)).

11. Letter from Thomas Jefferson to Isaac H. Tiffany (April 4, 1819).

12. Ronald Dworkin, Political Judges and the Rule of Law, 64 Proceedings of the British Academy, 259, 262 (1978).

13. Frederick A. Hayek, The Road to Serfdom 83–84 (1944).

14. American Bar Association, Model Rules of Professional Conduct, Scope (2000).

15. Black's Law Dictionary "Natural law" (5th ed.) (emphasis in original).

16. Uniform Commercial Code § 382-A:1–201(19).

17. *Id.* at § 382-A:2–302.

18. James J. White & Robert S. Summers, Uniform Commercial Code § 4–9 (4th ed. 1995).

19. Long v. City of Charlotte, 293 S.E.2d 101, 107–08 (N.C. 1982).

20. 378 U.S. 184 (1964).

21. *Id.* at 197 (Stewart, J., concurring).

22. United States v. Dougherty, 473 F.2d 1113, 1130 (D.C. Cir. 1972).

23. United States v. Adams, 126 F.2d 774, 776 (2d Cir. 1942).

24. *See, e.g.*, Peter J. Hill, Markets and Morality, in The Morality of Capitalism 57, 59 (Mark Hendrickson, ed. 1992) (discussing the incentives for cooperative behavior).

25. Amartya Sen, Development As Freedom 263 (1999).

26. Oliver Wendell Holmes, Jr., The Path of The Law, 10 Harv. L. Rev. 457 (1897).

27. *Id.* at 457.

28. Lon L. Fuller, The Morality of Law 4 (rev. ed. 1969).

29. Aristotle, The Nicomachean Ethics bks. IV–V, at 79–136 (Oxford Univ. Pres 1991).

30. Leszek Kołakowski, Freedom, Fame, Lying, and Betrayal 48 (1999).

31. Aristotle, *supra* note 29, bk. II, ch. 9, at 45.

32. *Id.* bk. IV, Ch. 7, at 101.

33. *Id.* bk. V, Chs. 1–11, at 106–36.

34. Immanuel Kant, The Metaphysic of Morals 17 (Cambridge Univ. Press ed. 1996).

35. William Shakespeare, Hamlet act I, sc. 3.

36. Kołakowski, *supra* note 30, at 52.

37. Epictetus, The Handbook, No. 46, at 26 (Hackett Pub. Co. 1983).

38. Rene A. Wormser, The Story of The Law 3–32 (1962).

39. *Id.* at 39; John Zane, The Story of Law 102–61 (1927).

40. Wormser, *supra* note 38, at 147.

41. *Id.*

42. Zane, *supra* note 39, at 162–88.

43. *Id.* at 250–51.

44. The Federalist No. 51, at 262 (James Madison) (Bantam Books ed. 1982).

45. FMC Corp. v. Holliday, 498 U.S. 52, 56–57 (1990).

46. Letter from Thomas Jefferson to George Washington (Feb. 15, 1791).

47. Letter from Edmund Randolph to George Washington (Feb. 12, 1791); Letter from James Madison to George Washington (Feb. 21, 1791).

48. Letter from Alexander Hamilton to George Washington (Feb. 23, 1791).

49. 17 U.S. 316 (1819).

50. *Id.* at 421.

51. 22 U.S. 1 (1824).

52. G. Alan Tarr, The State of State Constitutions, 62 La. L. Rev. 3, 9 (2001).

53. G. Alan Tarr, Understanding State Constitutions, 65 Temple L. Rev. 1169, 1170–71 (1992).

54. Fla. Const. Art. I, § 23.

55. N.C. Const. Art. I, § 15.

56. Idaho Const. art. 9, § 1; *see generally* Tarr, Understanding State Constitutions, *supra* note 53, at 1177–78.

57. John F. Dillon, Treatise on the Law of Municipal Corporations § 55 (1872).

58. U.S. Census Bureau, 2007 Census of Governments.

59. *See, e.g.*, Republican Party of Minnesota v. White, 536 U.S. 765 (2002) (considering a judicial conduct canon prohibiting a candidate form "announc[ing] his or her views on disputed legal or political issues").

60. William H. Taft, Recent Criticism of the Federal Judiciary, 34 American Law Reg. & Rev. 576, 577 (1895).

61. 22 U.S. 1 (1824).

62. *See* Greenman v. Yuba River Products, Inc., 377 P.2d 897 (Cal. 1963) (holding that a manufacturer may be held liable for a defective produce despite having no contract with the injured party).

63. 343 U.S. 483 (1954).

64. 384 U.S. 436 (1966).

Chapter 2

Constitutional Principles

*In framing a government, which is to be administered by men over men,
the great difficulty lies in this: you must first enable the government
to control the governed, and in the next place, oblige it to control itself.*

James Madison

CHAPTER OBJECTIVES

After studying this chapter you should better understand:

- The basic allocation of power in the U.S. Constitution to Congress, the president, and the judiciary
- The basic nature of constitutionally protected individual rights
- The principle of judicial review as expressed in *Marbury v. Madison*
- The basic interpretative approaches that U.S. Supreme Court justices articulated when considering a "right of privacy" in *Griswold v. Connecticut*
- The nature of the "originalist" and "living constitution" approaches to constitutional interpretation

The constitutional framers' world was very different than ours. They came from 13 colonies with British heritage, all near the Atlantic coast. The colonies had a combined population of less than 4 million, and only five cities of more than 10,000, and few of the inhabitants could hold office, vote, or pursue higher education. The framers could not have envisioned the dimensions of a country of more than 300 million people of diverse races and cultures living across several time zones. They also could not have anticipated a global economy of heavy industries, consumer markets, and instantaneous electronic communications, median human life spans of more than 70 years, or widespread agreement that gender and race should not limit legal rights and political participation.

The framers could not have foreseen how the country would change, but they knew that it would. The also knew they had a precious opportunity. They sought to invent a government based on libertarian principles that would endure in changing economic and social conditions. The framers were not of a single mind about how to go about accomplishing these ambitious goals. They held views that differed in important ways. Amazingly, they succeeded in building a foundational legal framework that survives into its third century, and they did it with only 4,400 words.

This chapter provides an overview of the main features of the U.S. Constitution and the approaches that judges have employed to interpret it. Judges' understanding of their roles can be best understood in their own words. Accordingly this chapter includes the opinions of two of the most illuminating U.S. Supreme Court cases regarding judicial interpretation, *Marbury v. Madison* and *Griswold v. Connecticut*, and a discussion of their significance.

Text of the Constitution

The U.S. Constitution is a statement of fundamental formal law to which all other formal laws are subject. Article VI, the Supremacy Clause, provides, "This Constitution, and the laws of the United States which shall be made in pursuance thereof; and all treaties made, or which shall be made, under the authority of the United States, shall be the supreme law of the land; and the judges in every state shall be bound thereby, anything in the Constitution or laws of any State to the contrary notwithstanding." Ultimately even this supreme formal law is subject to the power of those who can change it. Article V provides that amendments may be proposed by either two thirds of both houses of Congress or through a convention called by two thirds of the state legislatures, and the amendments become effective if three fourths of the states or state conventions approve. The Constitution can be changed, but the task was purposely made difficult.

The text of the Constitution often describes governmental powers or individual rights only in general terms. The Constitution gives the federal government limited powers, and it provides assurances that those powers may not be exercised at the expense of protected individual rights.

Federal Government

The first three articles of the Constitution establish the legislative, executive, and judicial branches. These articles are the source of authority for Congress, the president, and the federal judges.

Congress

Article I established Congress and empowered it to make laws. The article's sequential preeminence reflects the framers' political philosophy that among the three branches the body of representatives elected from all of the states is most closely connected to the people. Through the "Great Compromise" two bodies were established to balance power between large and small states, with House of Representatives membership based on population but each state having two members of the Senate. Initially citizen voters elected representatives, and state legislators elected senators. With the Seventeenth Amendment, ratified in 1913, the people also elected senators.

Congress was given power over the matters most likely to be subject to abuse: taxation, raising an army and navy, and declaring war. An income tax was not authorized until 1913 with the Sixteenth Amendment, which funded a vast expansion of the federal government. As noted in Chapter 1, in the original Constitution, Congress was also given powers later construed to be very broad, including the power to "regulate commerce . . . among the several states" and "[t]o make all laws which shall be necessary and proper for carrying into execution" the enumerated powers.

In the interwoven system of checks and balances the House of Representatives has the sole power to subject another official to impeachment, and the Senate has the sole power to hold a trial to determine whether the official is to be removed. This process for removing a president and federal judges has rarely been invoked, but it reflects the framers' concern about the tendency of those with power to want to expand their influence.

President

Article II provides for a president in whom the "executive power" is vested. No explanation is given about what constitutes the executive power. The Constitution's text does state that the president is the military's commander in chief. A number of other specific presidential powers are listed: to grant pardons for offenses against the United States, to make treaties with the approval of two thirds of the Senate, and to appoint ambassadors and judges "with the advice and consent of the Senate."

Article II also provides that the president and other civil officers "shall be removed from office on impeachment for, and conviction of, treason, bribery, or other high crimes and misdemeanors." This set a standard for Congress's exercise of its power to remove the president.

Judiciary

Article III only generally describes the federal judiciary and its powers. It says, "The judicial Power of the United States shall be vested in one supreme Court, and in such inferior Courts as the Congress may from time to time ordain and establish." The Constitution lets Congress set the number of the Court's justices and its procedural rules, as well as the configuration of inferior federal appellate courts and trial courts.

The Constitution provided further guidance about federal court jurisdiction. In addition to specifying a number of types of cases that the federal courts would decide, such as maritime disputes and cases involving treaties and ambassadors, it gave federal courts jurisdiction over cases arising under the Constitution and federal law, cases in which the United States is a party, and disputes between states and between citizens of different states.

Article III also provides that federal judges have life tenure "during good behavior," which tends to insulate judges from the influences that could affect them if they were subject to elections. Life tenure has been criticized for allowing judges to remain on the bench for too long, preventing an infusion of better attuned and more energetic younger judges.

Individual Rights

Framers James Madison, Alexander Hamilton, and others argued that mention of specific individual rights in the Constitution was unnecessary because the federal government has only the limited powers expressly given. Enumeration of certain rights became a political necessity when Thomas Jefferson and others insisted that fundamental rights were at risk of encroachment unless explicitly stated. Madison eventually agreed and introduced the first 10 amendments, known as the Bill of Rights, in the first session of Congress.[1]

Fundamental religious and speech rights are stated in the First Amendment in simple terms: "Congress shall make no law respecting an establishment of religion, or prohibiting the free exercise thereof; or abridging the freedom of speech, or of the press; or the right of the people peaceably to assemble, and to petition the Government for a redress of grievances." Some of the difficult interpretive issues that have arisen regarding these prohibitions are discussed in Chapter 4 of this book.

The Second and Third Amendments reflect the framers' experience with oppressive British military occupation and concern about expansion of federal power over the states and individuals. The Second Amendment provides, "A well regulated Militia, being necessary to the security of a free State, the right of the people to keep and bear Arms, shall not be infringed." Although this clause refers to the militia, the courts have interpreted it as guarantying a right of personal gun ownership. The Third Amendment prohibits military occupation of homes without the owner's consent "but in a manner to be prescribed by law," addressing one of the abuses that had been cited as inspiring the American Revolution.

Several amendments address rights in connection with police actions and criminal prosecutions, as discussed in more detail in Chapter 10 of this book. The Fourth Amendment prohibits "unreasonable searches and seizures" and requires that warrants for searches be issued only "upon probable cause, supported by Oath or affirmation, and particularly describing the place to be searched, and the persons or things to be seized." The Fifth Amendment requires a grand jury indictment for certain serious crimes, prohibits compelling criminal defendants to testify against themselves, and prohibits a trial of the same person more than once for the same offense. In addition, the Fifth Amendment contains what is known as the Due Process Clause, broadly providing that no one may "be deprived of life, liberty, or property, without due process of law," which is discussed in Chapter 3. Additional criminal prosecution provisions are in the Sixth Amendment, which assures defendants of "a speedy and public trial" by "an impartial jury," as well as guarantying a right to be informed of the accusation, to confront accusing witnesses and call witnesses, and to have defense counsel. The Eighth Amendment prohibits "excessive bail" and "cruel and unusual punishments."

The Fifth Amendment prohibits private property from being taken for public use "without just compensation." This clause implicitly confirmed the power of government to take private property but only if for "public use" and only if the owner is paid for the value of what is taken. The courts' notion of what constitutes public use has evolved over time to include more than just actual use but also uses providing a "public benefit," an interpretation that recently has received much public attention and is discussed in Chapter 6.

The Seventh Amendment guaranties a jury trial for "suits at common law," which includes cases in which private legal rights are determined, but not "equity cases" in which a court is asked to grant an injunction or to decide a case based on basic fairness.

The final two amendments of the Bill of Rights were included in response to the concern that the list could be considered to be exclusive and that other rights would not be protected. The Ninth Amendment provides that the listed rights "shall not be construed to deny or disparage others retained by the people." The Tenth Amendment provides that "[t]he powers not delegated to the United States by the Constitution, nor prohibited by it to the states, are reserved to the states respectively, or to the people." This statement made explicit the idea that the federal government is limited only to the powers granted in the Constitution.

The Constitution was amended only twice after the Bill of Rights was ratified and before the Civil War. In 1795 the Eleventh Amendment made clear that a state could not be sued in the federal courts by a citizen of another state or country. In 1804 the Twelfth Amendment required voters to choose a president and vice president rather than having the presidential runner up become the vice president. The next three amendments are known as the Civil War Amendments. The Thirteenth Amendment and Fifteenth Amendment, respectively, simply abolished slavery and prohibited the states from denying the vote on the basis of race. The intervening Fourteenth Amendment was more complex and proved to be laden with the potential for considerable interpretive disagreement. In addition to assuring individuals in previously rebellious states of the same rights as individuals in the loyal states, the Fourteenth Amendment provides, "No State shall make or enforce any law which shall abridge the privileges or immunities of citizens of the United States; nor shall any State deprive any person of life, liberty, or property, without due process of law; nor deny to any person within its jurisdiction the equal protection of the laws." This language includes what are known as the Due Process Clause and the Equal Protection Clause, both of which were to be later employed by the U.S. Supreme Court in invalidating state legislation. These clauses are discussed in the next chapter.

In the 1900s several amendments addressed specific fundamental rights. The vote was at last extended to women in 1920 with the Nineteenth Amendment, almost a century and a half after the Constitution was ratified. Previously the U.S. Supreme Court had held that the Constitution did not extend the right of suffrage to anyone. The Twenty-Fourth Amendment, ratified in 1964, prohibited a poll tax in a federal election. In 1971 the Twenty-Sixth Amendment mandated an 18-year-old voting age.

History also has proved that amending the Constitution may not be an effective way to alter behaviors despite apparent popular agreement about the desirability of change. In 1920 the Eighteenth Amendment prohibited the manufacture, sale, or transportation of liquor. Prohibition was ineffective in eradicating liquor consumption. Instead it resulted in a lucrative illegal liquor market that heavily burdened law enforcement resources and, in 1933, during the Great Depression, the Twenty-First Amendment was ratified to repeal the Eighteenth Amendment.

There have been a total of 27 amendments—only 17 since the Bill of Rights was ratified in 1791. As the discussion above shows, few of the amendments were instruments for change.

Law has shifted fundamentally over time through another process—judicial interpretation—which is not reflected in the constitutional text.

Who Decides What the Law Means?

Within a very short time after ratification of the Constitution national leaders disagreed about key provisions governing the powers of the branches of government. What does it mean for Congress to have the power "[t]o regulate commerce . . . among the several states" and "[t]o make all laws which shall be necessary and proper for carrying into execution the" enumerated powers, for the president to have "[t]he executive power," and for the U.S. Supreme Court to have "[t]he judicial power of the United States"? The framers also left much room for disagreement about individual rights, such as what it means to prohibit any person from being "deprived of life, liberty, or property, without due process of law." There is nothing in the Constitution that says that the legislature and executive must look to the courts as the sole interpreter of the Constitution.

Judicial Review: *Marbury v. Madison*

As the United States underwent its first serious shift in the political orientation of its national leadership, a case came before the U.S. Supreme Court to test how a challenge to a law's constitutionality would be addressed. As Federalist John Adams was relinquishing power to Republican Thomas Jefferson in 1801, Adams made last-minute appointments of loyal Federalists to government posts, including William Marbury as a justice of the peace in the District of Columbia. Adams' secretary of state, John Marshall, signed a commission for Marbury before leaving office. Jefferson, looking to keep Federalists from office during his term, directed his secretary of state not to complete delivery of commissions. Marbury and other appointees looked to the Court, of which the same John Marshall was now chief justice, for a writ of mandamus to order the president to deliver the commissions.

Marshall took up several issues that were central to the newly established government. One basic question was this: Who decides whether an act of Congress exceeds the powers entrusted to that body in the Constitution?

Marbury v. Madison
5 U.S. (1 Cranch) 137 (1803)

Chief Justice Marshall, writing for the Court.

At the last term, on the affidavits then read and filed with the clerk, a rule was granted in this case, requiring the Secretary of State to show cause why a mandamus should not issue directing him to deliver to William Marbury his commission as a justice of the peace for the county of Washington, in the District of Columbia.

No cause has been shown, and the present motion is for a mandamus. The peculiar delicacy of this case, the novelty of some of its circumstances, and the real difficulty attending the points which occur in it require a complete exposition of the principles on which the opinion to be given by the Court is founded.

The first object of inquiry is,

1st. Has the applicant a right to the commission he demands?

In order to determine whether he is entitled to this commission, it becomes necessary to inquire whether he has been appointed to the office. For if he has been appointed, the law continues him in office for five years, and he is entitled to the possession of those evidences of office, which, being completed, became his property.

The appointment, being the sole act of the President, must be completely evidenced when it is shown that he has done everything to be performed by him.

Some point of time must be taken when the power of the Executive over an officer, not removable at his will, must cease. That point of time must be when the constitutional power of appointment has been exercised. And this power has been exercised when the last act required from the person possessing the power has been performed. This last act is the signature of the commission.

The commission being signed, the subsequent duty of the Secretary of State is prescribed by law, and not to be guided by the will of the President. He is to affix the seal of the United States to the commission, and is to record it.

It is therefore decidedly the opinion of the Court that, when a commission has been signed by the President, the appointment is made, and that the commission is complete when the seal of the United States has been affixed to it by the Secretary of State.

The discretion of the Executive is to be exercised until the appointment has been made. But having once made the appointment, his power over the office is terminated in all cases, where by law the officer is not removable by him. The right to the office is then in the person appointed, and he has the absolute, unconditional power of accepting or rejecting it.

Mr. Marbury, then, since his commission was signed by the President and sealed by the Secretary of State, was appointed, and as the law creating the office gave the officer a right to hold for five years independent of the Executive, the appointment was not revocable, but vested in the officer legal rights which are protected by the laws of his country.

To withhold the commission, therefore, is an act deemed by the Court not warranted by law, but violative of a vested legal right.

This brings us to the second inquiry: which is,

2d. If he has a right, and that right has been violated, do the laws of his country afford him a remedy?

The very essence of civil liberty certainly consists in the right of every individual to claim the protection of the laws whenever he receives an injury. One of the first duties of government is to afford that protection.

The Government of the United States has been emphatically termed a government of laws, and not of men. It will certainly cease to deserve this high appellation if the laws furnish no remedy for the violation of a vested legal right.

By the Constitution of the United States, the President is invested with certain important political powers, in the exercise of which he is to use his own discretion, and is accountable only to his country in his political character and to his own conscience. To aid him in the performance of these duties, he is authorized to appoint certain officers, who act by his authority and in conformity with his orders.

In such cases, their acts are his acts; and whatever opinion may be entertained of the manner in which executive discretion may be used, still there exists, and can exist, no power to control that discretion. The subjects are political. They respect the nation, not individual rights, and, being entrusted to the Executive, the decision of the Executive is conclusive.

But when the Legislature proceeds to impose on that officer other duties; when he is directed peremptorily to perform certain acts; when the rights of individuals are dependent on the performance of those acts; he is so far the officer of the law, is amenable to the laws for his conduct, and cannot at his discretion, sport away the vested rights of others.

The conclusion from this reasoning is that, where the heads of departments are the political or confidential agents of the Executive, merely to execute the will of the President, or rather to act in cases in which the Executive possesses a constitutional or legal discretion, nothing can be more perfectly clear than that their acts are only politically examinable. But where a specific duty is assigned by law, and individual rights depend upon the performance of that duty, it seems equally clear that the individual who considers himself injured has a right to resort to the laws of his country for a remedy.

The question whether a right has vested or not is, in its nature, judicial, and must be tried by the judicial authority. If, for example, Mr. Marbury had taken the oaths of a magistrate and proceeded to act as one, in consequence of which a suit had been instituted against him in which his defence had depended on his being a magistrate; the validity of his appointment must have been determined by judicial authority.

So, if he conceives that, by virtue of his appointment, he has a legal right either to the commission which has been made out for him or to a copy of that commission, it is equally a question examinable in a court, and the decision of the Court upon it must depend on the opinion entertained of his appointment.

That question has been discussed, and the opinion is that the latest point of time which can be taken as that at which the appointment was complete and evidenced was when, after the signature of the President, the seal of the United States was affixed to the commission.

It is then the opinion of the Court: That, having this legal title to the office, he has a consequent right to the commission, a refusal to deliver which is a plain violation of that right, for which the laws of his country afford him a remedy.

It remains to be inquired whether,

3d. He is entitled to the remedy for which he applies.

Blackstone, in the 3d volume of his Commentaries, page 110, defines a mandamus to be "a command issuing in the King's name from the Court of King's Bench, and directed to any person, corporation, or inferior court of judicature within the King's dominions requiring them to do some particular thing therein specified which appertains to their office and duty, and which the Court of King's Bench has previously determined, or at least supposes, to be consonant to right and justice."

This writ, if awarded, would be directed to an officer of government, and its mandate to him would be, to use the words of Blackstone, "to do a particular thing therein specified, which appertains to his office and duty and which the Court has previously determined or at least supposes to be consonant to right and justice."

These circumstances certainly concur in this case.

Still, to render the mandamus a proper remedy, the officer to whom it is to be directed must be one to whom, on legal principles, such writ may be directed, and the person applying for it must be without any other specific and legal remedy.

This, then, is a plain case of a mandamus, either to deliver the commission or a copy of it from the record, and it only remains to be inquired . . . whether it can issue from this Court.

The act to establish the judicial courts of the United States authorizes the Supreme Court "to issue writs of mandamus, in cases warranted by the principles and usages of law, to any courts appointed, or persons holding office, under the authority of the United States."

The Secretary of State, being a person, holding an office under the authority of the United States, is precisely within the letter of the description, and if this Court is not authorized to issue a writ of mandamus to such an officer, it must be because the law is unconstitutional, and therefore absolutely incapable of conferring the authority and assigning the duties which its words purport to confer and assign.

The Constitution vests the whole judicial power of the United States in one Supreme Court, and such inferior courts as Congress shall, from time to time, ordain and establish. This power is expressly extended to all cases arising under the laws of the United States; and consequently, in some form, may be exercised over the present case, because the right claimed is given by a law of the United States.

In the distribution of this power it is declared that "the Supreme Court shall have original jurisdiction in all cases affecting ambassadors, other public ministers and consuls, and those in which a state shall be a party. In all other cases, the Supreme Court shall have appellate jurisdiction."

If it had been intended to leave it in the discretion of the Legislature to apportion the judicial power between the Supreme and inferior courts according to the will of that body, it would certainly have been useless to have proceeded further than to have defined the judicial power and the tribunals in which it should be vested. The subsequent part of the section is mere surplusage—is entirely without meaning—if such is to be the construction. If Congress remains at liberty to give this court appellate jurisdiction where the Constitution has declared their jurisdiction shall be original, and original jurisdiction where the Constitution has declared it shall be appellate, the distribution of jurisdiction made in the Constitution, is form without substance.

When an instrument organizing fundamentally a judicial system, divides it into one Supreme and so many inferior courts as the Legislature may ordain and establish; then enumerates its powers, and proceeds so far to distribute them, as to define the jurisdiction of the Supreme Court by declaring the cases in which it shall take original jurisdiction, and that in others it shall take appellate jurisdiction; the plain import of the words seems to be, that in one class of cases, its jurisdiction is original, and not appellate; in the other it is appellate, and not original. If any other construction would render the clause inoperative, that is an additional reason for rejecting such other construction, and for adhering to the obvious meaning.

To enable this court then to issue a mandamus, it must be shown to be an exercise of appellate jurisdiction, or to be necessary to enable them to exercise appellate jurisdiction.

It has been stated at the bar that the appellate jurisdiction may be exercised in a variety of forms, and that, if it be the will of the Legislature that a mandamus should be used for that purpose, that will must be obeyed. This is true; yet the jurisdiction must be appellate, not original.

It is the essential criterion of appellate jurisdiction that it revises and corrects the proceedings in a cause already instituted, and does not create that case. Although, therefore, a mandamus may be directed to courts, yet to issue such a writ to an officer for the delivery of a paper is, in effect, the same as to sustain an original action for that paper, and therefore seems not to belong to appellate, but to original jurisdiction. Neither is it necessary in such a case as this to enable the Court to exercise its appellate jurisdiction.

The authority, therefore, given to the Supreme Court by the act establishing the judicial courts of the United States to issue writs of mandamus to public officers appears not to be warranted by the Constitution, and it becomes necessary to inquire whether a jurisdiction so conferred can be exercised.

The question whether an act repugnant to the Constitution can become the law of the land is a question deeply interesting to the United States, but, happily, not of an intricacy proportioned to its interest. It seems only necessary to recognise certain principles, supposed to have been long and well established, to decide it.

That the people have an original right to establish for their future government such principles as, in their opinion, shall most conduce to their own happiness is the basis on which the whole American fabric has been erected. The exercise of this original right is a very great exertion; nor can it nor ought it to be frequently repeated. The principles, therefore, so established are deemed fundamental. And as the authority from which they proceed, is supreme, and can seldom act, they are designed to be permanent.

This original and supreme will organizes the government and assigns to different departments their respective powers. It may either stop here or establish certain limits not to be transcended by those departments.

The Government of the United States is of the latter description. The powers of the Legislature are defined and limited; and that those limits may not be mistaken or forgotten, the Constitution is written. To what purpose are powers limited, and to what purpose is that limitation committed to writing, if these limits may at any time be passed by those intended to be restrained? The distinction between a government with limited and unlimited powers is abolished if those limits do not confine the persons on whom they are imposed, and if acts prohibited and acts allowed are of equal obligation. It is a proposition too plain to be contested that the Constitution controls any legislative act repugnant to it, or that the Legislature may alter the Constitution by an ordinary act.

Between these alternatives there is no middle ground. The Constitution is either a superior, paramount law, unchangeable by ordinary means, or it is on a level with ordinary legislative acts, and, like other acts, is alterable when the legislature shall please to alter it.

If the former part of the alternative be true, then a legislative act contrary to the Constitution is not law; if the latter part be true, then written Constitutions are absurd attempts on the part of the people to limit a power in its own nature illimitable.

If an act of the Legislature repugnant to the Constitution is void, does it, notwithstanding its invalidity, bind the Courts and oblige them to give it effect? Or, in other words, though it be not law, does it constitute a rule as operative as if it was a law? This would be to overthrow in fact what was established in theory, and would seem, at first view, an absurdity too gross to be insisted on. It shall, however, receive a more attentive consideration.

It is emphatically the province and duty of the Judicial Department to say what the law is. Those who apply the rule to particular cases must, of necessity, expound and interpret that rule. If two laws conflict with each other, the Courts must decide on the operation of each.

So, if a law be in opposition to the Constitution, if both the law and the Constitution apply to a particular case, so that the Court must either decide that case conformably to the law, disregarding the Constitution, or conformably to the Constitution, disregarding the law, the Court must determine which of these conflicting rules governs the case. This is of the very essence of judicial duty.

Those, then, who controvert the principle that the Constitution is to be considered in court as a paramount law are reduced to the necessity of maintaining that courts must close their eyes on the Constitution, and see only the law.

This doctrine would subvert the very foundation of all written Constitutions. It would declare that an act which, according to the principles and theory of our government, is entirely void, is yet, in practice, completely obligatory. It would declare that, if the Legislature shall do what is expressly forbidden, such act, notwithstanding the express prohibition, is in reality effectual. It would be giving to the Legislature a practical and real omnipotence with the same breath which professes to restrict their powers within narrow limits. It is prescribing limits, and declaring that those limits may be passed at pleasure.

Thus, the particular phraseology of the Constitution of the United States confirms and strengthens the principle, supposed to be essential to all written Constitutions, that a law repugnant to the Constitution is void, and that courts, as well as other departments, are bound by that instrument.

Marshall expressed a notion that has become synonymous with the rule of law: that everyone, including the highest executive, is subject to the enacted laws. As Marshall famously said in *Marbury v. Madison*, "The Government of the United States has been emphatically termed a government of laws, and not of men." He explained that in some matters a president has political discretion but in others is as much bound by the law as anyone else. This was not in dispute. The more difficult question was this: Who decides when an act exceeds constitutional authority?

Even those who think they understand the legal system may be surprised to know that the Constitution does not say that the judiciary interprets it, as Marshall concluded. Nor did the leaders at the time agree that this was so. Revolutionary intellectual Jefferson did not believe that the federal courts had the power to declare an act of Congress to be unconstitutional. He believed that giving judges the power to override legislative acts would be "very dangerous" and tend to "place us under the despotism of an oligarchy."[2] His view was that each branch must decide for itself about the validity of its actions, with the ultimate check on excess resting with change through the election process.[3] Jefferson, Madison, and others also believed that state autonomy within the federalist arrangement would constrain Congress from assuming powers not granted in the Constitution. According to this view, the states were not bound by acts of the national government that exceeded the limited powers granted to it. Jefferson invoked this power of state nullification in his Kentucky Resolution of 1799, which declared void the federal alien sedition laws that among other things allowed for the arrest of those who published "malicious" statements about the government. Jefferson argued that the states that ratified the Constitution had the "the unquestionable right to judge of its infraction" and to nullify an unauthorized act.

Jefferson could have challenged Marshall's position that the Court had the authority to refuse to enforce an act of Congress. The executive, not the judiciary, had force at its disposal. But Marshall brilliantly crafted the decision in a way that did not call for any action by any of the other branches. He said that although the president must honor the judicial appointments, the Court had no power to issue a writ of mandamus, so it could do nothing about it. Jefferson did not publicly contest the Court's interpretation of its powers, and over time the principle of judicial review became a foundation of the constitutional system. The courts do not often declare a statute to be unconstitutional, but the assumption that they have the power to do so stems from the analysis in *Marbury*.

How Is the Constitution Interpreted?

The U.S. Constitution often describes governmental powers or individual rights only in general terms. How do judges decide what the generalities mean? For most of the U.S. Supreme Court's history justices did not address this question directly. They began to do so in the second half of the 1900s, when they disagreed about their authority to invalidate statutes affecting evolving notions of individual rights. The 1960s in particular were a turbulent period during which judges staked out opposing points of view. *Griswold v. Connecticut* is an excellent example.

Molding the Constitution: *Griswold v. Connecticut*

In *Griswold v. Connecticut* the defendants were medical professionals who were fined for violating a Connecticut statute by giving advice about contraception. The U.S. Supreme Court justices agreed that such a prohibition was a bad law, but they disagreed about whether the Court had the constitutional authority to strike down the Connecticut legislation. The justices' opinions illustrate the main differing views about constitutional interpretation.

Griswold v. Connecticut
381 U.S. 479 (1965)

Justice Douglas, writing for the Court.

Appellant Griswold is Executive Director of the Planned Parenthood League of Connecticut. Appellant Buxton is a licensed physician and a professor at the Yale Medical School who served as Medical Director for the League at its Center in New Haven—a center open and operating from November 1 to November 10, 1961, when appellants were arrested.

They gave information, instruction, and medical advice to married persons as to the means of preventing conception. They examined the wife and prescribed the best contraceptive device or material for her use. Fees were usually charged, although some couples were serviced free.

The statutes whose constitutionality is involved in this appeal are 53-32 and 54-196 of the General Statutes of Connecticut. The former provides: "Any person who uses any drug, medicinal article or instrument for the purpose of preventing conception shall be fined not less than fifty dollars or imprisoned not less than sixty days nor more than one year or be both fined and imprisoned."

Section 54-196 provides: "Any person who assists, abets, counsels, causes, hires or commands another to commit any offense may be prosecuted and punished as if he were the principal offender."

The appellants were found guilty as accessories and fined $100 each, against the claim that the accessory statute as so applied violated the Fourteenth Amendment. The Appellate Division of the Circuit Court affirmed. The Supreme Court of Errors affirmed that judgment.

Coming to the merits, we are met with a wide range of questions that implicate the Due Process Clause of the Fourteenth Amendment. We do not sit as a super-legislature to determine the wisdom, need, and propriety of laws that touch economic problems, business affairs, or social conditions. This law, however, operates directly on an intimate relation of husband and wife and their physician's role in one aspect of that relation.

The right of "association," like the right of belief, is more than the right to attend a meeting; it includes the right to express one's attitudes or philosophies by membership in a group or by affiliation with it or by other lawful means. Association in that context is a form of expression of opinion; and while it is not expressly included in the First Amendment its existence is necessary in making the express guarantees fully meaningful.

The [Court's] cases suggest that specific guarantees in the Bill of Rights have penumbras, formed by emanations from those guarantees that help give them life and substance. Various guarantees create zones of privacy. The right of association contained in the penumbra of the First Amendment is one, as we have seen. The Third Amendment in its prohibition against the quartering of soldiers "in any house" in time of peace without the consent of the owner is another facet of that privacy. The Fourth Amendment explicitly affirms the "right of the people to be secure in their persons, houses, papers, and effects, against unreasonable searches and seizures." The Fifth Amendment in its Self-Incrimination Clause enables the citizen to create a zone of privacy which government may not force him to surrender to his detriment. The Ninth

Amendment provides: "The enumeration in the Constitution, of certain rights, shall not be construed to deny or disparage others retained by the people."

The Fourth and Fifth Amendments were described in *Boyd v. United States*, 116 U.S. 616, 630 (1886), as protection against all governmental invasions "of the sanctity of a man's home and the privacies of life." We recently referred in *Mapp v. Ohio*, 367 U.S. 643, 656 (1961), to the Fourth Amendment as creating a "right to privacy, no less important than any other right carefully and particularly reserved to the people."

We have had many controversies over these penumbral rights of "privacy and repose." These cases bear witness that the right of privacy which presses for recognition here is a legitimate one.

The present case, then, concerns a relationship lying within the zone of privacy created by several fundamental constitutional guarantees. And it concerns a law which, in forbidding the use of contraceptives rather than regulating their manufacture or sale, seeks to achieve its goals by means having a maximum destructive impact upon that relationship. Such a law cannot stand in light of the familiar principle, so often applied by this Court, that a "governmental purpose to control or prevent activities constitutionally subject to state regulation may not be achieved by means which sweep unnecessarily broadly and thereby invade the area of protected freedoms." *NAACP v. Alabama*, 377 U.S. 288, 307 (1964). Would we allow the police to search the sacred precincts of marital bedrooms for telltale signs of the use of contraceptives? The very idea is repulsive to the notions of privacy surrounding the marriage relationship.

We deal with a right of privacy older than the Bill of Rights—older than our political parties, older than our school system. Marriage is a coming together for better or for worse, hopefully enduring, and intimate to the degree of being sacred. It is an association that promotes a way of life, not causes; a harmony in living, not political faiths; a bilateral loyalty, not commercial or social projects. Yet it is an association for as noble a purpose as any involved in our prior decisions.

Justice Goldberg, concurring.

I agree with the Court that Connecticut's birth-control law unconstitutionally intrudes upon the right of marital privacy, and I join in its opinion and judgment. Although I have not accepted the view that "due process" as used in the Fourteenth Amendment incorporates all of the first eight Amendments . . . I do agree that the concept of liberty protects those personal rights that are fundamental, and is not confined to the specific terms of the Bill of Rights. My conclusion that the concept of liberty is not so restricted and that it embraces the right of marital privacy though that right is not mentioned explicitly in the Constitution is supported both by numerous decisions of this Court, referred to in the Court's opinion, and by the language and history of the Ninth Amendment. In reaching the conclusion that the right of marital privacy is protected, as being within the protected penumbra of specific guarantees of the Bill of Rights, the Court refers to the Ninth Amendment. I add these words to emphasize the relevance of that Amendment to the Court's holding.

This Court, in a series of decisions, has held that the Fourteenth Amendment absorbs and applies to the States those specifics of the first eight amendments which express fundamental personal rights. The language and history of the Ninth Amendment reveal that the Framers of the Constitution believed that there are additional fundamental rights, protected from governmental infringement, which exist alongside those fundamental rights specifically mentioned in the first eight constitutional amendments.

The Ninth Amendment reads, "The enumeration in the Constitution, of certain rights, shall not be construed to deny or disparage others retained by the people." The Amendment is almost entirely the work of James Madison. It was introduced in Congress by him and passed the House and Senate with little or no debate and virtually no change in language. It was proffered to quiet expressed fears that a bill of specifically enumerated rights could not be sufficiently broad to cover all essential rights and that the specific mention of certain rights would be interpreted as a denial that others were protected.

The Ninth Amendment to the Constitution may be regarded by some as a recent discovery and may be forgotten by others, but since 1791 it has been a basic part of the Constitution which we are sworn to uphold. To hold that a right so basic and fundamental and so deep-rooted in our society as the right of privacy in marriage may be infringed because that right is not guaranteed in so many words by the first eight amendments to the Constitution is to ignore the Ninth Amendment and to give it no effect whatsoever.

In determining which rights are fundamental, judges are not left at large to decide cases in light of their personal and private notions. Rather, they must look to the "traditions and [collective] conscience of our people" to determine whether a principle is "so rooted [there] . . . as to be ranked as fundamental." *Snyder v. Massachusetts*, 291 U.S. 97, 105 (1934). The inquiry is whether a right involved "is of such a character that it cannot be denied without violating those 'fundamental principles of liberty and justice which lie at the base of all our civil and political institutions.'" *Powell v. Alabama*, 287 U.S. 45, 67 (1932) (quoting *Hebert v. Louisiana*, 272 U.S. 312, 316 (1926)).

The entire fabric of the Constitution and the purposes that clearly underlie its specific guarantees demonstrate that the rights to marital privacy and to marry and raise a family are of similar order and magnitude as the fundamental rights specifically protected.

Finally, it should be said of the Court's holding today that it in no way interferes with a State's proper regulation of sexual promiscuity or misconduct. As my Brother Harlan so well stated in his dissenting opinion in *Poe v. Ullman*, 367 U.S. 497, 553 (1961):

> *Adultery, homosexuality and the like are sexual intimacies which the State forbids . . . but the intimacy of husband and wife is necessarily an essential and accepted feature of the institution of marriage, an institution which the State not only must allow, but which always and in every age it has fostered and protected. It is one thing when the State exerts its power either to forbid extra-marital sexuality . . . or to say who may marry, but it is quite another when, having acknowledged a marriage and the intimacies inherent in it, it undertakes to regulate by means of the criminal law the details of that intimacy.*

In sum, I believe that the right of privacy in the marital relation is fundamental and basic—a personal right "retained by the people" within the meaning of the Ninth Amendment. Connecticut cannot constitutionally abridge this fundamental right, which is protected by the

Fourteenth Amendment from infringement by the States. I agree with the Court that petitioners' convictions must therefore be reversed.

Justice Harlan, concurring.

I fully agree with the judgment of reversal, but find myself unable to join the Court's opinion. The reason is that it seems to me to evince an approach to this case very much like that taken by my Brothers Black and Stewart in dissent, namely: the Due Process Clause of the Fourteenth Amendment does not touch this Connecticut statute unless the enactment is found to violate some right assured by the letter or penumbra of the Bill of Rights.

In other words, what I find implicit in the Court's opinion is that the "incorporation" doctrine may be used to restrict the reach of Fourteenth Amendment Due Process. For me this is just as unacceptable constitutional doctrine as is the use of the "incorporation" approach to impose upon the States all the requirements of the Bill of Rights as found in the provisions of the first eight amendments and in the decisions of this Court interpreting them.

In my view, the proper constitutional inquiry in this case is whether this Connecticut statute infringes the Due Process Clause of the Fourteenth Amendment because the enactment violates basic values "implicit in the concept of ordered liberty," *Palko v. Connecticut*, 302 U.S. 319, 325 (1937). For reasons stated at length in my dissenting opinion in *Poe v. Ullman*, 367 U.S. 497 (1961), I believe that it does. While the relevant inquiry may be aided by resort to one or more of the provisions of the Bill of Rights, it is not dependent on them or any of their radiations. The Due Process Clause of the Fourteenth Amendment stands, in my opinion, on its own bottom.

Justice White, concurring.

In my view this Connecticut law as applied to married couples deprives them of "liberty" without due process of law, as that concept is used in the Fourteenth Amendment. I therefore concur in the judgment of the Court reversing these convictions under Connecticut's aiding and abetting statute. These decisions affirm that there is a "realm of family life which the state cannot enter" without substantial justification. *Prince v. Massachusetts*, 321 U.S. 158, 166 (1944).

The Connecticut anti-contraceptive statute deals rather substantially with this relationship. For it forbids all married persons the right to use birth-control devices, regardless of whether their use is dictated by considerations of family planning, health, or indeed even of life itself. The anti-use statute, together with the general aiding and abetting statute, prohibits doctors from affording advice to married persons on proper and effective methods of birth control. And the clear effect of these statutes, as enforced, is to deny disadvantaged citizens of Connecticut, those without either adequate knowledge or resources to obtain private counseling, access to medical assistance and up-to-date information in respect to proper methods of birth control. In my view, a statute with these effects bears a substantial burden of justification when attacked under the Fourteenth Amendment.

In these circumstances one is rather hard pressed to explain how the ban on use by married persons in any way prevents use of such devices by persons engaging in illicit sexual relations and thereby contributes to the State's policy against such relationships. Neither the state courts nor the State before the bar of this Court has tendered such an explanation. It is purely fanciful to believe that the broad proscription on use facilitates discovery of use by persons engaging in a prohibited relationship or for some other reason makes such use more unlikely and thus can be supported by any sort of administrative consideration.

I find nothing in this record justifying the sweeping scope of this statute, with its telling effect on the freedoms of married persons, and therefore conclude that it deprives such persons of liberty without due process of law.

Justice Black, dissenting.

I agree with my Brother Stewart's dissenting opinion. And like him I do not to any extent whatever base my view that this Connecticut law is constitutional on a belief that the law is wise or that its policy is a good one. In order that there may be no room at all to doubt why I vote as I do, I feel constrained to add that the law is every bit as offensive to me as it is to my Brethren of the majority and my Brothers Harlan, White and Goldberg who, reciting reasons why it is offensive to them, hold it unconstitutional.

My point is that there is no provision of the Constitution which either expressly or impliedly vests power in this Court to sit as a supervisory agency over acts of duly constituted legislative bodies and set aside their laws because of the Court's belief that the legislative policies adopted are unreasonable, unwise, arbitrary, capricious or irrational. The adoption of such a loose, flexible, uncontrolled standard for holding laws unconstitutional, if ever it is finally achieved, will amount to a great unconstitutional shift of power to the courts which I believe and am constrained to say will be bad for the courts and worse for the country. Subjecting federal and state laws to such an unrestrained and unrestrainable judicial control as to the wisdom of legislative enactments would, I fear, jeopardize the separation of governmental powers that the Framers set up and at the same time threaten to take away much of the power of States to govern themselves which the Constitution plainly intended them to have.

I realize that many good and able men have eloquently spoken and written, sometimes in rhapsodical strains, about the duty of this Court to keep the Constitution in tune with the times. The idea is that the Constitution must be changed from time to time and that this Court is charged with a duty to make those changes. For myself, I must with all deference reject that philosophy. The Constitution makers knew the need for change and provided for it. Amendments suggested by the people's elected representatives can be submitted to the people or their selected agents for ratification. That method of change was good for our Fathers, and being somewhat old-fashioned I must add it is good enough for me. And so, I cannot rely on the Due Process Clause or the Ninth Amendment or any mysterious and uncertain natural law concept as a reason for striking down this state law.

So far as I am concerned, Connecticut's law as applied here is not forbidden by any provision of the Federal Constitution as that Constitution was written, and I would therefore affirm.

Justice Stewart, dissenting.

Since 1879 Connecticut has had on its books a law which forbids the use of contraceptives by anyone. I think this is an uncommonly silly law. As a practical matter, the law is obviously unenforceable, except in the oblique context of the present case. As a philosophical matter, I believe the use of contraceptives in the relationship of marriage should be left to personal and private choice, based upon each individual's moral, ethical, and religious beliefs. As a matter of social policy, I think professional counsel about methods of birth control should be available to all, so that each individual's choice can be meaningfully made. But we are not asked in this case to say whether we think this law is unwise, or even asinine. We are asked to hold that it violates the United States Constitution. And that I cannot do.

In the course of its opinion the Court refers to no less than six Amendments to the Constitution: the First, the Third, the Fourth, the Fifth, the Ninth, and the Fourteenth. But the Court does not say which of these Amendments, if any, it thinks is infringed by this Connecticut law.

We are told that the Due Process Clause of the Fourteenth Amendment is not, as such, the "guide" in this case. With that much I agree. There is no claim that this law, duly enacted by the Connecticut Legislature is unconstitutionally vague. There is no claim that the appellants were denied any of the elements of procedural due process at their trial, so as to make their convictions constitutionally invalid.

As to the First, Third, Fourth, and Fifth Amendments, I can find nothing in any of them to invalidate this Connecticut law, even assuming that all those Amendments are fully applicable against the States. It has not even been argued that this is a law "respecting an establishment of religion, or prohibiting the free exercise thereof." And surely, unless the solemn process of constitutional adjudication is to descend to the level of a play on words, there is not involved here any abridgment of "the freedom of speech, or of the press; or the right of the people peaceably to assemble, and to petition the Government for a redress of grievances." No soldier has been quartered in any house. There has been no search, and no seizure. Nobody has been compelled to be a witness against himself.

The Court also quotes the Ninth Amendment, and my Brother Goldberg's concurring opinion relies heavily upon it. But to say that the Ninth Amendment has anything to do with this case is to turn somersaults with history. The Ninth Amendment, like its companion the Tenth, which this Court held "states but a truism that all is retained which has not been surrendered," *United States v. Darby*, 312 U.S. 100, 124 (1941), was framed by James Madison and adopted by the States simply to make clear that the adoption of the Bill of Rights did not alter the plan that the Federal Government was to be a government of express and limited powers, and that all rights and powers not delegated to it were retained by the people and the individual States. Until today no member of this Court has ever suggested that the Ninth Amendment meant anything else, and the idea that a federal court could ever use the Ninth Amendment to annul a law passed by the elected representatives of the people of the State of Connecticut would have caused James Madison no little wonder.

What provision of the Constitution, then, does make this state law invalid? The Court says it is the right of privacy "created by several fundamental constitutional guarantees." With all deference, I can find no such general right of privacy in the Bill of Rights, in any other part of the Constitution, or in any case ever before decided by this Court.

At the oral argument in this case we were told that the Connecticut law does not "conform to current community standards." But it is not the function of this Court to decide cases on the basis of community standards. If, as I should surely hope, the law before us does not reflect the standards of the people of Connecticut, the people of Connecticut can freely exercise their true Ninth and Tenth Amendment rights to persuade their elected representatives to repeal it. That is the constitutional way to take this law off the books.

In *Griswold* the majority concluded that the marital relationship was a private matter constitutionally protected against government control. A few years later in *Eisenstadt v. Baird*,[4] the Court built on the right of privacy and held that the Equal Protection Clause entitled unmarried couples to the same kind of privacy. Soon afterwards the right of privacy was invoked in one of the most controversial opinions that the Court ever issued. In the 1973 case of *Roe v. Wade*,[5] a majority of the Court held that a woman's decision about abortion was private during her first few months of pregnancy, with government having power to regulate or prohibit abortions in later stages. *Griswold* was a launching point for later judicial involvement in matters previously left to the legislature, following a course of expansive constitutional interpretation to which some judges and scholars continue to object.

The opinions in *Griswold* encapsulate the two prevailing opposing approaches to constitutional interpretation. A majority of the justices saw their proper role as including protection of rights not expressly stated in the constitutional text. The dissenting justices disagreed, restricting themselves to the constitutional text for protected rights and finding no authority for the judicial discretion assumed by the majority.

Writing for the majority, Justice Douglas did not tie his conclusion to any particular phrase in the Constitution. In his view the expressly protected rights "have penumbras, formed by emanations from those guarantees that help give them life and substance," including a "zone of privacy" into which the government may not interfere. Within that zone, he said, is the marriage relationship. Justice Goldberg cited the Ninth Amendment as a source of judges' authority to find rights not expressly enumerated. The Ninth Amendment, which provides that the enumerated rights "shall not be construed to deny or disparage others retained by the people," had previously been considered to be merely a truism reflecting that the federal government had no powers except as delegated by the Constitution. Justices Harlan and White pointed to the Due Process Clause of the Fourteenth Amendment. Harlan said that the Due Process Clause protects "basic values 'implicit in the concept of ordered liberty'" including contraceptive advice. Justice White said that the Connecticut law violated the Due Process Clause because it affected the behavior of those who are not appropriate targets of it. The common theme in all of these approaches is an assumption of authority by the justices to define what rights are protected by the Constitution.

The dissenters agreed that the prohibition against giving contraceptive advice even to married couples was a bad law, but they did not see the Court as having the authority to invalidate legislation except when it conflicted with something specific in the Constitution.

Approaches to Constitutional Interpretation

The disagreement in *Griswold* illustrates the contrast between two basic notions about the judges' proper role in interpreting the Constitution: on the one hand originalism, variants of which are called strict interpretation and textualism, and on the other hand living constitution, sometimes called nonoriginalism.

Originalism

Originalism is reflected in the *Griswold* dissenting opinions. As Justice Black explained this view, judges are not charged with updating the Constitution. As he said, "The Constitution makers knew the need for change and provided for it. Amendments suggested by the people's elected representatives can be submitted to the people or their selected agents for ratification." Originalists reject the notion that judges are better suited than legislators to plumb or respect fundamental law. U.S. Supreme Court Justice Antonin Scalia, described by many as a leading modern originalist but who prefers to be called a textualist, argues that judges are not empowered to "update" the Constitution by applying their notion of current societal values. He says, "Quite to the contrary, the legislature would seem a much more appropriate expositor of social values, and its determination that a statute is compatible with the Constitution should, as in England, prevail."[6]

Originalists look to the constitutional text and context to determine what its general terms mean. As Thomas Jefferson instructed, when interpreting the Constitution "[o]n every question of construction, [we] carry ourselves back to the time when the Constitution was adopted, recollect the spirit manifested in the debates, and instead of trying what meaning may be squeezed out of the text, or invented against it, conform to the probable one in which it was passed."[7] With an originalist approach judges consider the evident meaning of words, the way words were used at the time of adoption, the context within the rest of the Constitution, and records of the circumstances and debates surrounding adoption. Scalia acknowledges that interpreting original intent is "a task sometimes better suited to the historian than the lawyer." But originalists see this as a lesser evil than having judges apply their own notions of what the Constitution should be.[8]

Living Constitution

Judges who are characterized as nonoriginalists argue that the framers intended to create a broad and flexible document that would have meaning in unforeseen circumstances. Chief Justice Oliver Wendell Holmes, Jr., expressed this view in 1920, when he said:

> [W]hen we are dealing with words that also are a constituent act, like the Constitution of the United States, we must realize that they have called into life a being the development of which could not have been foreseen completely by the most gifted of its begetters. It was enough for them to realize or to hope that they had created an organism; it has taken a century and has cost their successors much sweat and blood to prove that they created a nation. The case before us must be considered in the light of our whole experience, and not merely in that of what was said a hundred years ago.[9]

The term "living constitution" can be traced to Howard Lee McBain's 1927 eponymously entitled book in which he described a constitution that is "elastic, expansile, and is constantly being renewed."[10] On what do the justices rely to determine just how elastic the Constitution can be? Justices in *Griswold* mentioned "the light of our whole experience," "basic values," "traditions," and the "conscience of our people" to determine whether a principle is "so rooted [there] . . . as to be ranked as fundamental." But as the dissenters asked, by what means are those sensibilities to be determined? Connecticut's elected assembly enacted the restrictive law in question and rejected efforts at its repeal, and the law was upheld by a state trial court and two state courts of appeals.[11] The judges in the majority in *Griswold* implicitly concluded that the Connecticut legislative process did not reflect the "conscience of our people," and said that in such a case it was their duty to invalidate the legislation.

Interpretive Balance

A judge's approach to constitutional interpretation rarely can simply be characterized as either entirely strict textualism or elastic interpretation. There are many variations of interpretative approaches, some of which offer guideposts for determining the extent to which judges should feel constrained by the text. For instance, some scholars argue that judges must be more protective when the issue affects a minority that cannot seek redress through the democratic process. Some judges seem to invoke various approaches depending on the issue. For example, some judges seem to employ an elastic interpretation to carve out social rights but seem more restrictive when considering property rights. Few cases require judges to choose an interpretive approach, and judges have no obligation to announce when they are doing so.

As with so many things involving the law, constitutional interpretation involves a tension between formally expressed rules and contemporary notions of basic right and wrong. The framers left room for much later disagreement about the meaning of the Constitution. We should not be surprised that a willingness to stray from textual support has increased as time has passed and conditions have continued to change. The room left for disagreement can be seen not as a shortcoming but as further evidence of the framers' genius. Their composition has allowed a gradual evolution of the law to accommodate shifts in norms and conditions while constraining lawmakers and judges sufficiently to prevent radical upheaval.

Review Questions

1. What are the main powers given to the U.S. Congress in the U.S. Constitution?
2. What is the nature of the president's powers as described in the U.S. Constitution?
3. What is the nature of the federal judiciary's powers as described in the U.S. Constitution?
4. What is the nature of judicial review as defined in *Marbury v. Madison*?
5. What alternative did Thomas Jefferson propose to judicial determination of the constitutionality of a federal law or action?

6. Based on what analysis did Justice Marshall develop the principle of judicial review in *Marbury v. Madison*?

7. What were the basic interpretative approaches that the U.S. Supreme Court justices articulated when considering a right of privacy in *Griswold v. Connecticut* and which approach prevailed in that case?

8. How do the opinions in *Griswold v. Connecticut* reflect justices' views about the roles of the judiciary and the legislature?

9. Describe the nature of the originalist approach to constitutional interpretation and why its proponents support it and its opponents object to it.

10. Describe the nature of the living constitution approach to constitutional interpretation and why its proponents support it and its opponents object to it.

Notes

1. David N. Mayer, The Constitutional Thought of Thomas Jefferson 146–58 (1994).

2. *Id.* at 271 [quoting Letter from Thomas Jefferson to William Charles Jarvis (Sept. 28, 1820)].

3. *Id.* at 270.

4. 405 U.S. 438 (1972).

5. 410 U.S. 113 (1973).

6. Antonin Scalia, Originalism: The Lesser Evil, 57 U. Cinn. L. Rev. 849, 854 (1988–89).

7. Letter from Thomas Jefferson to Supreme Court Justice William Johnson (June 12, 1823).

8. Scalia, *supra* note 6, at 857.

9. Missouri v. Holland, 252 U.S. 416, 433 (1920).

10. Howard Lee McBain, The Living Constitution 3 (1927).

11. Buxton v. Ullman, 156 A.2d 508, 513 (Conn. 1959).

Chapter 3

Due Process, Equal Protection, and Civil Rights

Those who deny freedom to others deserve it not for themselves.
Abraham Lincoln

CHAPTER OBJECTIVES

After studying this chapter you should better understand:

- The standards applied for determining whether a procedure satisfies the constitutional due process requirements
- The manner in which the restrictions on federal government action in the Bill of Rights have been incorporated into the due process guaranty that applies to state actions
- The U.S. Supreme Court's approach to determining whether classifications violate the constitutional equal protection requirements
- The classifications to which "strict scrutiny" is applied in the equal protection analysis
- The basic remedies available for civil rights violations

At the heart of the rule of law lie the ideals that everyone should be treated fairly and equally before the law. Toward this end the U.S. Constitution protects individual rights by constraining government. But fairness and equality cannot be reduced to prohibitions. To reach more broadly the Constitution also includes fundamental guaranties. Many important court decisions and legislative acts addressing individual rights have been based on the two most fundamental general guaranties: the Due Process Clause and the Equal Protection Clause.

A Due Process Clause was part of the Fifth Amendment in the original Bill of Rights and it was aimed at the federal government. It provides that no person shall be "deprived of life, liberty, or property, without due process." The original Bill of Rights did not mention equal protection of the laws in a general sense. The Fourteenth Amendment, added after the Civil War and aimed at former slave states, included the same due process provisions as the Fifth Amendment. The Fourteenth Amendment also included the Equal Protection Clause. It provides that no state shall "deny to any person within its jurisdiction the equal protection of the laws." Although nothing in the text said that equal protection applied to the federal government as well as to the states, the U.S. Supreme Court eventually held that it did. In 1954 in *Bolling v. Sharpe* the Court said that "the concepts of equal protection and due process, both stemming from our American ideal of fairness, are not mutually exclusive. The 'equal protection of the laws' is a more explicit safeguard of prohibited unfairness than 'due process of law,' and, therefore, we do not imply that the two are always interchangeable phrases. But, as this Court has recognized, discrimination may be so unjustifiable as to be violative of due process."[1] Consequently due process and equal protection apply to both federal and state laws.

The Due Process and Equal Protection Clauses address government action. They require that laws and legal procedures be fair. As discussed in the final section of this chapter, other constitutional provisions or laws may directly address unfair or discriminatory rules or procedures involving private individuals or companies. The constitutional limitations on government action also are relevant to private conduct that involves the government. In the famous 1948 case of *Shelley v. Kraemer*,[2] the U.S. Supreme Court held that the Equal Protection Clause barred a state court from enforcing racially restrictive private real estate covenants because state action would be involved. The Court also instructed that the constitutional prohibitions on government action apply to a private entity that is entrusted with authority that is "traditionally the exclusive prerogative of the State," as when a ship building company's governance of a town was the functional equivalent of a municipality.[3]

Due process and equal protection are broad concepts, but they are often the basis for invalidating specific governmental acts as well as for imposing substantial liabilities. Those who are entrusted with government authority must be mindful of these important legal principles. This chapter provides an introduction to the U.S. Supreme Court's interpretation of the Due Process and Equal Protection Clauses and to the remedies potentially available to those who suffer harm from violations of these and other fundamental rights.

Due Process

The Due Process Clauses of the Fifth and Fourteenth Amendments can readily be understood as prohibiting the government from incarcerating individuals or taking their property without legal authority or without affording a meaningful opportunity to contest the action. This is known as procedural due process. The U.S. Supreme Court has also found in the Due Process Clauses a prohibition against infringement on substantive rights regardless of the procedure employed, which is known as substantive due process.

Procedural Due Process

Individual rights are subject to state action in a wide variety of contexts as different as denial of a permit to burn trash, an elementary school suspension, and imposition of the death penalty for a heinous crime. What process is due in any given circumstance? The courts have taken an ad hoc approach to answering this question, weighing what is at stake and the nature of the opportunity to be heard.

At one end of the spectrum, courts impose rigorous requirements when someone is prosecuted for a crime, especially when the punishment can be severe. For example, in death penalty cases the U.S. Supreme Court's review has been described as super due process. In such cases courts closely scrutinize the details of the trial and sentencing procedure. At the other end of the spectrum the courts have not involved themselves much in the details of procedures for handling public benefit claims. In this context the courts allow more flexibility to the responsible officials to design a review process.

Minimum Procedure: *Mathews v. Eldridge*

The modern legal environment involves many proceedings that the Constitution's framers could not have envisioned. For example, local boards make decisions that restrict property development, and federal agencies make decisions about employment and disability benefits. As discussed in Chapter 11 of this book, a vast regulatory apparatus has developed to administer governmental economic and social programs. Although administrative authorities have been allowed considerable discretion to fashion their review procedures, courts still endeavor to insure that those involved in the procedures are afforded due process.

In 1970 in *Goldberg v. Kelly*,[4] the U.S. Supreme Court held that due process required a state agency to hold a hearing at which claimants could present evidence before their welfare benefits were terminated. The decision was widely criticized for creating a constitutional mandate for evidentiary hearings that would overwhelm administrative programs. A few years later, the Court clarified its requirement. In *Mathews v. Eldridge*, the Court examined what process was required before social security disability benefits could be terminated. The majority confined the pretermination hearing requirement and identified broad considerations for determining whether a process is sufficient.

Mathews v. Eldridge
424 U.S. 319 (1976)

Justice Powell, writing for the Court.

The issue in this case is whether the Due Process Clause of the Fifth Amendment requires that prior to the termination of Social Security disability benefit payments the recipient be afforded an opportunity for an evidentiary hearing.

Cash benefits are provided to workers during periods in which they are completely disabled under the disability insurance benefits program created by the 1956 amendments to Title II of the Social Security Act. Respondent Eldridge was first awarded benefits in June 1968. In March 1972, he received a questionnaire from the state agency charged with monitoring his medical condition. Eldridge completed the questionnaire, indicating that his condition had not improved and identifying the medical sources, including physicians, from whom he had received treatment recently. The state agency then obtained reports from his physician and a psychiatric consultant. After considering these reports and other information in his file the agency informed Eldridge by letter that it had made a tentative determination that his disability had ceased in May 1972. The letter included a statement of reasons for the proposed termination of benefits, and advised Eldridge that he might request reasonable time in which to obtain and submit additional information pertaining to his condition.

In his written response, Eldridge disputed one characterization of his medical condition and indicated that the agency already had enough evidence to establish his disability. The state agency then made its final determination that he had ceased to be disabled in May 1972. This determination was accepted by the Social Security Administration (SSA), which notified Eldridge in July that his benefits would terminate after that month. The notification also advised him of his right to seek reconsideration by the state agency of this initial determination within six months.

Instead of requesting reconsideration Eldridge commenced this action challenging the constitutional validity of the administrative procedures established by the Secretary of Health, Education, and Welfare for assessing whether there exists a continuing disability.

The District Court concluded that the administrative procedures pursuant to which the Secretary had terminated Eldridge's benefits abridged his right to procedural due process. We reverse.

Procedural due process imposes constraints on governmental decisions which deprive individuals of "liberty" or "property" interests within the meaning of the Due Process Clause of the Fifth or Fourteenth Amendment.

This Court consistently has held that some form of hearing is required before an individual is finally deprived of a property interest. The "right to be heard before being condemned to suffer grievous loss of any kind, even though it may not involve the stigma and hardships of a criminal conviction, is a principle basic to our society." *Joint Anti-Fascist Comm. v. McGrath*, 341 U.S. 123, 168 (1951) (Frankfurter, J., concurring). The fundamental requirement of due process is the opportunity to be heard "at a meaningful time and in a meaningful manner." *Armstrong v. Manzo*, 380 U.S. 545, 552 (1965).

In recent years this Court increasingly has had occasion to consider the extent to which due process requires an evidentiary hearing prior to the deprivation of some type of property interest even if such a hearing is provided thereafter. In only one case, *Goldberg v. Kelly*, 397 U.S. 254, 266–71 (1970), has the Court held that a hearing closely approximating a judicial trial is necessary. In other cases requiring some type of pretermination hearing as a matter of constitutional right the Court has spoken sparingly about the requisite procedures.

These decisions underscore the truism that "'[d]ue process,' unlike some legal rules, is not a technical conception with a fixed content unrelated to time, place and circumstances." *Cafeteria Workers v. McElroy*, 367 U.S. 886, 895 (1961). "[D]ue process is flexible, and calls for such procedural protections as the particular situation demands." *Morrissey v. Brewer*, 408 U.S.

471, 481 (1972). Accordingly, resolution of the issue whether the administrative procedures provided here are constitutionally sufficient requires analysis of the governmental and private interests that are affected. More precisely, our prior decisions indicate that identification of the specific dictates of due process generally requires consideration of three distinct factors: first, the private interest that will be affected by the official action; second, the risk of an erroneous deprivation of such interest through the procedures used, and the probable value, if any, of additional or substitute procedural safeguards; and, finally, the Government's interest, including the function involved and the fiscal and administrative burdens that the additional or substitute procedural requirement would entail.

Since a recipient whose benefits are terminated is awarded full retroactive relief if he ultimately prevails, his sole interest is in the uninterrupted receipt of this source of income pending final administrative decision on his claim.

Only in *Goldberg* has the Court held that due process requires an evidentiary hearing prior to a temporary deprivation. It was emphasized there that welfare assistance is given to persons on the very margin of subsistence . . . .

Eligibility for disability benefits, in contrast, is not based upon financial need.

As *Goldberg* illustrates, the degree of potential deprivation that may be created by a particular decision is a factor to be considered in assessing the validity of any administrative decision-making process. The potential deprivation here is generally likely to be less than in *Goldberg*, although the degree of difference can be overstated. As the District Court emphasized, to remain eligible for benefits, a recipient must be "unable to engage in substantial gainful activity." Thus, in contrast to the discharged federal employee in *Arnett v. Kennedy*, 416 U.S. 134 (1974), there is little possibility that the terminated recipient will be able to find even temporary employment to ameliorate the interim loss.

As we recognized last Term in *Fusari v. Steinberg*, 419 U.S. 379, 389 (1975), "the possible length of wrongful deprivation of . . . benefits [also] is an important factor in assessing the impact of official action on the private interests." The Secretary concedes that the delay between a request for a hearing before an administrative law judge and a decision on the claim is currently between 10 and 11 months. Since a terminated recipient must first obtain a reconsideration decision as a prerequisite to invoking his right to an evidentiary hearing, the delay between the actual cutoff of benefits and final decision after a hearing exceeds one year.

In view of the torpidity of this administrative review process, and the typically modest resources of the family unit of the physically disabled worker, the hardship imposed upon the erroneously terminated disability recipient may be significant. Still, the disabled worker's need is likely to be less than that of a welfare recipient. In addition to the possibility of access to private resources, other forms of government assistance will become available where the termination of disability benefits places a worker or his family below the subsistence level. In view of these potential sources of temporary income, there is less reason here than in *Goldberg* to depart from the ordinary principle, established by our decisions, that something less than an evidentiary hearing is sufficient prior to adverse administrative action.

An additional factor to be considered here is the fairness and reliability of the existing pretermination procedures, and the probable value, if any, of additional procedural safeguards.

Central to the evaluation of any administrative process is the nature of the relevant inquiry. In order to remain eligible for benefits, the disabled worker must demonstrate by means of "medically acceptable clinical and laboratory diagnostic techniques," 42 U.S.C. § 423(d)(3), that he is unable "to engage in any substantial gainful activity by reason of any *medically determinable physical or mental impairment. . . .*" § 423(d)(1)(A) (emphasis supplied by Court). In short, a medical assessment of the worker's physical or mental condition is required. This is a more sharply focused and easily documented decision than the typical determination of welfare entitlement. In the latter case, a wide variety of information may be deemed relevant, and issues of witness credibility and veracity often are critical to the decisionmaking process.

By contrast, the decision whether to discontinue disability benefits will turn, in most cases, upon "routine, standard, and unbiased medical reports by physician specialists," *Richardson v. Perales*, 402 U.S. 389, 404 (1971), concerning a subject whom they have personally examined. To be sure, credibility and veracity may be a factor in the ultimate disability assessment in some cases. But procedural due process rules are shaped by the risk of error inherent in the truthfinding process as applied to the generality of cases, not the rare exceptions. The potential value of an evidentiary hearing, or even oral presentation to the decisionmaker, is substantially less in this context than in *Goldberg*.

The decision in *Goldberg* also was based on the Court's conclusion that written submissions were an inadequate substitute for oral presentation because they did not provide an effective means for the recipient to communicate his case to the decisionmaker. Written submissions were viewed as an unrealistic option, for most recipients lacked the "educational attainment necessary to write effectively," and could not afford professional assistance. In addition, such submissions would not provide the "flexibility of oral presentations" or "permit the recipient to mold his argument to the issues the decisionmaker appears to regard as important." *Goldberg*, 397 U.S. at 269. In the context of the disability-benefits-entitlement assessment the administrative procedures under review here fully answer these objections.

The detailed questionnaire which the state agency periodically sends the recipient identifies with particularity the information relevant to the entitlement decision, and the recipient is invited to obtain assistance from the local SSA office in completing the questionnaire. More important, the information critical to the entitlement decision usually is derived from medical sources, such as the treating physician. Such sources are likely to be able to communicate more effectively through written documents than are welfare recipients or the lay witnesses supporting their cause. The conclusions of physicians often are supported by X-rays and the results of clinical or laboratory tests, information typically more amenable to written than to oral presentation.

A further safeguard against mistake is the policy of allowing the disability recipient's representative full access to all information relied upon by the state agency. In addition, prior to the cutoff of benefits, the agency informs the recipient of its tentative assessment, the reasons therefor, and provides a summary of the evidence that it considers most relevant. Opportunity is then afforded the recipient to submit additional evidence or arguments, enabling him to challenge directly the accuracy of information in his file, as well as the correctness of the agency's tentative conclusions. These procedures, again as contrasted with those before the Court in

Goldberg, enable the recipient to "mold" his argument to respond to the precise issues which the decisionmaker regards as crucial.

In striking the appropriate due process balance, the final factor to be assessed is the public interest. This includes the administrative burden and other societal costs that would be associated with requiring, as a matter of constitutional right, an evidentiary hearing upon demand in all cases prior to the termination of disability benefits. The most visible burden would be the incremental cost resulting from the increased number of hearings and the expense of providing benefits to ineligible recipients pending decision. No one can predict the extent of the increase, but the fact that full benefits would continue until after such hearings would assure the exhaustion in most cases of this attractive option. Nor would the theoretical right of the Secretary to recover undeserved benefits result, as a practical matter, in any substantial offset to the added outlay of public funds. The parties submit widely varying estimates of the probable additional financial cost. We only need say that experience with the constitutionalizing of government procedures suggests that the ultimate additional cost in terms of money and administrative burden would not be insubstantial.

Financial cost alone is not a controlling weight in determining whether due process requires a particular procedural safeguard prior to some administrative decision. But the Government's interest, and hence that of the public, in conserving scarce fiscal and administrative resources, is a factor that must be weighed. At some point the benefit of an additional safeguard to the individual affected by the administrative action and to society in terms of increased assurance that the action is just, may be outweighed by the cost. Significantly, the cost of protecting those whom the preliminary administrative process has identified as likely to be found undeserving may in the end come out of the pockets of the deserving since resources available for any particular program of social welfare are not unlimited.

The ultimate balance involves a determination as to when, under our constitutional system, judicial-type procedures must be imposed upon administrative action to assure fairness. In assessing what process is due in this case, substantial weight must be given to the good faith judgments of the individuals charged by Congress with the administration of social welfare programs that the procedures they have provided assure fair consideration of the entitlement claims of individuals. This is especially so where, as here, the prescribed procedures not only provide the claimant with an effective process for asserting his claim prior to any administrative action, but also assure a right to an evidentiary hearing, as well as to subsequent judicial review, before the denial of his claim becomes final.

We conclude that an evidentiary hearing is not required prior to the termination of disability benefits, and that the present administrative procedures fully comport with due process.

Justice Brennan, dissenting.

For the reasons stated in my dissenting opinion in *Richardson v. Wright*, 405 U.S. 208 (1972), I agree with the District Court and the Court of Appeals that, prior to termination of benefits, Eldridge must be afforded an evidentiary hearing of the type required for welfare beneficiaries . . . . I would add that the Court's consideration that a discontinuance of disability benefits may cause the recipient to suffer only a limited deprivation is no argument. It is speculative. Moreover, the very legislative determination to provide disability benefits, without any prerequisite determination of need in fact, presumes a need by the recipient which is not this Court's function to denigrate. Indeed, in the present case, it is indicated that because disability benefits were terminated there was a foreclosure upon the Eldridge home and the family's furniture was repossessed, forcing Eldridge, his wife and children to sleep in one bed.

The *Mathews* test balances three considerations to determine what process is due: the importance of the interest at stake to the individual; the extent to which additional procedures are likely to result in a more reliable determination; and the burdens additional procedures would impose on the government. Consideration of these factors seems logical, but their application leaves much room for unpredictability about required procedure, especially about whether a hearing must be conducted before action is taken. In *Goldberg* the Court held that a hearing must be held before welfare benefits could be terminated; in *Mathews* the Court said such a step was not required for termination of disability benefits. Applying the *Mathews* test the Court has held that a school security guard could be terminated without a prior hearing if given an opportunity to provide information before termination,[5] a police officer could be suspended for misconduct without a prior hearing,[6] and a medical student could be dismissed for poor clinical performance without a hearing based on a review by a panel of doctors and administrators.[7]

Due Process and Fundamental Rights

In the Due Process Clause the U.S. Supreme Court has found more than assurance that a meaningful procedure will be followed when government action affects someone's life, liberty, or property. The Court also has relied on the notion of due process for identification of other rights deemed fundamental.

Implied Fundamental Rights

As demonstrated in the discussion of *Griswold v. Connecticut* in Chapter 2, the U.S. Supreme Court has pointed to due process to protect implied fundamental rights, including the right to privacy described in *Griswold* and later cases. As Justice Harlan put it in *Griswold*, protection of fundamental rights is "implicit in the concept of ordered liberty" and required as part of due process. This notion of carving out fundamental rights as unassailable has been called substantive due process.

At first the substantive due process notion was applied to economic rights. In 1905 in *Lochner v. New York*,[8] the Court held that a New York law limiting bakers' working hours violated a "right to free contract" implicit in the Fourteenth Amendment's Due Process Clause, which the Court said protected the employer's right to make employment decisions as well as the employee's decisions about working. During the Great Depression the Court changed course under considerable pressure from President Franklin Roosevelt, whose administration's economic regulations were being invalidated by the Court as unconstitutional intrusions into the freedom of contract. In 1937 in *West Coast Hotel Co. v. Parrish*,[9] the Court shifted and upheld minimum wage legislation, saying that the freedom to contract was not "absolute and uncontrollable" and that economic "regulation which is reasonable in relation to its subject and is adopted in the interests of the community is due process."[10] The substance of economic restrictions therefore no longer much mattered provided they were the product of the legislative process. The Court also upheld labor regulations of steel industry,[11] adopting a deferential review of legislation regulating commerce and thereafter enabling vast expansion of economic regulations. For several decades substantive due process remained dormant.

As discussed in Chapter 2 of this book, substantive due process reemerged in *Griswold v. Connecticut* when a majority of the Court held that individuals had an implied fundamental right to privacy. As Justice Harlan put it in *Griswold*, the Due Process Clause protected basic values "implicit in the concept of ordered liberty," though the Court stopped referring to economic rights as among those basic values. The focus became a right of privacy, which later arose in *Roe v. Wade*,[12] the decision that continues to define the Court's approach to abortion laws. In *Roe* the Court held that the right of privacy was broad enough to cover a mother's abortion decision. The Court decided that a legal prohibition against abortion in the first trimester of pregnancy violated a mother's right of due process, but that abortions in the second trimester could be regulated and they could be prohibited in the third trimester. The notion of substantive due process as reinvigorated in *Griswold* therefore became the foundation for the Court's approach to one of the most controversial issues it has faced.

Incorporation Against the States

As previously noted the Bill of Rights was aimed at the federal government. The Fourteenth Amendment's due process guaranties against state infringement served as a springboard for the U.S. Supreme Court to apply the original Bill of Rights to state action. This expansion occurred in a series of cases through a judicial interpretative process known as incorporation.

The Court's justices have disagreed about the extent to which the Bill of Rights should be applied to state laws based on the Fourteenth Amendment. Some saw no authority for such a step, such as Justice Stanley Reed who said, "Nothing has been called to our attention that either the framers of the Fourteenth Amendment or the states that adopted intended its due process clause to draw within its scope the earlier amendments to the Constitution."[13] But Justice Hugo Black argued that the Fourteenth Amendment was intended to make all of the Bill of Rights applicable to the states. He said, "In my judgment that history conclusively demonstrates that the language of the first section of the Fourteenth Amendment, taken as a whole, was thought by those responsible for its submission to the people, and by those who opposed its submission, sufficiently explicit to guarantee that thereafter no state could deprive its citizens of the privileges and protections of the Bill of Rights."[14] Neither Reed's nor Black's view was accepted by a majority of the Court. The approach that the Court did follow is known as "selective incorporation," which as Justice Felix Frankfurter described it, required the Court to give the Due Process Clause of the Fourteenth Amendment an "independent function," applying protections in the Bill of Rights against the states according to "accepted notions of justice."[15]

By now the Court has incorporated almost all of the Bill of Rights into the Fourteenth Amendment's due process guaranty. The incorporated rights include the First Amendment protections for free speech, press, and assembly, and the right to exercise of religion and against establishment of religion; the Fourth Amendment protections against unreasonable searches and seizures; the Fifth Amendment's prohibitions against double jeopardy and self-incrimination; the Sixth Amendment's criminal procedure guaranties of a speedy and public trial, juries, witness confrontation, one's own witnesses, and a lawyer; and the Eighth Amendment's prohibition against cruel and unusual punishment. There is now little notable difference between the rights that have been found to be protected against federal and state action.

Equal Protection

Enacted in the aftermath of the Civil War, the Equal Protection Clause was aimed at state-sponsored racial discrimination in the formerly rebellious states. It did not achieve widespread social compliance. Nor did the U.S. Supreme Court readily embrace the principles of equal protection. Several decades later, in 1896 in *Plessy v. Ferguson*,[16] the Court still held the view that state law could segregate people by race as long as they had separate but equal facilities. For many years thereafter, the Equal Protection Clause served little function in constitutional interpretation. For instance, in 1927 in *Buck v. Bell*,[17] Justice Oliver Wendell Holmes said that Virginia's sterilization of state hospital inmates did not deny them equal protection, and referred to an equal protection contention as "the usual last resort of constitutional arguments to point out shortcomings of this sort."[18]

In 1954 the Court at last rescinded its approval of "separate but equal." In the landmark case of *Brown v. Board of Education*,[19] the Court held that separate state public schools were inherently unequal, and in *Bolling v. Sharpe*,[20] the Court held that the same was true under federal law with respect to the District of Columbia's public schools. Since *Brown v. Board of Education* the Court has subjected many other classifications to equal protection review according to an analytical framework for determining the degree to which such classifications will be scrutinized.

Legal Preferences: *Grutter v. Bollinger*

The consideration of race in a selection process for hiring or school admissions is among the most controversial legal issues. In the 2003 case of *Grutter v. Bollinger*, the U.S. Supreme Court reviewed the University of Michigan Law School's admission policy. The policy required consideration of a range of variables and declared a commitment to enrollment of a "critical mass" of underrepresented minority students. A white student who had high grades and test scores but who was denied admission challenged the policy, alleging that the law school discriminated against her on the basis of race in violation of the Fourteenth Amendment's Equal Protection Clause. According to the Court's equal protection analysis, racial classifications are subject to strict scrutiny. This case illustrates just how differently justices can go about applying such scrutiny.

Grutter v. Bollinger
539 U.S. 306 (2003)

Justice O'Connor, writing for the Court.

This case requires us to decide whether the use of race as a factor in student admissions by the University of Michigan Law School (Law School) is unlawful.

The Law School ranks among the Nation's top law schools. It receives more than 3,500 applications each year for a class of around 350 students. Seeking to "admit a group of students who individually and collectively are among the most capable," the Law School looks for individuals with "substantial promise for success in law school" and "a strong likelihood of succeeding in the practice of law and contributing in diverse ways to the well-being of others." More broadly, the Law School seeks "a mix of students with varying backgrounds and experiences who will respect and learn from each other."

The hallmark of that policy is its focus on academic ability coupled with a flexible assessment of applicants' talents, experiences, and potential "to contribute to the learning of those around them." The policy requires admissions officials to evaluate each applicant based on all the information available in the file, including a personal statement, letters of recommendation, and an essay describing the ways in which the applicant will contribute to the life and diversity of the Law School.

The policy does not restrict the types of diversity contributions eligible for "substantial weight" in the admissions process, but instead recognizes "many possible bases for diversity admissions." The policy does, however, reaffirm the Law School's longstanding commitment to "one particular type of diversity," that is, "racial and ethnic diversity with special reference to the inclusion of students from groups which have been historically discriminated against, like African-Americans, Hispanics and Native Americans, who without this commitment might not be represented in our student body in meaningful numbers." By enrolling a "'critical mass' of [underrepresented] minority students," the Law School seeks to "ensur[e] their ability to make unique contributions to the character of the Law School."

Petitioner Barbara Grutter is a white Michigan resident who applied to the Law School in 1996 with a 3.8 GPA and 161 LSAT score. The Law School initially placed petitioner on a waiting list, but subsequently rejected her application. Petitioner alleged that respondents discriminated against her on the basis of race in violation of the Fourteenth Amendment . . . .

Because the Fourteenth Amendment "protect[s] persons, not groups," all "governmental action based on race—a *group* classification long recognized as in most circumstances irrelevant and therefore prohibited—should be subjected to detailed judicial inquiry to ensure that the *personal* right to equal protection of the laws has not been infringed." *Adarand Constructors, Inc. v. Peña*, 515 U.S. 200, 227 (1995).

We have held that all racial classifications imposed by government "must be analyzed by a reviewing court under strict scrutiny." *Id*. This means that such classifications are constitutional only if they are narrowly tailored to further compelling governmental interests.

Before this Court, as they have throughout this litigation, respondents assert only one justification for their use of race in the admissions process: obtaining "the educational benefits that flow from a diverse student body." In other words, the Law School asks us to recognize, in the context of higher education, a compelling state interest in student body diversity.

The Law School's educational judgment that such diversity is essential to its educational mission is one to which we defer. Our scrutiny of the interest asserted by the Law School is no less strict for taking into account complex educational judgments in an area that lies primarily within the expertise of the university.

We have long recognized that, given the important purpose of public education and the expansive freedoms of speech and thought associated with the university environment, universities occupy a special niche in our constitutional tradition. Our conclusion that the Law School has a compelling interest in a diverse student body is informed by our view that attaining a diverse student body is at the heart of the Law School's proper institutional mission, and that "good faith" on the part of a university is "presumed" absent "a showing to the contrary." *Regents of Univ. of Cal. v. Bakke*, 438 U.S. 265, 318–19 (1978).

As part of its goal of "assembling a class that is both exceptionally academically qualified and broadly diverse," the Law School seeks to "enroll a 'critical mass' of minority students." The Law School's interest is not simply "to assure within its student body some specified percentage of a particular group merely because of its race or ethnic origin." *Bakke*, 438 U.S. at 307. That would amount to outright racial balancing, which is patently unconstitutional. Rather, the Law School's concept of critical mass is defined by reference to the educational benefits that diversity is designed to produce.

These benefits are substantial. As the District Court emphasized, the Law School's admissions policy promotes "cross-racial understanding," helps to break down racial stereotypes, and "enables [students] to better understand persons of different races." These benefits are "important and laudable," because "classroom discussion is livelier, more spirited, and simply more enlightening and interesting" when the students have "the greatest possible variety of backgrounds."

These benefits are not theoretical but real, as major American businesses have made clear that the skills needed in today's increasingly global marketplace can only be developed through exposure to widely diverse people, cultures, ideas, and viewpoints.

We have repeatedly acknowledged the overriding importance of preparing students for work and citizenship, describing education as pivotal to "sustaining our political and cultural heritage" with a fundamental role in maintaining the fabric of society. *Plyler v. Doe*, 457 U.S. 202, 221 (1982). For this reason, the diffusion of knowledge and opportunity through public institutions of higher education must be accessible to all individuals regardless of race or ethnicity.

Moreover, universities, and in particular, law schools, represent the training ground for a large number of our Nation's leaders. Individuals with law degrees occupy roughly half the state governorships, more than half the seats in the United States Senate, and more than a third of the seats in the United States House of Representatives. The pattern is even more striking when it comes to highly selective law schools. A handful of these schools accounts for 25 of the 100 United States Senators, 74 United States Courts of Appeals judges, and nearly 200 of the more than 600 United States District Court judges.

In order to cultivate a set of leaders with legitimacy in the eyes of the citizenry, it is necessary that the path to leadership be visibly open to talented and qualified individuals of every race and ethnicity.

Even in the limited circumstance when drawing racial distinctions is permissible to further a compelling state interest, government is still "constrained in how it may pursue that end: [T]he means chosen to accomplish the [government's] asserted purpose must be specifically and narrowly framed to accomplish that purpose." *Shaw v. Hunt*, 517 U.S. 899, 908 (1996).

To be narrowly tailored, a race-conscious admissions program cannot use a quota system— it cannot "insulat[e] each category of applicants with certain desired qualifications from competition with all other applicants." *Bakke*, 438 U.S. at 315. Instead, a university may consider race or ethnicity only as a "'plus' in a particular applicant's file," without "insulat[ing] the individual from comparison with all other candidates for the available seats." *Id.* at 317.

The Law School's goal of attaining a critical mass of underrepresented minority students does not transform its program into a quota. Nor, as Justice Kennedy posits, does the Law School's consultation of the "daily reports," which keep track of the racial and ethnic composition of the class (as well as of residency and gender), "sugges[t] there was no further attempt at individual review save for race itself" during the final stages of the admissions process. To the contrary, the Law School's admissions officers testified without contradiction that they never gave race any more or less weight based on the information contained in these reports. Moreover, as Justice Kennedy concedes, between 1993 and 2000, the number of African-American, Latino, and Native-American students in each class at the Law School varied from 13.5 to 20.1 percent, a range inconsistent with a quota.

We also find that, like the Harvard plan Justice Powell referenced in *Bakke*, the Law School's race-conscious admissions program adequately ensures that all factors that may contribute to student body diversity are meaningfully considered alongside race in admissions decisions. With respect to the use of race itself, all underrepresented minority students admitted by the Law School have been deemed qualified. By virtue of our Nation's struggle with racial inequality, such students are both likely to have experiences of particular importance to the Law School's mission, and less likely to be admitted in meaningful numbers on criteria that ignore those experiences.

We take the Law School at its word that it would "like nothing better than to find a race-neutral admissions formula" and will terminate its race-conscious admissions program as soon as practicable. It has been 25 years since Justice Powell first approved the use of race to further an interest in student body diversity in the context of public higher education. Since that time, the number of minority applicants with high grades and test scores has indeed increased. We expect that 25 years from now, the use of racial preferences will no longer be necessary to further the interest approved today.

Justice Thomas, concurring in part and dissenting in part.

Frederick Douglass, speaking to a group of abolitionists almost 140 years ago, delivered a message lost on today's majority:

> *[I]n regard to the colored people, there is always more that is benevolent, I perceive, than just, manifested towards us. What I ask for the negro is not benevolence, not pity, not sympathy, but simply* justice. *The American people have always been anxious to know what they shall do with us. . . . I have had but one answer from the beginning. Do nothing with us! Your doing with us has already played the mischief with us. Do nothing with us! If the apples will not remain on the tree of their own strength, if they are worm-eaten at the core, if they are early ripe and disposed to fall, let them fall! . . . And if the negro cannot stand on his own legs, let him fall also. All I ask is, give him a chance to stand on his own legs! Let him alone! . . . [Y]our interference is doing him positive injury.*

The Constitution abhors classifications based on race, not only because those classifications can harm favored races or are based on illegitimate motives, but also because every time the government places citizens on racial registers and makes race relevant to the provision of burdens or benefits, it demeans us all.

While legal education at a public university may be good policy or otherwise laudable, it is obviously not a pressing public necessity when the correct legal standard is applied. [T]he absence of a public, American Bar Association (ABA) accredited, law school in Alaska, Delaware, Massachusetts, New Hampshire, and Rhode Island, provides further evidence that Michigan's maintenance of the Law School does not constitute a compelling state interest.

The only cognizable state interests vindicated by operating a public law school are, therefore, the education of that State's citizens and the training of that State's lawyers.

The Law School today, however, does precious little training of those attorneys who will serve the citizens of Michigan. In 2002, graduates of the University of Michigan Law School made up less than 6% of applicants to the Michigan bar, even though the Law School's graduates constitute nearly 30% of all law students graduating in Michigan. Less than 16% of the Law School's graduating class elects to stay in Michigan after law school.

In sum, the Law School trains few Michigan residents and overwhelmingly serves students, who, as lawyers, leave the State of Michigan. The Law School's decision to be an elite institution does little to advance the welfare of the people of Michigan or any cognizable interest of the State of Michigan.

With the adoption of different admissions methods, such as accepting all students who meet minimum qualifications, the Law School could achieve its vision of the racially aesthetic student body without the use of racial discrimination.

The Court bases its unprecedented deference to the Law School—a deference antithetical to strict scrutiny—on an idea of "educational autonomy" grounded in the First Amendment. In my view, there is no basis for a right of public universities to do what would otherwise violate the Equal Protection Clause.

The absence of any articulated legal principle supporting the majority's principal holding suggests another rationale. I believe what lies beneath the Court's decision today are the benighted notions that one can tell when racial discrimination benefits (rather than hurts) minority groups, and that racial discrimination is necessary to remedy general societal ills.

It is uncontested that each year, the Law School admits a handful of blacks who would be admitted in the absence of racial discrimination. Who can differentiate between those who belong and those who do not? The majority of blacks are admitted to the Law School because of discrimination, and because of this policy all are tarred as undeserving. This problem of stigma does not depend on determinacy as to whether those stigmatized are actually the "beneficiaries" of racial discrimination. When blacks take positions in the highest places of government, industry, or academia, it is an open question today whether their skin color played a part in their advancement.

The Court also holds that racial discrimination in admissions should be given another 25 years before it is deemed no longer narrowly tailored to the Law School's fabricated compelling state interest. While I agree that in 25 years the practices of the Law School will be illegal, they are, for the reasons I have given, illegal now.

Chief Justice Rehnquist, dissenting.

From 1995 through 2000, the Law School admitted between 1,130 and 1,310 students. Of those, between 13 and 19 were Native American, between 91 and 108 were African-Americans, and between 47 and 56 were Hispanic. If the Law School is admitting between 91 and 108 African-Americans in order to achieve "critical mass," thereby preventing African-American students from feeling "isolated or like spokespersons for their race," one would think that a number of the same order of magnitude would be necessary to accomplish the same purpose for Hispanics and Native Americans. Similarly, even if all of the Native American applicants admitted in a given year matriculate, which the record demonstrates is not at all the case, how can this possibly constitute a "critical mass" of Native Americans in a class of over 350 students? In order for this pattern of admission to be consistent with the Law School's explanation of "critical mass," one would have to believe that the objectives of "critical mass" offered by respondents are achieved with only half the number of Hispanics and one-sixth the number of Native Americans as compared to African-Americans.

[T]he correlation between the percentage of the Law School's pool of applicants who are members of the three minority groups and the percentage of the admitted applicants who are members of these same groups is far too precise to be dismissed as merely the result of the school paying "some attention to [the] numbers." [F]rom 1995 through 2000 the percentage of admitted applicants who were members of these minority groups closely tracked the percentage of individuals in the school's applicant pool who were from the same groups.

The Law School cannot precisely control which of its admitted applicants decide to attend the university. But it can and, as the numbers demonstrate, clearly does employ racial preferences in extending offers of admission.

The Court, in an unprecedented display of deference under our strict scrutiny analysis, upholds the Law School's program despite its obvious flaws. We have said that when it comes to the use of race, the connection between the ends and the means used to attain them must be precise. But here the flaw is deeper than that; it is not merely a question of "fit" between ends and means. Here the means actually used are forbidden by the Equal Protection Clause of the Constitution.

Justice Kennedy, dissenting.

About 80% to 85% of the places in the entering class are given to applicants in the upper range of Law School Admissions Test scores and grades. An applicant with these credentials likely will be admitted without consideration of race or ethnicity. With respect to the remaining 15% to 20% of the seats, race is likely outcome determinative for many members of minority groups.

The Law School has not demonstrated how individual consideration is, or can be, preserved at this stage of the application process given the instruction to attain what it calls critical mass. In fact the evidence shows otherwise. There was little deviation among admitted minority students during the years from 1995 to 1998. The percentage of enrolled minorities fluctuated only by 0.3%, from 13.5% to 13.8%. The number of minority students to whom offers were extended varied by just a slightly greater magnitude of 2.2%, from the high of 15.6% in 1995 to the low of 13.4% in 1998.

The obvious tension between the pursuit of critical mass and the requirement of individual review increased by the end of the admissions season. Most of the decisions where race may decide the outcome are made during this period. The admissions officers consulted the daily reports which indicated the composition of the incoming class along racial lines. As Dennis Shields, Director of Admissions from 1991 to 1996, stated, "the further [he] went into the [admissions] season the more frequently [he] would want to look at these [reports] and see the change from day-to-day." These reports would "track exactly where [the Law School] st[ood] at any given time in assembling the class," and so would tell the admissions personnel whether they were short of assembling a critical mass of minority students. Shields generated these reports because the Law School's admissions policy told him the racial make-up of the entering class was "something [he] need[ed] to be concerned about," and so he had "to find a way of tracking what's going on."

The consultation of daily reports during the last stages in the admissions process suggests there was no further attempt at individual review save for race itself. The admissions officers could use the reports to recalibrate the plus factor given to race depending on how close they were to achieving the Law School's goal of critical mass. The bonus factor of race would then become divorced from individual review; it would be premised instead on the numerical objective set by the Law School.

There is no constitutional objection to the goal of considering race as one modest factor among many others to achieve diversity, but an educational institution must ensure, through sufficient procedures, that each applicant receives individual consideration and that race does not become a predominant factor in the admissions decisionmaking. The Law School failed to comply with this requirement, and by no means has it carried its burden to show otherwise by the test of strict scrutiny.

If universities are given the latitude to administer programs that are tantamount to quotas, they will have few incentives to make the existing minority admissions schemes transparent and protective of individual review.

As the majority in *Grutter v. Bollinger* noted, constitutional rights belong to individuals, not groups. The law school candidate before the Court was not accused of any wrongful conduct herself, and from her perspective she would have been admitted if her race were different. The justices who decided that the law school's consideration of race as a "plus factor" was nonetheless permissible obviously felt strongly that institutions needed some leniency from racial blindness to take steps to diversify. These justices said they would defer to the law school's judgment despite acknowledging that, according to their own cases, race classifications must always be subjected to strict scrutiny. The dissenting justices argued that upon close scrutiny the school's policy is revealed as a disguised process for ensuring that a minimum number of students of a particular race would be enrolled. They had a different version of what it meant to apply strict scrutiny. None of the justices' analytical approaches can be divorced from their policy perspectives.

Scrutiny of Classifications

Although the majority and dissenting justices in *Grutter* disagreed about how to scrutinize the law school's admissions policy, the law has been settled that under the Equal Protection Clause racial classifications are subject to something called "strict scrutiny." All agree that strict scrutiny is the least deferential of several levels of scrutiny that the Court applies in an equal protection analysis. The scrutiny gradations can be traced to a famous "Footnote Four" in *United States v. Carolene Products Co.*,[21] a 1938 case in which the Court upheld federal milk product regulations. In that footnote Justice Stone suggested legislation should be more closely scrutinized if it implicates a prohibition of the Bill of Rights or affects the rights of "discrete and insular minorities" who were not protected in the democratic process. The Court later followed this suggestion in its equal protection cases.

In the equal protection analysis the level of scrutiny depends on whether the Court deems the class to be suspect. A class is suspect if there are unlikely to be appropriate reasons for making distinctions based on membership in it. Strict scrutiny applies to racial classifications by local, state, and federal government, including in government contracting.[22] Strict scrutiny also has been applied to distinctions based on alienage,[23] citizenship,[24] and ethnicity.[25] As the test is described in *Grutter*, strict scrutiny requires that the classification be narrowly tailored to further a compelling governmental interest. The Court therefore examines both the classification's purpose and its manner of implementation. In *Grutter* and in the earlier affirmative action case *Bakke*, which was discussed at length in *Grutter*, a majority of the Court held that attaining a diverse student body was a compelling interest for a university admissions program. In *Bakke* the Court held that holding a prescribed number of seats for an ethnic minority was not a sufficiently narrow way to pursue this interest; in *Grutter* the Court held that the plus factor approach was adequately tailored.

Gender classifications are not subjected to strict scrutiny. Gender distinctions sometimes are common sense, but the Court has held that the Constitution does not allow "overbroad generalizations about the different talents, capacities, or preferences of males and females."[26] The Court applies an intermediate scrutiny that requires that classifications serve "important governmental objectives" and be "substantially related to the achievement of those objectives."[27] "Substantially related" obviously is a lower threshold than "narrowly tailored" as required under strict scrutiny. In *Michael M. v. Superior Court of Sonoma County*,[28] the Court upheld a statutory rape law that prohibited males from having sex with minor women but not vice versa, based on the state's legitimate objective of preventing teen pregnancies and the fact that only women can get pregnant. In *Craig v. Boren*,[29] however, the Court held that a different minimum age for males and females to purchase alcohol had not been shown to be connected to legitimate safety concerns. In *United States v. Virginia*,[30] the Court held that the Virginia Military Institute's policy of excluding women also failed intermediate scrutiny because the gender integration concerns were insufficient to outweigh the importance of allowing women to participate in the unique program. The Court also has applied a similar intermediate degree of scrutiny to legal classifications based on illegitimacy.[31]

Most other distinctions claimed to violate equal protection are reviewed only for a reasonable basis. In the 1970 case of *Dandridge v. Williams*,[32] the Court said, "In the area of economics and social welfare, a State does not violate the Equal Protection Clause merely because the classifications made by its laws are imperfect. If the classification has some 'reasonable basis,' it does not offend the Constitution simply because the classification 'is not made with mathematical nicety or because in practice it results in some inequality.'"[33] The reasonable basis need not have been articulated when the classification was set. Applying a reasonable basis test means a court is highly unlikely to find fault with the challenged classification.

So far the Court has not applied heightened scrutiny to sexual orientation classifications. In 1996 in *Romer v. Evans*,[34] the Court held that a state constitutional amendment forbidding legal protection based on sexual orientation had no identifiable legitimate purpose and therefore failed even minimal scrutiny. Sexual orientation classifications have been successfully challenged based on state constitutions as well. The California Supreme Court struck down a same-sex marriage law, employing strict scrutiny based on a fundamental right to marriage under the California Constitution, which was later overruled by a ballot proposition declaring that only a marriage between a man and a woman is valid in the state.[35] The Massachusetts Supreme Court held that a state law prohibition against same-sex marriages had no rational basis, violating both due process and equal protection under the Massachusetts Constitution.[36] The Connecticut Supreme Court reached the same conclusion applying intermediate scrutiny.[37] Other courts use various approaches to the issue under their constitutions.

Remedies for Civil Rights Violations

Many of the constitutional cases brought before the U.S. Supreme Court seek to invalidate a law. Invalidation may not address harm that individuals have suffered from violations of their constitutional rights. Sometimes the court can rectify the situation. For instance, if the Court in *Grutter* had determined that the admissions policy was unconstitutional the Court could have ordered the student's admission. In many contexts statutes authorize monetary remedies for those harmed by unconstitutional actions. Such remedies often include recovery of attorneys' fees and other costs, which not only could allow a more full recovery of financial loss but also encourage individuals of limited means to seek relief.

Civil rights monetary remedies were authorized soon after ratification of the Fourteenth Amendment, with the Ku Klux Klan Act of 1871. Some of its provisions remain law today, including 42 U.S.C. § 1983, often simply referred to as "Section 1983." Section 1983 provides that "[e]very person who, under color of any statute, ordinance, regulation, custom, or usage, of any State or Territory or the District of Columbia, subjects, or causes to be subjected, any citizen of the United States or other person within the jurisdiction thereof to the deprivation of any rights, privileges, or immunities secured by the Constitution and laws, shall be liable to the party injured in an action at law, suit in equity . . . ." Section 1983 actions therefore can be brought based on allegations of violations of any constitutional right under color of state law. Examples include claims for injuries resulting from excessive police force in violation of the Fourth Amendment prohibitions against unreasonable searches and seizures, or for injuries suffered by prisoners for cruel and unusual conditions prohibited by the Eighth Amendment.

In most cases a civil rights suit will be aimed at a government official or employee alleged to have acted wrongly. The Eleventh Amendment prohibits suits against the state governments but not against individual state officials. In *Monell v. Department of Social Services*,[38] the Court held that a local government could be liable under Section 1983 if it adopted a policy or custom that caused the deprivation. The local government is not responsible for its employees' self-motivated individual wrongful acts.

A second wave of civil rights legislation was highlighted by the Civil Rights Act of 1964, which broadly outlawed racial segregation in schools, public places, and employment. The Civil Rights Act of 1964 also created the Equal Employment Opportunity Commission, which has the power to bring enforcement actions. Title VII of the act prohibits discrimination in employment on the basis of race, color, religion, sex, or national origin.[39] It applies to employers with 15 or more regular employees. It also prohibits sexual harassment, which is treated as sex discrimination for purposes of Title VII. The Court has held that Title VII also applies to employment practices that have a "racially disparate impact" on protected groups, not just instances of individual discrimination.[40] There are exceptions from Title VII, including for certain occupations where the classification is appropriate, such as when a religious organization hires members of its own faith. Title VII is a very far-reaching law, applying to many private associations the equal protection that constitutionally applies to government actions.

Other parts of the Civil Rights Act prohibit discrimination in contexts other than employment, including Title II that forbids discrimination at hotels, motels, restaurants, theaters, and other public accommodations. Soon after Title II was enacted the Court addressed the constitutionality of applying antidiscrimination laws to actions not involving the government. In *Katzenbach v. McClung*,[41] the owners of an Alabama restaurant challenged the application of the law to their policy of giving inside service only to white customers. Citing Congress' power to regulate commerce and to enact necessary and property laws, Justice Tom Clark, writing for the Court, described Congress' power as virtually limitless:

> *The power of Congress in this field is broad and sweeping; where it keeps within its sphere and violates no express constitutional limitation it has been the rule of this Court, going back almost to the founding days of the Republic, not to interfere. The*

*Civil Rights Act of 1964, as here applied, we find to be plainly appropriate in the res-
olution of what the Congress found to be a national commercial problem of the first
magnitude. We find it in no violation of any express limitations of the Constitution
and we therefore declare it valid.*[42]

The Court also quickly upheld the constitutionality of applying antiracial discrimination laws to
private property agreements. In *Jones v. Alfred H. Mayer Co.*,[43] the Court held that Congress
could forbid racial discrimination in the sale of private property based on the Thirteenth Amendment's slavery prohibition. The Court said, "At the very least, the freedom that Congress is
empowered to secure under the Thirteenth Amendment includes the freedom to buy whatever a
white man can buy, the right to live wherever a white man can live."[44] The Thirteenth Amendment makes no mention of state action; it outlaws slavery anywhere and authorizes Congress to
enforce this prohibition.

There are now many federal and state statutes prohibiting various forms of discrimination in the
community as well as in the government. They include the federal Age Discrimination in Employment Act protecting those who are 40 or older,[45] and the federal Americans with Disabilities Act
of 1990 that requires certain accommodations to be made for a "physical or mental impairment
that substantially limits one or more of the major life activities of such individual."[46] Title IX prohibits gender exclusion from education and federal financial assistance programs, and it has
caused schools and colleges to redirect resources to make athletic programs available to women.[47]
Many state statutes similarly forbid discrimination based on various classifications.

Criminal laws also have been enacted to address civil rights violations. For example, federal
law makes it a crime for any person acting under color of law to willfully deprive someone of
constitutional or legal rights.[48] Other statutes address specific types of conduct, such as violating someone's right to vote,[49] or denial of access to fair housing.[50]

Review Questions

1. What is the substantive due process analysis and to what rights has it been applied?

2. What is the constitutional interpretive process of incorporation, and what has been the
   result of its application?

3. What kinds of actions are subject to the U.S. Constitution's due process requirements?

4. What is the test for determining whether a procedure for terminating government
   benefits satisfies the constitutional due process requirements?

5. What approach has the U.S. Supreme Court taken in applying the Equal Protection
   Clause to classifications?

6. To what classifications is strict scrutiny applied in the equal protection analysis?

7. What were the two principal opposing perspectives that justices expressed in *Grutter
   v. Bollinger* for determining whether consideration of race in admissions satisfied
   equal protection requirements?

8. To what classifications is the equal protection intermediate scrutiny applied?
9. To what is the equal protection reasonable basis test applied?
10. What are the principal laws on which civil rights claims may be made?

Notes

1. 347 U.S. 497, 499 (1954).
2. 334 U.S. 1 (1948).
3. Jackson v. Metropolitan Edison Co., 419 U.S. 345, 353 (1974).
4. 397 U.S. 254 (1970).
5. Cleveland Bd. of Ed. v. Loudermill, 470 U.S. 532 (1985).
6. Gilbert v. Homar, 520 U.S. 924 (1997).
7. Board of Curators v. Horowitz, 435 U.S. 78 (1978).
8. 198 U.S. 45 (1905).
9. 300 U.S. 379 (1937).
10. *Id*. at 391.
11. NLRB v. Jones & Laughlin Steel Corp., 301 U.S. 1 (1937).
12. 410 U.S. 113 (1973).
13. Adamson v. California, 332 U.S. 46, 54 (1947).
14. *Id*. at 74–75 (Black, J. dissenting).
15. *Id*. at 67–68 (Frankfurter, J., concurring).
16. 163 U.S. 537 (1896).
17. 274 U.S. 200 (1927).
18. *Id*. at 208.
19. 347 U.S. 483 (1954).
20. 347 U.S. 497 (1954).
21. 304 U.S. 144 (1938).
22. Adarand Constructors, Inc. v. Peña, 515 U.S. 200 (1995).
23. Graham v. Richardson, 403 U.S. 365 (1971).
24. Oyama v. California, 332 U.S. 633 (1948).
25. Hernandez v. Texas, 347 U.S. 475 (1954).
26. United States v. Virginia, 518 U.S. 515, 533 (1996).
27. Wengler v. Druggists Mut. Ins. Co., 446 U.S. 142, 150 (1980).
28. 450 U.S. 464 (1981).
29. 429 U.S. 190 (1976).

30. United States v. Virginia, 518 U.S. 515 (1996).

31. Mills v. Habluetzel, 456 U.S. 91 (1982).

32. 397 U.S. 471 (1970).

33. *Id.* at 485 (quoting Lindsley v. Natural Carbonic Gas Co., 220 U.S. 61, 78 (1911)).

34. 517 U.S. 620 (1996).

35. *In re* Marriage Cases 183 P.3d 384 (Cal. 2008), *overruled by* Cal. Const. art. I, § 7.5.

36. Goodridge v. Department of Public Health, 798 N.E.2d 941 (Mass. 2003).

37. Kerrigan v. Commissioner of Public Health, 957 A.2d 407 (Conn. 2008).

38. 436 U.S. 658 (1978).

39. 42 U.S.C. § 2000e-2 (2000).

40. Griggs v. Duke Power Co., 401 U.S. 424 (1971).

41. 379 U.S. 294 (1964).

42. *Id.* at 305.

43. 392 U.S. 409 (1968).

44. *Id.* at 443.

45. 42 U.S.C. §§ 6101–6107 (2000 & Supp. 2006).

46. *Id.* §§ 12101–12213.

47. 20 U.S.C. §§ 1681(2000).

48. 18 U.S.C. § 242 (2000).

49. *Id.* § 245.

50. 42 U.S.C. § 3631 (2000).

Chapter 4

Freedom of Speech and Religion

Liberty is meaningless where the right to utter one's thoughts and opinions has ceased to exist. That, of all rights, is the dread of tyrants. It is the right which they first of all strike down.

Frederick Douglass

CHAPTER OBJECTIVES

After studying this chapter you should better understand:

- The nature of constitutionally permissible government restrictions on speech
- The extent to which the First Amendment protects provocative expressions
- The constitutional requirements for a public official or figure, or a private figure, to recover for defamation
- The religious freedoms that the First Amendment protects
- The U.S. Supreme Court's test for determining whether a religious display on public property violates the First Amendment

Among the most potent of the enumerated constitutional rights are the First Amendment's prohibitions against laws "respecting an establishment of religion, or prohibiting the free exercise thereof; or abridging the freedom of speech." These guaranties of individual rights constrain government from dictating matters of conscience. Liberal government toleration of opinion and expression are essential; as founder Thomas Jefferson said, "[T]ruth is great and will prevail if left to herself, that she is the proper and sufficient antagonist to error, and has nothing to fear from the conflict, unless by human interposition disarmed of her natural weapons, free argument and debate, errors ceasing to be dangerous when it is permitted freely to contradict them."[1]

The First Amendment declares freedom of speech and religion in seemingly absolute terms. It does not forbid only unreasonable government acts as does the Fifth Amendment constraint on searches and seizures. But experience shows that simple declarations usually cannot be applied as absolutely as they may appear, and this is so even with expressive freedom. One person's right to practice religion must be reconciled with another's right not to be compelled to do so; one person's right to speak must be reconciled with the need for reasonable rules about time and place to protect others from abuse. This chapter provides an introduction to freedom of speech and religion and to the difficult interpretative questions that arise when competing rights must be reconciled.

Free Speech

Historically freedom of speech is among the most cherished of all constitutional rights. The framers saw free speech as essential for repelling the tyrannical tendencies of those who can wield government power. As the U.S. Supreme Court said, "[T]he freedom to speak one's mind is not only an aspect of individual liberty—and thus a good unto itself—but also is essential to the common quest for truth and the vitality of society as a whole."[2] But not all speech is protected.

Speech Regulation

We do not have an unfettered right to speak wherever and whenever we please. In a public forum speech may be subjected to restrictions on time, place, and manner provided that the restrictions are content neutral. Public administrators may set agendas and time limits; protestors may be subjected to reasonable restrictions to protect public safety. The restrictions must be drawn narrowly to achieve a significant government interest and to allow for communication on public issues through other channels. But a limitation need not be the least restrictive means available as long as it "promotes a substantial government interest that would be achieved less effectively absent the regulation."[3] A restriction does not lose its neutrality merely because it has an incidental effect on some speakers but not others.

Content Prohibitions

Notwithstanding the First Amendment's unqualified statement of a freedom of speech, the U.S. Supreme Court has held that government may restrict or prohibit some kinds of speech based on content. As Justice Oliver Wendell Holmes famously said, "The most stringent protection of free speech would not protect a man in falsely shouting fire in a theatre and causing a panic."[4] The Court has upheld obscenity restrictions that protect individuals from unwelcome exposure to highly offensive material. As the Court explained, "The States have the power to make a morally neutral judgment that public exhibition of obscene material, or commerce in such material, has a tendency to injure the community as a whole, to endanger the public safety, or to jeopardize . . . the States' 'right to maintain a decent society.'"[5] In the

1973 case of *Miller v. California*,[6] the Court outlined requirements for constitutionally permissible obscenity regulations. The Court declined to define obscenity, leaving this question to community standards based on the impact on an average person within the community. Still the court set some basic constraints on defining the community's standard. Obscenity regulation must be confined "to works which depict or describe sexual conduct."[7] The regulation "must also be limited to works which, taken as a whole, appeal to the prurient interest in sex, which portray sexual conduct in a patently offensive way, and which, taken as a whole, do not have serious literary, artistic, political, or scientific value."[8] Of course there is much room for argument about what has serious artistic value; public debate raged about the artistic value of a portrayal of a crucifix immersed in urine and about lurid homoerotic photographs. The Court did give examples of what could be proscribed as obscenity: "Patently offensive representations or descriptions of ultimate sexual acts, normal or perverted, actual or simulated," or of "masturbation, excretory functions, and lewd exhibition of the genitals."[9] Of course, what is patently offensive also varies widely among communities and is subject to serious disagreement even within a community.

Another form of expression that the Court has not shielded is use of "fighting words." In 1942 in *Chaplinsky v. State of New Hampshire*,[10] the Court upheld a state law forbidding anyone from addressing "any offensive, derisive or annoying word to any other person who is lawfully in any street or other public place" and from calling someone "any offensive or derisive name." The person charged with violating the law stood before city hall and, using foul language, called the city marshal a "racketeer," "fascist," and other names. The Court said that government may prohibit use of words that "by their very utterance inflict injury or tend to incite an immediate breach of the peace."[11] Subsequent cases make clear that statements are not fighting words merely because they are annoying, offensive, derisive, or outrageous. *Chaplinsky*, which occurred during wartime, is a rare instance in which words alone were found to be bad enough to be prohibited.

Provocative Expression: Texas v. Johnson

Freedom of expression would be impotent if lawmakers could prohibit statements that might offend their political sensibilities. A representative government relies on citizens' ability to express their disapproval of government actions, and the more important the issue the more likely passions will be high and aggressive tones will be used to get attention and to make the point. The Court has tended to protect political expression regardless of how offensive listeners may perceive it to be.

Flag burning is an act that many people find to be offensive. Congress and state legislatures have enacted laws to prohibit flag desecration. In 1984 Gregory Lee Johnson burned an American flag on a street in Dallas while protesters chanted. He was convicted of desecrating a venerated object in violation of a state statute. The U.S. Supreme Court justices certainly were not of a single mind about whether the First Amendment protected flag burning. The following are excerpts from some of the opinions.

Texas v. Johnson
491 U.S. 397 (1989)

Justice Brennan, writing for the Court.

After publicly burning an American flag as a means of political protest, Gregory Lee Johnson was convicted of desecrating a flag in violation of Texas law. This case presents the question whether his conviction is consistent with the First Amendment. We hold that it is not.

While the Republican National Convention was taking place in Dallas in 1984, respondent Johnson participated in a political demonstration dubbed the "Republican War Chest Tour." As explained in literature distributed by the demonstrators and in speeches made by them, the purpose of this event was to protest the policies of the Reagan administration and of certain Dallas-based corporations. The demonstrators marched through the Dallas streets, chanting political slogans and stopping at several corporate locations to stage "die-ins" intended to dramatize the consequences of nuclear war. On several occasions they spray-painted the walls of buildings and overturned potted plants, but Johnson himself took no part in such activities. He did, however, accept an American flag handed to him by a fellow protestor who had taken it from a flagpole outside one of the targeted buildings.

The demonstration ended in front of Dallas City Hall, where Johnson unfurled the American flag, doused it with kerosene, and set it on fire. While the flag burned, the protestors chanted, "America, the red, white, and blue, we spit on you." After the demonstrators dispersed, a witness to the flag burning collected the flag's remains and buried them in his backyard. No one was physically injured or threatened with injury, though several witnesses testified that they had been seriously offended by the flag burning.

Of the approximately 100 demonstrators, Johnson alone was charged with a crime. The only criminal offense with which he was charged was the desecration of a venerated object. After a trial, he was convicted, sentenced to one year in prison, and fined $2,000.

Johnson was convicted of flag desecration for burning the flag rather than for uttering insulting words. This fact somewhat complicates our consideration of his conviction under the First Amendment. We must first determine whether Johnson's burning of the flag constituted expressive conduct, permitting him to invoke the First Amendment in challenging his conviction. If his conduct was expressive, we next decide whether the State's regulation is related to the suppression of free expression.

The First Amendment literally forbids the abridgment only of "speech," but we have long recognized that its protection does not end at the spoken or written word.

Johnson burned an American flag as part—indeed, as the culmination—of a political demonstration that coincided with the convening of the Republican Party and its renomination of Ronald Reagan for President. The expressive, overtly political nature of this conduct was both intentional and overwhelmingly apparent.

The government generally has a freer hand in restricting expressive conduct than it has in restricting the written or spoken word. It may not, however, proscribe particular conduct because it has expressive elements. It is, in short, not simply the verbal or nonverbal nature of the expression, but the governmental interest at stake, that helps to determine whether a restriction on that expression is valid.

Thus, although we have recognized that, where "'speech' and 'nonspeech' elements are combined in the same course of conduct, a sufficiently important governmental interest in regulating the nonspeech element can justify incidental limitations on First Amendment freedoms," *United States v. O'Brien*, 391 U.S. 367, 376 (1968), we have limited the applicability of *O'Brien's* relatively lenient standard to those cases in which "the governmental interest is unrelated to the suppression of free expression." *Id.* at 377.

In order to decide whether *O'Brien's* test applies here, therefore, we must decide whether Texas has asserted an interest in support of Johnson's conviction that is unrelated to the suppression of expression. The State offers two separate interests to justify this conviction: preventing breaches of the peace and preserving the flag as a symbol of nationhood and national unity. We hold that the first interest is not implicated on this record and that the second is related to the suppression of expression.

Although the State stresses the disruptive behavior of the protestors during their march toward City Hall, it admits that "no actual breach of the peace occurred at the time of the flagburning or in response to the flagburning." The State's emphasis on the protestors' disorderly actions prior to arriving at City Hall is not only somewhat surprising, given that no charges were brought on the basis of this conduct, but it also fails to show that a disturbance of the peace was a likely reaction to *Johnson's* conduct. The only evidence offered by the State at trial to show the reaction to Johnson's actions was the testimony of several persons who had been seriously offended by the flag burning.

The State's position, therefore, amounts to a claim that an audience that takes serious offense at particular expression is necessarily likely to disturb the peace, and that the expression may be prohibited on this basis. Our precedents do not countenance such a presumption. On the contrary, they recognize that a principal "function of free speech under our system of government is to invite dispute. It may indeed best serve its high purpose when it induces a condition of unrest, creates dissatisfaction with conditions as they are, or even stirs people to anger." *Terminiello v. Chicago*, 337 U.S. 1, 337 U.S. 4 (1949).

Thus, we have not permitted the government to assume that every expression of a provocative idea will incite a riot, but have instead required careful consideration of the actual circumstances surrounding such expression, asking whether the expression "is directed to inciting or producing imminent lawless action and is likely to incite or produce such action." *Brandenburg v. Ohio*, 395 U.S. 444, 395 U.S. 447 (1969) (reviewing circumstances surrounding rally and speeches by Ku Klux Klan). To accept Texas' arguments that it need only demonstrate "the potential for a breach of the peace," and that every flag burning necessarily possesses that potential, would be to eviscerate our holding in *Brandenburg*. This we decline to do.

Nor does Johnson's expressive conduct fall within that small class of "fighting words" that are "likely to provoke the average person to retaliation, and thereby cause a breach of the peace." *Chaplinsky v. New Hampshire*, 315 U.S. 568, 574 (1942). No reasonable onlooker would have regarded Johnson's generalized expression of dissatisfaction with the policies of the Federal Government as a direct personal insult or an invitation to exchange fisticuffs.

We thus conclude that the State's interest in maintaining order is not implicated on these facts.

It remains to consider whether the State's interest in preserving the flag as a symbol of nationhood and national unity justifies Johnson's conviction.

Johnson was not, we add, prosecuted for the expression of just any idea; he was prosecuted for his expression of dissatisfaction with the policies of this country, expression situated at the core of our First Amendment values.

Moreover, Johnson was prosecuted because he knew that his politically charged expression would cause "serious offense." If he had burned the flag as a means of disposing of it because it was dirty or torn, he would not have been convicted of flag desecration . . . . The Texas law is thus not aimed at protecting the physical integrity of the flag in all circumstances, but is designed instead to protect it only against impairments that would cause serious offense to others.

If there is a bedrock principle underlying the First Amendment, it is that the government may not prohibit the expression of an idea simply because society finds the idea itself offensive or disagreeable.

To conclude that the government may permit designated symbols to be used to communicate only a limited set of messages would be to enter territory having no discernible or defensible boundaries. Could the government, on this theory, prohibit the burning of state flags? Of copies of the Presidential seal? Of the Constitution? In evaluating these choices under the First Amendment, how would we decide which symbols were sufficiently special to warrant this unique status? To do so, we would be forced to consult our own political preferences, and impose them on the citizenry, in the very way that the First Amendment forbids us to do.

We reject the suggestion, urged at oral argument by counsel for Johnson, that the government lacks "any state interest whatsoever" in regulating the manner in which the flag may be displayed. Congress has, for example, enacted precatory regulations describing the proper treatment of the flag, and we cast no doubt on the legitimacy of its interest in making such recommendations. To say that the government has an interest in encouraging proper treatment of the flag, however, is not to say that it may criminally punish a person for burning a flag as a means of political protest.

We are fortified in today's conclusion by our conviction that forbidding criminal punishment for conduct such as Johnson's will not endanger the special role played by our flag or the feelings it inspires. To paraphrase Justice Holmes, we submit that nobody can suppose that this one gesture of an unknown man will change our Nation's attitude towards its flag.

We are tempted to say, in fact, that the flag's deservedly cherished place in our community will be strengthened, not weakened, by our holding today. Our decision is a reaffirmation of the principles of freedom and inclusiveness that the flag best reflects, and of the conviction that our toleration of criticism such as Johnson's is a sign and source of our strength. Indeed, one of the proudest images of our flag, the one immortalized in our own national anthem, is of the bombardment it survived at Fort McHenry. It is the Nation's resilience, not its rigidity, that Texas sees reflected in the flag—and it is that resilience that we reassert today.

The way to preserve the flag's special role is not to punish those who feel differently about these matters. It is to persuade them that they are wrong.

Chief Justice Rehnquist, dissenting.

For more than 200 years, the American flag has occupied a unique position as the symbol of our Nation, a uniqueness that justifies a governmental prohibition against flag burning in the way respondent Johnson did here.

The flag is not simply another "idea" or "point of view" competing for recognition in the marketplace of ideas. Millions and millions of Americans regard it with an almost mystical reverence, regardless of what sort of social, political, or philosophical beliefs they may have. I cannot agree that the First Amendment invalidates the Act of Congress, and the laws of 48 of the 50 States, which make criminal the public burning of the flag.

The result of the Texas statute is obviously to deny one in Johnson's frame of mind one of many means of "symbolic speech." Far from being a case of "one picture being worth a thousand words," flag burning is the equivalent of an inarticulate grunt or roar that, it seems fair to say, is most likely to be indulged in not to express any particular idea, but to antagonize others.

Uncritical extension of constitutional protection to the burning of the flag risks the frustration of the very purpose for which organized governments are instituted. The Court decides that the American flag is just another symbol, about which not only must opinions pro and con be tolerated, but for which the most minimal public respect may not be enjoined. The government may conscript men into the Armed Forces where they must fight and perhaps die for the flag, but the government may not prohibit the public burning of the banner under which they fight. I would uphold the Texas statute as applied in this case.

Justice Stevens, dissenting.

Respondent was prosecuted because of the method he chose to express his dissatisfaction with [national] policies. Had he chosen to spray-paint—or perhaps convey with a motion picture projector—his message of dissatisfaction on the facade of the Lincoln Memorial, there would be no question about the power of the Government to prohibit his means of expression. The prohibition would be supported by the legitimate interest in preserving the quality of an important national asset. Though the asset at stake in this case is intangible, given its unique value, the same interest supports a prohibition on the desecration of the American flag.

The ideas of liberty and equality have been an irresistible force in motivating leaders like Patrick Henry, Susan B. Anthony, and Abraham Lincoln, schoolteachers like Nathan Hale and Booker T. Washington, the Philippine Scouts who fought at Bataan, and the soldiers who scaled the bluff at Omaha Beach. If those ideas are worth fighting for—and our history demonstrates that they are—it cannot be true that the flag that uniquely symbolizes their power is not itself worthy of protection from unnecessary desecration.

The justices said they agreed that the flag is a cherished symbol for many. For this reason the flag is also an attractive object for showing contempt. Justice Brennan saw no constitutional basis for exempting the flag from being an object of demonstration. In holding that Johnson's flag burning was constitutionally protected expression, Justice Brennan took comfort in the idea, as expressed by Jefferson in the quote appearing in the introduction to this chapter, that error in thought will be contradicted if debate is protected. As Justice Brennan wrote, "[O]ur toleration of criticism such as Johnson's is a sign and source of our strength." In *Johnson* some-one picked up the remains of the flag and buried it, a counter-protest that may itself have made a point in the public debate.

The dissenting justices saw the flag as a worthy exception, in a sense property in which the public has rights that can be protected by legislative act. Others have agreed that expressive rights need not extend to the national symbol and have sought a constitutional amendment to prohibit flag desecration, but so far no such amendment has been made.

Ultimately toleration cannot be decreed by constitutional declaration; it depends on societal norms. Societal orthodoxies can erode expressive freedoms. Attempts to enforce orthodoxies are subject to challenge on First Amendment grounds. For example, some public universities have adopted speech codes that forbid use of words that the university deems offensive, equating them with sexual harassment or fighting words. Courts have held such codes to be unconstitutionally overbroad. Federal courts have stricken university prohibitions against "demeaning or slurring individuals" or use of "slogans that infer negative connotations about the individual's racial or ethnic affiliation,"[12] as well as a university policy that prohibited "acts of intolerance" toward others.[13] A federal court overturned a university's sanctions imposed on a fraternity for conducting an "ugly woman contest" with "racist and sexist themes."[14] The courts have made clear that just as with flag desecration offensive ideas are to be met with others' rights to express their disagreement. As the Court said in *Johnson*, "If there is a bedrock principle underlying the First Amendment, it is that the government may not prohibit the expression of an idea simply because society finds the idea itself offensive or disagreeable."

Liability for Harming Reputation

"Defamation" is a cause of action for harm to reputation as a result of false statements. "Libel" refers to a written or printed defamatory statement, and "slander" refers to an oral defamatory statement. Claims for damage to reputation are based on a state rule of law and as such the U.S. Supreme Court has held that such claims must comport with the First Amendment's free speech protections. The Court has instructed that truth is absolutely protected, but under some circumstances false statements can result in liability. In the landmark 1964 case of *New York Times Co. v. Sullivan*,[15] the Court held that a public figure may hold a speaker liable for damage to reputation caused by publication of a defamatory falsehood if the statement was made with "actual malice," which the Court described as "knowledge that it was false or with reckless disregard of whether it was false or not."[16] Three years later in *Curtis Publishing Co. v. Butts*,[17] the Court said that a showing of actual malice also was required for suits brought by a "public figure," which is someone who has sought the public's attention or who has gained notoriety. Some individuals have roles of sufficient influence in society that they are deemed to be public figures for all purposes. Others are considered "limited purpose public figures" only within the context of particular subjects for which they have become notorious. In *Gertz v. Robert Welch, Inc.*,[18] the Court instructed that the actual malice standard was not required when the subject is a private figure. The Court said that states could establish their own standards provided they required at least that the statement was made negligently. In other words, someone is not liable for merely being mistaken, even about a private figure.

Defamation cases often turn on the distinction between opinion and fact. As the Court said in *Gertz*, "Under the First Amendment there is no such thing as a false idea. However pernicious an opinion may seem, we depend for its correction not on the conscience of judges and juries but on the competition of other ideas. But there is no constitutional value in false statements of fact."[19] If a statement is not capable of being proved false it is likely to be opinion. "Smith is a lousy mayor" is opinion; "Smith used city funds to build a swimming pool at his house" is a statement of fact that could be proved true or false.

By definition parody is not a faithful portrayal and cannot be a misleading representation of fact. The outer limits of First Amendment protection were tested in *Hustler Magazine, Inc. v. Falwell*,[20] involving a mock liquor advertisement depicting Evangelist leader Jerry Falwell as a drunken hypocrite who had sex with his mother in an outhouse, a characterization that obviously was not meant to be a factual representation. The mock advertisement had a small-print disclaimer that it was a parody and "not to be taken seriously." The Court characterized the portrayal as protected political commentary, a "distant cousin" of traditional political cartoons "and a rather poor relation at that." The Court also said that it could not make an exception based on outrageousness:

> *If it were possible by laying down a principled standard to separate the one from the other, public discourse would probably suffer little or no harm. But we doubt that there is any such standard, and we are quite sure that the pejorative description "outrageous" does not supply one. "Outrageousness" in the area of political and social discourse has an inherent subjectiveness about it which would allow a jury to impose liability on the basis of the jurors' tastes or views, or perhaps on the basis of their dislike of a particular expression. An "outrageousness" standard thus runs afoul of our longstanding refusal to allow damages to be awarded because the speech in question may have an adverse emotional impact on the audience.*[21]

Liability for defamation is based on the notion that maliciously false statements do not warrant protection. Someone also can suffer reputational harm from publication of truthful information that should reasonably be expected to be private. This could occur, for example, with publication of the identity of a youth who was a victim of a sex crime, or of a photograph surreptitiously taken in private space. The states have recognized a cause of action for invasion of privacy or public disclosure for the harm of unwanted publicity of private information as it affects a person of ordinary sensibilities. The Court has held that the First Amendment protects publication of truthful information obtained from public records even if the person to whom it pertains wished the information to be private, but the Court has not addressed the validity of state law causes of action based on publication of private information obtained from other sources.[22]

Immunity from Liability

The law extends considerable immunity from liability to public officials for statements made in courtrooms, legislative chambers, and executive offices. Statements made in a legislative context are afforded the greatest protection. Article I, Section 6 of the U.S. Constitution provides that U.S. senators and representatives "shall in all Cases, except Treason, Felony, and Breach of the Peace, be privileged from Arrest during their attendance at the Session of their

Respective Houses, and in going to and from the same, and for any Speech or Debate in either House, they shall not be questioned in any other Place." Consequently legislators and their staff have absolute immunity for legislative acts. This immunity does not extend to communications that are unconnected to legislative acts. In *Hutchinson v. Proxmire*,[23] the U.S. Supreme Court held that Senator William Proxmire was not immune from liability for his "Golden Fleece of the Month Award," which he circulated publicly to illuminate what he perceived to be the most egregious examples of wasteful governmental spending. The senator's commentary was deemed to be too far removed from his legislative prerogative.

Executive officials have only qualified immunity. An executive official against whom a claim has been made must show good faith in making the allegedly defamatory statement. Officials do not act in good faith if they knew or reasonably should have known that a false statement would violate the subject's constitutional rights or if the false statement was made with a malicious intent to deprive the subject of constitutional rights.

Judges are immune from liability for their actions within their judicial functions, even if accused of acting maliciously or corruptly. Those who testify in judicial proceedings also have immunity from defamation liability. But this immunity does not protect someone from prosecution for perjury for testifying falsely, nor does it protect someone from liability for filing baseless and malicious lawsuits.

Members of the public who make false statements in government proceedings can be held liable for defamation. Everyone has a First Amendment right to "to petition the Government for a redress of grievances," but this right does not absolutely cloak those who make false statements. In *McDonald v. Smith*,[24] a petitioner claimed absolute immunity from libel claims based on letters he sent to the president accusing a candidate for U.S. attorney of civil rights violations, fraud, conspiracy, blackmail, and other illegal and unethical acts. The U.S. Supreme Court held that communications with public officials are subject to the same requirements as are applied to libel in general. Accordingly, individuals petitioning the government or speaking at government meetings may be held liable for malicious false statements about public officials or figures and false statements about private figures that are made negligently.

To enable the media to inform citizens about public affairs, courts recognize a "fair report privilege." The privilege shields reporters from liability for repeating others' false statements if the report is a fair and accurate summary of public proceedings or a public document. The privilege extends to reports about government meetings and judicial proceedings. Accordingly, a reporter would not be liable for reporting a false statement made at a public hearing if the characterization is fair and accurate and correctly attributed to the speaker. The privilege is unlikely to be extended to reports about off-the-record or anonymous statements.

Religious Freedom

Religious intolerance was on the founders' minds when they composed the Bill of Rights. They conceived of religious belief as a matter of conscience not to be dictated by government decree.

Their experience taught that government involvement in religious affairs tended to result in coercion. The First Amendment contains two clauses affecting religion. One is the Establishment Clause, which prohibits laws "respecting an establishment of religion." The other forbids laws that prohibit the free exercise of religion, known as the Free Exercise Clause.

Establishment Clause

The First Amendment prohibits Congress from adopting laws "respecting an establishment of religion." This prohibition is applied to state laws through the Fourteenth Amendment. The Establishment Clause is easily understood as forbidding government from declaring an official religion. More difficult questions arise about religious practices in a public context.

Government Entanglement with Religious Practices

In Establishment Clause cases the U.S. Supreme Court usually applies a test it described in the 1971 case of *Lemon v. Kurtzman*.[25] The *Lemon* test involves examination of three requirements. As the Court said, "First, the statute must have a secular legislative purpose; second, its principal or primary effect must be one that neither advances nor inhibits religion; finally, the statute must not foster 'an excessive government entanglement with religion.'"[26] To survive scrutiny a law must therefore be secular in purpose and not "excessively" religious in effect.

Establishment Clause objections have been made to prayer in public schools. The courts have tried to accommodate voluntary prayer while affording a prerogative to be a full part of the community without having to attend prayer. The U.S. Supreme Court has instructed that nothing in the Constitution "prohibits any public school student from voluntarily praying at any time before, during, or after the school day. But the religious liberty protected by the Constitution is abridged when the State affirmatively sponsors the particular religious practice of prayer."[27] This approach leaves considerable room for disagreement about what constitutes state sponsorship of religious practices.

The courts similarly have not drawn neat lines when considering First Amendment challenges to public recitations of the Pledge of Allegiance and its reference to a nation "under God." In *Newdow v. U.S. Congress*,[28] a school boy's atheist father filed suit alleging that the pledge was religious indoctrination. In a split decision a federal court of appeals held that the pledge was impermissible religious compulsion in public school even if students could choose not to recite it. The appeals court said that the pledge "places students in the untenable position of choosing between participating in an exercise with religious content or protesting," and the coercive effect "is particularly pronounced in the school setting given the age and impressionability of schoolchildren, and their understanding that they are required to adhere to the norms set by their school, their teacher and their fellow students."[29] Some other courts have disagreed, holding that the reference to God in the pledge is primarily a secular reference to a historic tradition and the First Amendment is not violated if children are not forced to participate.[30] So far the U.S. Supreme Court has declined to resolve the disagreement.

Public Religious Display: Van Orden v. Perry

Christian symbols have always appeared in public venues in the United States. Religious practices may have become more diverse but most people in the country are Christian and share fundamental beliefs that make them receptive to Christian symbols. But not everyone readily accepts religious displays that they associate with government. Christmas nativity scenes have been challenged as violating the Establishment Clause, sometimes successfully. Courts generally allow public displays of scenes often associated with religion if their message is not construed as government endorsement. In *County of Allegheny v. American Civil Liberties Union*,[31] the U.S. Supreme Court considered several religious displays in public spaces. The Court held that a Christian nativity display in the main staircase of a county courthouse too strongly endorsed Christianity. The scene included an angel proclaiming "Gloria in Excelsis Deo," which means "Glory to God in the Highest." The Court held that a closer constitutional question was presented with a large Hanukkah menorah placed outside a government building next to a decorated Christmas tree at which a sign appeared declaring the city's "salute to liberty." The Court held that Christmas trees are not themselves impermissibly religious, and the combined display of the tree, the sign, and the menorah was not an "endorsement" of religious choices.

Judges who consider Establishment Clause challenges to public displays associated with religion must reconcile the First Amendment with the ubiquitous presence of such symbols. Judges also are challenged to keep their own religious beliefs from controlling their constitutional interpretation. The potential for differing perspectives is well illustrated in *Van Orden v. Perry*, in which the Court considered a challenge to a monument on state capitol grounds depicting the Ten Commandments. Eight of the nine justices wrote opinions, three of which were dissents. The following are excerpts from some of the opinions.

Van Orden v. Perry
545 U.S. 677 (2005)

Chief Justice Rehnquist, writing for the Court.

The question here is whether the Establishment Clause of the First Amendment allows the display of a monument inscribed with the Ten Commandments on the Texas State Capitol grounds. We hold that it does.

The 22 acres surrounding the Texas State Capitol contain 17 monuments and 21 historical markers commemorating the "people, ideals, and events that compose Texan identity." The monolith challenged here stands 6-feet high and 3-1/2 feet wide. It is located to the north of the Capitol building, between the Capitol and the Supreme Court building. Its primary content is the text of the Ten Commandments. An eagle grasping the American flag, an eye inside of a pyramid, and two small tablets with what appears to be an ancient script are carved above the text of the Ten Commandments. Below the text are two Stars of David and the superimposed Greek letters Chi and Rho, which represent Christ. The bottom of the monument bears the inscription "PRESENTED TO THE PEOPLE AND YOUTH OF TEXAS BY THE FRATERNAL ORDER OF EAGLES OF TEXAS 1961."

Petitioner Thomas Van Orden is a native Texan and a resident of Austin. At one time he was a licensed lawyer, having graduated from Southern Methodist Law School. Van Orden testified that, since 1995, he has encountered the Ten Commandments monument during his frequent visits to the Capitol grounds. His visits are typically for the purpose of using the law library in the Supreme Court building, which is located just northwest of the Capitol building.

Forty years after the monument's erection and six years after Van Orden began to encounter the monument frequently, he sued numerous state officials in their official capacities under Rev. Stat. § 1979, 42 U.S.C. § 1983, seeking both a declaration that the monument's placement violates the Establishment Clause and an injunction requiring its removal.

Our cases, Januslike, point in two directions in applying the Establishment Clause. One face looks toward the strong role played by religion and religious traditions throughout our Nation's history. The other face looks toward the principle that governmental intervention in religious matters can itself endanger religious freedom.

This case, like all Establishment Clause challenges, presents us with the difficulty of respecting both faces. Our institutions presuppose a Supreme Being, yet these institutions must not press religious observances upon their citizens. One face looks to the past in acknowledgment of our Nation's heritage, while the other looks to the present in demanding a separation between church and state.

As we explained in *Lynch v. Donnelly*, 465 U.S. 668 (1984): "There is an unbroken history of official acknowledgment by all three branches of government of the role of religion in American life from at least 1789." *Id.* at 674. For example, both Houses passed resolutions in 1789 asking President George Washington to issue a Thanksgiving Day Proclamation to "recommend to the people of the United States a day of public thanksgiving and prayer, to be observed by acknowledging, with grateful hearts, the many and signal favors of Almighty God." President Washington's proclamation directly attributed to the Supreme Being the foundations and successes of our young Nation . . . .

Recognition of the role of God in our Nation's heritage has also been reflected in our decisions. This recognition has led us to hold that the Establishment Clause permits a state legislature to open its daily sessions with a prayer by a chaplain paid by the State. Such a practice, we thought, was "deeply embedded in the history and tradition of this country." *Marsh v. Chambers*, 463 U.S. 783, 786 (1983). With similar reasoning, we have upheld laws, which originated from one of the Ten Commandments, that prohibited the sale of merchandise on Sunday.

In this case we are faced with a display of the Ten Commandments on government property outside the Texas State Capitol. Such acknowledgments of the role played by the Ten Commandments in our Nation's heritage are common throughout America. We need only look within our own Courtroom. Since 1935, Moses has stood, holding two tablets that reveal portions of the Ten Commandments written in Hebrew, among other lawgivers in the south frieze. Representations of the Ten Commandments adorn the metal gates lining the north and south sides of the Courtroom as well as the doors leading into the Courtroom. Moses also sits on the exterior east facade of the building holding the Ten Commandments tablets.

Similar acknowledgments can be seen throughout a visitor's tour of our Nation's Capital.

Our opinions, like our building, have recognized the role the Decalogue plays in America's heritage. The Executive and Legislative Branches have also acknowledged the historical role of the Ten Commandments. These displays and recognitions of the Ten Commandments bespeak the rich American tradition of religious acknowledgments.

Of course, the Ten Commandments are religious—they were so viewed at their inception and so remain. The monument, therefore, has religious significance. According to Judeo-Christian belief, the Ten Commandments were given to Moses by God on Mt. Sinai. But Moses was a law-giver as well as a religious leader. And the Ten Commandments have an undeniable historical meaning, as the foregoing examples demonstrate. Simply having religious content or promoting a message consistent with a religious doctrine does not run afoul of the Establishment Clause.

The placement of the Ten Commandments monument on the Texas State Capitol grounds is a far more passive use of those texts than was the case in *Stone v. Graham*, 449 U.S. 39 (1980), where the text confronted elementary school students every day. Indeed, Van Orden, the petitioner here, apparently walked by the monument for a number of years before bringing this lawsuit. Texas has treated her Capitol grounds monuments as representing the several strands in the State's political and legal history. The inclusion of the Ten Commandments monument in this group has a dual significance, partaking of both religion and government. We cannot say that Texas' display of this monument violates the Establishment Clause of the First Amendment.

Justice Thomas, concurring.

This case would be easy if the Court were willing to abandon the inconsistent guideposts it has adopted for addressing Establishment Clause challenges, and return to the original meaning of the Clause. I have previously suggested that the Clause's text and history "resis[t] incorporation" against the States. If the Establishment Clause does not restrain the States, then it has no application here, where only state action is at issue.

Even if the Clause is incorporated, or if the Free Exercise Clause limits the power of States to establish religions, our task would be far simpler if we returned to the original meaning of the word "establishment" than it is under the various approaches this Court now uses. The Framers understood an establishment "necessarily [to] involve actual legal coercion." *Elk Grove Unified School Dist. v. Newdow*, 542 U.S. 1, 52 (2004) (Thomas, J., concurring). And "government practices that have nothing to do with creating or maintaining . . . coercive state establishments" simply do not "implicate the possible liberty interest of being free from coercive state establishments." *Id.* at 53.

There is no question that, based on the original meaning of the Establishment Clause, the Ten Commandments display at issue here is constitutional. In no sense does Texas compel petitioner Van Orden to do anything. The only injury to him is that he takes offense at seeing the monument as he passes it on his way to the Texas Supreme Court Library. He need not stop to read it or even to look at it, let alone to express support for it or adopt the Commandments as guides for his life. The mere presence of the monument along his path involves no coercion and thus does not violate the Establishment Clause.

Returning to the original meaning would do more than simplify our task. It also would avoid the pitfalls present in the Court's current approach to such challenges. This Court's precedent elevates the trivial to the proverbial "federal case," by making benign signs and postings subject to challenge. Yet even as it does so, the Court's precedent attempts to avoid declaring all religious symbols and words of longstanding tradition unconstitutional, by counterfactually declaring them of little religious significance. Even when the Court's cases recognize that such symbols have religious meaning, they adopt an unhappy compromise that fails fully to account for either the adherent's or the nonadherent's beliefs, and provides no principled way to choose between them. Even worse, the incoherence of the Court's decisions in this area renders the Establishment Clause impenetrable and incapable of consistent application. All told, this Court's jurisprudence leaves courts, governments, and believers and nonbelievers alike confused—an observation that is hardly new.

Justice Breyer, concurring.

The case before us is a borderline case. On the one hand, the Commandments' text undeniably has a religious message, invoking, indeed emphasizing, the Deity. On the other hand, focusing on the text of the Commandments alone cannot conclusively resolve this case. Rather, to determine the message that the text here conveys, we must examine how the text is used. And that inquiry requires us to consider the context of the display.

Here the tablets have been used as part of a display that communicates not simply a religious message, but a secular message as well. The circumstances surrounding the display's placement on the capitol grounds and its physical setting suggest that the State itself intended the latter, nonreligious aspects of the tablets' message to predominate. And the monument's 40-year history on the Texas state grounds indicates that that has been its effect.

The group that donated the monument, the Fraternal Order of Eagles, a private civic (and primarily secular) organization, while interested in the religious aspect of the Ten Commandments, sought to highlight the Commandments' role in shaping civic morality as part of that organization's efforts to combat juvenile delinquency. The tablets, as displayed on the monument, prominently acknowledge that the Eagles donated the display, a factor which, though not sufficient, thereby further distances the State itself from the religious aspect of the Commandments' message.

The physical setting of the monument, moreover, suggests little or nothing of the sacred. The setting does not readily lend itself to meditation or any other religious activity. But it does provide a context of history and moral ideals. It (together with the display's inscription about its origin) communicates to visitors that the State sought to reflect moral principles, illustrating a relation between ethics and law that the State's citizens, historically speaking, have endorsed.

If these factors provide a strong, but not conclusive, indication that the Commandments' text on this monument conveys a predominantly secular message, a further factor is determinative here. As far as I can tell, 40 years passed in which the presence of this monument, legally speaking, went unchallenged (until the single legal objection raised by petitioner). And I am not aware of any evidence suggesting that this was due to a climate of intimidation. Those 40 years suggest that the public visiting the capitol grounds has considered the religious aspect of the tablets' message as part of what is a broader moral and historical message reflective of a cultural heritage.

I recognize the danger of the slippery slope. Still, where the Establishment Clause is at issue, we must "distinguish between real threat and mere shadow." *School Dist. of Abington Township v. Schempp*, 374 U.S. 203, 308 (1963) (Ginsburg, J., concurring). Here, we have only the shadow.

Justice Stevens, dissenting.

When the Ten Commandments monument was donated to the State of Texas in 1961, it was not for the purpose of commemorating a noteworthy event in Texas history, signifying the Commandments' influence on the development of secular law, or even denoting the religious beliefs of Texans at that time. To the contrary, the donation was only one of over a hundred largely identical monoliths, and of over a thousand paper replicas, distributed to state and local governments throughout the Nation over the course of several decades.

The donors were motivated by a desire to "inspire the youth" and curb juvenile delinquency by providing children with a "code of conduct or standards by which to govern their actions." It is the Eagles' belief that disseminating the message conveyed by the Ten Commandments will help to persuade young men and women to observe civilized standards of behavior, and will lead to more productive lives. Significantly, although the Eagles' organization is nonsectarian, eligibility for membership is premised on a belief in the existence of a "Supreme Being."

The desire to combat juvenile delinquency by providing guidance to youths is both admirable and unquestionably secular. But achieving that goal through biblical teachings injects a religious purpose into an otherwise secular endeavor.

The reason this message stands apart is that the Decalogue is a venerable religious text. For many followers, the Commandments represent the literal word of God as spoken to Moses and repeated to his followers after descending from Mount Sinai. The message conveyed by the Ten Commandments thus cannot be analogized to an appendage to a common article of commerce ("In God we Trust") or an incidental part of a familiar recital ("God save the United States and this honorable Court").

The profoundly sacred message embodied by the text inscribed on the Texas monument is emphasized by the especially large letters that identify its author: "I AM the LORD thy God." It commands present worship of Him and no other deity. It directs us to be guided by His teaching in the current and future conduct of all of our affairs. It instructs us to follow a code of divine law, some of which has informed and been integrated into our secular legal code ("Thou shalt not kill"), but much of which has not ("Thou shalt not make to thyself any graven images. . . . Thou shalt not covet").

I do not doubt that some Texans, including those elected to the Texas Legislature, may believe that the statues displayed on the Texas Capitol grounds, including the Ten Commandments monument, reflect the "ideals . . . that compose Texan identity." Tex. H. Con. Res. 38, 77th Leg. 6473 (2001). But Texas, like our entire country, is now a much more diversified community than it was when it became a part of the United States or even when the monument was erected. Today there are many Texans who do not believe in the God whose Commandments are displayed at their seat of government. Many of them worship a different god or no god at all. Some may believe that the account of the creation in the Book of Genesis is less reliable than the views of men like Darwin and Einstein.

Our leaders, when delivering public addresses, often express their blessings simultaneously in the service of God and their constituents. Thus, when public officials deliver public speeches, we recognize that their words are not exclusively a transmission from the government because those oratories have embedded within them the inherently personal views of the speaker as an individual member of the polity. The permanent placement of a textual religious display on state property is different in kind; it amalgamates otherwise discordant individual views into a collective statement of government approval. Moreover, the message never ceases to transmit itself to objecting viewers whose only choices are to accept the message or to ignore the offense by averting their gaze. In this sense, although Thanksgiving Day proclamations and inaugural speeches undoubtedly seem official, in most circumstances they will not constitute the sort of governmental endorsement of religion at which the separation of church and state is aimed.

The plurality's reliance on early religious statements and proclamations made by the Founders is also problematic because those views were not espoused at the Constitutional Convention in 1787 nor enshrined in the Constitution's text. Thus, the presentation of these religious statements as a unified historical narrative is bound to paint a misleading picture. It does so here. In according deference to the statements of George Washington and John Adams, the Chief Justice and Justice Scalia fail to account for the acts and publicly espoused views of other influential leaders of that time. Notably absent from their historical snapshot is the fact that Thomas Jefferson refused to issue the Thanksgiving proclamations that Washington had so readily embraced based on the argument that to do so would violate the Establishment Clause.

Ardent separationists aside, there is another critical nuance lost in the plurality's portrayal of history. Simply put, many of the Founders who are often cited as authoritative expositors of the Constitution's original meaning understood the Establishment Clause to stand for a *narrower* proposition than the plurality, for whatever reason, is willing to accept. Namely, many of the Framers understood the word "religion" in the Establishment Clause to encompass only the various sects of Christianity.

The evidence is compelling. Prior to the Philadelphia Convention, the States had begun to protect "religious freedom" in their various constitutions. Many of those provisions, however, restricted "equal protection" and "free exercise" to Christians, and invocations of the divine were commonly understood to refer to Christ.

It is our duty, therefore, to interpret the First Amendment's command that "Congress shall make no law respecting an establishment of religion" not by merely asking what those words meant to observers at the time of the founding, but instead by deriving from the Clause's text and history the broad principles that remain valid today.

The principle that guides my analysis is neutrality. The basis for that principle is firmly rooted in our Nation's history and our Constitution's text. I recognize that the requirement that government must remain neutral between religion and irreligion would have seemed foreign to some of the Framers; so too would a requirement of neutrality between Jews and Christians.

Fortunately, we are not bound by the Framers' expectations—we are bound by the legal principles they enshrined in our Constitution.

The judgment of the Court in this case stands for the proposition that the Constitution permits governmental displays of sacred religious texts. This makes a mockery of the constitutional ideal that government must remain neutral between religion and irreligion. If a State may endorse a particular deity's command to "have no other gods before me," it is difficult to conceive of any textual display that would run afoul of the Establishment Clause.

In *Van Orden* the plurality chose not to apply the three-step *Lemon* analysis, instead relying on a conclusion that there was no impermissible entanglement with religion because the Ten Commandments had a sufficiently weighty nonreligious role. In a sense the Court decided that the display was permissible *because* of its entanglement with government rather than despite it. The other members of the Court had at least two fundamentally different views about the meaning of the Establishment Clause. From his viewpoint Justice Stevens saw the Commandments as overtly religious and their display on public grounds as an endorsement of religion. From a different viewpoint Justice Thomas also objected to downplaying the Commandments' religious significance, but he saw the display as unobjectionable because no one was coerced to pay heed to it. The test that will be applied to any given case is hardly clear. As Thomas said, "All told, this Court's jurisprudence leaves courts, governments, and believers and nonbelievers alike confused—an observation that is hardly new."

Free Exercise

The Free Exercise Clause forbids laws "prohibiting the free exercise" of religion. The U.S. Supreme Court has not seen many controversies about religious practices. As U.S. Supreme Court Justice Anthony Kennedy said, "The principle that government may not enact laws that suppress religious belief or practice is so well understood that few violations are recorded in our opinions."[32] Although laws aimed at suppressing a religion would quickly be seen as unconstitutional, laws that have an incidental impact on religious practices are not so easily analyzed. A law with an incidental impact on religious practices will not be unconstitutional if the law is neutral and of general application. For example, the Court held that bigamy may be prohibited even for those who believe it to be their religious duty.[33] As the Court explained, "Conscientious scruples have not, in the course of the long struggle for religious toleration, relieved the individual from obedience to a general law not aimed at the promotion or restriction of religious beliefs. The mere possession of religious convictions which contradict the relevant concerns of a political society does not relieve the citizen from the discharge of political responsibilities."[34]

Problems of constitutionality arise when a law that seems to govern nonreligious conduct is actually aimed at a religious practice. The Court has made clear that "religious beliefs need not be acceptable, logical, consistent, or comprehensible to others in order to merit First Amendment protection."[35] In the 1993 case of *Church of the Lukumi Babalu Aye, Inc. v. City of Hialeah*,[36] a Florida community encountered the Santeria faith practiced mostly by Cuban immigrants. Alarmed by animal sacrificial rituals in which the Santerians engaged, the municipal government adopted resolutions noting concern about "certain religions" that might engage in "practices which are inconsistent with public morals, peace or safety," and enacted ordinances effectively prohibiting the Santeria rituals. The Court held that the ordinances were not neutral—they were enacted in response to concerns raised within the community about the practices. The Court explained that a law targeted at a religion must be narrowly tailored to address a compelling government interest. The municipal ordinances did not survive this test. The Court said they were both underinclusive, allowing animal killing in other functionally indistinguishable contexts such as hunting, and overinclusive because concerns about animal cruelty could be addressed without forbidding the Santeria practice. The Court gave the following advice to public officials:

> *The Free Exercise Clause commits government itself to religious tolerance, and upon even slight suspicion that proposals for state intervention stem from animosity to religion or distrust of its practices, all officials must pause to remember their own high duty to the Constitution and to the rights it secures. Those in office must be resolute in resisting importunate demands and must ensure that the sole reasons for imposing the burdens of law and regulation are secular. Legislators may not devise mechanisms, overt or disguised, designed to persecute or oppress a religion or its practices.*[37]

Review Questions

1. What content may the government restrict without violating the First Amendment's guaranty of freedom of speech?

2. On what basis did the U.S. Supreme Court decide that flag burning was protected by the First Amendment in *Texas v. Johnson*?

3. By what standard may a public official or figure sue for defamation?

4. By what standard may a private figure sue for defamation?

5. What is the nature of immunity from liability for statements made in courts, legislatures, and executive proceedings?

6. What is the fair report privilege?

7. What are the two religious freedoms that the First Amendment protects?

8. What test did the U.S. Supreme Court apply in *Van Orden v. Perry* to determine whether a Ten Commandments public display violated the First Amendment's Establishment Clause?

9. On what basis do courts hold that religion-related displays on government property do not violate the First Amendment's Establishment Clause?

10. Under what circumstances would restrictions on religious practices likely be deemed to violate the First Amendment's Free Exercise Clause?

Notes

1. Virginia Act for Establishing Religious Freedom (1786).
2. Bose Corp. v. Consumers Union of U.S., Inc., 466 U.S. 485, 503–04 (1984).
3. United States v. Albertini, 472 U.S. 675, 689 (1985).
4. Schenck v. United States, 249 U.S. 47, 52 (1919).
5. Paris Adult Theatre I v. Slaton, 413 U.S. 49, 69 (1973) (quoting Jacobellis v. Ohio, 378 U.S. 184, 199 (1964) (Warren, C.J., dissenting)).
6. 413 U.S. 15 (1973).
7. *Id.* at 24.
8. *Id.*
9. *Id.* at 25.
10. 315 U.S. 568 (1942).
11. *Id.* at 571–72.
12. Dambrot v. Central Mich. Univ., 55 F.3d 1177 (6th Cir. 1995).
13. Bair v. Shippensburg Univ., 280 F. Supp. 2d 357 (M.D. Pa. 2003).
14. Iota XI Chapter of Sigma Chi Fraternity v. George Mason Univ., 993 F.2d 386 (4th Cir. 1993).
15. 376 U.S. 254 (1964).
16. *Id.* at 279–80.
17. 388 U.S. 130 (1967).
18. 418 U.S. 323 (1974).
19. *Id.* at 339–40.
20. 485 U.S. 46 (1988).
21. *Id.* at 55.
22. Cox Broadcasting Corp. v. Cohn, 420 U.S. 469 (1975).
23. 443 U.S. 111 (1979).
24. 472 U.S. 479 (1985).
25. 403 U.S. 602 (1971).
26. *Id.* at 612–13 (citation omitted).
27. Santa Fe Independent School District v. Doe, 530 U.S. 290, 313 (2000).
28. 328 F.3d 466 (9th Cir. 2003), *reversed on other grounds*, 542 U.S. 1 (2004).
29. 328 F.3d at 488.
30. Sherman v. Community Consolidated School District 21 of Wheeling Township, 980 F.2d 437 (7th Cir. 1992).
31. 492 U.S. 573 (1989).

32. Church of the Lukumi Babalu Aye, Inc. v. City of Hialeah, 508 U.S. 520, 523 (1993).

33. Reynolds v. United States, 98 U.S. 145 (1879).

34. Minersville School Dist. v. Gobitis, 310 U.S. 586, 594–95 (1940).

35. Thomas v. Review Bd. of Indiana Employment Security Div., 450 U.S. 707, 714 (1981).

36. 508 U.S. 520 (1993).

37. *Id*. at 547.

Chapter 5

Freedom of Information

And liberty cannot be preserved without a general knowledge among the people, who have a right, from the frame of their nature, to knowledge, as their great Creator, who does nothing in vain, has given them understandings, and a desire to know; but besides this, they have a right, an indisputable, unalienable, indefeasible, divine right to that most dreaded and envied kind of knowledge, I mean, of the characters and conduct of their rulers.

John Adams

CHAPTER OBJECTIVES

After studying this chapter you should better understand:

- The constitutionality of prior governmental restraints on investigative report publication
- The extent to which the press has any special right of access to public proceedings and records
- The kinds of records required to be made available to the public under the federal Freedom of Information Act and the principal exceptions to the requirements
- The kinds of records that are typically required to be maintained and made available to the public under state law and the common exceptions to the requirements
- The kinds of meetings that typically are required to be open to the public and the common exceptions to the requirement

A government cannot be "of the people" unless the people are well informed about public affairs. As Francis Bacon said and as authoritarian regimes know well, "Knowledge is power." The importance of publicly available information about government activities is reflected in the First Amendment's guaranty of a free press—from the nation's beginning the press was a vitally important forum for the kind of political commentary and public criticism necessary for a rule of law. The free press guaranty prevents government from controlling the dissemination of information. But official accountability depends not only on the availability of a public forum but also on public access to information. Toward this end federal and state lawmakers have enacted freedom of information laws.

There are two principal kinds of freedom of information laws. Open meeting laws are intended to insure that government deliberations occur in public as much as is reasonably possible. Public record or right-to-know laws require that the public be given access to government records. Both open meeting and public record laws are sometimes called sunshine laws, metaphorically referring to the goal of illuminating dark recesses of government decision making.

This chapter considers the nature of the laws aimed at insuring that the public has access to information about its government. It also considers the extent to which the courts have responded to restrictions on that access. As with most rights, freedom of information cannot be absolute. There are good reasons for some secrecy in matters such as national defense and law enforcement, and there are real practical concerns about how information can be shared as the nation and its government grow, the volume of available information explodes, and the technological means for maintaining and sharing it change. The future of the rule of law depends on how these modern realities can be reconciled with the enduring importance of an informed public.

Freedom of the Press

The First Amendment prohibits the federal government from "abridging the freedom . . . of the press." The U.S. Supreme Court has applied this prohibition to state laws by incorporation through the Fourteenth Amendment's Due Process Clause. The preeminence of a free press in the Bill of Rights reflects its importance to the founders' notion of a knowledgeable public and an accountable government. The press continues to play its important informational role.

Limits on Publication

The First Amendment prohibits government restrictions on the press. But it does not promise the press unfettered access to all information it seeks. Federal and state laws enable the government to keep some information secret. Public records laws contain exceptions, as discussed below, and statutes authorize confidentiality for certain kinds of information, such as for national security or law enforcement investigatory purposes. The First Amendment also does not guaranty free publication of all information. As discussed in Chapter 4 government may regulate the publication or broadcast of obscene material and the press is fully subject to those restrictions. Neither does the First Amendment guaranty publication in all contexts. For example, the U.S. Supreme Court held that school officials may censor student newspapers for legitimate educational purposes.[1]

Prepublication Restraint: *New York Times Co. v. United States*

The journalists' professional creed is to serve the public interest by seeking out and faithfully publishing enlightening information and perspectives even when others are made uncomfortable. Some information, including information about government activities, can do more than make others uncomfortable—its publication can endanger the lives of individuals and threaten national security. But public security cannot be a wild card for government secrecy. It is the excuse of first resort for an authoritarian government that benefits from an ignorant public. These considerations create something of a paradox: How can the same government about which the public needs to know be trusted to decide what information about its activities may be kept secret?

The intersection of a free press and national security came before the U.S. Supreme Court in the famous "Pentagon Papers" case. The Pentagon Papers were a secret U.S. Defense Department study of military involvement in Vietnam. Daniel Ellsburg, a Defense Department analyst who opposed continuation of the war, surreptitiously provided classified documents to the press that showed that executive officials publicly misrepresented their war activities. Publication was likely to harm diplomatic relations and to undermine support for the war. It also could have revealed intelligence sources. As the press began publication, President Richard Nixon's administration asked a federal court to prohibit disclosure of some of the information. In a case that quickly went to the Court, six of the nine justices agreed that the First Amendment prohibited courts from interfering with publication. The justices' differing points of view illustrate the seriousness with which they approached the question about whether prior restraint of the press can ever be justified.

New York Times Co. v. United States
403 U.S. 713 (1971)

Per curiam opinion for the Court.

We granted certiorari in these cases in which the United States seeks to enjoin the *New York Times* and the *Washington Post* from publishing the contents of a classified study entitled "History of U.S. Decision-Making Process on Viet Nam Policy."

"Any system of prior restraints of expression comes to this Court bearing a heavy presumption against its constitutional validity." *Bantam Books, Inc. v. Sullivan*, 372 U.S. 58, 70 (1963). The Government "thus carries a heavy burden of showing justification for the imposition of such a restraint." *Organization for a Better Austin v. Keefe*, 402 U.S. 415, 419 (1971). The District Court for the Southern District of New York in the *New York Times* case and the District Court for the District of Columbia and the Court of Appeals for the District of Columbia Circuit in the *Washington Post* case held that the Government had not met that burden. We agree.

Justice Black, concurring.

I adhere to the view that the Government's case against the *Washington Post* should have been dismissed, and that the injunction against the *New York Times* should have been vacated without oral argument when the cases were first presented to this Court. I believe that every moment's continuance of the injunctions against these newspapers amounts to a flagrant, indefensible, and continuing violation of the First Amendment.

In seeking injunctions against these newspapers, and in its presentation to the Court, the Executive Branch seems to have forgotten the essential purpose and history of the First Amendment. When the Constitution was adopted, many people strongly opposed it because the document contained no Bill of Rights to safeguard certain basic freedoms. They especially feared that the new powers granted to a central government might be interpreted to permit the government to curtail freedom of religion, press, assembly, and speech. In response to an overwhelming public clamor, James Madison offered a series of amendments to satisfy citizens that these great liberties would remain safe and beyond the power of government to abridge. Yet the Solicitor General argues and some members of the Court appear to agree that the general powers of the Government adopted in the original Constitution should be interpreted to limit and restrict the specific and emphatic guarantees of the Bill of Rights adopted later. I can imagine no greater perversion of history. Both the history and language of the First Amendment support the view that the press must be left free to publish news, whatever the source, without censorship, injunctions, or prior restraints.

In the First Amendment the Founding Fathers gave the free press the protection it must have to fulfill its essential role in our democracy. The press was to serve the governed, not the governors. The Government's power to censor the press was abolished so that the press would remain forever free to censure the Government. The press was protected so that it could bare the secrets of government and inform the people. Only a free and unrestrained press can effectively expose deception in government. And paramount among the responsibilities of a free press is the duty to prevent any part of the government from deceiving the people and sending them off to distant lands to die of foreign fevers and foreign shot and shell. In my view, far from deserving condemnation for their courageous reporting, the *New York Times*, the *Washington Post*, and other newspapers should be commended for serving the purpose that the Founding Fathers saw so clearly. In revealing the workings of government that led to the Vietnam war, the newspapers nobly did precisely that which the Founders hoped and trusted they would do.

To find that the President has "inherent power" to halt the publication of news by resort to the courts would wipe out the First Amendment and destroy the fundamental liberty and security of the very people the Government hopes to make "secure." No one can read the history of the adoption of the First Amendment without being convinced beyond any doubt that it was injunctions like those sought here that Madison and his collaborators intended to outlaw in this Nation for all time.

The word "security" is a broad, vague generality whose contours should not be invoked to abrogate the fundamental law embodied in the First Amendment. The guarding of military and diplomatic secrets at the expense of informed representative government provides no real security for our Republic.

Justice Douglas, concurring.

The dominant purpose of the First Amendment was to prohibit the widespread practice of governmental suppression of embarrassing information. It is common knowledge that the First Amendment was adopted against the widespread use of the common law of seditious libel to punish the dissemination of material that is embarrassing to the powers-that-be. The present cases will, I think, go down in history as the most dramatic illustration of that principle. A debate of large proportions goes on in the Nation over our posture in Vietnam. That debate antedated the disclosure of the contents of the present documents. The latter are highly relevant to the debate in progress.

Secrecy in government is fundamentally anti-democratic, perpetuating bureaucratic errors. Open debate and discussion of public issues are vital to our national health.

Justice Brennan, concurring.

The error that has pervaded these cases from the outset was the granting of any injunctive relief whatsoever, interim or otherwise. The entire thrust of the Government's claim throughout these cases has been that publication of the material sought to be enjoined "could," or "might," or "may" prejudice the national interest in various ways. But the First Amendment tolerates absolutely no prior judicial restraints of the press predicated upon surmise or conjecture that untoward consequences may result. Even if the present world situation were assumed to be tantamount to a time of war, or if the power of presently available armaments would justify even in peacetime the suppression of information that would set in motion a nuclear holocaust, in neither of these actions has the Government presented or even alleged that publication of items from or based upon the material at issue would cause the happening of an event of that nature. Thus, only governmental allegation and proof that publication must inevitably, directly, and immediately cause the occurrence of an event kindred to imperiling the safety of a transport already at sea can support even the issuance of an interim restraining order. In no event may mere conclusions be sufficient, for if the Executive Branch seeks judicial aid in preventing publication, it must inevitably submit the basis upon which that aid is sought to scrutiny by the judiciary. And therefore, every restraint issued in this case, whatever its form, has violated the First Amendment—and not less so because that restraint was justified as necessary to afford the courts an opportunity to examine the claim more thoroughly. Unless and until the Government has clearly made out its case, the First Amendment commands that no injunction may issue.

Justice Stewart, concurring.

In the governmental structure created by our Constitution, the Executive is endowed with enormous power in the two related areas of national defense and international relations. This power, largely unchecked by the Legislative and Judicial branches, has been pressed to the very hilt since the advent of the nuclear missile age. For better or for worse, the simple fact is that a President of the United States possesses vastly greater constitutional independence in these two vital areas of power than does, say, a prime minister of a country with a parliamentary form of government.

In the absence of the governmental checks and balances present in other areas of our national life, the only effective restraint upon executive policy and power in the areas of national defense and international affairs may lie in an enlightened citizenry—in an informed and critical public opinion which alone can here protect the values of democratic government. For this reason, it is perhaps here that a press that is alert, aware, and free most vitally serves the basic purpose of the First Amendment. For, without an informed and free press there cannot be an enlightened people.

Yet it is elementary that the successful conduct of international diplomacy and the maintenance of an effective national defense require both confidentiality and secrecy. Other nations can hardly deal with this Nation in an atmosphere of mutual trust unless they can be assured that their confidences will be kept. And, within our own executive departments, the development of considered and intelligent international policies would be impossible if those charged with their formulation could not communicate with each other freely, frankly, and in confidence. In the area of basic national defense, the frequent need for absolute secrecy is, of course, self-evident.

I think there can be but one answer to this dilemma, if dilemma it be. The responsibility must be where the power is. If the Constitution gives the Executive a large degree of unshared power in the conduct of foreign affairs and the maintenance of our national defense, then under the Constitution, the Executive must have the largely unshared duty to determine and preserve the degree of internal security necessary to exercise that power successfully. It is an awesome responsibility, requiring judgment and wisdom of a high order. I should suppose that moral, political, and practical considerations would dictate that a very first principle of that wisdom would be an insistence upon avoiding secrecy for its own sake. For when everything is classified, then nothing is classified, and the system becomes one to be disregarded by the cynical or the careless, and to be manipulated by those intent on self-protection or self-promotion. I should suppose, in short, that the hallmark of a truly effective internal security system would be the maximum possible disclosure, recognizing that secrecy can best be preserved only when credibility is truly maintained. But be that as it may, it is clear to me that it is the constitutional duty of the Executive—as a matter of sovereign prerogative, and not as a matter of law as the courts know law—through the promulgation and enforcement of executive regulations, to protect the confidentiality necessary to carry out its responsibilities in the fields of international relations and national defense.

We are asked, quite simply, to prevent the publication by two newspapers of material that the Executive Branch insists should not, in the national interest, be published. I am convinced that the Executive is correct with respect to some of the documents involved. But I cannot say that disclosure of any of them will surely result in direct, immediate, and irreparable damage to our Nation or its people. That being so, there can under the First Amendment be but one judicial resolution of the issues before us. I join the judgments of the Court.

Justice White, concurring.

It is not easy to reject the proposition urged by the United States and to deny relief on its good faith claims in these cases that publication will work serious damage to the country. But that discomfiture is considerably dispelled by the infrequency of prior-restraint cases. Normally, publication will occur and the damage be done before the Government has either opportunity or grounds for suppression. So here, publication has already begun, and a substantial part of the threatened damage has already occurred. The fact of a massive breakdown in security is known, access to the documents by many unauthorized people is undeniable, and the efficacy of equitable relief against these or other newspapers to avert anticipated damage is doubtful at best.

What is more, terminating the ban on publication of the relatively few sensitive documents the Government now seeks to suppress does not mean that the law either requires or invites newspapers or others to publish them or that they will be immune from criminal action if they do. Prior restraints require an unusually heavy justification under the First Amendment but failure by the Government to justify prior restraints does not measure its constitutional entitlement to a conviction for criminal publication.

Justice Marshall, concurring.

In these cases, we are not faced with a situation where Congress has failed to provide the Executive with broad power to protect the Nation from disclosure of damaging state secrets. Congress has on several occasions given extensive consideration to the problem of protecting the military and strategic secrets of the United States. This consideration has resulted in the enactment of statutes making it a crime to receive, disclose, communicate, withhold, and publish certain documents, photographs, instruments, appliances, and information.

Either the Government has the power under statutory grant to use traditional criminal law to protect the country or, if there is no basis for arguing that Congress has made the activity a crime, it is plain that Congress has specifically refused to grant the authority the Government seeks from this Court. In either case this Court does not have authority to grant the requested relief. It is not for this Court to fling itself into every breach perceived by some Government official nor is it for this Court to take on itself the burden of enacting law, especially a law that Congress has refused to pass.

Chief Justice Burger, dissenting.

The newspapers make a derivative claim under the First Amendment; they denominate this right as the public "right to know"; by implication, the *Times* asserts a sole trusteeship of that right by virtue of its journalistic "scoop." The right is asserted as an absolute. Of course, the First Amendment right itself is not an absolute, as Justice Holmes so long ago pointed out in his aphorism concerning the right to shout "fire" in a crowded theater if there was no fire. There are no doubt other exceptions no one has had occasion to describe or discuss. Conceivably such exceptions may be lurking in these cases and would have been flushed had they been properly considered in the trial courts, free from unwarranted deadlines and frenetic pressures. An issue of this importance should be tried and heard in a judicial atmosphere conducive to thoughtful, reflective deliberation, especially when haste, in terms of hours, is unwarranted in light of the long period the *Times*, by its own choice, deferred publication.

It is not disputed that the *Times* has had unauthorized possession of the documents for three to four months, during which it has had its expert analysts studying them, presumably digesting them and preparing the material for publication. During all of this time, the *Times*, presumably in its capacity as trustee of the public's "right to know," has held up publication for purposes it considered proper, and thus public knowledge was delayed. No doubt this was for a good reason; the analysis of 7,000 pages of complex material drawn from a vastly greater volume of material would inevitably take time and the writing of good news stories takes time. But why should the United States Government, from whom this information was illegally acquired by someone, along with all the counsel, trial judges, and appellate judges be placed under needless pressure? After these months of deferral, the alleged "right to know" has somehow and suddenly become a right that must be vindicated instanter.

Would it have been unreasonable, since the newspaper could anticipate the Government's objections to release of secret material, to give the Government an opportunity to review the entire collection and determine whether agreement could be reached on publication? Stolen or not, if security was not in fact jeopardized, much of the material could no doubt have been declassified, since it spans a period ending in 1968. With such an approach—one that great newspapers have in the past practiced and stated editorially to be the duty of an honorable press—the newspapers and Government might well have narrowed the area of disagreement as to what was and was not publishable, leaving the remainder to be resolved in orderly litigation, if necessary. To me it is hardly believable that a newspaper long regarded as a great institution in American life would fail to perform one of the basic and simple duties of every citizen with respect to the discovery or possession of stolen property or secret government documents. That duty, I had thought—perhaps naively—was to report forthwith, to responsible public officers. This duty rests on taxi drivers, Justices, and the *New York Times*. The course followed by the *Times*, whether so calculated or not, removed any possibility of orderly litigation of the issue. If the action of the judges up to now has been correct, that result is sheer happenstance.

The consequence of all this melancholy series of events is that we literally do not know what we are acting on. As I see it, we have been forced to deal with litigation concerning rights of great magnitude without an adequate record, and surely without time for adequate treatment either in the prior proceedings or in this Court.

We all crave speedier judicial processes but when judges are pressured, as in these cases, the result is a parody of the judicial function.

Justice Harlan, dissenting.

In a speech on the floor of the House of Representatives, Chief Justice John Marshall, then a member of that body, stated, "The President is the sole organ of the nation in its external relations, and its sole representative with foreign nations." 10 Annals of Cong. 613 (1800). From that time, shortly after the founding of the Nation, to this, there has been no substantial challenge to this description of the scope of executive power.

From this constitutional primacy in the field of foreign affairs, it seems to me that certain conclusions necessarily follow. Some of these were stated concisely by President Washington, declining the request of the House of Representatives for the papers leading up to the negotiation of the Jay Treaty:

> The nature of foreign negotiations requires caution, and their success must often depend on secrecy; and even when brought to a conclusion, a full disclosure of all the measures, demands, or eventual concessions which may have been proposed or contemplated would be extremely impolitic; for this might have a pernicious influence on future negotiations, or produce immediate inconveniences, perhaps danger and mischief, in relation to other powers.

The power to evaluate the "pernicious influence" of premature disclosure is not, however, lodged in the Executive alone. I agree that, in performance of its duty to protect the values of the First Amendment against political pressures, the judiciary must review the initial Executive determination to the point of satisfying itself that the subject matter of the dispute does lie within the proper compass of the President's foreign relations power. Constitutional considerations forbid "a complete abandonment of judicial control." Moreover, the judiciary may properly insist that the determination that disclosure of the subject matter would irreparably impair the national security be made by the head of the Executive Department concerned—here, the Secretary of State or the Secretary of Defense—after actual personal consideration by that officer. This safeguard is required in the analogous area of executive claims of privilege for secrets of state.

But in my judgment the judiciary may not properly go beyond these two inquiries and redetermine for itself the probable impact of disclosure on the national security.

Even if there is some room for the judiciary to override the executive determination, it is plain that the scope of review must be exceedingly narrow. I can see no indication in the opinions of either the District Court or the Court of Appeals in the *Post* litigation that the conclusions of the Executive were given even the deference owing to an administrative agency, much less that owing to a co-equal branch of the Government operating within the field of its constitutional prerogative.

Justice Blackmun, dissenting.

The *New York Times* clandestinely devoted a period of three months to examining the 47 volumes that came into its unauthorized possession. Once it had begun publication of material from those volumes, the New York case now before us emerged. It immediately assumed, and ever since has maintained, a frenetic pace and character. Seemingly, once publication started, the material could not be made public fast enough. Seemingly, from then on, every deferral or delay, by restraint or otherwise, was abhorrent, and was to be deemed violative of the First Amendment and of the public's "right immediately to know." Yet that newspaper stood before us at oral argument and professed criticism of the Government for not lodging its protest earlier than by a Monday telegram following the initial Sunday publication.

With such respect as may be due to the contrary view, this, in my opinion, is not the way to try a lawsuit of this magnitude and asserted importance. It is not the way for federal courts to adjudicate, and to be required to adjudicate, issues that allegedly concern the Nation's vital welfare.

I strongly urge, and sincerely hope, that these two newspapers will be fully aware of their ultimate responsibilities to the United States of America. Judge Wilkey, dissenting in the District of Columbia case, after a review of only the affidavits before his court (the basic papers had not then been made available by either party), concluded that there were a number of examples of documents that, if in the possession of the *Post* and if published, "could clearly result in great harm to the nation," and he defined "harm" to mean "the death of soldiers, the destruction of alliances, the greatly increased difficulty of negotiation with our enemies, the inability of our diplomats to negotiate. . . ." I, for one, have now been able to give at least some cursory study not only to the affidavits, but to the material itself. I regret to say that, from this examination, I fear that Judge Wilkey's statements have possible foundation. I therefore share his concern. I hope that damage has not already been done. If, however, damage has been done, and if, with the Court's action today, these newspapers proceed to publish the critical documents and there results therefrom "the death of soldiers, the destruction of alliances, the greatly increased difficulty of negotiation with our enemies, the inability of our diplomats to negotiate," to which list I might add the factors of prolongation of the war and of further delay in the freeing of United States prisoners, then the Nation's people will know where the responsibility for these sad consequences rests.

The Pentagon Papers case has become synonymous with a rule that courts may not constitutionally restrain press publication. Justice Black stated the rule in purest terms: "Both the history and language of the First Amendment support the view that the press must be left free to publish news, whatever the source, without censorship, injunctions, or prior restraints," and Justice Stewart essentially agreed. But Justice Brennan did not view the issue so simply. He indicated that extraordinary circumstances could justify prior restraint of publication, but not based only on the government's "surmise or conjecture that untoward consequences may result." Justice Harlan went a step further and proposed a process in which a court would prevent disclosure if it concluded that the executive's interest in confidentiality was within the scope of its constitutional foreign relations power and the responsible department head showed that disclosure would irreparably impair national security. Other justices saw such a process as beyond the scope of the judiciary's constitutional power to decide cases and controversies.

The Pentagon Papers case is also important for the distinction it makes between prepublication restraint and legal accountability. The Court has instructed that the First Amendment's prohibition against laws abridging the freedom of the press does not immunize the press from criminal or civil responsibility for wrongfully obtaining information or for making false statements.[2] As discussed in Chapter 4, those who publish information about others may be held civilly liable for defamation. Members of the press also face the same criminal responsibility as anyone else for illegally obtaining classified information or for other illegal steps taken to gain access to records. Several justices in the Pentagon Papers case noted the potential for criminal prosecution.

Press Access

The First Amendment does not require that the government make special accommodations for investigative reporting. The U.S. Supreme Court has instructed that "the First Amendment does not guarantee the press a constitutional right of special access to information not available to the public generally."[3] The press has the same rights as the public to acquire information including with the lawful methods described below.

Most legislative and judicial proceedings are open to the public and therefore accessible to the press. Some proceedings are not. For example, courts sometimes close portions of criminal trials. The U.S. Supreme Court has instructed that criminal trials historically have been open to the public and may be closed only to protect a compelling governmental interest in a manner narrowly tailored to that purpose.[4] For example, courts may close some proceedings to protect criminal defendants from prejudicial publicity and to protect endangered witnesses from being publicly identified. Courts also have customarily closed hearings involving juveniles to protect the subjects. The courts have held that the press has no special right of access to prisons or jails. The Court has not held that civil trials must be public, but some states require it and rules of civil procedure typically presume that trials will be public. Still, courts close civil trials for certain kinds of confidential matters such as testimony about trade secrets.

Sometimes the press acquires otherwise confidential information and the government seeks it for law enforcement. The press has no special right to withhold information and reporters may be compelled to testify in civil or criminal proceedings about what they have learned. Many states have enacted statutes, however, that provide reporters, publishers, and editors with a privilege not to disclose a source or information. Typically this privilege is subject to being overridden if certain conditions exist, such as a demonstration of the importance of the information and the impossibility of obtaining it by any other means.

Public Records Laws

The public's awareness of its government's activities depends on access to records about the public's business. The U.S. Constitution does not mention a right of access to public records nor has the U.S. Supreme Court held that the press has a special right of access to them. Beginning in the 1960s, Congress and state legislatures sought to increase public access to government records and have enacted public records laws.

Federal Public Records Laws

The federal Freedom of Information Act (FOIA)[5] became law in 1966. It requires federal agencies to disclose most kinds of records in response to a written request. The disclosure requirements do not apply to Congress, the courts, or to the White House executive offices. The statute requires agencies to provide information about the nature of their records and to describe the procedure that must be followed to obtain them. The FOIA also sets the procedure for someone to appeal a denial of record access to the agency, which can be further appealed in federal district court.

The FOIA requires that a record be provided upon request unless an exception applies. The FOIA exceptions include the following kinds of records:[6]

- Matters excepted from disclosure according to specific federal statutory criteria
- National defense and foreign policy information properly classified
- Matters solely related to internal agency rules and practices
- Privileged or confidential trade secrets or commercial or financial information obtained from a person
- Inter-agency and intra-agency memoranda or letters that would be subject to the attorney-client privilege or otherwise protected from disclosure in litigation
- Personnel or medical files protected by privacy rights
- Information collected in law enforcement when disclosure could reasonably be expected to endanger someone's safety, interfere with law enforcement, violate a right to a fair trial,

be an unwarranted invasion of personal privacy, disclose a confidential source, or disclose enforcement techniques and procedures in a way that could result in circumvention of the law

- Information related to the supervision of financial institutions
- Geological information about wells

For most of the information subject to these exceptions agencies may choose to disclose it if they wish. If they withhold it they must indicate the amount of information withheld. But the statute authorizes agencies to treat certain kinds of sensitive law enforcement and national security information as if it does not exist.

Electronic records are explicitly made subject to disclosure obligations. To comply agencies establish "electronic reading room" Web sites. Requests for information also may be submitted electronically according to the procedure described by the agency.

Federal law also addresses individuals' rights of access to information about themselves. The federal Privacy Act[7] restricts the federal government's collection of personal information and its disclosure. Under the statute an individual may obtain from federal agencies records that can be retrieved by the individual's name, social security number, or other personal identifier. The individual also has a right to change or delete incorrect, irrelevant, untimely, or incomplete information. The Privacy Act specifies a process for forcing disclosure of the information or for challenging unauthorized disclosure of the information to others.

As with the Freedom of Information Act, the Privacy Act has exceptions, including for information concerning national security, criminal investigations, and confidential sources. Requests must be made in writing to each agency from which the information is sought. The statute does not prescribe a time limit for responses, but agencies must respond within 10 working days to a letter indicating that obtained information is wrong. The agency may charge its copying costs.

State Public Records Laws

State public records laws vary in their details but in essence are similar to the federal FOIA. They typically mandate public access to all materials made or received by state agencies and local governments in connection with official business unless an exception under the statute applies. Authorities subject to the requirement likely include local boards, authorities, school districts, and public higher education authorities. Exceptions are similar to those in the FOIA including limitations on public access to personnel files, police investigatory files, and attorney–client communications, though the precise scope of the exceptions varies among jurisdictions. At the local government level, public records include more than records of public meetings; they also likely include such things as vendor contracts, financial records, insurance policies, permit applications, and databases. Documents, electronic files, and other media are all considered public records subject to inspection.

The laws typically require that the public be allowed access to records in their existing form. Typically agencies must provide copies in any medium in which the agency maintains the record. Public offices are not required to sort through information to identify subjects of interest. The public entity may charge prescribed fees, usually including actual costs of reproduction if special handling is required.

Record Retention and Disposal

An obligation to provide the public with access to government records would be meaningless if the government had no obligation to keep the records. The records laws oblige public offices to maintain records of their activities in a manner in which they can be retrieved and to dispose of them only according to retention schedules. Some kinds of records with historic value, or that provide useful information about decisions, may be required to be maintained indefinitely, while documents routinely generated or received with only transitory value may be authorized for disposal on an ongoing basis. Within the federal government both the National Archives and Records Administration and the General Services Administration have responsibilities for records management.[8] State archives or similar offices carry out such responsibilities and issue schedules and regulations for records retention and disposal.

E-mails, word processing files, scanned images, and other electronic records have introduced complications for those who make records retention policies. Electronic records are easily generated in many formats. They can be stored in centralized databases within or outside the organization, as well as in local computer drives or media. Federal and state authorities are developing rules for which electronic records must be maintained and how they must be stored.

Open Meetings

Governmental accountability depends on more than access to records about past activities. The opportunity to participate meaningfully in government activities also depends on access to the decision making process. The U.S. Constitution does not guaranty a right of public access to legislative sessions. The Constitutional Convention met in secret and both houses of Congress hold closed door meetings. Authority for the chambers to hold these closed sessions is implied in Article I, Section 5 of the Constitution, which says, "Each House shall keep a journal of its proceedings, and from time to time publish the same, excepting such parts as may in their judgment require secrecy." Secret sessions still occur, but recently, especially after the era of Watergate, legislators have enacted measures to require that most meetings be open to the public.

Federal Open Meetings Law

In 1976 Congress enacted a federal open meetings law called the Government in the Sunshine Act.[9] It requires federal agencies to conduct meetings in public if they involve a sufficient number of governing members to take action. It also requires that at least a week's prior public notice be given of such meetings. The statute allows deliberations to be conducted during closed meetings if protected information is being discussed. The exceptions cover subjects similar to those protected from disclosure under the federal Freedom of Information Act, as well as a general exception if premature disclosure is "likely to significantly frustrate implementation of a proposed agency action."[10] The courts have addressed many subtle interpretive issues, including to whom the law applies, what constitutes a meeting, and the application of the exceptions. Agencies may have other obligations under statutes specifically applying to them.

State Open Meetings Laws

In 1967 Forida became the first state to pass an open meetings law in modern form. Article I, Section 24(b) of the State's Constitution provides that "[a]ll meetings of any collegial public body of the executive branch of state government or of any collegial public body of a county, municipality, school district, or special district, at which official acts are to be taken or at which public business of such body is to be transacted or discussed, shall be open and noticed to the public . . . ." Other state constitutions similarly contain a right to open meetings and all states now have some form of an open meeting law. These laws vary but typically they have three main components: giving the public an opportunity to observe the deliberations of public bodies, requiring advance notice of such meetings, and requiring that records be kept of the meetings.

Typical state open meeting laws apply to state and local government deliberative bodies. Some states extend this requirement to publicly funded organizations. The meetings to which the requirement applies usually include not only regularly scheduled sessions but also spontaneous gatherings of decision makers. The open meeting rule would apply, for example, to a gathering at someone's house where decision makers discuss upcoming votes on a pending matter. Most states do not require that meetings of less than a quorum of members be held in public, but some apply the requirement to any gathering of two or more members of the body at which the public business is discussed. Some states apply the requirement only when action may be taken, or when the members are deliberating a decision, while others extend the requirement to gatherings at which any public business will be discussed.

Some states require that opportunity for public comment be afforded at public meetings but most do not and the U.S. Constitution does not require it. As the U.S. Supreme Court observed, "Policymaking organs in our system of government have never operated under a constitutional constraint requiring them to afford every interested member of the public an opportunity to present testimony before any policy is adopted."[11] The Court explained that such a requirement would encumber government and excessively involve judges in executive and legislative affairs.[12]

Open meeting laws require that advance notice be given to the public of a meeting at which deliberations may occur. The notice must specify date, time, and place, and laws typically also require that the notice include an agenda of the matters to be discussed. Notices typically are posted in the public offices and on the Internet but state law may also require publication in a newspaper of general circulation within the jurisdiction. Sometimes open meetings laws require only that notice must be "reasonable," but more commonly they require following a regular schedule and posting agendas well in advance. Open meetings laws allow special sessions on short notice to address emergencies.

Open meeting laws also require that records of the meetings be kept and made available for public review. Records commonly are kept on video or tape, but some bodies continue to keep minutes. The records should give those who could not physically attend the meeting sufficient information so that they can apprise themselves of the substance of the discussion and any action taken.

Open meeting laws specify the procedure to contest the conduct of a meeting that occurred outside a public forum. In general any member of the public, including the press, may file an action in court to seek to prevent a closed meeting from occurring. If the meeting has already occurred members of the public, as well as certain executive officials such as the attorney general, may have authority to challenge any action that was taken in violation of the open meeting law. Laws may also provide for civil penalties against those who violate the law and may allow removal of someone from office for intentional violations.

Some bodies are exempt from open meetings laws, such as legislative and judicial ethics committees, grand juries, and investigatory bodies. Open meeting laws allow deliberative bodies to meet without public access in "executive sessions" to hear or discuss certain matters. Executive sessions are convened by a vote taken in an open session and typically the body must state the reason for holding a closed meeting. Records must be kept of such sessions but are not made public unless later circumstances require it. The authorized reasons for executive sessions vary among the states but typically include consideration of the following:

- Matters affecting personal privacy, such as discussion of a crime victim's identity
- Qualifications, performance, character, or fitness of public employees
- Obtaining legal advice from an attorney
- Terms of contract negotiations or discussion of trade secrets that are part of contracts
- Reports of police investigations
- Matters involving security
- Economic development incentive proposals

What Is a Meeting?: *Beck v. Shelton*

When open meeting laws were first enacted the notion of a "meeting" was a fairly simple concept: individuals gathered together in a room and conversed. Times have changed. When do communications through such mechanisms as chat rooms and video conferencing implicate the public's interest in openness? The following Virginia Supreme Court case illustrates a few of the thorny questions that can arise about what constitutes a meeting and what form of communication triggers the public forum requirement.

Beck v. Shelton
593 S.E.2d 195 (Va. 2004)

Justice Lemons, writing for the Virginia Supreme Court.

In this appeal, we consider several issues relating to The Virginia Freedom of Information Act ("FOIA" or the "Act"), Code §§ 2.2-3700 to -3714, including: 1) whether "members-elect" are "members" of a public body for the purpose of application of FOIA; 2) whether the use of electronic mail ("e-mail") for communication between three or more members of a public body constitutes a "meeting" for the purposes of FOIA; and, 3) whether a particular gathering of citizens attended by three members of the Fredericksburg City Council constituted a "meeting" under the Act.

Gordon Shelton, Anthony Jenkins, and Patrick J. Timpone (collectively, "Shelton") filed an 18-count petition for writ of mandamus and injunction against William M. Beck, Mayor of the City of Fredericksburg; W. Scott Howson III, Vice-Mayor of the City of Fredericksburg; and three Councilmen, Thomas P. Fortune, William C. Withers, Jr., and Matthew J. Kelly (collectively, "Defendants" or "Beck"). While citing multiple incidents of alleged violations of FOIA, the gravamen of the complaint was that Defendants "deliberately e-mailed each other in a knowing, willful and deliberate attempt to hold secret meetings, avoid public scrutiny" and "discuss City business and decide City issues without the input of all the council members and the public." Shelton asserted that various exchanges of e-mail, face-to-face meetings, and one public gathering on the streets of Fredericksburg constituted "meetings" under FOIA for which there was no notice pursuant to Code § 2.2-3707 and no emergency or other exception which would relieve the Defendants from the obligations imposed upon them concerning public meetings.

Under Code § 2.2-3701, the definition of "public body" is extended to:

> *(ii) any committee, subcommittee, or other entity however designated, of the public body created to perform delegated functions of the public body or to advise the public body. It shall not exclude any such committee, subcommittee or entity because it has private sector or citizen members.*

This provision simply includes committees, subcommittees, or entities within the types of public bodies covered by FOIA, irrespective of participation by private sector or citizen members. It does not expand the meaning of "members" in the definition of "meetings" also contained in Code § 2.2-3701.

We will not rewrite Code § 2.2-3701 to change the word "members" to the phrase "members or members-elect." It is not our prerogative. If the legislature chooses to do so, it is properly within its power to do so.

It is not disputed that on several occasions after July 1, 2002, more than three members of City Council corresponded with each other concerning specific items of public business by use of e-mail. It would serve no useful purpose to relate the particular subjects of the communications because the issue before us involves the method of communication. Succinctly stated, assuming all other statutory requirements are met, does the exchange of e-mails between members of a public body constitute a "meeting" subject to the provisions of FOIA?

Indisputably, the use of computers for textual communication has become commonplace around the world. It can involve communication that is functionally similar to a letter sent by ordinary mail, courier, or facsimile transmission. In this respect, there may be significant delay before the communication is received and additional delay in response. However, computers can be utilized to exchange text in the nature of a discussion, potentially involving multiple participants, in what are euphemistically called "chat rooms" or by "instant messaging." In these forms, computer generated communication is virtually simultaneous.

In the case before us, the e-mail communications did not involve virtually simultaneous interaction. Rather, the e-mail communications at issue in this case were more like traditional letters sent by ordinary mail, courier, or facsimile. The record contains printed copies of the e-mails in question. The shortest interval between sending a particular e-mail and receiving a response was more than four hours. The longest interval was well over two days.

By definition, a violation under § 2.2-3708 presumes a "meeting" as defined in FOIA. Code § 2.2-3701 provides in part:

> *"Meeting" or "meetings" means the meetings including work sessions, when sitting physically, or through telephonic or video equipment pursuant to § 2.2-3708, as a body or entity, or as an informal assemblage of (i) as many as three members or (ii) a quorum, if less than three, of the constituent membership, wherever held, with or without minutes being taken, whether or not votes are cast, of any public body. The gathering of employees of a public body shall not be deemed a "meeting" subject to the provisions of this chapter.*

Clearly, the conduct in question did not involve "sitting physically" in a "work session." Consequently, the key to resolving the question before us is whether there was an "assemblage." The term "assemble" means "to bring together" and comes from the Latin simul, meaning "together, at the same time." *Webster's Third New International Dictionary* 131 (1993). The term inherently entails the quality of simultaneity. While such simultaneity may be present when e-mail technology is used in a "chat room" or as "instant messaging," it is not present when e-mail is used as the functional equivalent of letter communication by ordinary mail, courier, or facsimile transmission. The General Assembly anticipated this type of communication when it provided:

> *nothing contained herein shall be construed to prohibit (i) separately contacting the membership, or any part thereof, of any public body for the purpose of ascertaining a member's position with respect to the transaction of public business, whether such contact is done in person, by telephone or by electronic communication, provided the contact is done on a basis that does not constitute a meeting as defined in this chapter . . .*

Code § 2.2-3710(B). Under the terms of this provision, it is anticipated that some electronic communication may constitute a "meeting" and some may not. As previously stated, the key difference between permitted use of electronic communication, such as e-mail, outside the notice and open meeting requirements of FOIA, and those that constitute a "meeting" under FOIA, is the feature of simultaneity inherent in the term "assemblage."

We hold that the trial court erred in its determination that the e-mail communications at issue in this case constituted a "meeting" under FOIA.

In July, 2002, citizens living near the intersection of Charlotte and Weedon Streets in the City of Fredericksburg were concerned about the lack of a stop sign at the intersection and other issues related to traffic safety. Two city employees and three members of City Council were separately invited by concerned citizens to attend a gathering at the intersection in the middle of the day on July 25, 2002. Approximately 20 people were in attendance.

On appeal, Shelton maintains that such a gathering was a "meeting" under the terms of FOIA. We disagree. The public policy of the Commonwealth "ensures the people of the Commonwealth ready access to public records in the custody of a public body or its officers and employees, and free entry to meetings of public bodies wherein the business of the people is being conducted." Code § 2.2-3700(B). But FOIA "shall not be construed to discourage the free discussion by government officials or employees of public matters with the citizens of the Commonwealth." *Id.* Obviously, the balance between these values must be considered on a case-by-case basis according the facts presented. Here, FOIA gives additional guidance:

> *Nothing in this chapter shall be construed to prohibit the gathering or attendance of two or more members of a public body (i) at any place or function where no part of the purpose of such gathering or attendance is the discussion or transaction of any public business, and such gathering or attendance was not called or prearranged with any purpose of discussing or transacting any business of the public body or (ii) at a public forum, candidate appearance, or debate, the purpose of which is to inform the electorate and not to transact public business or to hold discussions relating to the transaction of public business, even though the performance of the members individually or collectively in the conduct of public business may be a topic of discussion or debate at such public meeting.*

Code § 2.2-3707(G).

The trial court was not plainly wrong or without evidence to support its judgment that the Charlotte Street gathering was a citizen-organized "informational forum" and that no part of the purpose of the gathering or attendance was the discussion or transaction of any public business. The undisputed evidence at trial was that City Council did not have any business pending before it on the issue of traffic controls, nor was it likely to have such matters come before it in the future.

Most common questions that arise about open meeting laws can be answered by reading the statutes. *Beck v. Shelton* illustrates that lawmakers cannot anticipate every nuance of public deliberation. In most situations members of bodies subject to the open meeting laws can avoid complications by confining their discussions to scheduled public meetings. But as *Beck v. Shelton* shows, circumstances can arise in which public officials and citizens will have different views about the nature of discussions in other contexts.

The Virginia Supreme Court read the statute as not applying to members-elect, only to current members of government bodies who have power to make decisions. Other state lawmakers have determined that open meeting concerns are raised if members-elect participate in a meeting at which they commit to later deliberative action. Accordingly, some open meeting statutes include members-elect in the definition of those to whom the statute applies.

Answering the question of whether an electronic exchange might constitute a meeting similarly begins with examination of the language of applicable statutes. In *Beck v. Shelton* the Virginia Supreme Court focused on simultaneity to decide whether e-mail exchanges were a meeting subject to the statute. The court concluded that the exchanges were more like correspondence than a meeting, but noted that use of a chat room or instant messaging could be the equivalent of a meeting. The distinctions are blurry because modern modes of communication do not fit into traditional concepts of what it means to deliberate together. Lawmakers therefore must think creatively when they seek to give clear guidance about what kinds of modern communications trigger a public right of participation. They also need to consider the means by which the public is to be afforded an opportunity to participate. The governing body could enable interested persons to observe message exchanges in real time, but this passive observation is different than being present in a room during a presentation or deliberation. Must the public have the opportunity to object or contribute to the exchange? The need to revisit open meeting concepts is likely to persist as new technologies continue to emerge in the future.

Review Questions

1. What was the U.S. Supreme Court's reaction to the Nixon Administration's efforts to restrain newspaper publication of the Pentagon Papers?

2. Under what circumstances would the U.S. Supreme Court likely allow prepublication restraint?

3. To what extent does the press have a special right of access to public proceedings and records?

4. Does the First Amendment protect the press from criminal or civil liability for violations of the law in gaining access to information?

5. What does the federal Freedom of Information Act generally require of federal agencies?

6. What are the basic exceptions allowing agencies to withhold information identified in a Freedom of Information Act request?

7. What does the federal Privacy Act generally require?

8. What kinds of records are typically required to be maintained and made available to the public under state law and what are the common exceptions to the requirements?

9. What do open meetings laws generally require and what are the common exceptions to the requirement?

10. What are the considerations for assessing whether electronic communications might be subject to open meetings requirements?

Notes

1. Hazelwood School District v. Kuhlmeier, 484 U.S. 260 (1988).
2. Near v. Minnesota, 283 U.S. 697, 713–14 (1931).
3. Branzburg v. Hayes, 408 U.S. 665, 684 (1972).
4. Globe Newspaper Co. v. Superior Court, 457 U.S. 596, 606–07 (1982).
5. 5 U.S.C. § 552 (2006).
6. *Id.* § 552(b).
7. *Id.* § 552a.
8. 44 U.S.C. § 2904 (2000); 36 C.F.R. pt. 1228 (2008).
9. 5 U.S.C. § 552b (2006).
10. *Id.* § 552b(c)(9)(B).
11. Minn. State Bd. for Community Colleges v. Knight, 465 U.S. 271, 284 (1984).
12. *Id.* at 285.

Chapter 6

Property

Before I built a wall I'd ask to know
What I was walling in or walling out,
And to whom I was like to give offense.
Robert Frost, "Mending Wall"

CHAPTER OBJECTIVES

After studying this chapter you should better understand:

- The constitutional constraints on government taking of private property
- The constitutional constraints on government regulation of property use and requirements for payment of exactions as a condition to development
- The basic nature of real estate interests and conveyances
- The basic nature of the real estate recording system
- The basic forms of intellectual property and the nature of legal protection available for them

Property law is important to individuals and communities. Homes, investment, economic development, and government operations all depend on the value of property rights. Most people have a sense of their basic nature but rely on real estate professionals to understand the details. The details can be difficult to understand. Even basic property law concepts are defined by archaic terms and obscure common-law presumptions, made more complicated by idiosyncratic variations among the governing state laws. But, as with many areas of the law, a better grasp of the basics is useful for making good decisions and for avoiding difficulties and disputes.

This chapter is intended to alleviate some of the common mystery and confusion about property law. The focus is on "real property"—land and the improvements built on it, including the nature of ownership, the limits of government control over it, and the laws of conveyances. This chapter also provides an overview of intellectual property, which shares some basic features with real property law but also has unique attributes that are commonly misunderstood.

Property Rights and Responsibilities

Surprisingly to many, the U.S. Constitution does not mention rights to private property. But it does protect them. The Fifth Amendment prohibits private property from being "taken for public use without just compensation." As the U.S. Supreme Court said early on, the right to own property is "a primary object of the social compact" and "one of the natural, inherent, and unalienable rights of man."[1] These unalienable rights entail two interrelated concepts: exclusivity and alienability. Exclusivity enables owners to make reasonable choices about how to use and enjoy their property. Alienability is the right to sell or give it to others. The U.S. Constitution and judicial interpretations of it impose obligations that run with these benefits, including the obligation to pay a fair share of taxes to contribute to the public fund and the need to abide by reasonable use restrictions to protect the rights of others.

Eminent Domain

The ultimate government power to which property is subject is the power to take it for public use, known as the power of eminent domain. Exercise of eminent domain is sometimes referred to as a "condemnation," which derives from the act of exacting something from a landowner, or a "taking," which refers to the compulsion that is involved. The U.S. Constitution does not mention any power of eminent domain, but its legal legitimacy for a representative government's use has never been seriously challenged. Legal authorities have interpreted the Constitution's silence as a reflection of the eminent domain power's assumed existence rather than any intent to withhold it. The question of constitutional limits on the power has been the subject of much judicial interpretation and debate.

The Fifth Amendment restricts use of eminent to domain to takings for public use. Courts generally have deferred to legislatures for determinations about when an intended use is sufficiently tied to a legitimate public need. This deference attracted much public attention in the 2005 case of *Kelo v. City of New London*,[2] in which the U.S. Supreme Court held that Connecticut law could constitutionally permit use of eminent domain to acquire land for conveyance to a private party as part of an economic redevelopment plan. The Court said its "public use jurisprudence has wisely eschewed rigid formulas and intrusive scrutiny in favor of affording legislatures broad latitude in determining what public needs justify the use of the takings power."[3] In *Kelo*, and in other opinions, the Court has made it clear that legislatures not only have broad discretion to designate proper public purposes for use of eminent domain but also that they can decline to invoke this power or restrict its application as narrowly as they choose. Legislatures have customarily authorized their jurisdiction's government units, public educational bodies, public utilities, and public carriers to use eminent domain for many purposes, including for roads, public buildings and schools, parks, utility lines, and environmental protection.

To exercise eminent domain, the governing law usually requires the body authorized to use the power to first contact the owner and to attempt to negotiate an agreement. If agreement cannot be reached, the authority may file a condemnation action in court. The procedure usually requires that the authority deposit estimated full compensation in court when the action is filed, which the owner can withdraw without giving up a right to prove entitlement to more during the case. The required compensation is the fair market value of what is taken, which is either the value of acquired land or the diminished value of land remaining after a part of it is taken. This is determined by a jury, by a judge, or by appointed commissioners and is based on appraisal testimony that the parties submit. Although the amount of compensation commonly is determined in a contested hearing, disputes about the authority's determination about the need for the property are generally dismissed in deference to the government's discretion to determine the scope of public projects.

Land Use Controls

Private use of property also is subject to the government's police power to protect public health and safety. This power enables government to enact regulations that change the nature and extent of permissible property uses, and no compensation need be paid for the effect of reasonable use restrictions. The U.S. Supreme Court has recognized the possibility of a regulatory taking with overly aggressive restrictions. In the famous 1922 case of *Pennsylvania Coal Co. v. Mahon*,[4] Justice Oliver Wendell Holmes said, "The general rule at least, is that while property may be regulated to a certain extent, if regulation goes too far it will be recognized as a taking."[5] He warned that if the U.S. Constitution's protection against taking private property without compensation "is found to be qualified by the police power, the natural tendency of human nature is to extend the qualification more and more until at last private property disappears."[6] He also explained that an owner must be entitled to compensation if a restriction "goes too far." The challenge for the courts has been in determining when regulations go too far.

All land use regulations affect property values to some degree. The Court rejected "the proposition that diminution in property value, standing alone, can establish a 'taking.'"[7] In general, courts have expanded the notion of permissible regulations as governments have perceived more need to address harm from urbanization with land use controls.

Several cases have built a framework for making the difficult distinction between property restrictions that must be borne without compensation and those for which payment must be made. In 1978 in *Penn Central Transportation Co. v. New York City*,[8] the Court held that a historic preservation regulation prohibiting construction of an office building above Grand Central Station was not a taking because "[t]he regulations imposed are substantially related to the promotion of the general welfare and not only permit reasonable beneficial use of the landmark site but also afford [the owner] opportunities further to enhance not only the Terminal site property but also other properties."[9] The Court later described the proper degree of review as consideration of "a complex of factors including the regulation's economic effect on the landowner, the extent to which the regulation interferes with reasonable investment-backed expectations, and the character of the government action."[10] In 1987 in *First English Evangelical Lutheran Church of Glendale v. County of Los Angeles*,[11] the Court held that a prohibition against construction in a flood protection area was a taking because it "den[ied] a landowner all use of his property . . . for which the Constitution clearly requires compensation."[12] Five years later in

Lucas v. South Carolina Coastal Council,[13] the Court held that a prohibition against building within a coastal area unconstitutionally denied an owner of property without compensation, saying that a taking occurs when a regulation "declares 'off-limits' all economically productive or beneficial uses of land."[14] The Court explained that although government may enact regulations to address a harmful land use, mere legislative "recitation of a noxious-use justification cannot be the basis for departing from our categorical rule that total regulatory takings must be compensated. If it were, departure would virtually always be allowed."[15] The Court shifted its approach to regulatory takings somewhat in 2002 in *Tahoe-Sierra Preservation Council, Inc. v. Tahoe Regional Planning Agency*,[16] holding that a 32-month moratorium on development did not offend the Court's sense of "fairness and justice" for reasonable limitations. The Court said it would not attempt to devise a general rule about when a moratorium on development would go too far and suggested that such a limitation could be developed by a state's legislature.[17]

The Court therefore has established that there are limits to the government's ability to restrict property but has not provided a clear measure of those limits. The outcome can turn on particular justices' sense of fairness and justice.

Exaction Proportionality: Dolan v. City of Tigard

Exactions are requirements imposed on a development as a condition for regulatory approval, such as requiring an owner to dedicate land to public use or to build public improvements or pay to offset the cost of constructing them. Exactions can implicate the constitutional prohibition against the taking of property without compensation. In 1987 in *Nollan v. California Coastal Commission*,[18] the U.S. Supreme Court considered a requirement for donation of a lateral public easement on a beachfront lot as a condition for construction of a home. The easement was designed to connect public beaches on either side of the owner's property. The Court found that protection of visual access to the ocean is a legitimate public interest but that such an interest did not justify requiring donation of an easement across the property. The Court held that the requirement was a taking because it lacked an "essential nexus" between legitimate state interests and the government's exaction.

The *Nollan* decision did not explain how courts should determine whether an exaction is sufficiently connected to legitimate regulatory concerns. In 1994 a challenge came before the Court to a local requirement that an owner seeking to expand a hardware store exclude a portion of her land from development and donate land for a public pedestrian and bike pathway. In *Dolan v. City of Tigard*, an excerpt of which follows, the Court completed the modern analysis for the constitutionality of exactions.

Dolan v. City of Tigard
512 U.S. 374 (1994)

Chief Justice Rehnquist, writing for the Court.

The State of Oregon enacted a comprehensive land use management program in 1973. The program required all Oregon cities and counties to adopt new comprehensive land use plans that were consistent with the statewide planning goals. The plans are implemented by land use regulations which are part of an integrated hierarchy of legally binding goals, plans, and regulations. Pursuant to the State's requirements, the city of Tigard, a community of some 30,000 residents on the southwest edge of Portland, developed a comprehensive plan and codified it in its Community Development Code (CDC). The CDC requires property owners in the area zoned Central Business District to comply with a 15% open space and landscaping requirement, which limits total site coverage, including all structures and paved parking, to 85% of the parcel. After the completion of a transportation study that identified congestion in the Central Business District as a particular problem, the city adopted a plan for a pedestrian/bicycle pathway intended to encourage alternatives to automobile transportation for short trips. The CDC requires that new development facilitate this plan by dedicating land for pedestrian pathways where provided for in the pedestrian/bicycle pathway plan.

The city also adopted a Master Drainage Plan (Drainage Plan). The Drainage Plan noted that flooding occurred in several areas along Fanno Creek, including areas near petitioner's property. The Drainage Plan also established that the increase in impervious surfaces associated with continued urbanization would exacerbate these flooding problems. To combat these risks, the Drainage Plan suggested a series of improvements to the Fanno Creek Basin, including channel excavation in the area next to petitioner's property. Other recommendations included ensuring that the floodplain remains free of structures and that it be preserved as greenways to minimize flood damage to structures. The Drainage Plan concluded that the cost of these improvements should be shared based on both direct and indirect benefits, with property owners along the waterways paying more due to the direct benefit that they would receive.

Petitioner Florence Dolan owns a plumbing and electric supply store located on Main Street in the Central Business District of the city. The store covers approximately 9,700 square feet on the eastern side of a 1.67-acre parcel, which includes a gravel parking lot. Fanno Creek flows through the southwestern corner of the lot and along its western boundary. The year-round flow of the creek renders the area within the creek's 100-year floodplain virtually unusable for commercial development. The city's comprehensive plan includes the Fanno Creek floodplain as part of the city's greenway system.

Petitioner applied to the city for a permit to redevelop the site. Her proposed plans called for nearly doubling the size of the store to 17,600 square feet, and paving a 39-space parking lot. The existing store, located on the opposite side of the parcel, would be razed in sections as construction progressed on the new building. In the second phase of the project, petitioner proposed to build an additional structure on the northeast side of the site for complementary businesses, and to provide more parking. The proposed expansion and intensified use are consistent with the city's zoning scheme in the Central Business District. The City Planning Commission granted petitioner's permit application subject to conditions imposed by the city's CDC.

The CDC establishes the following standard for site development review approval:

> *Where landfill and/or development is allowed within and adjacent to the 100-year floodplain, the city shall require the dedication of sufficient open land area for greenway*

adjoining and within the floodplain. This area shall include portions at a suitable elevation for the construction of a pedestrian/bicycle pathway within the floodplain in accordance with the adopted pedestrian/bicycle plan.

Thus, the Commission required that petitioner dedicate the portion of her property lying within the 100-year floodplain for improvement of a storm drainage system along Fanno Creek and that she dedicate an additional 15-foot strip of land adjacent to the floodplain as a pedestrian/bicycle pathway. The dedication required by that condition encompasses approximately 7,000 square feet, or roughly 10% of the property. In accordance with city practice, petitioner could rely on the dedicated property to meet the 15% open space and landscaping requirement mandated by the city's zoning scheme. The city would bear the cost of maintaining a landscaped buffer between the dedicated area and the new store.

Petitioner contends that the city has forced her to choose between the building permit and her right under the Fifth Amendment to just compensation for the public easements. Petitioner does not quarrel with the city's authority to exact some forms of dedication as a condition for the grant of a building permit, but challenges the showing made by the city to justify these exactions. She argues that the city has identified "no special benefits" conferred on her, and has not identified any "special quantifiable burdens" created by her new store that would justify the particular dedications required from her which are not required from the public at large.

In evaluating petitioner's claim, we must first determine whether the "essential nexus" exists between the "legitimate state interest" and the permit condition exacted by the city. If we find that a nexus exists, we must then decide the required degree of connection between the exactions and the projected impact of the proposed development.

Undoubtedly, the prevention of flooding along Fanno Creek and the reduction of traffic congestion in the Central Business District qualify as the type of legitimate public purposes we have upheld. It seems equally obvious that a nexus exists between preventing flooding along Fanno Creek and limiting development within the creek's 100-year floodplain. Petitioner proposes to double the size of her retail store and to pave her now-gravel parking lot, thereby expanding the impervious surface on the property and increasing the amount of stormwater run-off into Fanno Creek.

The same may be said for the city's attempt to reduce traffic congestion by providing for alternative means of transportation. In theory, a pedestrian/bicycle pathway provides a useful alternative means of transportation for workers and shoppers. . . ."

The second part of our analysis requires us to determine whether the degree of the exactions demanded by the city's permit conditions bear the required relationship to the projected impact of petitioner's proposed development. Here the Oregon Supreme Court deferred to what it termed the "city's unchallenged factual findings" supporting the dedication conditions and found them to be reasonably related to the impact of the expansion of petitioner's business.

The city required that petitioner dedicate "to the city as Greenway all portions of the site that fall within the existing 100-year floodplain [of Fanno Creek] . . . and all property 15 feet above [the floodplain] boundary." In addition, the city demanded that the retail store be designed so as not to intrude into the greenway area. The city relies on the Commission's rather tentative findings that increased stormwater flow from petitioner's property "can only add to the public need to manage the [floodplain] for drainage purposes" to support its conclusion that the "requirement of dedication of the floodplain area on the site is related to the applicant's plan to intensify development on the site."

The city made the following specific findings relevant to the pedestrian/bicycle pathway:

> *In addition, the proposed expanded use of this site is anticipated to generate additional vehicular traffic thereby increasing congestion on nearby collector and arterial streets. Creation of a convenient, safe pedestrian/bicycle pathway system as an alternative means of transportation could offset some of the traffic demand on these nearby streets and lessen the increase in traffic congestion.*

The question for us is whether these findings are constitutionally sufficient to justify the conditions imposed by the city on petitioner's building permit. Since state courts have been dealing with this question a good deal longer than we have, we turn to representative decisions made by them.

In some States, very generalized statements as to the necessary connection between the required dedication and the proposed development seem to suffice. We think this standard is too lax to adequately protect petitioner's right to just compensation if her property is taken for a public purpose.

Other state courts require a very exacting correspondence, described as the "specifi[c] and uniquely attributable" test. Under this standard, if the local government cannot demonstrate that its exaction is directly proportional to the specifically created need, the exaction becomes "a veiled exercise of the power of eminent domain and a confiscation of private property behind the defense of police regulations." *Pioneer Trust & Savings Bank v. Mount Prospect*, 176 N.E.2d 799, 802 (Ill. 1961). We do not think the Federal Constitution requires such exacting scrutiny, given the nature of the interests involved.

A number of state courts have taken an intermediate position, requiring the municipality to show a "reasonable relationship" between the required dedication and the impact of the proposed development.

We think the "reasonable relationship" test adopted by a majority of the state courts is closer to the federal constitutional norm than either of those previously discussed. But we do not adopt it as such, partly because the term "reasonable relationship" seems confusingly similar to the term "rational basis" which describes the minimal level of scrutiny under the Equal Protection Clause of the Fourteenth Amendment. We think a term such as "rough proportionality" best encapsulates what we hold to be the requirement of the Fifth Amendment. No precise mathematical calculation is required, but the city must make some sort of individualized determination that the required dedication is related both in nature and extent to the impact of the proposed development.

If petitioner's proposed development had somehow encroached on existing greenway space in the city, it would have been reasonable to require petitioner to provide some alternative greenway space for the public either on her property or elsewhere. But that is not the case here.

We conclude that the findings upon which the city relies do not show the required reasonable relationship between the floodplain easement and the petitioner's proposed new building.

With respect to the pedestrian/bicycle pathway, we have no doubt that the city was correct in finding that the larger retail sales facility proposed by petitioner will increase traffic on the streets of the Central Business District. The city estimates that the proposed development would generate roughly 435 additional trips per day. Dedications for streets, sidewalks, and other public ways are generally reasonable exactions to avoid excessive congestion from a proposed property use. But on the record before us, the city has not met its burden of demonstrating that the additional number of vehicle and bicycle trips generated by the petitioner's development reasonably relate to the city's requirement for a dedication of the pedestrian/bicycle pathway easement. The city simply found that the creation of the pathway "could offset some of the traffic demand . . . and lessen the increase in traffic congestion."

Cities have long engaged in the commendable task of land use planning, made necessary by increasing urbanization particularly in metropolitan areas such as Portland. The city's goals of reducing flooding hazards and traffic congestion, and providing for public greenways, are laudable, but there are outer limits to how this may be done. "A strong public desire to improve the public condition [will not] warrant achieving the desire by a shorter cut than the constitutional way of paying for the change." *Pennsylvania Coal Co. v. Mahon*, 260 U.S. 393, 416 (1922).

Justice Stevens, dissenting.

The record does not tell us the dollar value of petitioner Florence Dolan's interest in excluding the public from the greenway adjacent to her hardware business. The mountain of briefs that the case has generated nevertheless makes it obvious that the pecuniary value of her victory is far less important than the rule of law that this case has been used to establish. It is unquestionably an important case.

Certain propositions are not in dispute. The enlargement of the Tigard unit in Dolan's chain of hardware stores will have an adverse impact on the city's legitimate and substantial interests in controlling drainage in Fanno Creek and minimizing traffic congestion in Tigard's business district. That impact is sufficient to justify an outright denial of her application for approval of the expansion. The city has nevertheless agreed to grant Dolan's application if she will comply with two conditions, each of which admittedly will mitigate the adverse effects of her proposed development. The disputed question is whether the city has violated the Fourteenth Amendment to the Federal Constitution by refusing to allow Dolan's planned construction to proceed unless those conditions are met.

Not one of the state cases cited by the Court announces anything akin to a "rough proportionality" requirement. For the most part, moreover, those cases that invalidated municipal ordinances did so on state law or unspecified grounds roughly equivalent to *Nollan's* "essential nexus" requirement.

Applying its new standard, the Court finds two defects in the city's case. First, while the record would adequately support a requirement that Dolan maintain the portion of the floodplain on her property as undeveloped open space, it does not support the additional requirement that the floodplain be dedicated to the city. Second, while the city adequately established the traffic increase that the proposed development would generate, it failed to quantify the off-setting decrease in automobile traffic that the bike path will produce. Even under the Court's new rule, both defects are, at most, nothing more than harmless error.

The Court's rejection of the bike path condition amounts to nothing more than a play on words. Everyone agrees that the bike path "could" offset some of the increased traffic flow that the larger store *will* generate, but the findings do not unequivocally state that it will do so, or tell us just how many cyclists will replace motorists. Predictions on such matters are inherently nothing more than estimates. Certainly the assumption that there will be an offsetting benefit here is entirely reasonable and should suffice whether it amounts to 100 percent, 35 percent, or only 5 percent of the increase in automobile traffic that would otherwise occur. If the Court proposes to have the federal judiciary micro-manage state decisions of this kind, it is indeed extending its welcome mat to a significant new class of litigants. Although there is no reason to believe that state courts have failed to rise to the task, property owners have surely found a new friend today.

Even if Dolan should accept the city's conditions in exchange for the benefit that she seeks, it would not necessarily follow that she had been denied "just compensation" since it would be appropriate to consider the receipt of that benefit in any calculation of "just compensation." Particularly in the absence of any evidence on the point, we should not presume that the discretionary benefit the city has offered is less valuable than the property interests that Dolan can retain or surrender at her option. But even if that discretionary benefit were so trifling that it could not be considered just compensation when it has "little or no relationship" to the property, the Court fails to explain why the same value would suffice when the required nexus is present. In this respect, the Court's reliance on the "unconstitutional conditions" doctrine is assuredly novel, and arguably incoherent. The city's conditions are by no means immune from constitutional scrutiny. The level of scrutiny, however, does not approximate the kind of review that would apply if the city had insisted on a surrender of Dolan's First Amendment rights in exchange for a building permit.

In our changing world one thing is certain: uncertainty will characterize predictions about the impact of new urban developments on the risks of floods, earthquakes, traffic congestion, or environmental harms. When there is doubt concerning the magnitude of those impacts, the public interest in averting them must outweigh the private interest of the commercial entrepreneur. If the government can demonstrate that the conditions it has imposed in a land use permit are rational, impartial and conducive to fulfilling the aims of a valid land use plan, a strong presumption of validity should attach to those conditions. The burden of demonstrating that those conditions have unreasonably impaired the economic value of the proposed improvement belongs squarely on the shoulders of the party challenging the state action's constitutionality. That allocation of burdens has served us well in the past. The Court has stumbled badly today by reversing it.

States reacted to *Nollan* and to *Dolan* by revising exaction statutes to restrict compulsory land dedications to needs that the proposed development generates and to require demonstration that the nexus and rough proportionality requirements are met. State statutes now also commonly require that exaction payments, known as "impact fees," be based on a quantitative analysis of service needs resulting from the development, such as associated demands for additional space in schools or fire or police service. Communities that see development proposals as an opportunity to exact arbitrarily determined donations reach beyond their constitutional authority and face liability for unconstitutional takings.

Zoning and Planning

Modern land-use controls began early in the 1900s as a method to address haphazard growth and intermingled industry, commerce, and housing. In 1916 New York City enacted the first comprehensive zoning ordinance in the United States. In 1926 in *Village of Euclid v. Ambler Realty Co.*,[19] the U.S. Supreme Court approved a New York City–type plan adopted by Euclid, Ohio. The Court held that because zoning keeps dangers away from residential districts, it "bears a rational relation to the health and safety of the community" and is therefore constitutionally permissible.[20] Zoning by geometrically shaped districts thereafter conveniently became known as "Euclidean zoning." Other states followed the same approach, especially in urban areas, enacting zoning districts and establishing regulatory boards to review development for compliance.

Sound land-use regulations are based on expert analysis of many factors, including existing property uses, environmental conditions, and growth patterns. Zoning ordinances regulate the location and use of buildings by designating use zones for various categories of commercial, industrial, residential, agricultural, and other uses. They also regulate building dimensions, lot sizes, building placement, and densities. Subdivision ordinances typically require that any division of land into smaller parts be approved by a planning board, which considers proposed street access, drainage, water and sewage facilities, and other use features. The procedure usually requires submission of plans and public hearings, including an opportunity for neighbors to protest the proposal.

Environmental Regulations

There are many federal and state laws that restrict property use to protect the environment. Included among the most far reaching are the following federal statutes:

The National Environmental Policy Act[21] requires that environmental assessments and impact statements be undertaken before construction of major projects such as airports, highways, and parklands. The Resource Conservation and Recovery Act[22] gives the Environmental Protection Agency (EPA) authority to control the generation, transportation, treatment, storage, and disposal of hazardous waste. It also imposes requirements on underground storage tanks. The Clean Water Act[23] regulates discharges into the waters of the United States and sets quality standards for surface waters. The Clean Air Act[24] regulates air emissions and authorizes the EPA to establish standards for sources of air pollutants. The Comprehensive Environmental Response, Compensation, and Liability Act,[25] also known as "CERCLA" or "Superfund," provides federal funds to clean up hazardous waste sites and gives the EPA authority to recover costs from responsible parties.

States have their own laws regulating development and discharges into the land, water, and air within the state. They also may aim at protection of state-specific resources, such as coastal areas or mines. The EPA often coordinates its activities through state environmental protection agencies.

Property Taxes

Private property has always carried with it the burden of taxation. In most states property taxes are the principal source of revenue for local governments and school districts. To address the constitutional requirement of fair allocation, real estate taxes are based on market values. A typical real property tax is in the range of 2% of market value. Certain kinds of property—such as educational, religious, and charitable facilities—may be exempt under state law. Property taxes are an effective means of revenue collection because the taxing authorities are empowered to sell owners' property to collect if they fail to pay. Statutes give the authorities a lien that is superior to mortgages and other owner-financing arrangements.

Real Estate Transactions

Almost six million existing and more than one million new single-family homes are transferred annually, and the development and exchange of commercial and industrial properties account for a substantial part of the national economy.[26] The government is not involved in most transactions, other than providing a means for the parties to make a public record of their ownership. The parties are left to structure and consummate their exchanges. They do so within a mysterious legal regime and rely on real estate professionals to help them navigate the process. Although real estate law is fundamentally the same in every state, terms can mean different things in different jurisdictions, with important consequences. Nonetheless, basic familiarity with real estate law and the nature of real estate transactions helps minimize the risk of loss due to unintended consequences.

Interests

Real estate ownership interests are based on a combination of centuries-old common-law rules and evolving statutory variations. Ultimately property owners may define ownership interests as they wish, but in the vast majority of transactions common forms are employed.

Owners

Title to real estate may be held by an individual or by a legal entity such as a government unit or a private trust or corporation. Ownership often is shared. In many states spouses can own as "tenants by the entireties," by which one spouse becomes sole owner upon the other's death and neither spouse may convey or mortgage the property without the other's consent. A similar form of common ownership for two or more owners is "joint tenants with rights of survivorship," in which a survivor becomes sole owner upon the other's death. With a "tenancy in common," each of multiple owners has a full right of possession, but each has an interest that may be transferred separately. Real estate purchasers choose their form of ownership to suit their interests.

Fee Ownership

Fee ownership is the common notion of what it means to be an owner, including rights to possess and to convey. Fee ownership can be made subject to others' rights, including security interests given to lenders and easement rights enjoyed by neighbors.

Security Interests

Property owners give security instruments, such as mortgages and deeds of trust, to a lender as security for repayment of a loan. Mortgages involve a mortgagor, who is the property owner and borrower, and a mortgagee, who is the lender. Deeds of trust are essentially the same but involve three parties—the borrower, who conveys the property to a third party, known as the trustee, and the beneficiary, who is the lender. All security instruments give a lender the right to foreclose the owner's rights and sell the property if there is a default in the loan agreement. There are other forms of security instruments, but they share the same essential right of foreclosure and sale. Although parties may define the terms of this relationship as they wish, statutes provide a mechanism for a lender to exercise rights to foreclose. The courts have completed the landscape by defining common law rules to insure that this process is conducted fairly with respect to the owner's equity in the property and the rights of other interest holders.

Term Estates

A real estate interest can be limited in time, as occurs when one person is given a life estate and the property automatically transfers to a remainder person upon the life tenant's death. Such arrangements are used for estate planning, often to shift the value of the property to enable the life estate holder to qualify for financial assistance.

Leases

Leases are real estate conveyances governed by the common law rules for land transfers. Legislatures and courts have intervened in the landlord–tenant relationship, mostly on behalf of residential tenants, imposing limitations on evictions and providing tenants with tools to compel landlords to improve housing quality. These laws typically prescribe the advanced notice that landlords must give to tenants before an eviction can become effective, as well as defenses that tenants may raise to evictions.

Easements and Covenants

An easement is a limited right to another's land, such as a right to cross or a right to install and maintain a utility line. Easements also can prohibit landowners from doing something, such as a restriction against removing trees or installing a tall building. Such negative easements are also called "restrictive covenants." Developers commonly impose restrictive covenants on subdivided parcels to create a neighborhood in which individual properties benefit from an overall scheme. The goal of such restrictive covenants can be as simple as insuring that property is only used for a residence within a residential neighborhood, or as complex as establishing detailed rules about the construction styles within a community.

Easements and covenants usually are described in recorded instruments. Easements can also be created by implication. For example, a conveyance of a lot in a subdivision may be deemed to include conveyance of rights to use roads shown on the approved subdivision plan even if those rights are not included in deeds. The most contentious type of easement is one acquired by prescription, which arises by obvious use without the owner's permission for a long time, usually a minimum of 20 years.

Time Shares, Cooperatives, and Condominiums

State laws provide various frameworks for shared ownership regimes such as time shares, cooperatives, and condominiums. A time share is a right to occupy a unit for separate time periods over a span of years. These rights can be defined by lease agreements or in deeds. In a cooperative, an organization of owners owns a building, and the individual unit owners are shareholders with rights of occupancy. Condominiums allow conveyance of units and shared interests in common land and facilities managed by a homeowners' association. All of these forms of ownership are created through compliance with state statutory requirements, which usually entails recording defining instruments and plans. State governments have seen need to protect purchasers of some forms of shared interests and regulate the manner in which the communities can be created and units can be advertised and conveyed.

Manufactured Housing

Another special form of ownership involves buildings that are constructed off site and brought onto the land—manufactured housing. Manufactured housing includes prefabricated structures and mobile homes that are placed on foundations and attached to utilities. State laws specify the documents that must be recorded in the real estate records and regulate many aspects of homeownership in such arrangements.

Instruments

For centuries the law has required that those claiming an interest in real estate have some written evidence of the conveyance. This rule stems from the English "Statute of Frauds," which was imported into the American legal system and is firmly embedded in state laws. Little is required for a document to meet the requirement—only enough to identify the property and the parties and a signature by the person making the conveyance. The matter becomes more complicated when more than one person claims ownership based on separate documents, in which case the state recording laws control the outcome as discussed below.

Lawyers usually prepare real estate instruments. Many use standard forms produced by lawyer associations. Increasingly real estate instruments, especially those used in connection with institutional financing, are prepared according to a standard form used nationally, to insure compliance with federal regulations and to facilitate resale in security markets. Even when standard forms are used, some parts of the instruments—such as descriptions of the parties and the property being conveyed—must be carefully tailored to suit the particular circumstances.

Deeds are instruments of conveyance by which real estate owners, or grantors, convey property interests to others, or grantees. The most common type of deed is a warranty deed, which contains warranties about title to the real estate and the grantors' obligation to defend it. Less common is a special warranty deed or a quitclaim deed, which limits the grantors' warranties usually only to defects that the grantors themselves caused and does not extend to any defects generated by preceding owners. Deeds contain the parties' names, a property description, the grantors' signatures, and a notary acknowledgement for each signature. Deeds commonly do not include the grantees' signatures.

Security instruments, including mortgages and deeds of trust, contain the owners' names, the terms and conditions, descriptions of the covered property, the grantors' signatures, and a notary acknowledgment for each signature. When the obligations subject to security instruments are satisfied the lender records a notice to this effect, usually called a satisfaction, discharge, or release.

Plans, also called "plats," are commonly recorded with registers of deeds. Plans depict boundaries, site conditions, and the location and nature of land features, objects, and structures. Plans usually are prepared by licensed land surveyors, but sometimes they are prepared by engineers or architects. Land use laws regulate the contents of plans and the permissibility of recording them with registers of deeds. Typically the approval of a local land-use regulatory board is required before a plan showing a subdivision or a new development can be recorded.

Specialized documents are created for particular transactions. In all cases, the precise contents of each real estate instrument should be designed to accomplish its intended specific purpose.

Recording

States' real estate instrument recording systems are intended to provide a mechanism for buyers to confirm the rights being offered and to protect themselves against claims by later purchasers of the same property. Real estate instruments are recorded with registers of deeds, sometimes called recorders or registrars, and in some states the function is performed by court or municipal clerks. If someone conveys the same real estate twice, and only recording matters, a second buyer who knew of the prior conveyance is rewarded by recording first, which may seem unfair, because the rule could reward someone who knew someone else was being defrauded. Most states address this problem by subordinating the rights of a buyer who had actual knowledge of a prior transfer to the person who, in good faith, purchased first.

The recording statutes are described as one of three types: race, notice, or race-notice. A typical race recording statute simply provides that an instrument takes priority only when properly recorded. Only three states still have statutes that ostensibly base priority purely on recording: Delaware, Louisiana, and North Carolina. Based on the statute alone, those who record first will prevail even if they knew someone else already purchased the same property. Most states' statutes are different and expressly make someone's knowledge about an unrecorded instrument a factor in determining priority. Twenty states have statutes making an unrecorded instrument void against someone who acquires an interest in the same real estate without actual knowledge of the unrecorded instrument. This is known as a notice statute. Twenty-six states have statutes that make an unrecorded instrument void against someone who acquires an interest in the same real estate without actual knowledge of the prior conveyance, provided that the person without such knowledge also records first. This is known as a race-notice statute. Although the statutes may seem like riddles, they are intended to accomplish essentially the same thing: they give priority in a competition of claims to the party who first records, unless that party acquired the interest knowing about a prior, unrecorded conveyance.

Recording Priorities: *Grose v. Sauvageau*

Wyoming is among the states with a race-notice recording law. In the excerpt that follows the Wyoming Supreme Court considered how much notice a neighbor must have about someone else's unrecorded claim to override winning the race to record.

Grose v. Sauvageau
942 P.2d 398 (Wyo. 1997)

Chief Justice Taylor, writing for the Wyoming Supreme Court.

Appellants challenge the district court's grant of summary judgment quieting title in favor of appellee. Appellants acknowledge that their quitclaim deed to the subject property was not without defects, but claim the district court erred when it determined that appellee's conduct did not preclude her claim of title. Despite the allegations of inappropriate conduct, appellants' failure to acquire or record a valid deed to the property necessitates the legal recognition of the quitclaim deed filed by appellee as a subsequent good faith purchaser without notice pursuant to Wyo. Stat. § 34-1-120 (1997).

According to Mrs. Grose's affidavit submitted in support of summary judgment, the story began when the Groses became interested in obtaining land for their children's 4-H projects. In July 1991, Mrs. Grose went to the courthouse in Converse County, Wyoming to research several lots which were of interest to her family. She emerged with the name of "Ryberg Construction." The record does not explain how Mrs. Grose found this name, since it is undisputed that the record owner of the subject lot was H. Carl Ryberg. Mrs. Grose then contacted Mr. Ryberg via telephone and discussed two lots he owned in Rolling Hills which had been acquired by Converse County for back taxes in 1989. Mrs. Grose and Mr. Ryberg agreed that Mr. Ryberg would send two quitclaim deeds for the lots and the Groses would pay the back taxes. The lot which is the subject of this controversy, Lot 153, is located in Rolling Hills adjacent to the

Groses' business property and between their business property and the land belonging to Sauvageau.

On July 26, 1991, the Groses paid the back taxes on Lot 153 and received a Certificate of Purchase. True to his word, Mr. Ryberg signed and sent a quitclaim deed. However, the quitclaim deed professing to transfer Mr. Ryberg's interest in Lot 153 had numerous deficiencies: it was undated; it incorrectly named Ryberg Construction Co. as the grantor; it lacked a description of the property; and it lacked a completed or dated notarization of Mr. Ryberg's signature. In addition, Mr. Ryberg's signature did not contain any reference to the relationship between Mr. Ryberg and the grantor, Ryberg Construction Co. Undaunted by these technicalities, Mr. Grose entered a description of the property and back-dated the documents to August 25, 1989 in order to reflect a date shortly after the tax sale to Converse County. The Groses made no attempt to record the deed or redeem the property.

The Groses built improvements on the property, including fences, a barn, and installation of water, as well as a riding arena and a corral. They seeded the property and informed the town council of their intent to plant trees. Unfortunately, the operation of the premises was not without incident.

In 1993, the Grose children inadvertently left one of the gates ajar, allowing several pigs to escape and roam through nearby properties. After the pigs were apprehended and returned by officers of the sheriff's department, the Groses were notified that Sauvageau believed that during their short-lived freedom, the pigs had routed Sauvageau's horses through a fence. Although skeptical about the guilt of their pigs, the Groses paid half of Sauvageau's veterinarian bill. This is the first incident in the record which portends the hostile relationship between the Groses and Sauvageau.

In August 1994, the Groses again had the misfortune of an errant swine seeking liberation through an open gate. This escape resulted in the Groses receiving a citation for having an animal at large. One week earlier, the Groses had been cited for exceeding the number of animals allowed on their lot. At a hearing held in September 1994 on the citations, the Groses eventually pled guilty to both charges and, under the judge's instruction to secure an animal variance for Lot 153, the Groses prepared an application and obtained the required signatures of adjacent landowners.

At the next regular Rolling Hills town council meeting, however, the Groses allege that Councilwoman Sauvageau was instrumental in preventing approval of their application. When the subject of the variance was raised, the Groses submitted their application for the Lot 153 variance and then informed the town council of their intent to request another variance for their adjoining property in the future. At that point, the discussion regarding the current application was tabled. The Groses were then brought to task by Councilwoman Sauvageau regarding the legality of the water installation on the property. Later in the evening after the town council members met in executive session, the town council reconvened only to pass an emergency ordinance which expanded the variance ordinance to include an annual review of the application and the signed approval of all property owners within 500 feet of the land at issue. The requirements contained in the new ordinance gave Councilwoman Sauvageau the ability to veto the Groses' variance by withholding her signature.

Hostilities continued, and in November 1994 prior to Councilwoman Sauvageau's bid for re-election, Mrs. Grose penned a letter to the local newspaper "questioning some of the people running for council." Sauvageau was not re-elected.

Shortly thereafter, allegedly because "the difficulties between [Sauvageau] and the Groses had become so bad," Sauvageau "determined to check on the ownership of the property, in the off chance that the Groses were mere lessees of the property." When Sauvageau inquired at the County Clerk's recording office, she discovered that the record owner of the property was H. Carl Ryberg. Upon contacting the County Treasurer's office, Sauvageau learned that the Groses held the property by virtue of a Certificate of Purchase. She then confirmed there had been no notice of application for a tax deed and subsequently hired legal counsel to investigate whether she could purchase and redeem the property. Sauvageau states that her purpose was to "acquire . . . a buffer lot between the [Groses] and their livestock, and [herself]."

On November 28, 1994, Sauvageau and Mr. Ryberg executed a contract to purchase Lot 153 for $50.00, with the agreement to pay an additional $200.00 if Sauvageau was successful in redeeming the property. In return, Sauvageau received a quitclaim deed from Mr. Ryberg transferring all his interest in the property to Sauvageau. During these negotiations, Mr. Ryberg did not inform Sauvageau or her attorney about the quitclaim deed he previously had signed and sent to the Groses. Sauvageau freely admits, however, that her actions were secretive in hopes that the Groses would not be alerted and apply for a tax deed before she could redeem the property.

The next day, November 29, 1994, Sauvageau recorded her deed, paid Converse County the amount required by statute, and obtained a certificate of redemption. Sauvageau then demanded that the Groses vacate the property. The Groses refused, claiming ownership by virtue of the unrecorded quitclaim deed from Ryberg Construction Co., executed by Mr. Ryberg and dated prior to the deed recorded by Sauvageau.

Sauvageau filed a quiet title and ejectment action. The Groses responded by denying Sauvageau's title and counterclaiming to quiet title. The Groses also counterclaimed for intentional infliction of emotional distress, for tortious interference with contract, and asserted a lien on the property for improvements. The parties then filed cross motions for summary judgment. The district court granted summary judgment quieting title in favor of Sauvageau, and dismissed the remaining counterclaims. After their motion for rehearing was denied, the Groses timely filed this appeal challenging only the district court's decision regarding title to the property.

In this case, the parties agree that the Groses were in possession of the property, that Sauvageau knew they were in possession, and that if Sauvageau had inquired of the Groses, the Groses would have told her of the quitclaim deed they had obtained from Mr. Ryberg. As the district court stated, "the only questions are the legal conclusions to be drawn from these facts."

The Groses' claim that Sauvageau's failure to make direct inquiry of the Groses interests, and her admitted efforts to acquire the property without notifying the Groses, defeats her status as a bona fide purchaser in good faith, and therefore, her entitlement to the property. Wyo. Stat. § 34-1-120 provides:

> *Every conveyance of real estate within this state, hereafter made, which shall not be recorded as required by law, shall be void, as against any subsequent purchaser or purchasers in good faith and for a valuable consideration of the same real estate or any portion thereof, whose conveyance shall be first duly recorded.*

To prevail in a contest under Wyo. Stat. § 34-1-120, Sauvageau must show that she is a "bona fide purchaser," which is: (1) a purchaser in good faith; (2) for a valuable consideration, not by gift; (3) with no actual, constructive or inquiry notice of any alleged or real infirmities in the title; and (4) who would be prejudiced by the cancellation or reformation.

The purpose of the recording statutes is to provide protection for those diligent enough to conduct a search of title records. However, "failure to record a deed does not render it void where prior to the conveyance subsequent purchasers are put on due inquiry and with reasonable investigation the existence of the deed could have been determined." *Doenz v. Garber*, 665 P.2d 932, 936 (Wyo. 1983).

A subsequent purchaser must take "with[out] actual, constructive, or inquiry notice . . . ." *First Interstate Bank of Sheridan v. First Wyoming Bank, N.A. Sheridan*, 762 P.2d 379, 383 (Wyo. 1988). Sauvageau did not have actual notice of the Groses' unrecorded quitclaim deed. Neither did she have constructive notice of the deed, since even if the Groses' deed was recorded, the improper acknowledgment defeats constructive notice. The district court concluded, however, that the Groses' possession of the property put Sauvageau on inquiry notice which required her to inquire directly of the Groses as to their claimed interest in the property.

The district court relied on the concurring opinion of Justice Raper, Retired, in *Van Patten v. Van Patten*, 784 P.2d 218, 222 (Wyo. 1989), wherein he quoted *Healy v. Wostenberg*, 38 P.2d 325, 333–34 (Wyo. 1934):

> *Possession of real property by a person other than the vendor is notice to the purchaser of whatever rights or interests, legal or equitable, in the fee which the occupant has or claims and which would be disclosed on a proper and reasonable inquiry of him. Indeed, such possession is notice of all facts in reference to the title which due and diligent inquiry of the occupant would disclose. Therefore possession is notice of the rights of those under whom the possessor claims.*

(Emphasis added by court.) The facts of that case, however, are easily distinguished from the undisputed facts in this record. In *Van Patten*, Justice Raper, Retired, went on to state: "No reasonable inquiry whatsoever was made to determine the occupants', appellants', claims of right. . . . Possession by others puts the subsequent claimant on notice and *requires reasonable investigation* of the rights of such possessors." (Emphasis added by court.) We do not agree that a reasonable investigation requires direct inquiry of the occupant in every case.

Inquiry notice is based on the premise that the failure to make inquiry by someone with sufficient knowledge to create a duty to do so will be attributed to their own negligence. The loss resulting from such negligence will not be relieved in a court of equity. While Sauvageau was well aware that the Groses had possession of the property and had made improvements upon it, she diligently searched the records only to discover that the Groses' possession of the property was entirely consistent with the rights of the record owner. Therefore, the Groses' possession of the property did not create a situation which would put Sauvageau on guard as to the possibility of an unrecorded instrument or an alternative claim to the property. Thus, there was not "sufficient knowledge" to create a duty to further investigate the Groses' claims.

Public policy requires that subsequent purchasers be able to rely on the title shown in public records. While in some cases a search of the record may not be sufficient, third-party possession of property constitutes inquiry notice to a subsequent purchaser only when "it is an 'actual, open, visible, and exclusive possession' inconsistent with the title of the record owner." *Nussbaumer v. Fetrow*, 556 N.W.2d 595, 598 (Minn. App. 1996). Since the Groses possession of the property was fully explained in the public records, Sauvageau had no duty to search further.

The Groses contend that "Sauvageau's claim to having acted in 'good faith' is destroyed by her own words":

> *The Defendants and I are not on good terms, and the less I speak to them the better. As such, when I wanted to determine what right they had to the property, I researched the real estate records and found that they were the holders of a certificate of purchase on the property, and that they could apply for a tax deed. I consulted with my attorney, and subsequent to such consultation determined that I would try to purchase the property and redeem it, hopefully before the Defendant's [sic] were able to get a tax deed. After investigation, I determined that I did not want the Defendant's [sic] to know I was interested in the property, since they might have been able to get a tax deed before I redeemed the property.*

The term "good faith" is not defined in the statute. Prior Wyoming cases addressing the elements of a subsequent purchaser within Wyo. Stat. § 34-1-120 describe "good faith" as an element separate from that of "notice." The facts of those cases, however, did not require the court to distinguish one from the other.

The Groses argue that "good faith" under Wyo. Stat. § 34-1-120 requires more than merely lack of notice, but cite to no supporting case law. Instead, they point to the definition of good faith as addressed in cases involving the implied covenant of good faith and fair dealing in contracts. Unfortunately, the definitions of the duty owed to another party in a contractual relationship give little guidance in the context of the "good faith" required under a "race-notice" statute.

While we agree that Sauvageau's conduct was hardly a model of good sportsmanship, we do not believe her actions constitute "bad faith" removing her from the protection afforded by Wyo. Stat. § 34-1-120. The Groses do not allege that Sauvageau made representations upon which they relied in their claim to title. Neither do the Groses claim that Sauvageau's actions, prior to the time she recorded her deed, prevented them from attempting to record their deed or apply for a tax deed as contemplated by statute. Finally, there are no allegations [of] any illegal or fraudulent conduct. Consequently, the Groses allege no affirmative actions which would preclude a finding of "good faith" under Wyo. Stat. § 34-1-120.

The Groses have been reimbursed in full with interest for the taxes which they paid for possession of the property. They also have an undisputed right to recover for the value of the improvements which they placed upon the property. As between the quitclaim deed held by the Groses and the deed recorded by Sauvageau, the latter must prevail.

The Groses surely would have looked like owners to passersby—they made improvements, troubled their neighbors, and applied for permits. They lost the property because they had not recorded a deed. Despite some good reasons to see the Groses as rightful owners, the Wyoming Supreme Court seemed persuaded to conclude otherwise by the fact that Sauvageau, who recorded first, had found a "certificate of purchase" to explain "the Groses' possession of the property." In Wyoming such a certificate is given to someone who buys property at a tax sale. Under Wisconsin law an owner has 3 months after the tax sale to get the property back by paying the taxes and other charges, a right that enabled Ryberg to sell the property to someone else and preempt the Groses' rights.

Recording laws were intended to make the public record a complete statement of real estate ownership interests, but *Grose v. Sauvageau* illustrates that the law is far more complicated. There are many ways for someone to acquire property rights that are not shown in the public deed records, and the following are some of the most common. Ownership can be acquired without a deed by adverse possession based on open and continuous occupation to the exclusion of others, without permission, for at least 20 years. This may occur, for example, if someone builds a garage over a boundary and for more than 20 years treats it as fully part of the garage owner's other property. As mentioned above, easement rights can be acquired by implication, such as based on a development plan to which a deed refers. A *lis pendens* or litigation lien, available in many states, binds later purchasers and creditors to the outcome of pending litigation, but in some states a litigation lien is recorded only in the court records. State statutes grant parties who provide labor or materials a lien on the property that becomes effective before anything need be recorded. Similarly, a lien for real estate taxes usually automatically attaches when taxes are due and the automatic lien has priority over later security interests. Also, rights commonly are acquired by inheritance according to estate planning instruments and laws of succession rather than through instruments in the real estate records. Because of these and other exceptions, real estate title examiners must look beyond the register's records to assess the nature of various possible claims to ownership. Nevertheless, the records are important evidence of rights, and real estate purchasers should be careful about complying promptly with recording requirements.

Conveyances

The event at which a real estate transfer is consummated is called a "closing." In some jurisdictions closings are held at the office of the register of deeds, historically a focus of real estate transactions and a convenient location for attending to recording requirements. Today it is more likely to occur at an attorney's or a bank's office. The typical closing involves at least three parties: an owner who is conveying real estate, a buyer who is acquiring it, and a lender who is providing financing and getting a security interest in the real estate. Others also may have a substantial interest in the closing, such as a broker expecting a commission. In the typical sale the deed and security instrument will be signed before a notary. Many other papers will be prepared before the closing and signed during the closing to comply with disclosure or documentation requirements, including a settlement statement of all charges and disbursements.

Usually the real estate to be conveyed will already be subject to a security instrument—a deed of trust or mortgage—that will be satisfied with the proceeds from a new loan to the buyer. The buyer's attorney will search the title before the closing to confirm the seller's rights and to identify any current security instruments affecting the property. The new lender will not want to make the new loan until the buyer has clear title and can convey a security interest to the new lender. The closing therefore essentially involves simultaneous exchanges of funds and interests, and each step of the process depends on completion of another step. Those who handle a closing must ensure that these steps are taken in proper order without anything intervening that might affect the buyer's or lender's rights.

Title Insurance

Title insurance protects the interests of owners and lenders. It is fundamentally different from other forms of insurance because it focuses on risk prevention rather than risk assumption. It provides a property owner or lender with assurance that the real property described in the policy, based on an examination of the title records before the conveyance, is accurate. Problems unearthed during the examination are brought to light before the transfer is made.

Title insurance protects against undisclosed title claims, liens, and encumbrances, problems that make the title unmarketable to a reasonable purchaser, and the lack of a right of access to a road. A loan policy insures a lender against the invalidity or unenforceability of the insured security interest as a result of title problems, not against an insured's inability or refusal to pay. In addition to the basic coverage of owner's and loan policies, title insurers offer coverage for certain other matters by means of endorsements and special packages of supplemental coverage.

There are several exclusions from coverage in title insurance policies. They reflect the fact that title insurance is based on what can be found in the real estate records. Coverage does not apply to loss due to government land-use restrictions, eminent domain, problems that policy owners agree to assume, or bankruptcy rights. Other exceptions that usually apply to homeowner residential policies include rights based on possessing the property that are not shown in the public records such as adverse possession, automatic liens for construction, and tax liens. Additionally, policies are often subject to a survey exception, which means coverage does not apply to boundary problems, such as mismatched boundaries, that are not shown in recorded documents and could be identified only with a survey. Lenders and commercial purchasers usually can obtain coverage against such problems based on a survey.

Title insurance has become an expected part of almost all real estate acquisitions and mortgages. Residential mortgage lenders require owners to pay for loan policies to protect the lender's interest, and owners can usually get coverage for their interests for a relatively small additional premium. Premiums typically are several hundred dollars, which in a transaction involving substantial other charges usually is not perceived as significant.

Intellectual Property

"Intellectual property" refers to various legal protections afforded inventions and creations—principally patents, copyrights, trademarks, and trade secrets. While the role of intellectual property in the economy has intensified, its importance has always been recognized. Article I, Section 8 of the U.S. Constitution gives Congress the power "[t]o promote the Progress of Science and useful Arts, by securing for limited Times to Authors and Inventors the exclusive Right to their respective Writings and Discoveries." Such rights are in the national interest because they give inventors and creators economic incentives to invest in innovation that ultimately may benefit others.

Patents

Patents can be obtained for inventions such as articles of manufacture, devices, compositions, new plant varieties, and industrial processes. The federal Patent and Trademark Office (PTO), an agency of the Department of Commerce, examines patent applications and grants patents when the legal conditions have been met. A patent is granted only for something new as defined in the patent law. The subject must not be obvious to someone with ordinary skill in the pertinent area of technology. Inventions must be specifically and clearly described, usually by means of technical drawings.

A patent grants the owner the exclusive right to make or sell the invention for 20 years from the date of filing, provided periodic fees are paid to the PTO. Infringement occurs by manufacture, use, or sale without the patent owner's permission. To stop infringement an owner may bring an action in federal court. Available relief includes injunctions to prohibit further use and damage awards for lost profits.

Copyrights

A copyright may exist for original works of authorship fixed in any tangible medium of expression including literary works, music, dramatic works, choreography, sculptures, paintings, motion pictures, sound records, or architecture. A copyright protects the form of expression, not the subject of the expression. As U.S. Supreme Court Justice Oliver Wendell Holmes put it, "Others are free to copy the original. They are not free to copy the copy."[27] Everyone is free to paint the same landscape but not to sell reproductions of an artist's rendition of that scene.

A copyright owner has the exclusive right to reproduce, distribute, and display the work publicly. In general, a copyright exists for 70 years after the author's death. For works made for hire, and for anonymous works, copyright generally lasts for the shorter of 95 years from publication or 120 years from creation. A copyright owner's rights are subject to exceptions, including "fair use" for criticism, news reporting, teaching, scholarship, and research. There also are exceptions for certain kinds of educational, religious, and charitable uses, as well as limited permitted uses upon payment of specified royalties.

Copyrights exist automatically when the work is created. Registration with the Copyright Office of the PTO is not required but triggers additional protections including a record of the claim, authority to bring an infringement suit in federal court, and certain monetary remedies not otherwise available.

Trademarks

A trademark is a distinctive word, phrase, symbol, design, or combination of such marks that indicates the source of goods. A mark identifying a service is called a service mark. The word or symbol must be distinctive—not a common name or simple product description, or solely a surname. Mark rights can last indefinitely. They can be lost if they become generic, as occurred with the name "aspirin" that Bayer Company once owned.

A registered mark gives exclusive rights for 10 years and can be renewed. Anyone who claims rights in a mark may use TM (trademark) or SM (service mark) to give public notice of the claim. The federal registration symbol ® may be used only after the mark is registered with the PTO. Trademark infringement actions are brought in federal court and afford remedies similar to those for copyright infringement as described above.

Trade Secrets

Owners of patents, copyrights, and trademarks retain exclusive rights while the protected material becomes known publicly. A trade secret is an innovation that is not intended to be shared with others, such as the formula for a soft drink. A trade secret can be any information of economic value, including data and techniques, not generally known to others and the subject of reasonable efforts to maintain secrecy. To satisfy these requirements employers typically limit access to protected information and require confidentiality agreements with employees and others with whom the information is entrusted. Someone whose trade secrets have been misappropriated may recover lost profits and other damages. Trade-secret protection originated in common law and has since become statutory law. Some states allow attorneys' fees awards and multiple damages if the misappropriation was willful and malicious.

Review Questions

1. What does the U.S. Constitution require for the taking of private property?
2. Under what circumstances may the government require a developer to pay fees or donate property in connection with construction?
3. What basic limits does the U.S. Constitution impose on government regulation of land use?
4. What kinds of activities are subject to federal environmental regulations?
5. What are easements, and for what purposes are they commonly used?
6. What is the difference between a warranty deed and a quitclaim deed?
7. How do recording laws protect good faith purchasers of real estate interests?
8. What is the good faith requirement under a race-notice real estate recording statute?

9. What does the typical title insurance policy cover?

10. What can be the subject of patent, copyright, trademark, and trade secret protection, and what laws protect them?

Notes

1. Vanhorne's Lessee v. Dorrance, 2 U.S. 304, 310 (1795).
2. 545 U.S. 469 (2005).
3. *Id*. at 483.
4. 260 U.S. 393 (1922).
5. *Id*. at 415.
6. *Id*.
7. Penn. Central Transp. Co. v. New York City, 438 U.S. 104, 131 (1978).
8. 438 U.S. 104 (1978).
9. *Id*. at 138.
10. Palazzolo v. Rhode Island, 533 U.S. 606, 617 (2001).
11. 482 U.S. 304 (1987).
12. *Id*. at 318.
13. 505 U.S. 1003 (1992).
14. *Id*. at 1030.
15. *Id*. at 1026.
16. 535 U.S. 302 (2002).
17. *Id*. at 342.
18. 483 U.S. 825 (1987).
19. 272 U.S. 365 (1926).
20. *Id*. at 391–94.
21. 42 U.S.C. §§ 4321–4370f (2000 & Supp. 2005).
22. *Id*. §§ 6901–6992k.
23. 33 U.S.C. §§ 1251–1387(2000 & Supp. 2005).
24. 42 U.S.C. §§ 7401–7671q (2000 & Supp. 2005).
25. *Id*. §§ 9601–9675.
26. U.S. Census Bureau, Statistical Abstract of the United States, Tables 939, 942, 1161 (2006).
27. Bleistein v. Donaldson Lithographic Co., 188 U.S. 239, 249 (1903).

Chapter 7

Contracts and Companies

*Anyone who doesn't take truth seriously in small matters
cannot be trusted in large ones either.*
Albert Einstein

CHAPTER OBJECTIVES

After studying this chapter you should better understand:

- General considerations about forming contracts
- Basic legal rules governing contract breach and termination
- The types of remedies available for a breach of contract
- The nature of public contracting requirements including bidding
- The common organizational forms for business and nonprofit companies and the principal considerations in choosing a form

Individuals commonly enter into contracts. They understand that a commitment is involved, but they rarely consider the fine legal details. Consumer goods purchases, insurance policies, home purchases and leases, mortgages, loans, cable and phone service—all are governed by formal contracts that more often than not are signed without even a full reading. Entering into contracts without worrying about the legal details can be explained by the reality that the vast majority of agreements are consummated without need for resort to formal laws for enforcement. The parties are left to align their commercial rights and obligations and the law fills in gaps only when necessary. But when someone becomes responsible for completing a project that depends on another's compliance with a contract—such as a public official managing a supplier or service provider agreement—ignoring contract law becomes very risky business.

Similarly individuals commonly deal with companies—as managers, employees, investors, and contractual partners—without considering the legal details. Corporations, partnerships, limited liability companies, and other forms of business and nonprofit organizations have restricted powers and limited liabilities under the law that could affect the enforceability of an agreement and the ability to recover a loss if something goes wrong. Failure to understand these potential consequences creates significant risk that may not be appreciated until serious damage has become unavoidable.

This chapter discusses contract law basics including the special considerations that apply to public contracts. It also describes the nature of corporations, partnerships, limited liability companies, and other business organizations that commonly are parties to contracts. Understanding basic contract law and business organizations enables those who enter into agreements, in their own behalf or in behalf of organizations or the public, to better accomplish their objectives and avoid costly disputes.

General Contract Considerations

A contract is a mechanism for enforcing promises. Honest people feel morally committed to honor contracts. They may recognize that a reputation for breaking promises can cause problems with other prospective business partners. Also they may seek to avoid the unproductive loss of resources likely to result from dispute and litigation. Despite these excellent reasons for caring about contracts, many responsible individuals prefer to avoid thinking about them. They may feel the weight of seemingly more urgent and less contingent demands on their attention, or they may fear that insisting on a well-drafted contract signals mistrust of others. But contracts can be viewed in a different light: as a process for reaching better agreements and for avoiding disputes.

Common misconceptions contribute to a tendency to avoid thinking carefully about contracts. Even experienced managers may incorrectly assume that good contracts should have magical language that only expensive attorneys can craft and decipher. Familiarity with customary contract language does have its benefits. Dispute-tested provisions may be effective for anticipating issues that tend to arise and for clarifying the parties' rights and obligations in view of how courts have resolved those issues. But ultimately the goal with any contract is to express *the parties' intent* clearly and this is accomplished when *the parties* understand the terms to which they are agreeing.

Documenting an agreement often illuminates issues that are important to the parties that, if left unaddressed, might later result in a dispute. Failing to address an issue means that if disagreement arises, the parties' rights and obligations will be determined by interpretive rules of which the parties may be wholly unaware and to which they would not have consciously agreed. Formalizing an agreement can focus attention on ambiguity and can result in a better agreement.

Expressing interest in the details of a contract should not endanger a worthwhile agreement. Committing to a contract without understanding its terms invites problems. Attempts to invalidate contracts based on lack of understanding or unfairness are rarely successful. Courts regularly remind parties that the law does not save parties from bad bargains or authorize judges to rewrite contracts with the benefit of hindsight. Similarly, courts do not generally allow lack of understanding to be used to avoid enforcement of even a harsh contractual provision. The very rare exceptions usually involve consumers whom legislatures or courts have determined to need special protection from unscrupulous trade practices. For example, in *Williams v. Walker-Thomas Furniture Co.*,[1] the District of Columbia federal court of appeals held that a trial court could properly invalidate a furniture store's installment sale contract provision that allowed the store to spread payments across balances owed on multiple consumer items so that a single default triggered forfeiture of all. The court said the clause could be stricken as "unconscionable" in a sale of goods context due to "an absence of meaningful choice on the part of one of the parties together with contract terms which are unreasonably favorable to the other party."[2] In less egregious circumstances courts regularly hold parties to contracts without regard to perceived fairness.

A contract should not lock parties into unmovable positions. It should be seen as part of an ongoing process. Contracts often involve performance that is to occur in the future, and things change. If disagreements arise, the parties should revisit the contract. Parties risk later problems if they allow their eagerness to complete a project to obscure the need for adjustments. To avoid disputes the parties should clarify their agreement whenever they depart from the original contract.

Contract Formation

Contracts can be formed expressly or impliedly. An express contract arises when parties assent to the material terms of an agreement in writing or orally. An implied contract arises when someone undertakes an obligation through performance, such as by eating a meal at a restaurant or filling a car's tank with gas. Some contracts must be in writing to be enforceable. The Statute of Frauds, which every state imported from English law, requires written proof of agreement for the sale of land, wills, contracts for the sale of goods above a minimum amount (typically $5,000), contracts requiring performance longer than one year, and a few other kinds of contracts. There are exceptions to this written agreement requirement, including when someone admits that a contract exists or demonstrates its existence through performance. But many kinds of substantial arrangements may be unenforceable without a written contract.

Many contracts are formed only after the parties have exchanged offers and counter-offers and have negotiated an agreement. Whether communications constitute an offer that can be accepted depends on both the words and actions of their maker. For instance, an advertisement normally is not considered to be an offer but rather an invitation for someone to offer to buy the advertised item. Unless an offer provides otherwise, the offeror may revoke it before it has been accepted. Revocation is not always simple. According to the "mailbox rule," unless the offer otherwise specifies, an acceptance of an offer becomes effective when sent even though not yet received. To avoid confusion and dispute the parties should be very clear about their intent when they communicate about potential contracts.

Sometimes both parties contend that a contract was concluded but disagree about the terms to which they believe they have agreed. A variation of this conflict is what is called a "battle of the forms," which arises when a response to an offer expresses acceptance but also contains new or different terms. This may occur, for example, if someone accepts an offer with an invoice containing boilerplate, or standardized, terms. The new or different terms may become part of the contract even without a reply from the original offeror. Under the Uniform Commercial Code that all states have enacted, additional or different terms become part of the contract unless the prior offer was expressly limited only to its terms, the additional or different terms materially alter the contract, or the person who made the prior offer rejects the additional or different terms within a reasonable time. Again, to avoid unexpected results the parties should communicate their intent clearly.

No contract arises if the parties did not in fact agree to the material, or essential, terms. What is material depends on the circumstances. In many contexts, the law will enforce a contract even though some aspects of it are unclear. For example, for the sale of goods the Uniform Commercial Code will supply rules to fill in gaps in agreements by allowing for a reasonable price and a reasonable time and place for delivery if these matters are unspecified. There are many cases in which parties have been surprised to learn of the extent to which they incurred liability for contracts that might have seemed too uncertain to be enforceable. An enforceable contract does not exist if the parties are mutually mistaken about the material terms. In the famous British case of *Raffles v. Wichelhouse*,[3] the parties agreed to a sale of cotton arriving from India "ex Peerless from Bombay," but two ships named *Peerless* arrived from Bombay, 2 months apart. The seller had in mind the later ship and the buyer the earlier. The court held that no contract had been formed. According to this rule the mistake must be mutual—one party cannot avoid a contract based on a unilateral mistake such as one person's wrong assumption about an item's value. Once again, the parties can protect themselves against surprises by expressing their intent clearly in their contracts.

Contract Breach and Termination

A party suffering a loss from a breach of contract may be entitled to compensation. Its measure is described in the next section. If a contract involves performance over time and one party breaches, the other may wish to terminate any further performance obligation. Usually a party may terminate performance only for the other party's "material breach" or "failure of substantial performance." The parties may define in their contract what constitutes a material breach and specify their rights if it occurs, including whether the nonbreaching party has any further obligations. In most circumstances the contract is not entirely clear, and the parties may disagree about whether the nonperformance is material. The party seeking to terminate the contract runs the risk of liability if a court later deems the breach to be too insubstantial to warrant termination.

Noncompliance with a contract is not likely to be considered a material breach if the other party still receives the essence of the bargain. The parties' common understanding of what is a material breach may be quite different than the rules that the courts apply. For example, a date for a real estate conveyance closing ordinarily is not viewed as requiring strict compliance unless the parties have clearly expressed such an intent in the contract. A delay of a few days or longer may be deemed legally inconsequential even though one or both parties would have thought the delay mattered.

The ability to insist on strict compliance with a contractual condition can be lost by going along without objection. Whether such a waiver of strict compliance has occurred depends on the nature of the contract and the parties' conduct. Contracts commonly provide that waiver of a condition in one instance is not to be deemed to be a waiver in future performance. Such provisions are generally enforced.

A party may be excused from performance if it becomes impossible. For example, someone may be legally excused from a contract for future building repairs if the building is destroyed. Changes in conditions that make performance more expensive generally are not considered impossibilities. Other rare circumstances may be a basis for overriding a contract, such as a war or catastrophe. But generally, swings in markets or material costs are risks that the parties bear when they enter into a contract.

Drafting Contracts

Contracts often are compilations of standard form language. Unfortunately many parties to contracts examine only specifically drawn provisions without paying attention to what appears in the forms. Yet form clauses are fully part of the contract and may be the key to the success or failure of a contractual relationship.

The appropriate terms and conditions to be included in a contract depend on the nature of the parties' undertakings and their interests. Both the whole and the parts matter. When a particular provision is unclear, the courts will look to the contract as a whole to determine the parties' intent. When the contractual language is clear, except in unusual circumstances such as fraud, courts will not look beyond the language to determine whether the parties meant something different.

Many of the basic elements to be included in any contract will be readily apparent, and their composition will require no special drafting expertise. The parties should scrutinize the language of their proposed contract with the mindset of an objective third party who might later be asked to interpret it. The following are some of the many issues that commonly result in dispute and therefore may warrant particular attention when drafting or reviewing a contract:

Parties   Contracts are often unclear about the extent to which rights and obligations may be transferred to or assumed by others. For example, to what extent may a party subcontract the work? Rules of contract interpretation often allow the parties to assign their rights to others unless the contract provides otherwise.

Approvals for Changes   Parties to contracts are not always clear about the need for approval of variation from the originally described expected performance. For example, disputes regularly arise with construction and machinery assembly contracts about compensation for extra work or material. Although such contracts commonly provide that no additional compensation will be owed unless the parties agree in writing before the additional work is done, courts tend to look past such restrictions and to award compensation for what is actually done. To avoid dispute, the parties therefore should not only address the procedure for changes to the contract but also follow those procedures during the course of performance.

Conditions Precedent Some obligations are not intended to be triggered unless something first occurs. For example, a real estate purchase agreement may be contingent on receipt of an environmental inspection report that shows no contamination. Parties entering into contracts tend to be optimistic about performance and not to consider what can go wrong. Silence about conditions precedent or the consequences of their nonoccurrence leaves room for complication and dispute.

Representations Negotiations leading to contracts usually involve representations about capabilities and intentions. If those representations are not stated in the contract, they may not be part of the contract. This is especially likely if the contract has the typical integration or merger clause that provides that previous negotiations between the parties are deemed to be superseded by what is stated in writing. The parties should therefore recite the nature of any representations that are intended to be legally binding and specify the consequences if they turn out not to be correct.

Rights Upon Default As described above, usually only a material breach of contract relieves the nondefaulting party from further obligations under the contract. Reasonable parties can disagree about what constitutes a material default, especially if the contract language is unhelpful. Specifying these matters can avoid dispute.

Risk of Loss and Insurance If a contract requires performance over time, losses can occur, and liabilities can arise as a result of accidents or other unforeseen circumstances. The law governing responsibility for losses during performance is complicated and not necessarily intuitive. Addressing these matters in the contract allocates responsibility for loss and helps the parties to focus on getting insurance or taking other steps to address the risks.

Indemnification Parties to contracts often undertake obligations on which third parties rely. Those third parties may have rights if the contractual parties directly intend to extend them. More commonly, third parties may not successfully sue based on the breach of someone else's contract. Parties may address these matters in a number of ways, including with indemnification agreements. With indemnification one party agrees to protect the other against claims by a third party. For example, if a public authority engages a private vendor to provide a service, the agreement could provide that the vendor will pay any claims made against the authority in connection with the service.

Disclaimers and Limitations of Liability The law will supply liability rules for breaches of contract when the parties do not specify them. In general, the rules are aimed at holding parties accountable for reasonable expectations. The parties can manage expectations with contracts, including with disclaimers of warranties or liability. Not all disclaimers are enforceable.

For example, courts are reluctant to enforce clauses that exclude or limit liability for negligence, particularly when the waiver was signed by a consumer who had no realistic opportunity to negotiate about it. Such a clause may be fully enforceable as part of a negotiated commercial contract in which the disclaimer is stated clearly and conspicuously.

Dispute Resolution   The contract can specify the steps that must be taken to attempt to resolve disputes. For example, a contract could provide that disputes about the need for work or price adjustments will be referred to a neutral third party. The parties also may wish to commit to mediation or other alternative dispute resolution, and to agree to the location at which it will occur.

Contract Remedies

When one party breaches a contract, the other may simply wish to rescind the agreement and become free of any further obligations to the breaching party. More commonly the victim of the breach has suffered an economic loss and seeks compensation. Often the parties reach a settlement. If they do not they may pursue their contract law remedies.

The basic principle of contract law is that damages are compensatory. The party seeking damages must therefore be able to prove economic loss and will recover only to the extent of it. Furthermore, in general a party that breaches a contract is responsible only for economic losses that were foreseeable at the time the obligation was undertaken. There is no recovery for pain and suffering from breach of contract.

Expectation Damages

In the usual contract dispute the measure of damages will be the loss of bargain, which is the difference between the outcome if the contract had been performed and what the party otherwise must pay to achieve the same result. These are called expectation damages.

In the "hairy hand" case of *Hawkins v. McGee*[4] made famous in the movie *Paper Chase* about Harvard Law School, the New Hampshire Supreme Court considered the measure of damages when a doctor grafted hairy skin onto the plaintiff's hand contrary to a promise to give "a hundred per cent perfect hand." The case became famous for how the court explained contract damages. The court said, "The measure of recovery 'is based upon what the defendant should have given the plaintiff, not what the plaintiff has given the defendant or otherwise expended.' 'The only losses that can be said fairly to come within the terms of a contract are such as the parties must have had in mind when the contract was made, or such as they either knew or ought to have known would probably result from a failure to comply with its terms.'"[5] The court explained, "We therefore conclude that the true measure of the plaintiff's damage in the present case is the difference between the value to him of a perfect hand or a good hand, such as the jury found the defendant promised him, and the value of his hand in its present condition, including any incidental consequences fairly within the contemplation of the parties when they made their contract."[6] The court overruled an award of pain and suffering, which may be appropriate for a tort claim but not for a contract claim.

Sometimes the difference between what was promised and what was delivered can be measured by the cost of substitute performance. For example, if a contractor fails to complete a project as promised, the owner will be able to recover the actual cost of having someone else complete it. For a breach of a contact for the sale of goods subject to the Uniform Commercial Code, if the buyer was able to find substitute goods, the buyer may recover the difference between the cost of the substitute and the contract price, together with incidental or consequential damages. If the buyer was able to find cheaper goods as a substitute, there will be no loss of expectancy, although the buyer may be able to recover the costs of having to find and transport the substitute. Or the buyer may recover the difference between the market price at the time of the breach and the contract price, together with any incidental or consequential damages. Although these rules may seem complicated, they are all simply intended to give the nonbreaching party the benefit of the bargain.

Lost profits may also be recovered for a breach of contract if the loss is the direct and natural consequence of the breach, the profits were likely to have been earned, they were reasonably foreseeable to the breaching party, and the amount can be shown with reasonable certainty. For example, the U.S. Supreme Court affirmed an award of lost profits when the federal government breached a contract to purchase a 4-year supply of envelopes for the postal service. The envelope company had already made arrangements to purchase the necessary materials and proved the difference between costs and the contract price.[7] On the other hand, the Court reversed an award of lost profits for the manufacture and sale of naval gun mounts when the record did not show that the manufacturer had the capacity to perform the contract and when there was no evidence of costs from which lost profits could be calculated.[8] Parties often specifically address liability for lost profits in their contracts because such an amount can be substantial and subject to serious disagreement.

Reliance Damages

Another measure of damages sometimes available for breach of contract is the amount of a party's loss resulting from reliance on the other party's performance, called reliance damages. This amount would include foreseeable expenses in anticipation of the breached promise. The purpose of reliance damages is to restore the victim of the breach to the position before entering into the contract. For example, if an organization rents a concert hall and the performer breaches an agreement to appear, the organization may recover rent that was paid for the hall even if the event was not going to be profitable.

Liquidated Damages

Liquidated damages, which are sometimes called a penalty, are a fixed amount to be paid if a party breaches. Many construction contracts contain liquidated damages clauses that give owners a right to a daily sum for delays. Courts do not favor liquidated damage clauses because they can be arbitrary and therefore inconsistent with the compensatory goal of contract damages. Courts therefore are not inclined to enforce such clauses if the amount is unreasonable in relation to estimates of actual loss. Liquidated damages clauses tend to be enforced only when the parties knew from the start that actual damages would be hard to calculate and the liquidated amount turns out to be not clearly far in excess of actual loss.

Specific Performance

Specific performance is compelled consummation of the contract. Traditionally courts see payment of damages as the appropriate remedy for a breach of contract based on the notion that everyone is made whole as long as the party suffering the breach is paid what was lost economically. In rare situations a court will compel a party to perform the contract if payment of damages is not an adequate remedy. This may occur if the subject of the contract is unique, such as a unique parcel of real estate or an antique. The party seeking specific performance must be able to perform its part of bargain.

Unjust Enrichment

In the vast majority of contract disputes, the amount of damages to be awarded will be measured by the expectancy or reliance methods described above. Occasionally courts will employ their equitable powers to fashion yet another type of damages known as unjust enrichment. This is measured by the amount by which the breaching party was enriched at the non-breaching party's expense. A variant of unjust enrichment is *quantum meruit*, or the value of what is provided, which can be awarded even if there was no contract. Unjust enrichment damages are awarded only when the court concludes that basic fairness requires it, such as when someone silently but willingly accepts an offer of a service for a fee but then refuses to pay for it.

Duty to Mitigate

When someone breaches a contract, the other party ordinarily is required to take reasonable action to prevent avoidable losses, which is called a duty to mitigate. Someone who fails to do so will be unable to recover damages from the breaching party for the avoidable losses. In a contract dispute the party that breached the contract who seeks to avoid liability based on a failure to mitigate must show that the nonbreaching party did not take steps that would have been reasonable under the circumstances. For example, a landlord generally has a duty to make reasonable efforts to find a substitute tenant if a tenant vacates before the lease term is up. The tenant will not prevail in using this defense against liability for unpaid rent for the remainder of the lease term if the landlord did take reasonable steps to find a new tenant but was unsuccessful.

Government Contracts

Generally government authorities have the legal power to enter into contracts for the same public purposes for which they are authorized to spend public funds. Statutes and regulations usually specify their legal authority and the procedure for entering into contracts, including who must approve the undertaking. Typically statutes authorize governing or executive bodies to enter into contracts for permitted purposes and often allow delegation of this authority to an officer. The capacity to enter into a contract also is tied to budget or appropriations requirements for meeting the financial obligations to be undertaken in the contract. The following is an overview of the federal and state laws governing public contracting and bidding.

Public Contracting Requirements

The federal government spends hundreds of billions of dollars annually for goods and services. One set of elaborate statutes governs armed forces procurement and another governs civilian agencies. Multitudinous regulations are issued regarding specific contracting procedures.

The Federal Procurement Policy Act gives the Office of Federal Procurement Policy, in the Office of Management and Budget, authority to shape policies and practices for federal contracts. The bulk of these policies are in the Federal Acquisition Regulation (FAR), which is in Title 48 of the Code of Federal Regulations. The Office of Management and Budget also coordinates particular agencies' supplemental procurement regulations with the FAR. The FAR has rules for general contracting requirements, competition and acquisition procedures, socioeconomic programs, and contract management. It also contains contract model clauses and forms. Some agencies and departments have extensive supplemental regulations. Some agencies are exempt from the FAR and have their own regulations, such as the U.S. Postal Service and the Tennessee Valley Authority.

State government contracting is subject to various constitutional, statutory, and regulatory requirements. The American Bar Association developed a Model Procurement Code that has been adopted by more than a dozen states and many local governments.[9] The states that have not adopted the Model Procurement Code have similar statutory regimes. The Model Procurement Code provides for a policy office and centralized procurement authority. The model contains detailed provisions for bidding and procurement, contract modifications and price adjustments, surplus property disposal, and dispute resolution. It also has special provisions for involving small and disadvantaged businesses as well as ethical standards.

Those managing government procurement, and those proposing to enter into contracts with the government, should be familiar with the particular contracting statutes and rules that apply. The courts' tendency to leave commercial parties to define their rights and obligations is tempered in the public contract sphere by concern about the taxpayers' interest. Failure to comply with requirements can result in complications and court intervention.

Taxpayers and Public Contracts: *Thompson v. Voldahl*

Any public contract depends on the availability of funds. Sometimes the funds are drawn from general revenues; sometimes they are raised with special funding methods. The taxpayers who must meet the financial burden tend to expect that their interests will be protected. The connection is readily identifiable when the public project benefits particular individuals or areas.

The following Iowa Supreme Court case illustrates some common issues that arise concerning payment for public contracts. In *Thompson v. Voldahl*, two Iowa counties initially spent about $275,000 to build and improve ditches. Years later when they made $25,000 in additional improvements, they taxed the costs in special assessments to the landowners in the subdistricts who directly benefitted. A state statute required that the authority must hold a public hearing if the work will be for more than 25% of "original cost." The district interpreted "original cost" as the prior cost for the entire district, but in an earlier case the Iowa Supreme Court had interpreted it as costs only for the affected subdistrict. When the assessment was declared void, the contractors had already been paid for part of their work. The assessed taxpayers sued to recover it. In the excerpt that follows, the Iowa Supreme Court took up questions about a contractor's rights to payment when public contracting laws are not followed.

Thompson v. Voldahl
188 N.W.2d 377 (Iowa 1971)

Justice Becker, writing for the Iowa Supreme Court.

Plaintiff taxpayers seek judgment in favor of Winnebago County for special assessment funds paid by the county to defendants as partial payment on void contracts. Plaintiffs seek eventual repayment of such funds to them as the special assessment taxpayers. Trial court dismissed plaintiffs' petition. We reverse and remand.

[T]he trial court had held the Board of Supervisors in making the contracts (with defendants here) acted without jurisdiction and enjoined collection of the special assessments levied pursuant to the void proceedings. We affirmed.

The parties here agree defendant contractors acted in good faith in entering into the contracts subsequently declared void. The charges made by defendants were reasonable and the warrants issued in payment of work partially completed were for the contested project.

Where a public contract is declared void by the courts the contractor-claimant cannot recover unpaid claims from the public coffers. We have held that one who contracts with a municipality or a political subdivision is bound at its peril to take cognizance of statutory limitations upon the authority of the government agency. Recovery is denied under the . . . public policy that the taxpayers should be protected from the evasion of statutory prerequisites by the public body and from the opportunity for fraud or collusion between public officials and contracting parties.

Defendants do not dispute this Iowa law and do not seek to recover the balance of their claims. But they maintain their right to keep what they have already been paid. They are able to cite many cases throughout the country where courts have refused to compel repayment of funds paid on a void public contract. Recovery in such cases is usually denied on broad equitable principles. He who seeks equity must do equity. The parties cannot, under the circumstances, be restored to the *status quo ante bellum*. Restitution is impossible. Plaintiffs (or the taxing body) will be unjustly enriched if recovery back is allowed. Therefore equity will not aid plaintiffs to recover the money illegally paid but will leave the parties where it finds them.

An annotation found at 140 A.L.R. 583, 585, entitled Recovery Back-Invalid Public Contract, collects a large number of cases dealing with this problem. The author warns, " . . . the formulation of any general principles of purportedly universal application, with respect to the right of public body to recover back sums paid under an invalid or unenforceable contract, is an exceedingly dangerous undertaking." We agree. The myriad fact situations and consequent diverse results defy formulation of general principles.

The money now held by defendants is plaintiffs' money. If returned it will not go to the general fund for general use after the taxing body has had the benefit of defendants' efforts. Rather, it will go to the special assessment taxpayers who contend they were never afforded the opportunity to test the necessity for the work performed. Plaintiffs here have claims for special assessments ranging as high as $2492. The ordinary case examined usually involves relatively modest tax burdens spread among a large number of taxpayers. This is pertinent to the equities to be examined because only strong equitable grounds will allow an illegal contractor to keep what has been illegally paid. Hence the entire factual situation is of paramount importance.

In considering the equities of the situation we find both the contractors and the taxpayers, if left in their present posture, will have been treated in grossly disparate manners. This is a direct aftermath of the illegal contracts to which defendants were party. We can see no equity in allowing these disparate treatments to continue.

Ordinarily the loss must fall on contractors who enter these public contracts charged with knowledge that if the contract is void they cannot recover. In the absence of strong countervailing equities the accident of prepayment in whole or in part does not change the rule. In this case the loss must be borne by defendant contractors.

Justice Uhlenhopp, dissenting.

Several circumstances are important. The supervisors and the contractors acted in good faith; no fraud or concealment existed. The contractors did not hasten to the courthouse to get their money, knowing that the public's proceedings were invalid. The contractors' charges were fair and reasonable. The landowners received the benefit of the contractors' work and have not and cannot restore the status quo ante.

The great weight of authority, including Iowa authority since 1872, simply denies recovery back under such conditions.

When governmental officials do not correctly follow procedural statutes and let a purported contract which is actually invalid, the contractor, though he be ever so innocent and his performance be ever so workmanlike, cannot recover on the purported contract, and he gets nothing. This result is necessary or the court would affirmatively use its powers to aid in the avoidance of the statutory procedural requirements. The court simply leaves the parties where it finds them. The policy has been carried a step farther. If the contractor admits the contract is invalid and merely asks for the reasonable value of his work, he is also denied relief. This result is necessary for the same reason.

The recovery back situation involves yet another step. The contract has been let, the work has been done, the contractor has been paid, and then the governmental subdivision or landowners seek to recover back without restoring the contractor's performance to him. This time the governmental subdivision or landowners are the ones asking the court to exercise its powers. But this time by the exercise of its powers the court would work a positive injustice—

through the court's own affirmative action the subdivision or landowners would end up with both the contractor's performance and the money. Again the court should simply leave the parties where it finds them.

Fundamentally, two conflicting interests are involved: those of the public under the procedural statutes relating to public improvements, and those of the good-faith contractor who furnishes value. The task is to balance those interests. When the contractor has not been paid, the procedural statutes are vindicated by denying him relief on contract or quantum meruit. But when the contractor has been paid and the landowners retain his performance, the interests of the public are adequately protected by allowing recovery back only if the landowners show one or more circumstances, such as bad faith by the contractor, disentitling him to retain the payments in good conscience. Thus the court does not affirmatively use its powers to take the money from the contractor unless as a matter of justice he should not keep it.

The result in this case is not changed by a couple additional features—partial payment of the contractors and partial payment of the assessments. All of the contractors received only part of their money and they respectively received varying proportions of their money. This does not alter the general principle allowing a good faith contractor to keep the money to the extent he has been paid. All this means is that the contractors who received a smaller proportion of their money are less fortunate than those who received a larger proportion.

Nor is the general principle denying recovery back changed by the varying proportions of the assessments actually paid by the respective landowners. All this means is that not all landowners receive the same windfall. Granting the landowners recovery back from the contractors would simply work a complete windfall to all landowners—the money and the performance both.

Our general rule preventing an unpaid, good faith contractor from recovering anything at law or in equity is harsh enough. We ought not extend the rule to the case of the paid or partly paid contractor, and thus affirmatively use the power of the courts to make a harsh result more harsh.

If the dispute in *Thompson v. Voldahl* did not involve a public contract, the contractors likely would have been entitled not only to keep what was paid to them but also to recover expectancy damages. The contractor's remedies were limited by the public's interest in the contract. The justices' differing views illustrate a common theme in court decisions in contract disputes: a tendency in cases that do not involve fraud to see both sides' positions as having some merit, and a tendency to arrive at a compromise of those positions. Regardless of which view of the equities is accepted, the case illustrates the mess that can result when a government authority does not adhere to the public contracting laws.

Bidding

Federal and state laws require that many public contracts be awarded through competitive bidding. Bidding is intended to discourage favoritism and to get the lowest price for expenditure of public funds. Bidding requirements usually apply to purchase of supplies and equipment and to construction and repair work above a certain threshold, typically in the range of $20,000 for purchases and $100,000 for construction. The thresholds apply to a project's total cost.

Statutes or regulations may provide direction about how to determine when a contract is separate or part of a larger project, such as when work is completed in stages. Contracts for less than the threshold may still be subject to less rigorous competitive requirements. For example, North Carolina requires that local governments use an informal bidding procedure for finding the lowest responsible bidder for supplies and materials costing more than $5,000 but less than the $30,000 threshold for formal bidding, without requiring advertisement or any minimum number of bids.[10]

Bidding requirements usually do not apply to professional services such as those provided by lawyers or engineers or to equipment leases or real estate purchases. Government authorities often are authorized to use sole source or single source procurement when there is only one reasonable source for an item or service. Bidding laws also have exceptions for emergencies. For example, Massachusetts makes an exception to the usual bidding requirements when taking the time to solicit bids "would endanger the health or safety of the people."[11]

In the public bidding process the contracting authority publishes an invitation for bids or request for proposals based on specifications. Bidder proposals must offer to provide the work or materials at a maximum price. Depending on the project the price may be a fixed amount, may be based on time and materials at certain rates and charges, may be equal to cost plus a profit percentage, or may be a combination of these or other methods. Bidders also must provide information to show their capacity to perform. Typically they must also provide a bond to protect the bidding authority in connection with the bidding procedure, such as for losses if the bidder improperly withdraws after being selected. The Model Procurement Code, for example, suggests a bond of 5% of the amount of a bid that exceeds $100,000, which the authority may apply to its costs if the bidder fails to honor the bid.[12]

The government authority requesting bids publicly opens them after the deadline for submission has passed. The contract is awarded to the lowest responsible bidder. Determining the lowest responsible bidder usually involves a number of factors other than price. For example, Connecticut defines "lowest responsible qualified bidder" as "the bidder whose bid is the lowest of those bidders possessing the skill, ability and integrity necessary to faithful performance of the work based on objective criteria considering past performance and financial responsibility."[13] Bidding laws may also allow consideration of social factors such as involvement of a local work force or minorities.

Unsuccessful bidders may learn of a mistake in a bid and seek reconsideration. Generally an unsuccessful bidder is not allowed to change a bid after it is opened based on an error in judgment. Applicable law may allow correction if the mistake is readily evident when the bid is reviewed, such as if there is an obvious error in adding component prices. The government authority may be obliged to inquire about obvious errors in successful bids rather than accept the bid with them.

Despite a government authority's best efforts to anticipate the full scope of work with an invitation to bid, the need for changes commonly arises. Bidding laws and regulations usually empower the authority to agree to changes in the ordinary course without having to undertake another public bidding process. Government authorities may be required to undertake further public bidding if the changes would result in a substantially different contract.

Bidder Remedies: *Lawrence Brunoli, Inc. v. Town of Bradford*

The public contracting laws are intended to protect the public's interest in having the best contract for the lowest possible price. This goal makes the dynamics of a public contract different than a purely commercial agreement. When the government authority fails to follow the proper procedure, the public's interest is likely to figure in the resolution of a dispute.

One recurring situation that results in complications is a claim that a bidding authority improperly awarded the bid to a favored company rather than to the lowest responsible bidder. Government authorities usually are allowed to consider a variety of factors other than just price, including prior experiences with the bidders. But they may not simply play favorites. Claims of favoritism tend to arise when the authorities seem to have relied on technicalities to award the contract to a higher bidder. In the following Connecticut case, an initially successful bidder was disqualified for not attending a prebid conference. The bidding authority had not objected at the time of the conference and the unsuccessful bidder alleged favoritism. In this opinion the Connecticut Supreme Court considers a bidder's available remedies when such allegations arise.

Lawrence Brunoli, Inc. v. Town of Branford
722 A.2d 271 (Conn. 1998)

Justice Norcott, writing for the Connecticut Supreme Court.

According to the allegations of the plaintiff's revised complaint, which for purposes of this appeal we assume to be true, the defendant published an invitation to bid on a municipal construction project for renovations to and alterations of Branford High School, in response to which the plaintiff submitted a bid. The plaintiff further alleged that, on February 3, 1997, it was informed that it was the "lowest qualified bidder," but that the defendant subsequently withdrew its award of the contract to the plaintiff because the plaintiff had failed to attend a prebid conference regarding details of the work to be performed under the contract. In addition, the complaint alleged that the defendant had permitted the plaintiff to bid on the project although the defendant knew that the plaintiff had not attended the prebid conference, and that the defendant therefore had waived any attendance requirement by accepting the bid. According to the complaint, the defendant later awarded the contract to the second lowest bidder, in violation of § 75-2 of the code of the town of Branford. The plaintiff alleged further that the defendant's conduct constituted favoritism toward the ultimate contract awardee. Finally, the plaintiff alleged that the defendant had breached its agreement to award the contract to the lowest qualified bidder, causing the plaintiff to suffer damages.

It is axiomatic that a party cannot be liable for breaching a contract with another party unless a contract exists between the parties that could be breached. In the realm of competitive municipal bidding, it is well settled that a contract is created through the municipality's action of awarding a contract, not through the submission of a bid by the contractor.

If an unsuccessful bidder has standing to bring a claim against a municipality, therefore, such standing must be derived from a source other than its bid submitted in response to the invitation to bid. That source is the municipal bidding statutes themselves. "Only 'where fraud, corruption or favoritism has influenced the conduct of the bidding officials or when the very object and integrity of the competitive bidding process is defeated by the conduct of municipal officials,' does an unsuccessful bidder have standing to challenge the award." *Ardmare Constr. Co. v. Freedman*, 467 A.2d 674, 676 (Conn. 1983) (quoting *Spiniello Constr. Co. v. Manchester*, 456 A.2d 1199, 1201 (Conn. 1983)). A review of our prior cases illustrates, however, that the only remedy afforded to unsuccessful bidders under the municipal bidding statutes has been injunctive relief against the awarding of the contract to the illegally favored bidder.

To grant standing to unsuccessful bidders who seek to bring actions for money damages would undermine the purpose underlying the municipal bidding statutes. If a municipality is found to have committed fraud, corruption or favoritism and is accordingly enjoined from awarding the bid to the designated awardee, the public is protected because the municipality is barred from paying more than the best price for the work to be performed. If, however, an unsuccessful bidder is permitted to assert a claim for money damages, rather than injunctive relief against awarding the contract to the successful bidder, the taxpayers of the municipality would be subject to paying once to have the work performed by the successful bidder and, if the unsuccessful bidder were successful, again for damages above and beyond the cost of the project. Such extra costs clearly are not in the public interest.

Further, a municipality must know, in advance of awarding a contract, what the ultimate costs of the project will be. If an unsuccessful bidder were able to eschew a claim for injunctive relief and assert a claim for damages, the municipality would not know with certainty what those costs are until the limitations period for such a claim for damages had passed.

The plaintiff contends, nevertheless, that the threat of public discontent at paying damages would provide a more effective deterrent to keep bidding officials from committing fraud, corruption or favoritism than does the threat of an injunction. We do not find this argument to be persuasive. Our cases, in which unsuccessful bidders sought injunctive relief in circumstances of fraud, corruption or favoritism, constitute persuasive evidence that money damages are not required as an incentive for unsuccessful bidders to act as watchdogs on the municipal bidding process. There already exists in the realm of injunctive relief sufficient incentive for unsuccessful bidders to seek judicial intervention, which in turn acts as a deterrent upon bidding officials to violate the bidding statutes, without the detriment to the public interest that an action for money damages would cause.

We reaffirm the conclusion that this court consistently has maintained: where a municipality has engaged in fraud, corruption or favoritism, an unsuccessful bidder does have standing under the applicable, competitive municipal bidding provision to bring an action for injunctive relief. We hold, however, that an unsuccessful bidder does not have standing to seek money damages. To conclude otherwise would run counter to the sound and established purpose of protecting the public interest that underlies the municipal bidding statutes.

Justice Berdon, dissenting.

This case involves an important public policy consideration—whether a municipality should be subject to liability for damages because it rejected the bid of the lowest qualified bidder in violation of the town code that requires the town to award contracts to such a bidder.

According to the plaintiff, the defendant engaged in favoritism when it awarded the contract to the second lowest bidder, whose bid was $344,000 higher than the plaintiff's, in violation of § 75-2 of the Branford code. The plaintiff brought the present action for money damages that it allegedly suffered as a result of this violation.

In my view, the assessment of monetary damages against the defendant would best serve the public interests at stake. I agree with those jurisdictions that have determined that "[a]n award of money damages would be in the public interest because it would deter such misconduct by public entities in the future." *Marbucco Corp. v. Manchester*, 632 A.2d 522, 524 (N.H. 1993). As the plaintiff asserts, the specter of public discontent at paying monetary damages is more likely to deter any potential official misconduct than if only injunctive relief is at stake. Moreover, such a deterrent would encourage more bidders, which would increase competition and thereby lower costs to the taxpayers. Lastly, awarding monetary damages would also compensate the plaintiff for its justifiable reliance upon the municipal code.

The law of contract does not necessarily start with an offer and end with the acceptance of that offer, for we have always recognized that variations are often required in order to do justice. In this matter, the plaintiff reasonably relied on the defendant's promise that if there was to be an award, the bid would be awarded to the lowest qualified bidder.

This court has long recognized that a "'promise which the promisor should reasonably expect to induce action . . . on the part of the promisee . . . and which does induce such action . . . is binding if injustice can be avoided only by enforcement of the promise.'" *D'Ulisse-Cupo v. Board of Directors of Notre Dame High School*, 520 A.2d 217, 221 (Conn. 1987) (quoting Restatement (Second) of Contracts § 90 (1973)) (omissions by the court). When government officials fail to award a contract to the lowest qualified bidder in violation of a code, ordinance or statute, "injustice to [the low bidder], the promisee, can be avoided only by at least the partial enforcement of the [government's] promise . . . . [Furthermore, t]o hold that [the low bidder] was not entitled to rely upon this promise . . . would make the [government's] promise an illusory one and render the whole competitive bidding process nugatory." *Swinerton & Walberg Co. v. Inglewood-Los Angeles County Civic Center Auth.*, 114 Cal. Rptr. 834, 838 (Cal. App. 1974). Such reasoning has encouraged other jurisdictions to award damages to low bidders who have claimed damages directly attributable to their reliance on a low bidder statute. Similarly, I would hold that, based upon the contractual theory of promissory estoppel, the plaintiff has alleged a cause of action for money damages over which the court has jurisdiction. Therefore, the trial court should not have dismissed the action.

The measure of damages with respect to an action predicated on promissory estoppel "may be limited as justice requires." 1 Restatement (Second) of Contracts § 90 (1981). I would adopt the New Hampshire approach as follows: "In the ordinary case, the damages that an unsuccessful low bidder may recover should be limited to those it sustained directly by reason of its justifiable reliance upon the municipality's promise to award the contract to the lowest responsible bidder submitting all essential information prior to the bidding deadline, if it awarded it at all. Hence, damages ordinarily should be limited to the expenses incurred by the lowest bidder in its fruitless participation in the competitive bidding process, i.e., its bid preparation costs. To permit the recovery of greater damages in such cases could drain the public fisc in response to mere carelessness on the part of low level government officials. If a disappointed low bidder complies with all requirements of the bid instructions but is deprived of the contract through some conduct of the awarding authority tantamount to bad faith, however, then the recovery of lost profits should be the measure of damages. The greater deterrence resulting from an entitlement to lost profits is justified when bad faith is proven because a municipality's bad faith undermines the purpose of competitive bidding. . . . [P]ublic confidence in government is eroded when municipal officials act in bad faith." *Marbucco Corp*, 632 A.2d at 525 (omissions by the court).

The opinions in *Lawrence Brunoli, Inc. v. Town of Branford* describe three different views courts have adopted about an aggrieved bidder's remedies for bidding law violations. One view limits the bidder to an injunction to compel the contract. A second allows recovery of reliance damages. A third allows recovery of lost profits particularly when there is evidence of fraud. A court's inclination to accept one of these views includes consideration that the loss probably will not be borne by the officials who violated procedure, but rather by the public. This is one reason courts have been reluctant to allow lost profit claims in public contract cases even when officials acted recklessly. Responsible public officials are more careful with the public's money than with their own. Unfortunately some are more willing to take chances when someone else will pay the bill. Public officials who intentionally harm others or engage in fraud may have personal liability.

Business and Nonprofit Organizations

Most people who work with corporations and other businesses or nonprofit organizations have only a vague sense of the organization's legal powers and limitations on its investors' liability for organizational debts. They may assume that those with whom they are dealing are legally capable of entering into contracts, raising capital, and being held accountable for liabilities. These may be correct assumptions but every organizational form has statutorily defined characteristics that can be different than is commonly assumed.

Organizational Objectives

The choice of a legal form of organization depends on the organizers' objectives. Common considerations include limiting investor liability for the organization's debts, the need for raising capital, the extent of control over organizational decisions, tax consequences, and the burdens of complying with legal formalities.

Limiting investor liability usually is a primary concern for enterprise organizers. During industrialization legislatures gave some enterprises charters so that only assets invested in the company—not investors' personal assets—were exposed to meet the company's liabilities. Industrial enterprises have financial risks so large that few would be willing to invest if doing so exposed them to personal liability. The courts upheld the enforceability of these limitations, and legislatures later enacted statutes to enable organizers to create entities through a filing process without need for specifically granted legislative authority. The benefits of limited liability depend on compliance with the statutory requirements. In rare circumstances courts have "pierced the corporate veil," disregarding the entity shield and holding an investor liable. This has occurred, for example, when someone merely used the shell of an entity name as a sham to shield assets from creditors.

Raising capital is another principal concern for business organizations. Major enterprises require substantial financial resources beyond what a few individuals are able to contribute. Corporations and some other entity forms allow passive investments that may individually be small but collectively are large. Other organizational forms also have various methods for allocating shares of the profits and increases in company value to investors based on their interests.

Entities also allow variation in control over organizational and operational matters. Someone who does not form an entity and instead operates as a sole proprietor will control the business. The owner of a few shares in a multinational corporation will have no effective control over the entity's decisions. The various entity forms have different layers of control, and organizers have some capacity to tailor authority within and across each layer.

Possible tax consequences are also an important consideration in the choice of entity. Sole proprietorships and simple organizations tend to be taxed in the same way and at the same rates as individuals. More sophisticated organizations have more complex tax consequences. Most organizations involve expert tax advisors for guidance about organizational structure and tax compliance.

Different entity forms also require different legal formalities. Modest companies entail only a few simple initial organizational documents and periodic reports. Large-scale enterprises likely require complex organizational documents and ongoing disclosure requirements such as federal and state securities reports, which are intended to give passive investors basic information about the enterprise so they can make sound investment decisions.

Common Organizational Forms

Although business and nonprofit organizations are governed by state law, most states have adopted the model or uniform laws developed by the American Bar Association or the National Conference of Commissioners on Uniform State Laws. The basic nature of the organizational forms is similar in all states.

Corporations

A corporation is a traditional form of business entity favored because it allows the accumulation of capital with investors liable only to the extent of their contributions. A corporation only exists when the necessary steps for incorporation have been accomplished, which among other things involves filing articles of incorporation with a state's secretary of state. The articles of incorporation define the corporation's basic structure including the number of authorized shares and the rights of various classes of shareholders. Corporations also have bylaws that prescribe other details of corporate business including the conduct of shareholder and director meetings. Corporations must identify their status in their entity names, usually with "corporation," "incorporated," "company," or "limited," or an authorized abbreviation. Once duly formed, corporations are considered "persons" under the law for most purposes and may enter into contracts, own property, and incur liabilities to the same extent as individuals.

Corporate shareholders have the legal authority to make the fundamental decisions about corporate existence. Corporations usually have directors to whom the shareholders delegate most managerial decisions. Daily affairs are further delegated to officers, who may or may not be directors, including a president or other presiding officer, treasurer or other chief financial officer, secretary, and, in larger corporations, other officers including vice presidents. For most significant transactions, with resolutions the directors authorize officers to take action in behalf of the corporation.

Large corporations typically have very complex forms for raising capital in exchange for equity in the form of stock and debt in the form of bonds. Shareholders purchase stock expecting that its value will increase. Corporations use their revenues to meet operational and investment needs, pay salaries and wages, and pay bonds and other debt. Net profits are available for distribution to shareholders as determined by the directors.

In theory a major disadvantage of the corporate form is its "double" taxation. Profits are subject to a tax on the corporate income and again when distributions are made to shareholders. But the tax laws afford many opportunities to minimize or avoid corporate taxes with deductions, carry-forwards, and other offsets.

A nonprofit corporation also is created with the filing of articles of incorporation; it may enter into contracts, own property, and incur liabilities to the same extent as an individual; and generally it has the same attributes and requirements as a business corporation. It may have members rather than shareholders who, like shareholders, are not personally liable for the corporation's obligations. They also may have directors and officers.

There are other varieties of corporate forms for particular purposes. For example, with a professional corporation or professional association the stock must be owned and held only by licensees of a particular professional service such as attorneys, accountants, architects, or physicians. The shareholders, directors, and officers are not individually liable for errors or omissions of the other shareholders, directors, or officers.

Limited Liability Companies

The limited liability company is a relatively new form of business entity that emerged in the 1990s as a popular form because it offers the liability protections of a corporation, but there is no tax at the entity level. A limited liability company is formed with articles of organization filed with a state. It is identified in its name with the words "limited liability company" or an authorized abbreviation. The company is comprised of members who automatically are considered to be managers unless the articles of organization provide otherwise.

Partnerships

A partnership is an association of two or more persons to carry on as co-owners of a business for profit. Unlike other entity forms, no formal agreement or filing is required to form a partnership.

A partnership is governed by an agreement that spells out the partners' rights and obligations, including their liability for the partnership's debts and their rights to share in the partnership's profits. Partnerships may use an assumed name, which must be filed with a state office. Title to real property may be held in a partnership name, with a general partner executing the instrument in behalf of the partnership. Each partner is individually liable for the acts and obligations of the partnership, which is a major reason why partnerships are not as common for most business purposes as limited liability companies and corporations. Also, partnership taxation is very complex, especially the rules for allocating profits and losses among partners.

Limited Partnerships

The ordinary partnership described above is sometimes referred to as a general partnership. Another form of partnership is the limited partnership, which consists of one or more general partners who have rights and obligations similar to partners in general partnerships, and one or more limited partners whose authority is more limited and who are liable only to the extent of their investment. Unlike a general or ordinary partnership, a limited partnership cannot exist without filing a certificate of limited partnership with the state. It will be identified in its name with the words "limited partnership" or an authorized abbreviation. The general partner of a limited partnership has the power and authority to bind the entity.

Trusts

A trust is not a legal entity but rather an agreement between someone transferring property or rights to property to another with the intent that it be held for the transferor's benefit. The person who makes the transfer is called the settlor, grantor, trustor, or creator. The person who is entrusted is called the trustee. Trustees may be individuals, groups of individuals, or institutions, such as banks. The person or entity for whose benefit the property is entrusted is called the beneficiary. Trusts are governed by trust agreements, which may be separate documents or contained within wills. Trustees, as fiduciaries, are subject to strict statutory and common law obligations.

Other Organizations

There are many other organizational forms. For example, each state has laws for nonprofit organizations that afford limited liability but have less rigorous filing requirements than business organizations. States also typically authorize use of unincorporated associations for nonprofits, with limited liability, that can be formed by filing a simple declaration. State laws typically also authorize religious organizations to appoint trustees to acquire, hold, and convey property in trust and to act through their ecclesiastical officers.

These are the basic features of the most common organizational forms. The powers and responsibilities of companies and their investors and managers depend on applicable state law and the organizational documents. Those entering into arrangements with organizations need to consult the applicable law and documents to understand a particular company's legal capacity and characteristics and to assess the risks involved with entering into agreements with them.

Review Questions

1. What kinds of contracts must be in writing for them to be enforceable?
2. What is the nature of a contract breach that is likely to enable the other party to terminate further performance obligations?
3. By what basic steps can parties to contracts protect themselves against having their rights governed by interpretative rules of which they are not aware?
4. What are the measures of expectation and reliance damages?
5. What are liquidated damages, and under what circumstances are they enforceable?
6. What is specific performance, and when is it available?
7. What is the duty to mitigate in connection with a contract breach?
8. What kinds of public contracts are generally subject to bidding requirements?
9. What are a public contract bidder's likely remedies if improperly denied an opportunity to do the work?
10. What are the common organizational forms for business and nonprofit companies and the principal considerations in choosing a form?

Notes

1. 350 F.2d 445 (D.C. Cir. 1965).
2. *Id.* at 449.
3. 2 Hurlstone & Coltman 906 (Court of Exchequer 1864).
4. 146 A. 641 (N.H. 1929).
5. *Id.* at 643 (quoting 3 Williston on Contracts § 1341 and Davis v. New England Cotton Yard Co., 77 N.H. 403, 404 (1914)).
6. *Id.* at 644.
7. United States v. Purcell Envelope Co., 249 U.S. 313 (1919).
8. United States v. Penn Foundry & Mfg. Co., 337 U.S. 198 (1949).
9. American Bar Association, Model Procurement Code (2000).
10. N.C. Gen. Stat. § 143–131 (2007).
11. Mass. Gen. Laws ch. 30B, § 8 (2007).
12. American Bar Association, Model Procurement Code § 5–301 (2000).
13. Conn. Gen. Stat. § 2-71p (f) (2007).

Chapter 8

Employment

Coming together is a beginning; keeping together is progress; working together is success.
Henry Ford

CHAPTER OBJECTIVES

After studying this chapter you should better understand:

- The basic statutory rights protecting employees
- The common noncontractual legal limitations on employment termination
- The constitutional protections accorded to public employee speech
- The basic federal and state laws and regulations governing pay, benefits, and work conditions
- The basic nature of the legal prohibitions against sexual harassment

All employees have legitimate expectations about their pay, benefits, and working conditions. All employers have legitimate expectations about their employees' work. The employment legal relationship was once almost entirely considered to be a matter of private agreement, with few restrictions on pay or permissible grounds for firing. Since the 1930s the landscape has changed dramatically, first with rules for maximum hours and minimum wages, and later with extensive laws and regulations that affect nearly every aspect of employment. Many employers and employees now find themselves among the thousands involved with claims of wrongful termination or for compensation or benefits. Claims sometimes arise from employers' egregious conduct and sometimes from employees' opportunistic abuse of the law. Many result from lack of knowledge about the law. This chapter introduces the most prominent employment laws including those specifically governing public employment.

Employer Approaches to Avoiding Employment Law Problems

This chapter can provide only an overview of the most prominent among a daunting array of employment laws. The details of these laws are important but an employer's successful navigation of the legal terrain also depends on effective leadership and management. This book is not intended to give management advice. But a review of common employment disputes indicates that serious problems are less likely to arise when employers take the following approaches:

- Cultivate a supportive work environment in which everyone understands their roles in achieving a compelling mission
- Model sincerely compassionate interest in employee success and welfare
- Make only promises that can be honored and are intended to be
- Provide clear rules of conduct that are enforced consistently and fairly
- Maintain a credible process for legitimate concerns to be brought to the attention of someone who can cause change without retribution
- Handle problems by collecting all available information with an open mind, including directly from those concerned, before making irreversible decisions whenever feasible
- Diligently investigate legal requirements by consulting information made available by federal and state agencies such as the U.S. Department of Labor and Equal Employment Opportunity Commission, and state labor departments, and regularly self-audit compliance

Impermissible Employment Decisions

Until recent decades employment was considered to be "at will" and terminable by either the employer or employee for any reason—or for no apparent reason—unless they agreed to conditions in a contract. Most employment relationships are not the subject of detailed written contracts, but courts have found contractual rights to exist based on other circumstances such as employer policies. The nature of the employment relationship has been further changed by legislative and judicial innovations restricting employment decisions. The following summarizes the law regarding contractual, statutory, and policy restrictions on employers' decisions to hire, promote, and terminate employees. These restrictions may seem like a bewildering tangle, but a collective message is apparent: lawmakers and judges are inclined to provide remedies to those who lose work opportunities as a result of employer animosities unrelated to work qualifications and performance.

Statutory Rights

Federal and state laws make some factors impermissible grounds for employment decisions. Employers who violate these prohibitions face penalties as well as claims for reinstatement and lost compensation.

Title VII of the Civil Rights Act of 1964[1] prohibits employers from discriminating against an individual with respect to "compensation, terms, conditions, or privileges of employment" because of an "individual's race, color, religion, sex, or national origin." It also prohibits discrimination on the basis of pregnancy, childbirth, or related medical condition. It applies to all employers with 15 or more regular employees.[2] The U.S. Supreme Court has held that Title VII applies not just to instances of intentional discrimination aimed at an individual but also to employment practices that are discriminatory in operation.[3] Title VII has exceptions, including for certain occupations where the classification is appropriate such as for a religious organization hiring members of its own faith. As discussed below, the Court has held that abuse or hostility in the work environment caused by sexual harassment is a form of prohibited sexual discrimination under Title VII.

The Age Discrimination in Employment Act[4] (ADEA) prohibits employers with 20 or more regular employees from discriminating against those who are 40 years old or older. The ADEA does not prohibit use of age in occupational classifications reasonably necessary to the normal operation of the organization or as part of a bona fide seniority system.

The Uniformed Services Employment and Reemployment Rights Act[5] prohibits any employer from denying employment or discriminating in pay or benefits against employees because of federal military service obligations. In general, the law requires employers to reinstate veterans who serve in the military not more than 5 years if the veteran employee gave notice before leaving for service and reapplies within 90 days after discharge. Qualified veterans must be reinstated in the same or comparable jobs with the same benefits they would have attained if they had not left for service.

The Americans with Disabilities Act[6] (ADA) prohibits employers with 15 or more employees from discriminating against individuals with a serious disability if they can perform the essential functions of the job with no special accommodations or if they can perform such functions with reasonable special accommodations without an undue hardship on the operation of the employer's business. Factors considered in determining undue hardship include the organization's size, the nature of the job, and the costs of the accommodations. An individual with a disability as defined by the statute is someone with an impairment that substantially limits one or more major life activities, someone who has a record of such an impairment, or someone who is regarded as having such an impairment. The statute also prohibits employers from asking employees about possible disabilities except in connection with their ability to perform specific job functions. Employers also may make a job offer contingent on a medical examination if it is required of all entering employees in similar jobs. Many of the recurring interpretive issues are addressed in the statutes or in the regulations issued by the U.S. Equal Opportunities Commission.

Antiretaliation or "whistleblower" laws prohibit employers from taking action against employees who pursue a legally protected right, such as for making a workers' compensation claim, or who disclose truthful information reasonably believed to concern a violation of a law or regulation. Dozens of federal statutes have such provisions, including major laws regarding antidiscrimination, safety, the environment, and contracting. States also have their own antiretaliation laws, some of which apply specifically to public employees who report improper use of office, gross waste of funds, or certain other abuses. Antiretaliation laws for government employees commonly require those who allege a violation to complete an administrative complaint process before commencing court action. Available relief typically includes reinstatement, compensation for lost wages and benefits, and recovery of reasonable costs and attorneys' fees. Employers may recover costs and fees for defending against frivolous complaints.

The Employee Polygraph Protection Act[7] prohibits consideration of a lie detector test or the refusal to take one to discipline or terminate an employee except in certain statutorily authorized contexts, such as for defense contractors and security companies. The law also has requirements about how permissible tests must be conducted.

Many government employers are subject to personnel statutes that set requirements for hiring, promotion, and termination of public employees. These laws typically prescribe allowable causes for disciplinary termination and the methods for terminating employees for non-disciplinary reasons such as layoffs due to organizational or financial constraints. The U.S. Supreme Court has held that public employees who have a justifiable expectation of continued government employment based on a statute or policy have a protected property interest, and due process may require that they be afforded at least with an opportunity to respond to charges of improper conduct before being terminated.[8] Personnel statutes commonly prescribe a process that complies with this requirement.

Contract Rights

As described in Chapter 7, each state has a statute of frauds that makes unwritten contracts unenforceable if they call for performance longer than 1 year, with some exceptions. Most courts have applied this rule to employment contracts for longer than 1 year. But a formal contract is not the only way to create an enforceable employment agreement. Courts have found binding contracts to exist based on other forms of expression, such as policy manuals. Many employers use handbooks or policy manuals to inform their employees about work expectations and procedures, pay and benefits, and grounds for disciplinary action or termination. Such policies may be deemed to be contractual commitments. Under some circumstances when employees have justifiably relied on written policies, employers have been held to them despite an express disclaimer that they were not intended to be a contract.

In a few cases courts have held that an employer's oral statements about job security created an enforceable contract. For example, in *Toussaint v. Blue Cross & Blue Shield of Michigan*,[9] the Michigan Supreme Court said, "When a prospective employee inquires about job security and the employer agrees that the employee shall be employed as long as he does the job, a fair construction is that the employer has agreed to give up his right to discharge at will without assigning cause and may discharge only for cause (good or just cause). The result is that the employee, if discharged without good or just cause, may maintain an action for wrongful discharge."[10] This view has not been widely accepted. Courts generally have rejected claims that a contract was formed solely based on an employee's actions taken in reliance on an expectation of employment.

Good Faith Covenant: *Berube v. Fashion Centre, Ltd.*

State courts vary in the extent to which they will examine employers' reasons for terminating an employee who has no contract. In the following case the Utah Supreme Court considered a store employee's claim that she was wrongfully terminated when she refused to take a polygraph examination about missing inventory. She had already taken two examinations that did not reveal any reason to believe she had done something wrong. The court considered whether an employer is restricted by an implied obligation not to insist on polygraph examinations that seem unreasonable.

Berube v. Fashion Centre, Ltd.
771 P.2d 1033 (Utah 1989)

Justice Durham, writing for the Utah Supreme Court.

Plaintiff Shirley Berube was employed by Fashion Centre, Ltd., dba Fashion Gal (Fashion Centre), in its Ogden, Utah store beginning in April 1979. She was initially hired as a sales clerk and was eventually promoted to the position of assistant manager in 1981. Her promotions were based on demonstrated ability and job performance evaluations which ranged from good to superior. Plaintiff was uniformly pleased with her experience at Fashion Centre and anticipated a long career with the company. The accuracy of her expectations was confirmed by one of her managers, who told her that she could expect to be a store manager someday.

At or near the time she was hired by Fashion Centre, plaintiff became aware of Fashion Centre's written disciplinary action policy. This policy stated that Fashion Centre, in attempting to act equitably, would not terminate employment without prior warning except for specific reasons, including failure to pass or refusal to take a polygraph examination. In all other circumstances, Fashion Centre promised employees a warning and an opportunity to improve performance prior to termination.

Plaintiff admits that she and Fashion Centre did not agree to a specified term of employment. Indeed, she understood that her employment was of no set duration and could be terminated by either party. However, based on a number of representations and procedures, she believed that Fashion Centre would only terminate her for cause.

In the fall of 1981, an apparent inventory shortage of over 3 percent occurred in Fashion Centre's Ogden store. This was an unusually large shortage, and Fashion Centre investigated. The investigation was inconclusive, and Fashion Centre requested that all employees of the Ogden store submit to a polygraph examination. Three employees were allowed to quit rather than undergo the polygraph examination. All others, including plaintiff, agreed to participate.

Fashion Centre provided the polygraph examiner with fifteen questions upon which to base the examination. Defendant Western States Polygraph (Western States) administered this exam to the employees. The examiner found that plaintiff's data suggested deception when she responded negatively to the question, "Do you know for certain who has cheated or stolen anything from that Fashion Gal store?" In a post-test interview, the examiner ascertained that plaintiff had "suspicions of others—especially those who threatened to quit rather than take the polygraph exam." Thus, plaintiff's "stress" reaction was apparently based on her suspicions of others and not on a disloyal withholding of relevant or incriminating information.

Western States forwarded a copy of plaintiff's test results to Fashion Centre headquarters in St. Louis, stating that plaintiff had shown "deception" on only one of fifteen relevant questions and explaining the apparent source of the "deception" result, as revealed in the post-test interview. Even in light of this explanation, Fashion Centre told plaintiff she would be required to take a second examination. Fashion Centre did not tell her why or say that she had failed the first examination.

Although disturbed by the request, plaintiff agreed to submit to the second examination, which was administered by a different polygraph company. She showed no signs of deception and "passed" the exam. A pretest interview, however, revealed that she had, from time to time, rounded off figures of a "class count" when she believed her employees had erred. This information was conveyed to Fashion Centre along with the test results.

Although the first and second polygraph examinations showed no unexplained deception on the part of plaintiff, Fashion Centre demanded that plaintiff undergo a third examination. Plaintiff was not given a reason for the third exam, and she believed, based on comments by the polygraph examiners, that she had "passed" the first two tests. She was distraught at the prospect of enduring another polygraph and by the implicit accusation that accompanied Fashion Centre's request that she submit to it. She sought advice from co-workers, friends, and relatives as to whether she should submit to the examination.

On the scheduled day of the exam, plaintiff called Fashion Centre's district manager, Jerry Brooks, and told him she was too nervous to take the exam and asked that it be postponed. Mr. Brooks informed her that Fashion Centre could require her to take any number of polygraphs and that she must call Bennett Lerner, Fashion Centre's personnel director, to seek a postponement. Plaintiff immediately called Mr. Lerner and told him she was extremely nervous and upset and could obtain a doctor's statement to that effect. In light of her condition, she asked Mr. Lerner to postpone her examination. Mr. Lerner told her she must take the exam or she would be terminated.

Plaintiff worked her usual shift that day and, at the scheduled time of the exam, called Mr. Brooks to tell him she could not take the exam. He told her to come to work the next day to sign her termination papers. When plaintiff arrived the next morning, she indicated her willingness to submit to the exam in order to retain her position. Mr. Brooks said that was impossible but she might try to reapply within two weeks. She did so, but despite repeated attempts on her part, Fashion Centre failed to respond to her inquiries.

Nineteenth century English courts employed the general presumption that an employment relationship created without any specific duration amounted to a general hiring of one-year duration. With the advent of the industrial revolution, courts in the United States began to rely increasingly on notions of freedom of contract in construing employment relationships.

In the last several decades, judicial decisions have resulted in the development of three primary categories of exceptions to the at-will rule. First, where an employee is fired in a manner or for a reason that contravenes a recognized and established public policy, the at-will rule will not serve to insulate the employer from liability. Second, courts have clarified the requirements for finding an express or implied contract term for employment for a certain period or a covenant for dismissal only with cause. Finally, many courts have relied upon the implied covenant of good faith and fair dealing and have granted the discharged employee a cause of action to sue when the employer's conduct breaches that implied covenant. This cause of action may sound in tort, contract, or both, depending upon the jurisdiction. We will examine these categories in turn.

Perhaps the most logical exception to the at-will rule is based upon public policy. Where an employee is discharged for a reason or in a manner that contravenes sound principles of established and substantial public policy, the employee may typically bring a tort cause of action against his employer.

Legitimate reliance on a public policy exception to the at-will rule requires an attempt to identify the proper sources of public policy and the principles which underlie it. Public policy is most obviously, but not exclusively, embodied in legislative enactments. The legislature, acting in consonance with constitutional principles and expressing the will of the people, determines that which is in the public interest and serves the public good. Not every legislative enactment, of course, embodies public policy; only those which protect the public or promote public interest qualify.

The legislature is not the only source of public policy, however. Limiting the scope of public policy to legislative enactments would necessarily eliminate aspects of the public interest which deserve protection but have limited access to the political process. Judicial decisions can also enunciate substantial principles of public policy in areas which the legislature has not treated.

In recognizing and following principles of public policy, we must be careful to avoid overextension of the principles involved. As the United States Supreme Court has stated:

> The truth is that the theory of public policy embodies a doctrine of vague and variable quality, and, unless deducible in the given circumstances from constitutional or statutory provisions, should be accepted as the basis of a judicial determination, if at all, only with the utmost circumspection. The public policy of one generation may not, under changed conditions, be the public policy of another.

Patton v. United States, 281 U.S. 276, 306 (1930). This principle applies equally in employment litigation. Although a given employee may feel that his or her termination violates a fundamental tenet of public policy, a court must carefully evaluate whether the public policy identified is fundamental and permanent or superficial and transitory. In fact, even those principles which are widely held values may not be sufficient to justify wrongful termination recovery. For example, although it is this state's expressed policy to provide and promote job security and full employment for its citizens, this public policy would be insufficient grounds upon which to maintain a wrongful termination action.

We acknowledge that a public policy exception has no application in this case. We also stress that actions for wrongful termination based on this exception must involve *substantial* and *important* public policies. To this end, we will construe public policies narrowly and will generally utilize those based on prior legislative pronouncements or judicial decisions, applying only those principles which are so substantial and fundamental that there can be virtually no question as to their importance for promotion of the public good.

An employee may demonstrate that his at-will termination breached an express or implied agreement with the employer to terminate him for cause alone. The at-will rule, after all, is merely a rule of contract construction and not a legal principle. The rule creates a presumption that any employment contract which has no specified term of duration is an at-will relationship. This presumption can be overcome by an affirmative showing by the plaintiff that the parties expressly or impliedly intended a specified term or agreed [to] terminate the relationship for cause alone. Such evidence may be found in employment manuals, oral agreements, and all circumstances of the relationship which demonstrate the intent to terminate only for cause or to continue employment for a specified period. Although in the past the presumption in favor of at-will employment has been difficult to overcome, rigid adherence to the at-will rule is no longer justified or advisable.

The conclusion that a promise exists may arise from a variety of sources, including the conduct of the parties, announced personnel policies, practices of that particular trade or industry, or other circumstances which show the existence of such a promise. Nevertheless, the determination of whether sufficient indicia of an implied-in-fact promise exists is a question of fact for the jury, with the burden of proof residing upon the plaintiff-employee.

Some courts have refused to accept an implied-in-fact alteration of the at-will rule because it would eliminate mutuality of obligation under the contract. These concerns, however, are unfounded. The ostensible need for mutuality arises from the nature of the at-will rule itself, in that a fundamental assumption is that because an employee may terminate the employment relationship at any time, the employer should likewise be free to do so. In a modern economy, however, this "freedom" of the employee is largely illusory. Indeed, the fact that one party, the employee, can terminate a contract at his or her will does not serve to invalidate the contract where the second party, the employer, is bound to continue the contract for a specified time or period. Therefore, mutuality of obligation should not be a barrier to the enforcement of an implied-in-fact promise made by the employer to provide employment for a specified term or to terminate the employee for cause alone.

Similarly, independent consideration should not be required for implied-in-fact promises by the employer which are made after the employee has commenced work. If the employee has given consideration apart from the services he has agreed to render for a contract of set duration, then that contract provision will be enforceable. The lack of separate consideration, however, is not fatal to a cause of action based upon an express or implied-in-fact promise by the employer that moves the employee's contract from at-will status. Instead, separate consideration merely signals the parties' intent more clearly.

The ability of employees to bring causes of action based upon express or implied-in-fact promises by the employer will not eliminate the at-will construction of most employment contracts. Courts have expressed concern that due deference be paid to managerial discretion and normal employment decisions. Nonetheless, where an enforceable promise has been made, employees should be able to find redress when it is breached.

Utah has recognized that all contracts contain a covenant of good faith and fair dealing. This includes, in this writer's view, employment contracts. Other jurisdictions have approached this exception to the at-will rule in a variety of ways. Indeed, there appears to be no clear majority rule; many jurisdictions have recently considered this issue and set forth their own approach.

I do not mean to suggest that any termination without cause of an at-will employee is tantamount to a breach of an implied covenant. The scope of the implied covenant is determined by the factual setting in which it is found. Indeed, where the reasonable expectations of the parties are met, there is no breach. Moreover, the motive of the employer in terminating the employee, although possibly relevant, is not necessarily a key issue. More important is the employer's conduct viewed in the context of the relevant contractual terms, express or implied, and the employee's reasonable expectations.

Admittedly, the concept of good faith and fair dealing is not susceptible to bright-line definitions and tests. It should therefore be used sparingly and with caution. Where true injustice has occurred, relief should be provided. Care must be exercised to avoid eclipsing the rule by expanding the exception.

In my view, plaintiff has stated a claim for relief under the second and third exceptions and is entitled to a jury determination of whether Fashion Centre breached the implied-at-law covenant of good faith and fair dealing as well as implied terms of its employment contract.

Fashion Centre terminated an experienced, motivated, and favorably reviewed employee who refused to submit to the third polygraph examination required of her in conjunction with a single inventory shortage, even though she had been exonerated by the previous two exams and had requested that the third exam be rescheduled for another day. This action occurred in light of Fashion Centre's own employment policy which essentially limited an employee's termination to just cause.

This matter is reversed and remanded. On remand, I would permit trial on both the theory of an implied-in-fact contract and the covenant of good faith and fair dealing. At trial, of course, Fashion Centre is free to attempt to demonstrate that there was no implied term in the employment contract or that it was expressly disavowed, or that for some reason the third polygraph was essential and reasonable and therefore not in breach of the contract.

The Utah Supreme Court relied on what it deemed to be the employer's implied promise about continued employment. In a later case the court explained its holding in *Berube* as follows: "If the parties actually intended such an agreement and the agreement is of such a nature that it is possible to operate as a contract term, a court will give effect to the parties' intentions by enforcing the agreement as an implied-in-fact contract provision. The existence of such an agreement is a question of fact which turns on the objective manifestations of the parties' intent."[11] Introduction of a "good faith" requirement seems to expose employers to liability unless they can point to an objective good faith basis for termination, eliminating the prerogative to terminate for no reason without liability. Such a superimposed good faith requirement is at the extreme of courts' willingness to find implied rights to continued employment.

Imputed Prohibitions against Termination

As demonstrated in *Berube v. Fashion Centre, Ltd.*, an employment decision that does not violate any statutory prohibition may still trigger a claim for wrongful termination if it is based on a reason that the courts deem impermissible. The implied prohibitions against termination include public policy and protection of constitutional rights.

Public Policy

In the late 1950s courts began to recognize claims for wrongful termination based on what they deemed to be an employer's violation of a public policy. Such a claim was first recognized in California for an employee who said that his union employer terminated him for refusing to give false testimony before a legislative committee.[12] The court explained,

> *It would be obnoxious to the interests of the state and contrary to public policy and sound morality to allow an employer to discharge any employee, whether the employment be for a designated or unspecified duration, on the ground that the employee declined to commit perjury, an act specifically enjoined by statute. . . . [I]n order to more fully effectuate the state's declared policy against perjury, the civil law, too, must deny the employer his generally unlimited right to discharge an employee whose employment is for an unspecified duration, when the reason for the dismissal is the employee's refusal to commit perjury.*[13]

A number of other state courts have agreed with this reasoning, particularly when employers seemingly punished their employees for refusing the employers' direction to do something illegal. The courts have not drawn very clear contours for the public policies they seek to protect. Most limit the public policy exception to something based on a constitution or statute, as the Utah Supreme Court said it would do in *Berube*. Others will also look to administrative rules and professional codes of ethics. Some even more broadly define public policy, as the New Jersey Supreme Court indicated it would do when it said, "Absent legislation, the judiciary must define the cause of action in case-by-case determinations."[14]

Political Partisanship in Public Employment

Making public employment decisions based on political affiliation has long been part of the American system, dating back at least to President Thomas Jefferson's removal of Federalists who had been appointed by his rival John Adams. A government employer's termination of an employee based on party membership implicates an employee's constitutional right to free speech and association. But there are circumstances when political affiliation has been deemed relevant to a public employer's ability to serve the *public's* interest. The U.S. Supreme Court said that "if an employee's private political beliefs would interfere with the discharge of his public duties, his First Amendment rights may be required to yield to the State's vital interest in maintaining governmental effectiveness and efficiency."[15] The Court explained that not every policymaking position is related to partisanship. It said that "the ultimate inquiry is not whether the label 'policymaker' or 'confidential' fits a particular position; rather, the question is whether the hiring authority can demonstrate that party affiliation is an appropriate requirement for the effective performance of the public office involved."[16]

Protected Speech in Public Employment: Garcetti v. Ceballos

More than 22 million people in the United States work for a government employer.[17] Public employees owe faithful service to carry out their supervisors' policies. At the same time public employees' knowledge and experience may equip them to promote better government in the public's interest and they have individual rights to free speech. How are these roles to be reconciled in determining the extent to which public employees may speak critically about their employers without being disciplined for it?

In *Pickering v. Board of Ed. of Township High School Dist. 205, Will County*,[18] the U.S. Supreme Court held that the First Amendment protected an English teacher from being dismissed for writing a critical letter to a newspaper about the school board's allocation of funds between educational and athletic programs. The Court held that the school district's legitimate interests were not sufficiently impaired by the teacher's participation in a public discussion about funding. What became known as the *"Pickering* test" was applied when a public employee spoke out on a matter of public concern, in which case the court would determine whether the government employer had a legitimate basis for controlling the employee's speech. The Court modified the analysis in the following 2006 case, *Garcetti v. Ceballos*, giving more deference to the government's interest in controlling employee speech. Ceballos, a county deputy district attorney, sued the district attorney for retaliating against him when he publicly said that misleading information was used to get a search warrant. The following excerpts from two of the opinions illustrate the justices' continuing divergent views about the interests involved in this malleable area of the law.

Garcetti v. Ceballos
547 U.S. 410 (2006)

Justice Kennedy, writing for the Court.

Respondent Richard Ceballos has been employed since 1989 as a deputy district attorney for the Los Angeles County District Attorney's Office. During the period relevant to this case, Ceballos was a calendar deputy in the office's Pomona branch, and in this capacity he exercised certain supervisory responsibilities over other lawyers. In February 2000, a defense attorney contacted Ceballos about a pending criminal case. The defense attorney said there were inaccuracies in an affidavit used to obtain a critical search warrant.

After examining the affidavit and visiting the location it described, Ceballos determined the affidavit contained serious misrepresentations. The affidavit called a long driveway what Ceballos thought should have been referred to as a separate roadway. Ceballos also questioned the affidavit's statement that tire tracks led from a stripped-down truck to the premises covered by the warrant. His doubts arose from his conclusion that the roadway's composition in some places made it difficult or impossible to leave visible tire tracks.

Ceballos spoke on the telephone to the warrant affiant, a deputy sheriff from the Los Angeles County Sheriff's Department, but he did not receive a satisfactory explanation for the perceived inaccuracies. He relayed his findings to his supervisors, petitioners Carol Najera and

Frank Sundstedt, and followed up by preparing a disposition memorandum. The memo explained Ceballos' concerns and recommended dismissal of the case. On March 2, 2000, Ceballos submitted the memo to Sundstedt for his review. A few days later, Ceballos presented Sundstedt with another memo, this one describing a second telephone conversation between Ceballos and the warrant affiant.

Based on Ceballos' statements, a meeting was held to discuss the affidavit. Attendees included Ceballos, Sundstedt, and Najera, as well as the warrant affiant and other employees from the sheriff's department. The meeting allegedly became heated, with one lieutenant sharply criticizing Ceballos for his handling of the case.

Despite Ceballos' concerns, Sundstedt decided to proceed with the prosecution, pending disposition of the defense motion to [challenge the warrant]. The trial court held a hearing on the motion. Ceballos was called by the defense and recounted his observations about the affidavit, but the trial court rejected the challenge to the warrant.

Ceballos claims that in the aftermath of these events he was subjected to a series of retaliatory employment actions. The actions included reassignment from his calendar deputy position to a trial deputy position, transfer to another courthouse, and denial of a promotion.

As the Court's decisions have noted, for many years "the unchallenged dogma was that a public employee had no right to object to conditions placed upon the terms of employment—including those which restricted the exercise of constitutional rights." *Connick v. Myers*, 461 U.S. 138, 143 (1983). That dogma has been qualified in important respects. The Court has made clear that public employees do not surrender all their First Amendment rights by reason of their employment. Rather, the First Amendment protects a public employee's right, in certain circumstances, to speak as a citizen addressing matters of public concern.

Pickering v. Board of Ed. of Township High School Dist. 205, Will Cty., 391 U.S. 563 (1968), provides a useful starting point in explaining the Court's doctrine. There the relevant speech was a teacher's letter to a local newspaper addressing issues including the funding policies of his school board. "The problem in any case," the Court stated, "is to arrive at a balance between the interests of the teacher, as a citizen, in commenting upon matters of public concern and the interest of the State, as an employer, in promoting the efficiency of the public services it performs through its employees." *Id.* at 568. The Court found the teacher's speech "neither [was] shown nor can be presumed to have in any way either impeded the teacher's proper performance of his daily duties in the classroom or to have interfered with the regular operation of the schools generally." *Id.* at 572–73. Thus, the Court concluded that "the interest of the school administration in limiting teachers' opportunities to contribute to public debate is not significantly greater than its interest in limiting a similar contribution by any member of the general public." *Id.* at 573.

Pickering and the cases decided in its wake identify two inquiries to guide interpretation of the constitutional protections accorded to public employee speech. The first requires determining whether the employee spoke as a citizen on a matter of public concern. If the answer is no, the employee has no First Amendment cause of action based on his or her employer's reaction to the speech. If the answer is yes, then the possibility of a First Amendment claim arises. The question becomes whether the relevant government entity had an adequate justification for treating the employee differently from any other member of the general public. This consideration reflects the importance of the relationship between the speaker's expressions and employment. A government entity has broader discretion to restrict speech when it acts in its role as employer, but the restrictions it imposes must be directed at speech that has some potential to affect the entity's operations.

When a citizen enters government service, the citizen by necessity must accept certain limitations on his or her freedom. Government employers, like private employers, need a significant degree of control over their employees' words and actions; without it, there would be little chance for the efficient provision of public services. Public employees, moreover, often occupy trusted positions in society. When they speak out, they can express views that contravene governmental policies or impair the proper performance of governmental functions.

At the same time, the Court has recognized that a citizen who works for the government is nonetheless a citizen. The First Amendment limits the ability of a public employer to leverage the employment relationship to restrict, incidentally or intentionally, the liberties employees enjoy in their capacities as private citizens. So long as employees are speaking as citizens about matters of public concern, they must face only those speech restrictions that are necessary for their employers to operate efficiently and effectively.

The Court's employee-speech jurisprudence protects, of course, the constitutional rights of public employees. Yet the First Amendment interests at stake extend beyond the individual speaker. The Court has acknowledged the importance of promoting the public's interest in receiving the well-informed views of government employees engaging in civic discussion.

The controlling factor in Ceballos' case is that his expressions were made pursuant to his duties as a calendar deputy. That consideration—the fact that Ceballos spoke as a prosecutor fulfilling a responsibility to advise his supervisor about how best to proceed with a pending case—distinguishes Ceballos' case from those in which the First Amendment provides protection against discipline. We hold that when public employees make statements pursuant to their official duties, the employees are not speaking as citizens for First Amendment purposes, and the Constitution does not insulate their communications from employer discipline.

Ceballos wrote his disposition memo because that is part of what he, as a calendar deputy, was employed to do. It is immaterial whether he experienced some personal gratification from writing the memo; his First Amendment rights do not depend on his job satisfaction. The significant point is that the memo was written pursuant to Ceballos' official duties. Restricting speech that owes its existence to a public employee's professional responsibilities does not infringe any liberties the employee might have enjoyed as a private citizen. It simply reflects the exercise of employer control over what the employer itself has commissioned or created.

Ceballos did not act as a citizen when he went about conducting his daily professional activities, such as supervising attorneys, investigating charges, and preparing filings. In the same way he did not speak as a citizen by writing a memo that addressed the proper disposition of a pending criminal case. When he went to work and performed the tasks he was paid to perform, Ceballos acted as a government employee. The fact that his duties sometimes required him to speak or write does not mean his supervisors were prohibited from evaluating his performance.

Proper application of our precedents thus leads to the conclusion that the First Amendment does not prohibit managerial discipline based on an employee's expressions made pursuant to official responsibilities. Because Ceballos' memo falls into this category, his allegation of unconstitutional retaliation must fail.

Exposing governmental inefficiency and misconduct is a matter of considerable significance. The dictates of sound judgment are reinforced by the powerful network of legislative enactments—such as whistle-blower protection laws and labor codes—available to those who seek to expose wrongdoing. Cases involving government attorneys implicate additional safeguards in the form of, for example, rules of conduct and constitutional obligations apart from the First Amendment. These imperatives, as well as obligations arising from any other applicable constitutional provisions and mandates of the criminal and civil laws, protect employees and provide checks on supervisors who would order unlawful or otherwise inappropriate actions.

Justice Souter, dissenting.

Open speech by a private citizen on a matter of public importance lies at the heart of expression subject to protection by the First Amendment. At the other extreme, a statement by a government employee complaining about nothing beyond treatment under personnel rules raises no greater claim to constitutional protection against retaliatory response than the remarks of a private employee. In between these points lies a public employee's speech unwelcome to the government but on a significant public issue. Such an employee speaking as a citizen, that is, with a citizen's interest, is protected from reprisal unless the statements are too damaging to the government's capacity to conduct public business to be justified by any individual or public benefit thought to flow from the statements. Entitlement to protection is thus not absolute.

Two reasons in particular make me think an adjustment using the basic *Pickering* balancing scheme is perfectly feasible here. First, the extent of the government's legitimate authority over subjects of speech required by a public job can be recognized in advance by setting in effect a minimum heft for comments with any claim to outweigh it. Thus, the risks to the government are great enough for us to hold from the outset that an employee commenting on subjects in the course of duties should not prevail on balance unless he speaks on a matter of unusual importance and satisfies high standards of responsibility in the way he does it.

My second reason for adapting *Pickering* to the circumstances at hand is the experience in Circuits that have recognized claims like Ceballos's here. First Amendment protection less circumscribed than what I would recognize has been available in the Ninth Circuit for over 17 years, and neither there nor in other Circuits that accept claims like this one has there been a debilitating flood of litigation. There has indeed been some: as represented by Ceballos's lawyer at oral argument, each year over the last five years, approximately 70 cases in the different Courts of Appeals and approximately 100 in the various District Courts. But even these figures reflect a readiness to litigate that might well have been cooled by my view about the importance required before *Pickering* treatment is in order.

All of the justices agreed that public employees have a right to participate in debates as citizens. They did not all agree about the extent to which government employers may restrict their employees' public commentary. Some of the justices seem to envision the public's interest as best served with vigorous public debate that includes disgruntled employees. Others seem to consider such an environment to be too disruptive and litigious. Based on *Ceballos*, government employers have substantial leeway to instruct their employees about the appropriateness of public comments pursuant to official duties and to discipline employees who do not adhere to the instructions.

Position Classification

After the Civil War, Congress sought to reform federal employment to address the problems of a spoils system in which presidents were seen as job brokers for their supporters. The new U.S. Civil Service Commission thereafter filled many federal jobs based on competitive examinations. In 1978 the Civil Service Reform Act[19] abolished the Civil Service Commission and assigned its responsibilities to three separate offices—the independent U.S. Office of Personnel Management to assist agencies with developing and managing position classification systems, the Merit Systems Protection Board to hear appeals of promotion decisions, and the Office of Special Counsel to investigate improprieties. Many federal jobs are now classified according to occupational series, title, and grade or pay bands, based on published minimum qualifications.

States also have position classification plans for state employees. They sometimes also apply to local government positions. The plans define the duties of each classified position and their minimum qualifications, and group jobs with similar expectations so that qualifications and pay ranges correspond. Classification is used for budgeting and for setting fair compensation across departments.

Pay, Benefits, and Work Conditions

There are many federal and state laws and regulations that govern pay, benefits, and work conditions. To comply, employers must continually investigate current rules and self-audit compliance. The following are among the most pervasive employment laws.

Wage and Hour Restrictions

The Fair Labor Standards Act[20] applies to both private and public employers. It has rules for minimum wages, overtime pay, child labor, and equal pay. The act affects more than 100 million workers. State law may impose additional requirements.

The minimum wage and overtime requirements apply to all employees unless an exemption applies. Some states set minimum wages higher than the federal rate. Under federal law overtime pay of at least 1.5 times the hourly rate must be paid after 40 hours of work in a workweek. Several categories of employees are exempt, such as sales personnel, computer professionals, drivers, farm workers, seasonal and recreational workers, and baby sitters, though certain minimum requirements may still apply with respect to such work. Some work is subject to special rules, such as firefighting and law enforcement. There also are exemptions for executive, administrative, and professional employees who are paid a salary, based on the nature of duties and responsibilities as set forth in U.S. Department of Labor regulations.[21]

The child-labor provisions restrict the hours of some kinds of work for 17 and 16 year olds. They more strictly limit work hours for 15 and 14 year olds. Fourteen is the minimum age for most work. There are exceptions and additional rules for farm work and other occupations. Some states have stricter laws.

The Equal Pay Act[22] prohibits paying lower pay to members of one gender for jobs of equal skill, effort, and responsibility performed under similar working conditions. As with most of the employment laws, there are exceptions.

Employment Taxes

Employers must withhold, deposit, report, and pay employment taxes for their employees. Federal and state laws impose many pay and benefits requirements.

Employer tax obligations usually apply only to employees. Characterization as employees—rather than as independent contractors who are responsible for their own employment tax compliance—is not always self-evident. Under common law, employee status was based on an employer's right to control the details of work regardless of whether the control was exercised. For example, doctors, lawyers, and construction contractors generally are not considered to be employees of those to whom they provide services. By statute, some kinds of workers are deemed to be employees or not regardless of the control test outcome.

In general employers must withhold and deposit federal income tax based on their employees' estimated taxable income as calculated on the Form W-4, Employee's Withholding Allowance Certificate. State income tax systems have similar requirements. Employers must also pay a federal social security and Medicare tax based on a percentage of employee wages, and they must withhold and deposit an additional percentage of such taxes from wages. Employers also must pay a Federal Unemployment Tax Act (FUTA) tax. Most pay both a federal and a state unemployment tax, but special rules apply to state and local government employers.

Medical and Retirement Benefits

In recent decades Congress has enacted many statutes governing medical and retirement benefits. Compliance requires in-depth knowledge of complex statutes and regulations. Among the most pervasive are the following federal laws.

The Employee Retirement Income Security Act[23] (ERISA) governs private industry employer-pension and health-benefit plans. It has rules for plan funding and requires plan sponsors and administrators to safeguard plan assets and to treat participants fairly. Examples of ERISA's many rules include restrictions on who may participate in retirement plans, how much may be contributed, when rights vest, and how benefits are to be handled after termination or retirement. ERISA also imposes requirements on health insurance plans.

ERISA has been amended, with federal statutes commonly referred to by separate names. These include the Consolidated Omnibus Budget Reconciliation Act[24] (COBRA), which applies to companies with 20 or more employees. It requires such employers to provide temporary continuing health insurance to employees and their dependents after employment termination and after certain other events such as divorce, legal separation, disability, and death. Coverage must be provided at the employer's cost plus a small administrative fee for up to 18 months in most cases and in some circumstances for longer periods. Under the Health Insurance Portability and Accountability Act[25] (HIPAA), a health insurance plan may exclude coverage for a preexisting health condition only if the condition was the subject of care within the 6 months prior to plan enrollment. In general, for conditions that may be excluded from coverage the duration of the exclusion can be no longer than 12 months. Some conditions, including pregnancy, may not be excluded. The preexisting condition exclusion is offset by an individual's "creditable coverage" under a prior health coverage plan if the break in coverage is less than 63 days. State laws may impose additional requirements. HIPAA and state laws also have rules about protecting medical record privacy.

The Family and Medical Leave Act (FMLA)[26] applies to private and public employers with 50 or more regular employees. It requires such employers to allow their employees who have worked for them for at least 1 year to have up to 12 weeks of unpaid leave for childcare or certain health reasons and for "any qualifying exigency," as defined by regulations, arising out of a family member's military service. The FMLA also requires employers to allow additional leave for a total of 26 weeks for giving care to an injured family member in military service. The statute describes permissible methods for employers to require proof of health conditions. There are limited exceptions from the FMLA requirements for key salaried employees.

The Health Maintenance Organization Act[27] requires employers with 25 or more employees who provide health insurance benefits to also offer a health maintenance organization (HMO) option if a qualified program is available.

Workers' Compensation

State workers' compensation insurance provides for payment of medical and rehabilitation costs, and reimbursement for lost income, to employees who suffer job-related injuries or illnesses. In exchange for the right to compensation, workers' compensation laws limit the employee's right to sue the employer or other employees for covered injuries. State laws require private employers to provide coverage through insurers or with approved self-insurance arrangements. Federal and state governments manage their own workers' compensation plans for their employees.

New Hire Reporting

The Immigration Reform and Control Act[28] prohibits employment of someone known not to be legally authorized to work in the country. Employers may protect themselves against claims of knowing violations by having applicants fill out a U.S. Citizenship and Immigration Services immigration form I-9 with supporting documentation. Federal law also requires employers to report new employees to a new-hire registry maintained by the states, for which the Internal Revenue Service W-4 form may be used in many states.[29]

Work Facilities

Federal and state laws require employers to maintain safe workplaces. They also prescribe many specific safety and structural accommodation measures.

The Occupational Safety and Health Act[30] requires all employers engaged in interstate commerce to maintain safe workplaces and to comply with specific workplace regulations. The act also imposes recordkeeping and reporting requirements. The Occupational Safety and Health Administration of the U.S. Labor Department (OSHA) inspects workplaces and imposes fines for noncompliant conditions or failure to keep required records. States may elect to regulate occupational health and safety by adopting standards at least as effective as federal standards.[31] More than half have done so. OSHA monitors compliance. Several of the state programs apply only to public employees, leaving private employers to the federal OSHA.

The public accommodation provisions of the Americans with Disabilities Act[32] require modifications to public areas of buildings, such as restrooms, elevators, and walkways, to allow the disabled access to the same services as the nondisabled. Department of Justice regulations prescribe disability accommodations in public and commercial facilities, including requirements for removing architectural barriers when readily achievable and for designing new and newly altered structures.[33]

Sexual Harassment

Sexual harassment is considered to be sexual discrimination under Title VII of the Civil Rights Act. The courts have described two categories of impermissible sexual harassment. *Quid pro quo* harassment occurs when supervisors make adverse employment decisions against employees who deny unwelcome sexual demands. "Hostile work environment" harassment occurs when severe or perverse sexual statements or conduct make the work environment intimidating, hostile, or offensive.

Even dirty jokes can be considered impermissible harassment if told in a manner intended to demean or harass someone because of sex, especially if there is a pattern that creates a pervasively demeaning atmosphere. The U.S. Supreme Court has said, however, that sexual harassment laws are not intended to be a "general civility code" and the law "does not reach genuine but innocuous differences in the ways men and women routinely interact with members of the same sex and of the opposite sex."[34] The Court gave the following illustration:

A professional football player's working environment is not severely or pervasively abusive, for example, if the coach smacks him on the buttocks as he heads onto the field—even if the same behavior would reasonably be experienced as abusive by the coach's secretary (male or female) back at the office. The real social impact of workplace behavior often depends on a constellation of surrounding circumstances, expectations, and relationships which are not fully captured by a simple recitation of the words used or the physical acts performed.[35]

The Court also explained that Title VII protects workers against sexually intimidating environments regardless of whether the harasser seeks to have sex, and the law forbids same-sex harassment.[36]

Many sexual harassment complaints follow failed personal relationships between supervisors and employees. Such relationships raise questions about the legitimacy of consent due to a supervisor's hierarchical power. Employers with effective antiharassment policies tend to be especially vigilant about such relationships.

Supervisors who harass employees are personally liable for their actions. Supervisors who become aware of harassing behavior by their subordinates but who fail to attempt to stop it may become liable for continuing harassment. The U.S. Supreme Court has held that employers are subject to liability for hostile environments their supervisors create even if unaware of it unless they can prove both "(a) that the employer exercised reasonable care to prevent and correct promptly any sexually harassing behavior, and (b) that the plaintiff employee unreasonably failed to take advantage of any preventive or corrective opportunities provided by the employer or to avoid harm otherwise."[37] Employers therefore can take steps to protect their employees against harassment, and themselves against liability, with clear antiharassment policies and realistically available complaint procedures.

Unions

The National Labor Relations Act of 1935 (NLRA)[38] gives private-sector employees the right to organize and bargain collectively with their employers. Recognized unions may negotiate with employers on wages, hours, and other terms and conditions of employment. Collective-bargaining agreements commonly contain restrictions on employee discipline and discharge. The NLRA does not apply to supervisors, agricultural workers, domestic home service, railroads, and employees of federal, state, or local government.

A union acquires the right to represent employees after a majority of employees vote to do so and after the National Labor Relations Board (NLRB) certifies the union as the qualified collective bargaining representative under the NLRA. The NLRB enforces the NLRA and prosecutes unfair labor practices with administrative proceedings. Although under the statute a bargaining unit can be as small as two employees, the NLRB has established standards for determining whether it will exercise its jurisdiction based on the volume and nature of a business.

Some federal public-sector employees have limited collective bargaining rights. By Executive Order 10988 issued in 1962, federal employee unions are authorized to represent members regarding matters such as transfers, promotions, termination, safety, and health, but not compensation. State laws governing public employee unions vary. Some state laws prohibit government units from entering into collective bargaining agreements with unions, but more than half of the states provide state employees with some rights to participate in union activity. Some authorize collective bargaining on conditions of employment, including wages and hours. States that allow unions to represent public employees commonly have state labor-relations boards that recognize appropriate bargaining units, consider unfair labor-practice charges, and arbitrate grievances. State laws typically prohibit public employees from striking or slowing down work.

Review Questions

1. What does Title VII prohibit?
2. What does the Age Discrimination in Employment Act prohibit?
3. What does the Americans with Disabilities Act prohibit and require?
4. What are whistleblower laws and whom do they protect?
5. What are the recognized exceptions to an employer's right to terminate an employee who does not have an employment contract?
6. To what extent may public employers base employment decisions on political partisanship without violating the First Amendment?
7. What is the test for determining whether public employees may be disciplined for publicly criticizing their employers?
8. What are the basic federal and state laws and regulations governing pay, benefits, and work conditions, and what do they require?
9. What is considered to be sexual harassment under Title VII?
10. What are the basic legal rights for unions, and to what extent may unions represent public sector employees?

Notes

1. 42 U.S.C. § 2000e-2 (2000).
2. *Id.* § 2000e-1(b).
3. Griggs v. Duke Power Co., 401 U.S. 424 (1971).
4. 29 U.S.C. §§ 621–634 (2000 & Supp. 2006).

5. 38 U.S.C. §§ 4301–4334 (2006).

6. 42 §§ U.S.C.A. 12101–12117 (2005 & Supp. 2008).

7. 29 U.S.C. §§ 20010–2009 (2000 & Supp. 2006).

8. *See* Cleveland Bd. of Educ. v. Loudermill, 470 U.S. 532, 542 (1985).

9. 292 N.W.2d 880 (Mich. 1980).

10. *Id.* at 890.

11. Johnson v. Morton Thiokol, Inc., 818 P.2d 997, 1001 (Utah 1991).

12. Petermann v. Int'l Brotherhood of Teamsters, 344 P.2d 25 (Cal. App. 1959).

13. *Id.* at 27.

14. Pierce v. Ortho Pharmaceutical Corp., 417 A.2d 505, 512 (N.J. 1980).

15. Branti v. Finkel, 445 U.S. 507, 517 (1980).

16. *Id.* at 518.

17. U.S. Dep't of Labor, Bureau of Labor Statistics, Current Employment Statistics Survey (National) (2008).

18. 391 U.S. 563 (1968).

19. Pub. L. 95-454, 92 Stat. 1111.

20. 29 U.S.C.A. §§ 201–219 (1998 & Supp. 2008).

21. 29 C.F.R. pt. 541 (2008).

22. 29 U.S.C. § 206(d) (2000).

23. 29 U.S.C.A. §§ 1001–1461 (1998 & Supp. 2008).

24. *Id.* §§ 1161–1168.

25. 42 U.S.C.A. §§ 300gg to 300gg-92 (2003 & Supp. 2008).

26. 29 U.S.C.A. §§ 2601–2654 (1998 & Supp. 2008).

27. 42 U.S.C.A. § 300e-9 (Supp. 2008).

28. 8 U.S.C. §§ 1324a–1324b (2006).

29. 42 U.S.C.A. § 653(a) (Supp. 2008).

30. 29 U.S.C.A. §§ 651–678 (1998 & Supp. 2008).

31. 29 U.S.C. § 667 (2000).

32. 42 U.S.C. §§ 12181–12189 (2000).

33. 28 C.F.R. pt. 36 (2008).

34. Oncale v. Sundowner Offshore Services, Inc., 523 U.S. 75, 81–82 (1998).

35. *Id.*

36. *Id.* at 80–81.

37. Burlington Indus., Inc. v. Ellerth, 524 U.S. 742, 765 (1998).

38. 29 U.S.C. §§ 151–168 (2000).

Chapter 9

Torts

The things that will destroy America are prosperity-at-any-price, peace-at-any-price, safety-first instead of duty-first, the love of soft living and the get-rich-quick theory of life.
Theodore Roosevelt

CHAPTER OBJECTIVES

After studying this chapter you should better understand:

- The legal elements on which negligence liability is based
- The types of damages that can be recovered for tort liability
- The common tort causes of action
- The nature of sovereign immunity for the government and public officials and employees and its exceptions
- The nature of statutes of limitations

The word "tort" seems foreign, but tort lawsuits are a conspicuous feature of the U.S. legal system. Torts are a broad range of legal causes of action for damages not based on contracts. The most common is for personal injuries as a result of car collisions, medical procedures, pedestrian falls, and product malfunctions. Although a few tort lawsuits result in widely reported multimillion dollar jury verdicts, most tort claims are settled without trials for not more than a few thousand dollars. But collectively personal injury tort claims consume substantial court resources, fuel major industries such as insurance and personal injury law practices, and have a significant impact on product research and development.

A defamation claim, which is addressed in the freedom of speech discussion in Chapter 4, also is a tort cause of action. Torts also include a variety of other civil wrongs such as assault, battery, intentional infliction of emotional distress, intentional interference with contractual relations, fraud and misrepresentation, and trespass and nuisance. Variations are constantly emerging. This chapter provides an introduction to personal injury claims and the other most common tort causes of action, and to special rules governing claims against the government.

Elements of a Negligence Action

Most tort claims are for personal injuries, and most personal injury claims are based on someone's negligence. To recover for negligence a plaintiff must prove that the defendant breached a duty to the plaintiff with an act or omission that was the legal cause of the plaintiff's injury. The following summarizes the elements of basic negligence claims. There are many complexities and variations depending on the circumstances and the state's law on which the claim is based.

Duty

Tort law is based on the notion that everyone has a duty not to carelessly endanger others. A duty in any given circumstance depends on whether the act or omission alleged to have been negligent created a risk of foreseeable harm. In tort law everyone has a general legal duty to act reasonably so as not to harm others who behave in ordinary ways. Individuals also can have legal duties as a result of particular relationships, such as a doctor's duty to a patient to provide competent medical care and a builder's duty to a customer to construct a house with ordinary skill. Legal duties stem from morality concepts, but they are not necessarily consistent with everyone's moral sensibilities. For example, drivers have a legal duty to other drivers and pedestrians not to drive at excessive speed, but they do not have a legal duty to assist someone in distress alongside the road. Views may differ about whether the moral duty is the same.

Assuming a Duty: *Biakanja v. Irving*

Those who provide services requiring specialized knowledge or skill assume a duty to perform those services as should be reasonably expected of someone in the field. Accordingly, those who plan to provide a service are expected to endeavor to acquire the knowledge and skill necessary to perform capably. They assume a greater risk of liability if they go beyond their areas of expertise. In the following California case a public official—a notary public—faces liability to someone who lost out on an inheritance because the notary gave faulty advice about a will. The notary was not a lawyer. Traditionally, based on contract principles, courts have been reluctant to extend liability for bad legal advice to anyone other than the client to whom the advice was given. This case illustrates the scope of potential liability based on negligence principles and the reasonable expectations of others.

Biakanja v. Irving
320 P.2d 16 (Cal. 1958)

Chief Justice Gibson, writing for the California Supreme Court.

Plaintiff's brother, John Maroevich, died, leaving a will which devised and bequeathed all of his property to plaintiff. The will, which was prepared by defendant, a notary public, was denied probate for lack of sufficient attestation. Plaintiff, by intestate succession, received only one-eighth of the estate, and she recovered a judgment against defendant for the difference between the amount which she would have received had the will been valid and the amount distributed to her.

Defendant, who is not an attorney, had for several years written letters and prepared income tax returns for Maroevich. The will was typed in defendant's office and "subscribed and sworn to" by Maroevich in the presence of defendant, who affixed his signature and notarial seal to the instrument. Sometime later Maroevich obtained the signatures of two witnesses to the will, neither of whom was present when Maroevich signed it. These witnesses did not sign in the presence of each other, and Maroevich did not acknowledge his signature in their presence.

An attorney who represented Maroevich's stepson in the probate proceedings testified that he had a telephone conversation with defendant shortly after Maroevich's death, in which defendant said he prepared the will and notarized it. According to the attorney, defendant, in discussing how the will was witnessed, "admonished me to the effect that I was a young lawyer, I'd better go back and study my law books some more, that anybody knew a will which bore a notarial seal was a valid will, didn't have to be witnessed by any witnesses."

The court found that defendant agreed and undertook to prepare a valid will and that it was invalid because defendant negligently failed to have it properly attested. The findings are supported by the evidence.

The principal question is whether defendant was under a duty to exercise due care to protect plaintiff from injury and was liable for damage caused plaintiff by his negligence even though they were not in privity of contract. In *Buckley v. Gray* 42 P. 900 (Cal. 1895), it was held that a person who was named as a beneficiary under a will could not recover damages from an attorney who negligently drafted and directed the execution of the will with the result that the intended beneficiary was deprived of substantial benefits. When *Buckley v. Gray* was decided in 1895, it was generally accepted that, with the few exceptions noted in the opinion in that case, there was no liability for negligence committed in the performance of a contract in the absence of privity. Since that time the rule has been greatly liberalized, and the courts have permitted a plaintiff not in privity to recover damages in many situations for the negligent performance of a contract.

The determination whether in a specific case the defendant will be held liable to a third person not in privity is a matter of policy and involves the balancing of various factors, among which are the extent to which the transaction was intended to affect the plaintiff, the foreseeability of harm to him, the degree of certainty that the plaintiff suffered injury, the closeness of the connection between the defendant's conduct and the injury suffered, the moral blame attached to the defendant's conduct, and the policy of preventing future harm. Here, the "end and aim" of the transaction was to provide for the passing of Maroevich's estate to plaintiff. Defendant must have been aware from the terms of the will itself that, if faulty solemnization caused the will to be invalid, plaintiff would suffer the very loss which occurred. As Maroevich died without revoking his will, plaintiff, but for defendant's negligence, would have received all of the Maroevich estate, and the fact that she received only one-eight[h] of the estate was directly caused by defendant's conduct.

Defendant undertook to provide for the formal disposition of Maroevich's estate by drafting and supervising the execution of a will. This was an important transaction requiring specialized skill, and defendant clearly was not qualified to undertake it. His conduct was not only negligent but was also highly improper. He engaged in the unauthorized practice of the law, which is a misdemeanor in violation of section 6126 of the Business and Professions Code. Such conduct should be discouraged and not protected by immunity from civil liability, as would be the case if plaintiff, the only person who suffered a loss, were denied a right of action.

Public officials are often perceived as being able to be helpful in ways that are not within their job descriptions. For example, a member of the public may ask a register of deeds to help interpret a title or draft a deed. But registers of deeds usually are not lawyers and, contrary to popular misconception, are not qualified to give legal advice. The privilege of authority carries with it a responsibility to act within its proper scope. Although most notaries do not work for government, they have official authority to give oaths and acknowledge signatures. They also often are the only person with official authority present when parties consummate a transaction. *Biakanja v. Irving* illustrates that those entrusted with official authority face potential liability if they undertake duties for which they are not properly qualified.

Breach of Standard of Care

Someone who is legally negligent breaches a standard of care. Sometimes conduct is so obviously negligent that identifying the standard of care is not an issue. But sometimes negligence liability turns on defining the appropriate standard of care. The courts' approach generally is reflected in the analysis that Judge Learned Hand explained in the 1947 case of *United States v. Carroll Towing Co.*[1] In *Carroll Towing* the court considered whether a barge operator was negligent for having no crew aboard when the barge broke loose in New York Harbor as a tug maneuvered vessels preparing for the Normandy invasion during World War II. Judge Hand formulated this equation: the negligence standard of care is breached if (A) the burden of preventing the harm was less than (B) the gravity of the harm multiplied by (C) the probability that it would occur. The court concluded that leaving the barge unattended breached the standard of care according to this formula. Courts rarely refer to the Judge Hand formula explicitly but its risk-utility balance underlies the liability analysis.

In cases involving ordinary negligence the analysis is based on an ordinary person. In cases alleging professional malpractice the standard of care is the skill and diligence that other professionals of ordinary competence would exercise in the same circumstances. Industry customs and safety regulations are commonly used to determine the standard of care. In cases involving professional malpractice expert testimony usually is necessary to prove that the standard of care was not met.

Legal Cause

Tort law requires a connection between the act alleged to have been negligent and the consequences for which recovery is sought. That is, the act or omission that breached a standard of care must be the legal or proximate cause of the harm. The test is variously described. Some courts apply a "but-for" rule and reject liability if the harm would have occurred even without the act or omission. Others require more than a link in the chain of events and require the act or omission to be at least a substantial factor in causing the harm. Regardless of how the linkage is defined, courts generally require that the harm be a foreseeable consequence of the allegedly negligent act or omission.

An opinion often cited for the foreseeability requirement is *Palsgraf v. Long Island Railroad Co.*,[2] written by New York Court of Appeals Chief Judge Benjamin Cardozo, who is among the most influential judges in the development of tort law. In *Palsgraf*, a passenger dropped a fireworks package while being pulled by a railroad guard onto a departing train. The explosion caused scales at the end of the platform to fall on the plaintiff, who sued the railroad company for the guard's alleged negligence. Judge Cardozo explained that an act or omission is legally "negligent" only in relation to reasonably foreseeable consequences, and the plaintiff's injury was seemingly random. Reasonable foreseeability has since been a touchstone for the proximate cause analysis. For example, in another famous tort case, *Smith v. Lampe*,[3] a federal court of appeals held that a man who honked his car's horn to warn a barge away from a fog-bound shore was not liable for negligence when the barge mistook the honking for a government directional signal, struck the rocky bottom, and sank. The court concluded that the well-intentioned man could not have reasonably anticipated that a tug captain would interpret honking as a signal to enter a harbor. The case illustrates that someone's allegedly negligent act or omission is assessed based on the risks to others that a reasonable person in the circumstances should have foreseen.

Damages

In tort cases all jurisdictions authorize compensatory damages based on the injured party's economic loss. Under some circumstances awards also can include an amount for less easily quantified harm such as pain and suffering. Some jurisdictions allow additional amounts to punish a wrongdoer and discourage future similar conduct.

Compensatory Damages

Compensatory damages are recoverable for actual loss that is fairly attributable to the injury, including such things as medical expenses and lost wages. Actual losses are sometimes called special damages. Damages may also include future losses, such as loss of earnings due to physical limitations, if they can be shown not to be speculative and if the amount can be proved with reasonable certainty.

Pain and Suffering and Punitive Damages

Awards for pain and suffering usually are allowed in tort actions, although most courts require that there be some physical or other medically identifiable manifestation of the pain and suffering. Some state courts allow enhanced compensatory or exemplary damages to reflect aggravating circumstance such as outrage or indignity. Typical jury awards for such intangibles are a multiple of compensatory damages or a per-day amount for the period of perceived suffering. These terms give little guidance about how to calculate the appropriate damage amounts. Courts vacate or reduce pain-and-suffering awards by juries that exceed a high threshold, the standard for which varies but typically is an amount judged to be "unreasonable," "irrational," or "shocking to the conscience."

Some states allow "punitive damages" to punish a defendant and to deter future similar conduct. These amounts also are not subject to well-defined parameters and can be wildly large numbers. Increasingly states prohibit punitive damages or limit them. Typical limits are a maximum specific figure, such as $200,000 or $300,000, or a maximum multiple of compensatory damages, such as three or five. The U.S. Supreme Court has held that punitive damages implicate due process concerns about the defendant's right to be treated fairly and are subject to constitutional challenge if they lack fundamental fairness or are the product of bias or passion.[4] For example, the Court overturned a punitive damages award of $145 million when compensatory damages were only $1 million, an award that the Court said was "an irrational and arbitrary deprivation of the property of the defendant."[5]

Pain-and-suffering awards, and especially punitive-damage awards, are the subject of much debate and calls for reform. Advocates of reform point to the "lottery" nature of the awards, the costs of passing them onto consumers, and the opportunistic behaviors they encourage. Supporters of allowing punitive damages point to their function as just retribution for egregious behavior and financial incentive for greater care. Reform proposals include caps on amounts as well as a requirement that punitive damages be awarded only when actual malice has been proved by clear and convincing evidence.

Loss of Consortium and Wrongful Death

If a negligence victim dies before recovering damages, the deceased's estate administrator or other legal representative will have rights as prescribed by statute to seek damages in behalf of someone who has died. Federal and state statutes also authorize families to bring claims for their own losses as a result of a death caused by negligence. Wrongful death statutes allow recovery for family support that the deceased had provided and would have been expected to continue. It is afforded to spouses and in some states to children but usually not to unmarried couples. Most states also allow claims for "loss of consortium" for spouses, and sometimes children, whose spouse or parent dies or survives with diminished capacity. Recovery typically is allowed for quantifiable losses such as lost income as well as for loss of "society," including sexual relations for spouses. Approaches to defining allowable damages vary in the statutes and common law.

Joint Responsibility

There can be more than one legal cause of the same harm. For example, if a manager sends out an obviously untrained equipment operator who negligently injures someone, both the manager's and the operator's acts could be considered to be legal causes of the injury. Those who are harmed by someone else's negligence may have been negligent themselves in the course of events. For instance, in the preceding example the injured person may have behaved negligently in coming in contact with the equipment. Allocating liability among more than one responsible party is a matter of both common-law tort principles and statutes.

Joint and Several Liability

As a general rule each person who negligently causes harm is fully liable for the consequences. If more than one person is potentially liable, the harmed person may pursue full recovery from each and need not pursue all. Those who represent tort claimants with a choice of potentially responsible parties often bring claims against the "deep pocket" who has the most resources or insurance coverage, and leave the target to pursue any rights that may exist for sharing the loss with others.

Comparative Negligence

Common law courts would deny negligence recovery to someone whose own contributory negligence was a factor in the harm regardless of relative fault. Most states now have a "comparative fault statute" that allocates responsibility based on the relative degrees of fault of those who legally cause the harm, with the plaintiff recovering a percentage based on the allocation to defendants. In some states damages are recoverable regardless of how much fault is attributed to the plaintiff, but in most states a plaintiff who is 50% or more negligent recovers nothing (or 51% or more in some states).

Contribution

As noted above, when two or more wrongdoers are responsible for negligently harming someone, the harmed person can sue either wrongdoer for all the loss. Common law courts generally would not allow someone who pays a judgment to recover from others who also may have been negligent and liable to the injured party, based on the theory that wrongdoers may not seek judicial relief from anyone, including each other. States now have contribution statutes that allow recovery from others in proportion to comparative negligence. They may prohibit such recovery from those who still face potential direct liability to the harmed party.

A liable party may also have a right of indemnity from someone else based on a contractual agreement or other direct relationship. An insurance policy is an indemnity contract. Sometimes claims for indemnity are brought after a judgment is paid, and in other cases potentially responsible parties bring into the case the others who owe indemnity. In some circumstances a right of indemnity can be lost if the party owing the duty of indemnity is not given the opportunity to participate in litigation or in settlement discussions. Accordingly, someone who expects to recover from an insurance company may have an obligation under the insurance contract to notify the insurance company as soon as the potential for the claim becomes apparent.

Strict Liability

Strict liability allows recovery of damages in tort for personal injuries without proof that the harm was caused by the defendant's negligence. Law commentators usually attribute the origins of strict liability to an English case from the 1800s, *Rylands v. Fletcher*,[6] in which the court held that the owner of a textile company was liable regardless of any proof of negligence for damage to coal mines that were flooded when the company built a reservoir. The court imposed liability on the reservoir owner on the theory that those who carry on "ultra-hazardous activities" pose such serious risks to others that they should be responsible for resultant loss. Many years later courts and legislatures adopted this risk-allocation approach and have applied it to such activities as construction blasting, explosives transportation, and rocket testing.

A series of California cases were influential in the expansion of strict liability beyond ultra-hazardous activities, in particular two opinions written by California Supreme Court Justice Roger Traynor. In the 1944 case of *Escola v. Coca-Cola Bottling Co.*,[7] the California Supreme Court affirmed a judgment for a woman who was injured when a soft drink bottle exploded. The court held that she did not have to prove negligence because an exploding bottle obviously is defective and poses an unreasonable risk to consumers. In his concurring opinion, Justice Traynor said that "public policy demands that responsibility be fixed wherever it will most effectively reduce the hazards to life and health inherent in defective products that reach the market."[8] This approach was further extended in 1963 in *Greenman v. Yuba Power Products, Inc.*,[9] when the California Supreme Court held that the manufacturer of a power tool could be held liable to someone injured when a piece of wood flew out of the machine. Justice Traynor said, "A manufacturer is strictly liable in tort when an article he places on the market, knowing that it is to be used without inspection for defects, proves to have a defect that causes injury to a human being."[10] He explained, "The purpose of such liability is to insure that the costs of injuries resulting from defective products are borne by the manufacturers that put such products on the market rather than by the injured persons who are powerless to protect themselves."[11]

Product liability is now widely recognized and is the basis for many lawsuits. To recover from a manufacturer, the injured person must prove that a product defect caused the injury and that the injury resulted from a use of the product that was reasonably foreseeable to the manufacturer. A product can be considered defective if an injury most likely would have been avoided had the manufacturer or someone later in the chain of distribution given reasonable warnings about risks that are not obvious to consumers but are known to the manufacturer. This "failure to warn" liability has resulted in conspicuous changes in product labeling. It was also an issue in the notorious case brought in the 1990s by a woman to whom a jury awarded almost $3 million from a fast-food restaurant for burns she suffered when she spilled hot coffee on her lap. The reported jury award demonstrates the potential of products liability but is not an accurate portrayal of the law. In fact the award did not stand—the judge reduced the total award to $640,000 and the parties eventually reached a confidential settlement. In another case a federal court of appeals, applying Indiana law, rejected a claim by a woman who was burned by coffee purchased from a convenience store against the coffee machine manufacturer for failure to warn.[12] With a conclusion that summarizes a commonly cited public policy concern with product liability, the court said, "Using the legal system to shift the costs of this injury to someone else may be attractive to the [plaintiffs], but it would have bad consequences for coffee fanciers who like their beverage hot. . . . First-party health and accident insurance deals with injuries of the kind [the plaintiff] suffered without the high costs of adjudication, and without potential side effects such as lukewarm coffee. We do not know whether the [plaintiffs] carried such insurance (directly or through an employer's health plan), but we are confident that Indiana law does not make [the coffee machine manufacturer] and similar firms insurers through the tort system of the harms, even grievous ones, that are common to the human existence."[13]

Intentional Harms

Tort causes of action also provide civil remedies for intentional harms against other people or their property. Many common-law causes of action have been refined by statute. The following are among the most commonly encountered.

Assault and Battery

An assault occurs when someone intentionally causes another person to reasonably apprehend immediate or harmful offensive contact. No actual contact is necessary—shaking a fist or making a threat is an assault if the target reasonably expects to be struck. Battery is actual harmful or offensive contact with a person or something closely associated, such as clothes, without the person's consent. Intentionally knocking something out of someone's hand or colliding with someone's car can be a battery.

False Imprisonment

False imprisonment is intentional confinement of another person without permission or legal authority. Legal authority includes a privilege recognized under the law, such as a police officer's power to arrest and confine someone suspected of committing a crime. The law also recognizes a "shopkeeper's privilege" that allows store personnel to detain for a reasonable time someone suspected of shoplifting.

Intentional Infliction of Emotional Distress

A claim for infliction of emotional distress arises when someone intentionally engages in outrageous conduct to cause emotional distress to another person. Outrageousness is judged according to an objective community standard. Courts tend to require some physical manifestation of harm. For example, the Virginia Supreme Court sustained dismissal of an intentional infliction of emotional distress claim by a woman who was subjected to hundreds of hang-up calls that she said caused her to be nervous, to lose sleep, and to be unable to concentrate at work. The court concluded that without evidence of medical attention or lost income "the alleged effect on the plaintiff's sensitivities is not the type of extreme emotional distress that is so severe that no reasonable person could be expected to endure it."[14]

Intentional Interference with Contractual Relations

A cause of action for intentional interference with contractual relations arises when someone who is not a party to an existing contract intentionally and unjustifiably interferes with that contract. For example, liability for intentional interference has been imposed for making false statements to an employer to cause an employee to be fired as part of a scheme to lure away customers. Competing with someone in business or protecting a legitimate business interest is not considered to be improper, nor is giving honest advice to breach a contract if the purpose is to protect the advice recipient's legitimate interests. Some states extend the cause of action to interference with a reasonably certain prospective contract as well as an existing one.

Trespass and Nuisance

In the words of the U.S. Supreme Court, the common law of trespass and nuisance is based on the notion of "a right thing in the wrong place—like a pig in the parlor instead of the barnyard."[15] Trespass law protects landowners against intrusions and nuisance law protects neighbors against unreasonable land uses.

Trespass is the intentional entry onto the property of another without permission or privilege. An involuntary or accidental entry onto another's property is not a trespass. A common remedy for trespass is an injunction to stop its continuance. Monetary damages can be awarded when the entry results in physical damage or economic loss such as destruction of trees or crops. Many states statutorily authorize multiple damages for loss of trees.

The tort of nuisance is a cause of action for unreasonable property use. Whether something is an unreasonable interference depends on the nature of the activity and the neighborhood in which it occurs. With urbanization activities that might once have been considered nuisances are now expected to be tolerated. Examples of activities that have been common subjects of nuisance actions are noisy dog kennels, septic ponds, and smoky incinerators. Damages include the diminished value of property and other economic losses attributable to the nuisance.

Fraud and Misrepresentation

Fraud occurs when someone causes harm with a misrepresentation about a material fact knowing it to be false and intending that it be relied upon. To have a tort claim the fraud victim must have been justified in relying on the misrepresentation; someone who easily could have investigated the truth cannot recover for fraud. Fraud can be either a false statement or a failure to disclose important known facts by someone with a duty to disclose them. A fiduciary such as a trustee can have such a duty.

The tort of negligent misrepresentation is similar to fraud, but the false representation need only be negligently made. A misrepresentation is negligently made if there is no reasonable basis for believing it to be true. The person making the misrepresentation need not actually know it is false.

Liability for Employees and Agents

In general, an employer is legally responsible for an employee's negligent acts performed within the scope of authority associated with the work. An act is considered to be within the scope of authority when it was actually authorized or incidental to other authorized conduct, or when it furthers the employer's business. An employer is not liable for an employee's acts committed outside the scope of employment even though the harm was made possible by use of the employer's facilities. For example, a municipal employee who drives negligently will be acting within the scope of authority if traveling for government purposes but probably not if the vehicle is being used after hours for a personal trip.

Employers also can be held liable for negligent hiring, retaining, or supervising based on the employer's actions in negligently empowering employees to harm others. As with other negligence claims the injured party must establish that the employer had a duty and breached it. The existence of a duty and the standard of care depend on the type of the work and its risk to others. For example, an employer probably has a duty to conduct a background investigation before hiring a day care supervisor or police officer but may reasonably hire an office worker without the same degree of scrutiny.

Government Immunity from Tort Liability

Sovereign immunity is among the most surprising legal principles for those who have not studied the law. Sovereign immunity and related principles protect federal and state government from damages liability unless the government waives its protection.

Nature of Sovereign Immunity

Sovereign immunity was adopted from the English law notion that a king can do no wrong and pays damages only by consent. Application of sovereign immunity to U.S. law initially was unclear. In 1793 in *Chisholm v. Georgia*,[16] the U.S. Supreme Court found no basis for state sovereign immunity and held that citizens of South Carolina could sue the State of Georgia to recover confiscated property. The decision was quickly reversed with the Eleventh Amendment to the U.S. Constitution that provides, "The Judicial power of the United States shall not be construed to extend to any suit in law or equity, commenced or prosecuted against one of the United States by Citizens of another State, or by Citizens or Subjects of any Foreign State." This language says nothing about citizens suing their own states, but the Court later held that such a prohibition was a "background principle" underlying the Constitution.[17] The Court also has held that Congress has the power to override the states' sovereign immunity when it does so unequivocally and when necessary to protect rights under the Fourteenth Amendment.[18] Congress has waived such immunity in the civil rights laws that authorize damage remedies.

Sovereign immunity applies to liability for monetary damages to be paid from public funds. The Court has held that sovereign immunity does not prohibit suits against state officials for injunctive relief for violating the Constitution because unconstitutional acts are not undertaken in behalf of the government. A claim seeking government funds is barred by immunity regardless of whether the government or an official is the named defendant.

Courts have drawn a distinction between "governmental" acts subject to immunity and "proprietary" acts that are not. Immunity clearly applies to governmental acts. Even a private entity may have sovereign immunity if its act is a traditional governmental service provided pursuant to statutory authority, such medical emergency services. A common distinction equates "governmental" to functions related to public health, safety, and welfare, and "proprietary" to functions traditionally or typically performed by private entities. The distinction is blurry, and courts have tended to take a broad view of governmental functions. For example, parking lots and recreational centers could be said to be both governmental and proprietary, but courts have tended to see them as governmental for sovereign immunity purposes.

Public officials also may have immunity from damage claims against them personally. Some public officials have absolute immunity from suits against them in connection with their official acts, such as legislators for their legislative acts and judges for their judicial acts, based on constitutional provisions or common law. Public officials also may be protected from personal tort liability based on the doctrine of a public duty. The doctrine evolved in common law to protect local governments and their employees from liability for failure to furnish police protection based on the unreasonableness of expecting law enforcement to prevent all harms. This doctrine also has been applied to such activities as fire fighting and building-code enforcement. Although it functions as immunity, it is analytically based on the tort principle that negligence liability must be based on breach of a duty to prevent foreseeable harm to a specific person, and official duties are sometimes owed to the public more generally. The public duty doctrine does not protect officials who voluntarily undertake a duty to a specific individual, such as when an official gives express assurances to an individual who justifiably relies on them.

Courts commonly also apply sovereign immunity to suits against public officials personally for their discretionary acts. The U.S. Supreme Court noted two reasons for this qualified immunity: the unfairness of subjecting officials to liability for decisions that are entrusted to their discretion, and the disincentive such liability would be to public service.[19] This form of immunity does not apply to "ministerial" or mandatory acts that involve no discretion.

Tort Claims Acts

Government waives its immunity from liability when it authorizes a damage claim. Legislatures authorize damage claims as a matter of policy to have the public rather than harmed individuals bear the cost of injuries resulting from government operations. Congress enacted the first major tort claim authorization in 1946 with the Federal Tort Claims Act (FTCA). The FTCA authorizes damage claims to be brought in federal district courts "for injury or loss of property, or personal injury or death caused by the negligent or wrongful act or omission of any employee of the Government while acting within the scope of his office or employment, under circumstances where the United States, if a private person, would be liable to the claimant in accordance with the law of the place where the act or omission occurred."[20] The FTCA retains immunity against certain kinds of claims traditionally barred, including those "based upon the exercise or performance or the failure to exercise or perform a discretionary function or duty on the part of a federal agency or an employee of the Government, whether or not the discretion involved be abused."[21] Before an action may be filed under the FTCA an administrative claim must be presented to the federal agency employing the person whose act or omission caused the injury. After an administrative claim is presented to the appropriate agency, the agency has 6 months to admit or deny the claim. A complaint cannot be filed in court against the agency until the administrative claim has been denied or until 6 months have passed without the agency acting on the claim.[22]

States have their own versions of tort claims acts with their own prerequisites and limitations. Additionally, other federal and state laws may authorize damage claims for violation of their prohibitions.

Scope of Waiver: *Dolan v. United States Postal Service*

The FTCA contains an exception from authorized tort damage claims for "[a]ny claim arising out of the loss, miscarriage, or negligent transmission of letters or postal matter." To protect themselves against lost packages, customers need to purchase insurance from the post office. Mail delivery operations also involve other risks to the public. In the following case the U.S. Supreme Court considered whether someone who tripped over packages could sue the post office for negligently leaving them in the way. It illustrates how claims against the government depend on statutory provisions and the courts' interpretation of them.

Dolan v. United States Postal Service
546 U.S. 481 (2006)

Justice Kennedy, writing for the Court.

Each day, according to the Government's submissions here, the United States Postal Service delivers some 660 million pieces of mail to as many as 142 million delivery points. This case involves one such delivery point—petitioner Barbara Dolan's porch—where mail left by postal employees allegedly caused her to trip and fall. Claiming injuries as a result, Dolan filed a claim for administrative relief from the Postal Service.

Under the Postal Reorganization Act, the Postal Service is "an independent establishment of the executive branch of the Government of the United States." 39 U.S.C. § 201. Holding a monopoly over carriage of letters, the Postal Service has "significant governmental powers," including the power of eminent domain, the authority to make searches and seizures in the enforcement of laws protecting the mails, the authority to promulgate postal regulations, and, subject to the Secretary of State's supervision, the power to enter international postal agreements. Consistent with this status, the Postal Service enjoys federal sovereign immunity absent a waiver.

The [Federal Tort Claims Act] qualifies its waiver of sovereign immunity for certain categories of claims (13 in all). If one of the exceptions applies, the bar of sovereign immunity remains. The 13 categories of exempted claims are set forth in 28 U.S.C. § 2680, and the relevant subsection for our purposes, pertaining to postal operations, is § 2680(b). It states:

> The provisions of this chapter and section 1346(b) of this title shall not apply to . . . [a]ny claim arising out of the loss, miscarriage, or negligent transmission of letters or postal matter.

As a consequence, the United States may be liable if postal employees commit torts under local law, but not for claims defined by this exception.

We assume that under the applicable state law a person injured by tripping over a package or bundle of papers negligently left on the porch of a residence by a private party would have a cause of action for damages. The question is whether, when mail left by the Postal Service causes the slip and fall, the § 2680(b) exception for "loss, miscarriage, or negligent transmission of letters or postal matter" preserves sovereign immunity despite the FTCA's more general statements of waiver.

If considered in isolation, the phrase "negligent transmission" could embrace a wide range of negligent acts committed by the Postal Service in the course of delivering mail, including creation of slip-and-fall hazards from leaving packets and parcels on the porch of a residence. After all, in ordinary meaning and usage, transmission of the mail is not complete until it arrives at the destination. The definition of words in isolation, however, is not necessarily controlling in statutory construction. A word in a statute may or may not extend to the outer limits of its definitional possibilities. Interpretation of a word or phrase depends upon reading the whole statutory text, considering the purpose and context of the statute, and consulting any precedents or authorities that inform the analysis. Here, we conclude both context and precedent require a narrower reading, so that "negligent transmission" does not go beyond negligence causing mail to be lost or to arrive late, in damaged condition, or at the wrong address. The phrase does not comprehend all negligence occurring in the course of mail delivery.

Starting with context, the words "negligent transmission" in § 2680(b) follow two other terms, "loss" and "miscarriage." Those terms, we think, limit the reach of "transmission." "[A] word is known by the company it keeps"—a rule that "is often wisely applied where a word is capable of many meanings in order to avoid the giving of unintended breadth to the

Acts of Congress." *Jarecki v. G. D. Searle & Co.*, 367 U.S. 303, 307 (1961). Here, as both parties acknowledge, mail is "lost" if it is destroyed or misplaced and "miscarried" if it goes to the wrong address. Since both those terms refer to failings in the postal obligation to deliver mail in a timely manner to the right address, it would be odd if "negligent transmission" swept far more broadly to include injuries like those alleged here—injuries that happen to be caused by postal employees but involve neither failure to transmit mail nor damage to its contents.

We think it more likely that Congress intended to retain immunity, as a general rule, only for injuries arising, directly or consequentially, because mail either fails to arrive at all or arrives late, in damaged condition, or at the wrong address. Illustrative instances of the exception's operation, then, would be personal or financial harms arising from nondelivery or late delivery of sensitive materials or information (e.g., medicines or a mortgage foreclosure notice) or from negligent handling of a mailed parcel (e.g., shattering of shipped china). Such harms, after all, are the sort primarily identified with the Postal Service's function of transporting mail throughout the United States.

Further supporting our interpretation, losses of the type for which immunity is retained under § 2680(b) are at least to some degree avoidable or compensable through postal registration and insurance. While the Government suggests other injuries falling outside the FTCA are also subject to administrative relief, even assuming that is true the provision the Government cites permits only discretionary relief, not an automatic remedy like postal insurance.

The postal exception is inapplicable, and Dolan's claim falls within the FTCA's general waiver of federal sovereign immunity.

Justice Thomas, dissenting.

The text of the postal exception, and every term therein, should be ascribed its ordinary meaning. The term in controversy here is "negligent transmission." The crux of my disagreement with the majority is its failure to assign the term "transmission" its plain meaning. Accordingly, I would interpret the term "transmission" consistent with its ordinary meaning, and conclude that the postal exception exempts the Government from liability for *any* claim arising out of the negligent delivery of the mail to a Postal Service patron, including Dolan's slip-and-fall claim.

The majority rationalizes its view by concluding that the terms "loss" and "miscarriage" necessarily limit the term "transmission." Applying the rule of *noscitur a sociis*—that a word is known by the company it keeps—the majority reasons that because both "loss" and "miscarriage" refer to "failings in the postal obligation to deliver mail in a timely manner to the right address, it would be odd if 'negligent transmission' swept more broadly." But there is nothing "odd" about interpreting the term "negligent transmission" to encompass more ground than the decidedly narrower terms "loss" and "miscarriage."

"[A] waiver of the Government's sovereign immunity will be strictly construed, in terms of its scope, in favor of the sovereign." *Lane v. Pena*, 518 U.S. 187, 192 (1996). These settled legal principles apply not only to the interpretation of the scope of the Government's waiver of immunity, but also to the interpretation of the scope of any exceptions to that waiver.

Accordingly, even if I were to conclude that the majority's interpretation of "negligent trans-mission" were as plausible as my own, I would still resolve this case in favor of the Government's sovereign immunity as mandated by our canons of construction.

The U.S. Postal Service delivers many packages, and problems inevitably will arise in connection with how they are left. Claims such as those made in *Dolan* are therefore predictable. Legislators could have been clear about the post office's liability for such claims, but the statute was so imprecise that a case went to the U.S. Supreme Court about its meaning and the justices disagreed about what it meant. The case illustrates that when the availability of a damages claim against the government is left unclear the outcome depends on how judges interpret the statutes and the judges' perspectives on the law of sovereign immunity.

Waiver by Insurance

Government units often purchase insurance to provide coverage against claims that otherwise might be subject to sovereign immunity. Insurance may be arranged because the contours of sovereign immunity are not very clear, or because of a decision to have the public bear the cost of insurance premiums rather than have individuals bear the cost of accidents. Some courts have refused to allow claims on insurance policies that the government did not have express statutory authority to obtain. Others have held that whenever the government purchases insurance it waives its sovereign immunity to the extent of the coverage.

Statutes of Limitations

Statutes of limitations require dismissal of lawsuits brought after a set time limit. The U.S. Supreme Court has explained that "although affording plaintiffs what the legislature deems a reasonable time to present their claims, [statutes of limitations] protect defendants and the courts from having to deal with cases in which the search for truth may be seriously impaired by the loss of evidence, whether by death or disappearance of witnesses, fading memories, disappearance of documents, or otherwise."[23] A court must dismiss a claim that is brought after the limitations period has passed unless there is an exception to application of the rule.

Under the Federal Tort Claims Act a tort victim has 2 years to bring a suit after the cause of action accrues.[24] State law typically requires tort actions to be brought within 2 or 3 years, but some periods are longer. Statutes of limitations typically provide that time begins to run when a cause of action accrues, although some statutes define commencement more specifically such as upon substantial completion of work for a negligent construction claim.

Identifying the date at which a cause of action has accrued is not always simple. For example, if the act or omission on which the claim is based was a continuing series of events, the cause of action may be deemed not to accrue until the last event. Complications also arise if the victim at first did not know about the harm, such as when someone learns that a drug was harmful many years after taking it. Similarly, issues arise if the victim did not have access to the facts needed to identify the source of the harm. In these situations some statutes authorize and courts apply a diligence discovery rule so that the limitations period is measured from when the injury is discovered, or in the exercise of reasonable diligence should have been discovered, rather than from when the harm occurred.

Review Questions

1. What are the legal elements for negligence liability?
2. What are the sources of a duty on which negligence liability can be based?
3. What is the "Learned Hand formula" for determining whether a standard of care has been breached?
4. How does foreseeability relate to legal cause for negligence liability?
5. What are compensatory damages, and when are pain and suffering and punitive damages available?
6. What is joint and several responsibility, comparative negligence, and contribution with respect to tort liability?
7. What are the main forms of strict liability?
8. What are the most common tort causes of action for intentional harms?
9. What is the nature of sovereign immunity and its exceptions?
10. How do statutes of limitations affect tort liability?

Notes

1. 159 F.2d 169 (2d Cir. 1947).
2. 162 N.E. 99 (N.Y. 1928).
3. 64 F.2d 201 (6th Cir. 1933).
4. Browning-Ferris Indus. of Vt., Inc. v. Kelco Disposal, Inc., 492 U.S. 257, 276–77 (1989).
5. State Farm Mutual Auto Ins. Co. v. Campbell, 538 U.S. 408, 429 (2003).
6. L.R. 3 H.L. 330 (1868).
7. 150 P.2d 436 (Cal. 1944).
8. *Id*. at 462.
9. 377 P.2d 897 (Cal. 1963).
10. *Id*. at 900.

11. *Id.* at 901.
12. McMahon v. Bunn-O-Matic Corp., 150 F.3d 651 (7th Cir. 1998).
13. *Id.* at 659.
14. Russo v. White, 400 S.E.2d 160, 163 (Va. 1991).
15. Village of Euclid v. Ambler Realty Co., 272 U.S. 365, 388 (1926).
16. 2 U.S. (2 Dall.) 419 (1793).
17. Hans v. Louisiana, 134 U.S. 1 (1890).
18. Seminole Tribe of Fla. v. Florida, 517 U.S. 44, 55 (1996).
19. Scheuer v. Rhodes, 416 U.S. 232, 240 (1974).
20. 28 U.S.C. § 1346(b)(1) (2000).
21. *Id.* § 2680(a).
22. *Id.* § 2675(a).
23. United States v. Kubrick, 444 U.S. 111, 117 (1979).
24. 28 U.S.C. § 2401(b) (2000).

Chapter 10

Criminal Law and Procedure

I think the first duty of society is justice.
Alexander Hamilton

CHAPTER OBJECTIVES

After studying this chapter you should better understand:

- The use of elements to define crimes and the common approaches to state of mind requirements
- The basic constitutional limitations on the government's authority to criminalize behavior
- The nature of the defenses of insanity, diminished capacity, and self-defense
- The basic constitutional limitations on searches, seizures, prosecution, and punishment
- The nature of the writ of habeas corpus and its availability

Criminal law counterposes two objectives of the rule of law: Empowering government to protect its citizens and constraining its tendency to oppress them. The founders were especially concerned about authoritarian tendencies—much of the Bill of Rights limits investigatory and prosecutorial powers. Courts and legislators have the difficult task of safeguarding this legacy in a world in which predators have plentiful opportunities to harm others and governments have enhanced arsenals for surveillance and internment.

There are practical as well as jurisprudential reasons to study basic criminal law and procedure. Millions work in the criminal justice system. Many others have personal experience as victims, witnesses, jurors, lawyers, or defendants. Over 1.1 million offenders are convicted of felonies every year in the United States.[1] Over 7 million people are in jail, prison, or on parole in the U.S.—this equates to 1 in 31 adults.[2] Most people have a sense of the very serious governmental challenges associated with these troubling realities that weigh on the delicate balance between individual liberties and public safety.

This chapter describes the fundamentals of criminal law and procedure and provides context for consideration of important criminal justice policy issues. The first part describes how legislatures define punishable offenses and the constitutional limitations on their discretion to do so. The second part describes the procedure by which courts attempt to protect the innocent and hold the guilty accountable.

Defining Criminal Offenses

State criminal laws originally were derived from the common laws of the English courts. States later adopted criminal statutes. Most states continue to recognize some common-law crimes though some states replaced them entirely with comprehensive criminal statutes. Most state criminal statutes reflect the American Law Institute's Model Penal Code that was promulgated in 1962. Federal criminal law is entirely statutory. Early on the U.S. Supreme Court held that the federal courts' limited powers do not include authority to recognize any federal common law crimes.[3] Federal criminal statutes concern federal or interstate matters such as the conduct of federal officials and protection of federal property, regulated institutions, intellectual property rights, interstate commerce, and crimes across state boundaries.

Each state has its own variations in criminal law, some of which are big differences such as the existence of a death penalty, and some are minor such as in the precise definition of a crime. Despite variation all criminal codes share some basic features.

Criminal laws make a categorical distinction in seriousness between "felonies" and "misdemeanors." In general "felonies" are punishable by imprisonment for 1 year or more, and "misdemeanors" are punishable by fine or imprisonment for less than 1 year. Some jurisdictions also have offenses or infractions punishable only by fine, such as a parking ticket.

Criminal offenses are composed of elements. Elements are acts committed with a state of mind. Comparison of three common crimes—theft, robbery, and burglary—illustrates how elements work. Someone is guilty of theft who unlawfully takes someone's property (act) with the purpose of depriving the lawful owner of it (state of mind). Robbery involves a theft in which the victim is injured or the thief purposely puts the victim in fear of immediate serious injury. A burglary occurs when someone enters a building for the purpose of committing a crime in it. The definitions of these crimes vary among the jurisdictions, but this description illustrates how the elements of different crimes can be related to each other.

States of Mind

A key element of any crime is the required state of mind, often referred to as *mens rea*, which means "guilty mind." Focusing on state of mind reflects criminal law's goal of deterrence. Accordingly, serious crimes involve intentional acts. The Model Penal Code employs four levels of culpability based on mental state: purposely, knowingly, recklessly, or negligently. In general, someone acts purposely when the offender has the wrongful conduct as a conscious object, knowingly when practically certain that conduct will cause a result, recklessly when consciously disregarding a substantial risk of the result, and negligently when the offender should have been aware of the risk of the result. For a few crimes someone can be strictly liable regardless of mental state, such as with statutory rape when an adult male has sex with a minor female.

Different mental-state requirements may apply to different elements of a crime. For example, a law may require one state of mind regarding conduct and another regarding attendant circumstances, such as defining the crime of receiving stolen property as purposely receiving property while knowing it has been stolen.

The Model Penal Code's treatment of homicide provides an example of how mental state requirements apply. A homicide occurs when someone causes the death of another human being. There are three kinds of homicide: murder, manslaughter, and negligent homicide. If the death is caused purposely or knowingly it is murder, which is a felony of the first degree. A homicide also is murder if it is "committed recklessly under circumstances manifesting extreme indifference to the value of human life," such as during a rape. Killing someone recklessly is manslaughter, a felony of the lesser second degree, and killing someone through negligence is negligent homicide, a felony of the third degree.[4] Criminal codes have many variations of homicide, but the Model Penal Code illustrates typical distinctions in grades of offenses based on states of mind.

Constitutional Limitations

Courts and legislatures cannot prohibit constitutionally protected behavior. For example, the U.S. Supreme Court's recognition of a privacy right in *Griswold v. Connecticut*, discussed in Chapter 2, meant that the state could not prosecute medical professionals for giving contraceptive advice. The courts' and legislatures' criminal law powers also are constrained by constitutional rights aimed directly at protecting those who might be arrested, prosecuted, and punished.

Conditions and Acts

The Eighth Amendment's prohibition against cruel and unusual punishments limits the government's criminal law powers. As the U.S. Supreme Court said, the Eighth Amendment prohibition means that "criminal penalties may be inflicted only if the accused has committed some act, has engaged in some behavior, which society has an interest in preventing, or perhaps, in historical common law terms, has committed some *actus reus*."[5] In *Robinson v. California*,[6] the Court held that a state could not punish someone just for being in a condition such as drug addict.[7] But someone can be convicted for behavior associated with a condition, such as for purchasing drugs or for being publicly intoxicated.

Knowing the Forbidden: Papachristou v. City of Jacksonville

A rule of law requires predictable rules including about what behavior is prohibited. In the following case the U.S. Supreme Court addresses the constitutionality of vagrancy laws, which have been known to be used as a tool to target individuals believed to fit profiles of being criminally inclined.

Papachristou v. City of Jacksonville
405 U.S. 156 (1972)

Justice Douglas, writing for the Court.

This case involves eight defendants who were convicted in a Florida municipal court of violating a Jacksonville, Florida, vagrancy ordinance.

The facts are stipulated. Papachristou and Calloway are white females. Melton and Johnson are black males. Papachristou was enrolled in a job-training program sponsored by the State Employment Service at Florida Junior College in Jacksonville. Calloway was a typing and shorthand teacher at a state mental institution located near Jacksonville. She was the owner of the automobile in which the four defendants were arrested. Melton was a Vietnam war veteran who had been released from the Navy after nine months in a veterans' hospital. On the date of his arrest, he was a part-time computer helper while attending college as a full-time student in Jacksonville. Johnson was a tow-motor operator in a grocery chain warehouse, and was a life-long resident of Jacksonville.

At the time of their arrest, the four of them were riding in Calloway's car on the main thoroughfare in Jacksonville. They had left a restaurant owned by Johnson's uncle, where they had eaten and were on their way to a nightclub. The arresting officers denied that the racial mixture in the car played any part in the decision to make the arrest. The arrest, they said, was made because the defendants had stopped near a used-car lot which had been broken into several times. There was, however, no evidence of any breaking and entering on the night in question.

Of these four charged with "prowling by auto," none had been previously arrested except Papachristou, who had once been convicted of a municipal offense.

Jimmy Lee Smith and Milton Henry (who is not a petitioner) were arrested between 9 and 10 a.m. on a weekday in downtown Jacksonville, while waiting for a friend who was to lend them a car so they could apply for a job at a produce company. Smith was a part-time produce worker and part-time organizer for a Negro political group. He had a common law wife and three children supported by him and his wife. He had been arrested several times but convicted only once. Smith's companion, Henry, was an 18-year-old high school student with no previous record of arrest.

This morning it was cold, and Smith had no jacket, so they went briefly into a dry cleaning shop to wait, but left when requested to do so. They thereafter walked back and forth two or three times over a two-block stretch looking for their friend. The store owners, who apparently were wary of Smith and his companion, summoned two police officers, who searched the men and found neither had a weapon. But they were arrested because the officers said they had no identification and because the officers did not believe their story.

Heath and a codefendant were arrested for "loitering" and for "common thief." Both were residents of Jacksonville, Heath having lived there all his life and being employed at an automobile body shop. Heath had previously been arrested but his codefendant had no arrest record. Heath and his companion were arrested when they drove up to a residence shared by Heath's girlfriend and some other girls. Some police officers were already there in the process of arresting another man. When Heath and his companion started backing out of the driveway, the officers signaled to them to stop and asked them to get out of the car, which they did. Thereupon they and the automobile were searched. Although no contraband or incriminating evidence was found, they were both arrested, Heath being charged with being a "common thief" because he was reputed to be a thief. The codefendant was charged with "loitering" because he was standing in the driveway, an act which the officers admitted was done only at their command.

Campbell was arrested as he reached his home very early one morning and was charged with "common thief." He was stopped by officers because he was traveling at a high rate of speed, yet no speeding charge was placed against him.

Brown was arrested when he was observed leaving a downtown Jacksonville hotel by a police officer seated in a cruiser. The police testified he was reputed to be a thief, narcotics pusher, and generally opprobrious character. The officer called Brown over to the car, intending at that time to arrest him unless he had a good explanation for being on the street. Brown walked over to the police cruiser, as commanded, and the officer began to search him, apparently preparatory to placing him in the car. In the process of the search he came on two small packets which were later found to contain heroin. When the officer touched the pocket where the packets were, Brown began to resist. He was charged with "disorderly loitering on street" and "disorderly conduct—resisting arrest with violence." While he was also charged with a narcotics violation, that charge was *nolled*.

Jacksonville's ordinance and Florida's statute were "derived from early English law," *Johnson v. State*, 202 So.2d 852, 854 (Fla. 1967), and employ "archaic language" in their definitions of vagrants. *Id.* at 855. The history is an often-told tale. The breakup of feudal estates in England led to labor shortages which, in turn, resulted in the Statutes of Laborers, designed to stabilize the labor force by prohibiting increases in wages and prohibiting the movement of workers from their home areas in search of improved conditions. Later vagrancy laws became criminal aspects of the poor laws. The series of laws passed in England on the subject became increasingly severe.

Living under a rule of law entails various suppositions, one of which is that "[all persons] are entitled to be informed as to what the State commands or forbids." *Lanzetta v. New Jersey*, 306 U.S. 451, 453 (1939).

The poor among us, the minorities, the average householder are not in business and not alerted to the regulatory schemes of vagrancy laws; and we assume they would have no understanding of their meaning and impact if they read them. Nor are they protected from being caught in the vagrancy net by the necessity of having a specific intent to commit an unlawful act.

The Jacksonville ordinance makes criminal activities which, by modern standards are normally innocent. "Nightwalking" is one. Florida construes the ordinance not to make criminal one night's wandering, only the "habitual" wanderer or, as the ordinance describes it, "common night walkers." We know, however, from experience that sleepless people often walk at night, perhaps hopeful that sleep-inducing relaxation will result.

Walkers and strollers and wanderers may be going to or coming from a burglary. Loafers or loiterers may be "casing" a place for a holdup. Letting one's wife support him is an intra-family matter, and normally of no concern to the police. Yet it may, of course, be the setting for numerous crimes.

The difficulty is that these activities are historically part of the amenities of life as we have known them. They are not mentioned in the Constitution or in the Bill of Rights. These unwritten amenities have been in part responsible for giving our people the feeling of independence and self-confidence, the feeling of creativity. These amenities have dignified the right of dissent and have honored the right to be nonconformists and the right to defy submissiveness. They have encouraged lives of high spirits rather than hushed, suffocating silence.

They are embedded in Walt Whitman's writings, especially in his "Song of the Open Road." They are reflected, too, in the spirit of Vachel Lindsay's "I Want to Go Wandering," and by Henry D. Thoreau.

Another aspect of the ordinance's vagueness appears when we focus, not on the lack of notice given a potential offender, but on the effect of the unfettered discretion it places in the hands of the Jacksonville police. We allow our police to make arrests only on "probable cause," a Fourth and Fourteenth Amendment standard applicable to the States as well as to the Federal Government. Arresting a person on suspicion, like arresting a person for investigation, is foreign to our system, even when the arrest is for past criminality. Future criminality, however, is the common justification for the presence of vagrancy statutes.

A direction by a legislature to the police to arrest all "suspicious" persons would not pass constitutional muster. A vagrancy prosecution may be merely the cloak for a conviction which could not be obtained on the real but undisclosed grounds for the arrest.

Where, as here, there are no standards governing the exercise of the discretion granted by the ordinance, the scheme permits and encourages an arbitrary and discriminatory enforcement of the law. It furnishes a convenient tool for "harsh and discriminatory enforcement by local prosecuting officials, against particular groups deemed to merit their displeasure." *Thornhill v. Alabama*, 310 U.S. 88, 97–98 (1940). It results in a regime in which the poor and the unpopular are permitted to "stand on a public sidewalk . . . only at the whim of any police officer." *Shuttlesworth v. Birmingham*, 382 U.S. 87, 90 (1965).

Of course, vagrancy statutes are useful to the police. Of course, they are nets making easy the roundup of so-called undesirables. But the rule of law implies equality and justice in its application. Vagrancy laws of the Jacksonville type teach that the scales of justice are so tipped that even-handed administration of the law is not possible. The rule of law, evenly applied to minorities as well as majorities, to the poor as well as the rich, is the great mucilage that holds society together.

The Jacksonville ordinance cannot be squared with our constitutional standards, and is plainly unconstitutional.

In addition to prohibiting loafing, the Jacksonville ordinance deemed "persons who use juggling" as prosecutable vagrants. Notwithstanding the silliness of such antiquated prohibitions, the Court's opinion illustrates the fundamental threat to liberty that exists if everyone is at risk of being arrested by means of an elastic criminal statute. Constitutional limits on criminalization echo the persistent theme of the balancing of public safety and individual liberties. Constitutional limitations protect liberty but also impede police actions that would in fact discourage activities associated with serious street problems such as drug dealing and gang activity.

The courts must not unduly constrain law enforcement, but they must still keep in mind Benjamin Franklin's warning, "They who can give up essential liberty to obtain a little temporary safety, deserve neither liberty nor safety."

Attempt

The law of attempt is aimed at those who take steps toward committing a crime but who do not complete it. If criminal law is meant to deter crime, then punishment need not depend on success. Many criminal laws reflect this view by authorizing the same punishment for attempting a crime as for completing it. The law of attempt is based on specific intent to commit a crime and therefore cannot be based on a reckless or negligent act. Someone must do more than just think about committing a crime, but laws vary about how close to completion an offender must come. Approaches include requiring an unequivocal act or a substantial act corroborative of criminal purpose. For example, an unequivocal corroborative act could be waiting in ambush or possessing something useful only for the intended crime.

Someone who has taken steps that would constitute criminal attempt may still be able to avoid legal responsibility by voluntarily abandoning the attempt. Jurisdictions vary in how they define sufficient abandonment. Typical statutes require a complete renunciation of the criminal purpose that is not motivated by fear of detection or by a decision to wait for a better opportunity.

Defenses

Criminal law recognizes that sometimes a person should not be punished despite having committed a prohibited act. Two of the most common defenses are diminished responsibility based on mental capacity and justification due to self-defense. The following is summary of these defenses. There are many variations in the criminal law.

Insanity and Diminished Capacity

The defense traditionally known as "insanity" stems from the notion that punishment is aimed at those who knew the nature of their criminal act. A legal determination of insanity does not necessarily result in the defendant's freedom from incarceration. Someone found not guilty by reason of insanity is subject to involuntary commitment for treatment until a court determines that the person is no longer dangerous. Someone who suffers from a mental disease or defect at the time of trial is not then subjected to trial but is instead committed to a mental health institution for so long as the condition continues. Although these consequences are involuntarily imposed, they are deemed more appropriate than the forms of punishment given to those who are considered mentally responsible for their actions.

The legal definition of insanity for purposes of responsibility is not the same as a medical definition of mental illness. The legal definition has been the subject of much debate, and its precise contours remain necessarily imprecise. For many years the test was known as the "*M'Naghten* Rule," based on a 1843 English case. M'Naghten, who shot another man in the back, and was said to suffer from periodic "morbid delusions" such that he "would all at once break out into the most extravagant and violent paroxysms."[8] The court said that "to establish a defence on the ground of insanity, it must be clearly proved that, at the time of the committing of the act, the party accused as labouring under such a defect of reason, from disease of the mind, as not to know the nature and quality of the act he was doing; or, if he did know it, that he did not know he was doing what was wrong."[9] This *M'Naghten* Rule, sometimes called the "right–wrong test," was widely adopted and is still applied in some jurisdictions. Some courts have retained the rule in essence but have modified it with an irresistible impulse test that requires a determination that mental disease overrode reason and judgment and the ability to choose between right and wrong.

The *M'Naghten* Rule has been criticized by scholars and courts as focusing too much on the morality of right and wrong and not enough on the realities of mental disease. A number of jurisdictions instead have applied what is known as the "*Durham* Test," which follows the 1954 federal court of appeals case of *Durham v. United States*.[10] Durham was convicted of housebreaking despite having had a history of hallucinations and psychosis. The court described the appropriate inquiry about responsibility as whether "the unlawful act was the product of mental disease or mental defect."[11] Some courts adopted and still follow this focus on disease.

The insanity defense drew much attention after the 1982 acquittal of John Hinckley, who shot President Ronald Reagan and other officials. Congress and about half of the states responded by legislatively changing their definitions of insanity. The federal Insanity Defense Reform Act of 1984 directed that the defense applies to federal crimes only if "the defendant, as a result of a severe mental disease or defect, was unable to appreciate the nature and quality or the wrongfulness of his acts,"[12] thereby requiring both a finding of mental disease and of an inability to appreciate wrongfulness. Federal law also was amended to require the defendant to prove the condition existed by clear and convincing evidence, a higher burden than proof by a preponderance of evidence as might otherwise be required.

Some jurisdictions also take into consideration a mental condition that does not meet the definition of legal insanity but that is deemed relevant to whether the defendant had the state of mind to satisfy the elements of the crime. This approach is known as "partial responsibility" or "diminished capacity" and is sometimes called "temporary insanity." The diminished capacity defense became notorious in the 1980s after Dan White relied on evidence of a chemical imbalance due to junk food to be convicted of the lesser crime of voluntary manslaughter of San Francisco Mayor George Mascone and Supervisor Harvey Milk. It became known derisively as the "Twinkie defense." California voters reacted to news of the defense with an initiative measure that bars evidence of diminished capacity except as it pertains to the sentence to be imposed.[13]

Someone who is intoxicated has limited mental capacity, but courts do not recognize voluntary intoxication as a form of temporary insanity or diminished responsibility. In 1968 in *Powell v. Texas*,[14] the U.S. Supreme Court upheld a statute making it a crime to be intoxicated in a public place. The defendant relied on a psychiatrist's testimony that alcoholism is a disease that results in compulsion. The Court said that it could not "cast aside the centuries-long evolution of the collection of interlocking and overlapping concepts which the common law has utilized to assess the moral accountability of an individual for his antisocial deeds."[15] Being intoxicated may still be deemed relevant to whether the defendant had the required state of mind to commit a particular crime, such as whether the defendant could have premeditated a murder.

Self-Defense

Self-defense is reasonable use of force for self-protection based on a reasonable belief of imminent danger. The amount of force must be measured to the threat. Self-defense does not allow use of deadly force without a reasonable sense of immediate serious danger. It also does not apply to someone who provokes the difficulty that led to use of force. In other words, someone may not kill in self-defense after inciting a fight.

In general, reasonable use of force is allowed to protect property but not deadly force absent a threat of physical harm. In most jurisdictions the person who claims self-defense must have had a reasonable belief that the force was necessary. In most jurisdictions someone must first try to retreat rather than strike if retreat seems possible with safety. But the law typically does not require retreat from a home. Many states allow greater discretion to use force for self-protection while at home.

Responsibility for Acts of Others

Several crimes punish those who help others commit a crime. An accomplice is someone who knowingly participates in a crime but who does not directly commit the criminal act, such as a driver in a bank robbery. Criminal laws typically subject accomplices to the same punishment as those who are more directly involved. An accessory is someone who is not present at the crime but who assists afterward, such as someone who helps hide stolen money. Accessories typically are subject to different punishment than those whom they assist. Solicitation occurs when someone attempts to get someone else to commit a crime. The crime is asking—the offender need not participate in the solicited act nor need the act be carried out. A typical solicitation statute addresses a particular intended act—such as prostitution or murder—and is assigned a particular punishment.

A conspiracy occurs when two or more individuals agree to commit a crime. Conspiracy responsibility existed at common law and is now the subject of federal and state statutes. For example, a federal statute provides that "[i]f two or more persons conspire either to commit any offense against the United States, or to defraud the United States, or any agency thereof in any manner or for any purpose, and one or more of such persons do any act to effect the object of the conspiracy, each shall be fined under this title or imprisoned not more than five years, or both."[16] Conspiracy is one of the most commonly charged federal crimes.

A conspiracy subjects its participants to prosecution based on their agreement to commit a crime rather than any direct involvement in carrying it out. Courts have upheld such responsibility based on the danger to society posed by those who join together to break the law. Conspirators need not personally know the other co-conspirators nor need they have contemplated the specific crimes actually committed in furtherance of the conspiracy. The conspiracy also need not be successful though most jurisdictions require some overt act toward its accomplishment. Someone can withdraw from further responsibility only with an affirmative step inconsistent with participation, such as by reporting upcoming crimes to the police.

Criminal Procedure

Criminal procedure is intended to insure that the guilty are treated fairly and the innocent are protected from unjust prosecution. Many statutes, judicial interpretations, and procedural and evidentiary rules protect fundamental constitutional rights in criminal procedure. The following are among the salient features of the law governing the actions of police, prosecutors, and others involved in the criminal justice system.

Investigation

Several clauses in the Bill of Rights constrain the power of the police to investigate. Police who violate an individual's rights may be prosecuted for illegal acts themselves and face civil rights liability to those whose rights were violated. As a result of U.S. Supreme Court decisions, misconduct can also affect prosecution of an offender. In some circumstances, evidence is excluded from the prosecution, making it possible for an obviously guilty person to escape criminal responsibility.

Warrants and Exceptions

The constitutional framers sought to protect individuals from police abuse by requiring warrants from judges before individuals or their property may lawfully be seized. The Fourth Amendment provides, "The right of the people to be secure in their persons, houses, papers, and effects, against unreasonable searches and seizures, shall not be violated, and no Warrants shall issue, but upon probable cause, supported by Oath or affirmation, and particularly describing the place to be searched, and the persons or things to be seized." Consistent with this requirement, a federal or state judge or magistrate issues a warrant only based on an application supported by an affidavit of facts about the case and the suspect sufficient to establish probable cause.

In the 1967 case of *Katz v. United States*,[17] the U.S. Supreme Court explained that the warrant requirement limits both the scope and the means of searches and protects that in which individuals have a reasonable expectation of privacy. The Court has decided many cases in which the parties argued about reasonable privacy expectations. The Court held that the Fourth Amendment does not apply to open fields or trash left on the road, but it does apply to listening in on someone's personal phone calls. The Court also has decided many cases involving questions about to whom the warrant requirement applies. For instance, it held that the Fourth Amendment applies to searches in public schools but that educational interests enable authorities to search students based on a reasonable suspicion about evidence of a violation of the law or school rules.[18] Searches and seizures will continue to be a common subject for judicial interpretation. Courts are struggling to delineate zones of privacy in computer files and electronic transmissions, which are now a common focus of police searches.

The Court has recognized exceptions to the warrant requirement for searches in which a reasonable expectation of privacy might otherwise exist. The police may conduct a search without a warrant based on probable cause that exists when the totality of the circumstances justifies a person of reasonable prudence to believe that evidence of a crime will be found.[19] Police also may conduct a search if given permission to do so with a voluntary waiver. Voluntariness is viewed in the totality of the circumstances. Someone can give consent with a gesture or an action such as opening a car trunk, or in some circumstances by failure to protest.

Police may conduct a search incident to an arrest to check for weapons and to prevent the destruction of evidence. Police also may stop and frisk someone to discover weapons based on reasonable suspicion that the person has been engaged in criminal activity, known as a *"Terry* stop" for the case in which the Court approved of the practice.[20] Probable cause is not required for such limited searches. Police also may seize immediately apparent evidence of a crime if the evidence is in plain view.

The Court has held that evidence seized in violation of the Fourth Amendment may not be used against the defendant, which is known as the exclusionary rule. In general, evidence obtained during an illegal search also is excluded as "fruit of the poisonous tree." The Court has explained that the exclusionary rule does not apply to evidence that inevitably would have been discovered regardless of the police error or misconduct.

Self-Incrimination and Miranda Warnings

The Fifth Amendment directs that no person "shall be compelled in any criminal case to be a witness against himself." As the U.S. Supreme Court explained, "Governments, state and federal, are thus constitutionally compelled to establish guilt by evidence independently and freely secured, and may not by coercion prove a charge against an accused out of his own mouth."[21] The protection against self-incrimination applies to civil as well as criminal proceedings whenever the answer might tend to subject the speaker to criminal responsibility.

In the famous case of *Miranda v. Arizona*,[22] the Court applied the exclusionary rule to situations in which suspects held in custody provided evidence without having been warned of their constitutional rights. The Court explained that custodial interrogation involves inherently compelling pressures that undermine a suspect's ability to exercise Fourth Amendment rights. The required Miranda Warnings, beginning with an instruction about a "right to remain silent," have become a familiar part of American culture. Any waiver of the right to the warnings must be given unequivocally, unambiguously, and with apparent understanding of the meaning of the waiver. If the suspect asserts a right to remain silent, the police must stop the interrogation until the suspect has a lawyer present or initiates new communications.

The Court has further explained that the exclusionary rule was meant to deter substantial and deliberate violations of the Fourth Amendment.[23] Accordingly, the Court held that a good faith exception applied when the police reasonably relied on a subsequently invalidated search warrant. The Court also held that truly spontaneous confessions after exercising the right to remain silent are admissible as are responses given to questions aimed not at interrogation but at the immediate safety of the police or the public, such as about the presence of a weapon that the police have reason to believe is nearby.[24]

According to common law, before entering someone's home the police are generally required to announce their presence and to provide residents an opportunity to open the door. Statutes also have been enacted to mandate this warning. The Court has held, however, that the exclusionary rule does not apply to a violation of this "knock and announce requirement." The Court instructed that the public must rely on civil suits and disciplinary action to deter violations of this rule.[25]

Eyewitness Identification

Police commonly use several methods for eyewitness identification of suspects. With a lineup, a witness is asked to identify someone among several people. With a show-up, the witness sees only the suspect. Photo identification also is used. Any of these methods is permissible if it is not unduly suggestive under the circumstances. In *Manson v. Brathwaite*,[26] the Court instructed that a suggestive procedure violates the Constitution only when reliability is compromised sufficiently to create a substantial likelihood of misidentification.

Common witness identification procedures have been widely criticized for failing to account for how easily human memory is affected by suggestion. Faulty witness identification techniques have been cited as a primary cause of wrongful convictions. Some state courts have tried to address these risks by prescribing disqualifying suggestive characteristics based on social science research. Some law enforcement agencies have undertaken to integrate this research into their practices.

Prosecution

Someone becomes a defendant in a criminal trial as a result of a grand jury indictment or a prosecutor's decision to bring charges after an arrest. In the U.S. criminal justice system the government has broad prosecutorial discretion. The U.S. Supreme Court explained that "so long as the prosecutor has probable cause to believe that the accused committed an offense defined by statute, the decision whether or not to prosecute, and what charge to file or bring before a grand jury, generally rests entirely in his discretion."[27] The Court noted that judges ordinarily should defer to prosecutors to consider such appropriate factors as "the strength of the case, the prosecution's general deterrence value, the Government's enforcement priorities, and the case's relationship to the Government's overall enforcement plan."[28] But prosecutors may not make decisions "deliberately based upon an unjustifiable standard such as race, religion, or other arbitrary classification."[29]

Charging and Arraignment

The Fifth Amendment to the U.S. Constitution provides, "No person shall be held to answer for a capital, or otherwise infamous crime, unless on a presentment or indictment of a Grand Jury, except in cases arising in the land or naval forces, or in the Militia, when in actual service in time of War or public danger." A crime is considered infamous based on the authorized punishment, which for federal crimes includes imprisonment for more than 1 year. When a right to a grand jury indictment does not apply, or a defendant waives it, the prosecution charges by filing an "information" in court.

Individuals also may become defendants without an indictment if they are arrested. The Court has held that a suspect arrested without a warrant must appear before a magistrate or judge promptly for a determination of whether there is probable cause that the individual committed a crime. This hearing must occur within 48 hours unless the prosecution can "demonstrate the existence of a bona fide emergency or other extraordinary circumstance."[30]

At an arraignment a defendant enters a plea of guilty, not guilty, or, in the federal courts and some other courts, *nolo contender*, meaning "no contest." A plea of no contest is intended to preserve rights for civil suits but usually is not permitted without the prosecution's cooperation, which is given only in rare circumstances. In most criminal cases defendants plead guilty before trial in a plea bargain for the prosecution's agreement to drop some charges or to recommend a lesser sentence. Before a judge accepts a defendant's guilty plea, the judge engages in a colloquy with the defendant, during which the judge advises the defendant about constitutional rights and the consequences of the plea and inquires whether the plea is truly voluntary. The judge also must determine that there is a factual basis for the guilty plea before accepting it.

At a pretrial hearing counsel will address such things as motions to suppress evidence and whether certain witnesses may testify. Often required hearings are combined and sometimes all occur at one time.

Bail

Bail protects the presumption of innocence by enabling a defendant to be free until the prosecution proves its case to the jury. A right to bail is based on the Eighth Amendment, which provides that "[e]xcessive bail shall not be required," and on the Due Process Clause guaranty that no one may be "deprived of life, liberty, or property, without due process of law."

Bail usually is a deposit of money or a bond provided by a third party that is forfeited if the defendant violates the bail conditions. Bail is set to assure the defendant's appearance at trial, and the amount is based on such things as the seriousness of the offense, the weight of the evidence, and the defendant's resources, ties to the community, and criminal record. The U.S. Supreme Court has held that not everyone is entitled to bail. Bail may be denied in death penalty cases or based on an ongoing threat to individuals or the community.

Prosecutor Disclosures: United States v. Agurs

In both civil and criminal trials a party must share information according to pretrial orders or in response to the other party's discovery requests. Despite disclosure obligations the civil process is fundamentally adversarial, and neither party has an obligation to educate the other.

In criminal trials prosecutors have an obligation to seek justice. As the U.S. Supreme Court said,

> *The United States Attorney is the representative not of an ordinary party to a controversy, but of a sovereignty whose obligation to govern impartially is as compelling as its obligation to govern at all; and whose interest, therefore, in a criminal prosecution is not that it shall win a case, but that justice shall be done. As such, he is in a peculiar and very definite sense the servant of the law, the twofold aim of which is that guilt shall not escape or innocence suffer. He may prosecute with earnestness and vigor—indeed, he should do so. But, while he may strike hard blows, he is not at liberty to strike foul ones.*[31]

Accordingly, statutes and rules of criminal procedure require the prosecution to share information, including evidence of innocence—called exculpatory evidence—with defendants. For example, several of the Federal Rules of Criminal Procedure require the prosecution to disclose evidence that belonged to the defendant or is material to the preparation of the defendant's case. Also, the Jenks Act[32] requires the prosecution in a federal case to produce statements previously made by a witness who testifies for the prosecution if the defendant requests it after the trial testimony.

Prosecutors' disclosure obligations have constitutional dimensions. In the famous case of *Brady v. Maryland*,[33] the Court made clear that prosecutors have a duty to disclose exculpatory evidence pertaining to guilt or punishment. Such evidence is now commonly known as "*Brady* material." Evidence that is withheld contrary to this obligation is inadmissible against the defendant at trial. In the following case the Court discusses the prosecutor's role and the extent to which nondisclosure endangers the defendant's fundamental right to a fair trial.

United States v. Agurs

427 U.S. 97 (1976)

Justice Stevens, writing for the Court.

After a brief interlude in an inexpensive motel room, respondent repeatedly stabbed James Sewell, causing his death. She was convicted of second-degree murder. The question before us is whether the prosecutor's failure to provide defense counsel with certain background information about Sewell, which would have tended to support the argument that respondent acted in self-defense, deprived her of a fair trial under the rule of *Brady v. Maryland*, 373 U.S. 83 (1963).

At about 4:30 p.m. on September 24, 1971, respondent, who had been there before, and Sewell, registered in a motel as man and wife. They were assigned a room without a bath. Sewell was wearing a bowie knife in a sheath, and carried another knife in his pocket. Less than two hours earlier, according to the testimony of his estranged wife, he had had $360 in cash on his person.

About 15 minutes later three motel employees heard respondent screaming for help. A forced entry into their room disclosed Sewell on top of respondent struggling for possession of the bowie knife. She was holding the knife; his bleeding hand grasped the blade; according to one witness he was trying to jam the blade into her chest. The employees separated the two and summoned the authorities. Respondent departed without comment before they arrived. Sewell was dead on arrival at the hospital.

Circumstantial evidence indicated that the parties had completed an act of intercourse, that Sewell had then gone to the bathroom down the hall, and that the struggle occurred upon his return. The contents of his pockets were in disarray on the dresser and no money was found; the jury may have inferred that respondent took Sewell's money and that the fight started when Sewell re-entered the room and saw what she was doing.

On the following morning respondent surrendered to the police. She was given a physical examination which revealed no cuts or bruises of any kind, except needle marks on her upper arm. An autopsy of Sewell disclosed that he had several deep stab wounds in his chest and abdomen, and a number of slashes on his arms and hands, characterized by the pathologist as "defensive wounds."

Respondent offered no evidence. Her sole defense was the argument made by her attorney that Sewell had initially attacked her with the knife, and that her actions had all been directed toward saving her own life. The support for this self-defense theory was based on the fact that she had screamed for help. Sewell was on top of her when help arrived, and his possession of two knives indicated that he was a violence-prone person. It took the jury about 25 minutes to elect a foreman and return a verdict.

The rule of *Brady v. Maryland* arguably applies in three quite different situations. Each involves the discovery, after trial, of information which had been known to the prosecution but unknown to the defense.

In the first situation, typified by *Mooney v. Holohan*, 294 U.S. 103 (1935), the undisclosed evidence demonstrates that the prosecution's case includes perjured testimony and that the prosecution knew, or should have known, of the perjury. In a series of subsequent cases, the Court has consistently held that a conviction obtained by the knowing use of perjured testimony is fundamentally unfair, and must be set aside if there is any reasonable likelihood that the false testimony could have affected the judgment of the jury.

The second situation, illustrated by the *Brady* case itself, is characterized by a pretrial request for specific evidence. In that case, defense counsel had requested the extrajudicial statements made by Brady's accomplice, one Boblit. This Court held that the suppression of one of Boblit's statements deprived Brady of due process, noting specifically that the statement had been requested and that it was "material." A fair analysis of the holding in *Brady* indicates that implicit in the requirement of materiality is a concern that the suppressed evidence might have affected the outcome of the trial.

Brady was found guilty of murder in the first degree. Since the jury did not add the words "without capital punishment" to the verdict, he was sentenced to death. At his trial, Brady did not deny his involvement in the deliberate killing, but testified that it was his accomplice, Boblit, rather than he, who had actually strangled the decedent. This version of the event was corroborated by one of several confessions made by Boblit but not given to Brady's counsel despite an admittedly adequate request.

The holding that the suppression of exculpatory evidence violated Brady's right to due process was affirmed, as was the separate holding that he should receive a new trial on the issue of punishment but not on the issue of guilt or innocence. The Court interpreted the Maryland Court of Appeals opinion as ruling that the confession was inadmissible on that issue. For that reason, the confession could not have affected the outcome on the issue of guilt, but could have affected Brady's punishment. It was material on the latter issue, but not the former. And since it was not material on the issue of guilt, the entire trial was not lacking in due process.

In *Brady*, the request was specific. It gave the prosecutor notice of exactly what the defense desired. Although there is, of course, no duty to provide defense counsel with unlimited discovery of everything known by the prosecutor, if the subject matter of such a request is material, or indeed if a substantial basis for claiming materiality exists, it is reasonable to require the prosecutor to respond either by furnishing the information or by submitting the problem to the trial judge. When the prosecutor receives a specific and relevant request, the failure to make any response is seldom, if ever, excusable.

In many cases, however, exculpatory information in the possession of the prosecutor may be unknown to defense counsel. In such a situation, he may make no request at all, or possibly ask for "all *Brady* material" or for "anything exculpatory." Such a request really gives the prosecutor no better notice than if no request is made. If there is a duty to respond to a general request of that kind, it must derive from the obviously exculpatory character of certain evidence in the hands of the prosecutor. But if the evidence is so clearly supportive of a claim of innocence that it gives the prosecution notice of a duty to produce, that duty should equally arise even if no request is made. The third situation in which the *Brady* rule arguably applies, typified by this case, therefore embraces the case in which only a general request for "*Brady* material" has been made.

We now consider whether the prosecutor has any constitutional duty to volunteer exculpatory matter to the defense, and if so, what standard of materiality gives rise to that duty.

As the District Court recognized in this case, there are situations in which evidence is obviously of such substantial value to the defense that elementary fairness requires it to be disclosed even without a specific request. For though the attorney for the sovereign must prosecute the accused with earnestness and vigor, he must always be faithful to his client's overriding interest that "justice shall be done." He is the "servant of the law, the twofold aim of which is that guilt shall not escape or innocence suffer." *Berger v. United States*, 295 U.S. 78, 88 (1935). This description of the prosecutor's duty illuminates the standard of materiality that governs his obligation to disclose exculpatory evidence.

The proper standard of materiality must reflect our overriding concern with the justice of the finding of guilt. Such a finding is permissible only if supported by evidence establishing guilt beyond a reasonable doubt. It necessarily follows that if the omitted evidence creates a reasonable doubt that did not otherwise exist, constitutional error has been committed. This means that the omission must be evaluated in the context of the entire record. If there is no reasonable doubt about guilt whether or not the additional evidence is considered, there is no justification for a new trial. On the other hand, if the verdict is already of questionable validity, additional evidence of relatively minor importance might be sufficient to create a reasonable doubt.

This statement of the standard of materiality describes the test which courts appear to have applied in actual cases although the standard has been phrased in different language. It is also the standard which the trial judge applied in this case. He evaluated the significance of Sewell's prior criminal record in the context of the full trial which he recalled in detail. Stressing in particular the incongruity of a claim that Sewell was the aggressor with the evidence of his multiple wounds and respondent's unscathed condition, the trial judge indicated his unqualified opinion that respondent was guilty. He noted that Sewell's prior record did not contradict any evidence offered by the prosecutor, and was largely cumulative of the evidence that Sewell was wearing a bowie knife in a sheath and carrying a second knife in his pocket when he registered at the motel.

Since the arrest record was not requested and did not even arguably give rise to any inference of perjury, since after considering it in the context of the entire record the trial judge remained convinced of respondent's guilt beyond a reasonable doubt, and since we are satisfied that his firsthand appraisal of the record was thorough and entirely reasonable, we hold that the prosecutor's failure to tender Sewell's record to the defense did not deprive respondent of a fair trial as guaranteed by the Due Process Clause of the Fifth Amendment.

Justice Marshall, dissenting.

Our overriding concern in cases such as the one before us is the defendant's right to a fair trial. One of the most basic elements of fairness in a criminal trial is that available evidence tending to show innocence, as well as that tending to show guilt, be fully aired before the jury; more particularly, it is that the State in its zeal to convict a defendant not suppress evidence that might exonerate him. This fundamental notion of fairness does not pose any irreconcilable conflict for the prosecutor, for as the Court reminds us, the prosecutor "must always be faithful to his client's overriding interest that justice shall be done." No interest of the State is served, and no duty of the prosecutor advanced, by the suppression of evidence favorable to the defendant. On the contrary, the prosecutor fulfills his most basic responsibility when he fully airs all the relevant evidence at his command.

Under today's ruling, if the prosecution has not made knowing use of perjury, and if the defense has not made a specific request for an item of information, the defendant is entitled to a new trial only if the withheld evidence actually creates a reasonable doubt as to guilt in the judge's mind. With all respect, this rule is completely at odds with the overriding interest in assuring that evidence tending to show innocence is brought to the jury's attention. The rule creates little, if any, incentive for the prosecutor conscientiously to determine whether his files contain evidence helpful to the defense. Indeed, the rule reinforces the natural tendency of the prosecutor to overlook evidence favorable to the defense, and creates an incentive for the prosecutor to resolve close questions of disclosure in favor of concealment.

More fundamentally, the Court's rule usurps the function of the jury as the trier of fact in a criminal case. The Court's rule explicitly establishes the judge as the trier of fact with respect to evidence withheld by the prosecution. The defendant's fate is sealed so long as the evidence does not create a reasonable doubt as to guilt in the judge's mind, regardless of whether the evidence is such that reasonable men could disagree as to its import—regardless, in other words, of how "close" the case may be.

Leaving open the question whether a different rule might appropriately be applied in cases involving deliberate misconduct, I would hold that the defendant in this case had the burden of demonstrating that there is a significant chance that the withheld evidence, developed by skilled counsel, would have induced a reasonable doubt in the minds of enough jurors to avoid a conviction. This is essentially the standard applied by the Court of Appeals, and I would affirm its judgment.

As representatives of the people, prosecutors should make decisions based on the facts and law and in the public's interest. They must honor constitutional rights, including the presumption of innocence. But prosecutors also have legal and often political careers and may be drawn toward choices benefitting self-interest. In addition to actions that are constitutionally required, such as the disclosure obligations described in *United States v. Agurs*, prosecutors are subject to many statutes, court rules, and professional codes of ethics. Those who abuse their positions face disciplinary action, civil lawsuits, and in egregious situations, criminal penalties.

Witnesses

The Sixth Amendment's Confrontation Clause provides that "in all criminal prosecutions, the accused shall enjoy the right . . . to be confronted with the witnesses against him." In a criminal prosecution a right to confront means a right to cross-examine an adverse witness at trial in an attempt to contradict, discredit, or explain. The U.S. Supreme Court has instructed that the Confrontation Clause also applies to interrogation aimed at securing testimony to be used against the accused at trial. The right to cross-examine at trial therefore applies not only to witnesses who appear at the trial for the prosecution but also those whose out-of-court statements will be used at trial, including by means of affidavits or statements given to police.[34]

Right to Counsel

The Sixth Amendment provides, "In all criminal prosecutions, the accused shall enjoy the right . . . to have the Assistance of Counsel for his defence." In *Gideon v. Wainwright*,[35] the U.S. Supreme Court held that the right to criminal defense counsel is fundamental. Someone who cannot afford a lawyer must be provided one at the government's expense. The right applies to defense of any charge that can result in incarceration, whether for a felony or a misdemeanor. It applies at all critical stages in the proceeding, including during custodial interrogation and all court proceedings after the first appearance.

The Court explained that the right to counsel means more than just having a lawyer in attendance. The right is to at least "reasonably effective assistance."[36] A conviction will be set aside if a lawyer is so incompetent in the representation as not to meet this standard if the failures deprived the defendant of a fair trial.

Jury Trial

Section 2 of Article III of the Constitution provides, "The Trial of all Crimes, except in Cases of Impeachment, shall be by Jury" and the Sixth Amendment states, "In all criminal prosecutions, the accused shall enjoy the right to a speedy and public trial, by an impartial jury." The U.S. Supreme Court has held that the jury trial right applies to all "serious" crimes but not to offenses that are considered "petty" under the law and practices. [37] The right to a jury applies to both federal and state trials when the possibility of incarceration is longer than 6 months and may apply to other penalties that are deemed similarly severe.

Speedy Trial

The Sixth Amendment provides, "In all criminal cases the accused shall enjoy the right to a speedy trial." The U.S. Supreme Court described this guaranty as "an important safeguard to prevent undue and oppressive incarceration prior to trial, to minimize anxiety and concern accompanying public accusation and to limit the possibility that long delay will impair the ability of an accused to defend himself."[38] The right to a speedy trial is necessarily relative,[39] and some delays in the interest of public justice may be tolerated depending on the circumstances. Appropriate considerations include the "[l]ength of delay, the reason for the delay, the defendant's assertion of his right, and prejudice to the defendant."[40] If someone has been denied a right to a speedy trial, the court will dismiss an indictment or overturn a conviction.

To insure compliance with the Sixth Amendment, legislatures prescribe time limits for criminal trials. The federal Speedy Trial Act requires trial in most cases no later than 70 days after the indictment or information is filed or the defendant first appears before a judge, whichever is later.[41] The defendant can waive the right or the judge can allow a trial later than the statute requires based on a finding that the interests of justice require it. State constitutions and statutes also prescribe time constraints for criminal trials. A typical state-law requirement may be for a trial within 6 months of indictment for a felony and 3 months for a misdemeanor. Often criminal trials occur later than the speedy trial time limit due to pretrial motions or requests by the defendant for more time to prepare.

Proof beyond a Reasonable Doubt

The U.S. Supreme Court has held that due process prohibits "conviction except upon proof beyond a reasonable doubt of every fact necessary to constitute the crime with which he is charged."[42] The Court explained that "a society that values the good name and freedom of every individual should not condemn a man for commission of a crime when there is reasonable doubt about his guilt. . . . It is critical that the moral force of the criminal law not be diluted by a standard of proof that leaves people in doubt whether innocent men are being condemned."[43] Judges and law scholars disagree about how to define proof beyond a reasonable doubt. The Court upheld a conviction after a jury instruction requiring "an abiding conviction, to a moral certainty, of the truth of the charge," rejecting an argument that the jury would view moral certainty as a lesser requirement than beyond a reasonable doubt.[44] State courts have varying views about the extent to which the jury should be left to define beyond a reasonable doubt itself according to community standards.

Double Jeopardy

The Fifth Amendment provides that no one may "be subject for the same offense to be twice put in jeopardy of life or limb." This Double Jeopardy Clause protects an individual against a second prosecution for the same offense after conviction or acquittal, and from multiple punishments for the same offense. Offenses are considered to be the same for double jeopardy purposes if they contain the same elements. To be different each offense must "require proof of an additional fact which the other does not."[45] State courts may impose additional requirements under their state constitutions.

Double jeopardy is triggered during a jury trial when the jury has been impaneled and sworn and in a trial without a jury when the judge begins to hear evidence. Double jeopardy is not triggered after a mistrial that was declared in response to the defendant's motion or by a dismissal due to manifest necessity such as when the jury is unable to reach a decision.

The U.S. Supreme Court has held that federal and state governments are separate sovereigns, and the Double Jeopardy Clause does not prevent either from prosecuting for the same act.[46] A number of federal statutes nonetheless prohibit dual federal and state convictions for particular crimes, and the U.S. Department of Justice has followed a practice of not prosecuting an offender for the same crime on which there has been a state conviction. Some states have similar statutes, and some courts interpret state constitutions as prohibiting dual federal and state convictions.

Punishment

Criminal codes prescribe minimum and maximum penalties based on the elements of the crime. There are a wide variety of sanctions that may be imposed including monetary fines, probation or suspended sentences with incarceration if conditions are violated, incarceration, mandatory payment of restitution to victims, community service, treatment programs, and other alternatives such as disciplinary training or educational programs. Many states also have the death penalty. Judges usually determine sentences only after post-trial sentencing hearings, which may include testimony by victims and their families.

The right to a jury trial means that the maximum sentence a judge may impose is the maximum based on the facts found by the jury or admitted by the defendant. A judge may not constitutionally impose an enhanced sentence beyond the statutory maximum based on the judge's finding of aggravated circumstances. The only fact on which a judge may base a sentence longer than the statutory maximum is criminal history. Below the maximum the judge may exercise sentencing discretion through an inquiry into any information bearing on the appropriateness of a sentence.[47]

Sentencing Guidelines

In the 1970s and 1980s federal and state governments enacted sentencing guidelines to promote consistency and fairness. Guidelines prescribe sentencing ranges based on the seriousness of the crime and the offender's criminal history. In 1984 Congress passed the Sentencing Reform Act that created the U.S. Sentencing Commission to establish mandatory guidelines. Many judges found the guidelines to be too constrictive and departed from them. The U.S. Supreme Court has since instructed that the sentencing guidelines must be considered as advisory and not truly mandatory.[48]

More than one third of the states have some form of sentencing guidelines. State sentencing guidelines vary with respect to whether they are characterized as mandatory, advisory, or voluntary. Mandatory state sentencing guidelines raise the same constitutionality concerns as the federal guidelines. Some states also have sentencing commissions that perform functions similar to those handled by the U.S. Sentencing Commission for the federal system.

Death Penalty

Nationally there are about 3,000 prisoners who have been given the death penalty, and about 50 prisoners are executed annually.[49] States with the death penalty impose it for murder, and a few authorize it for other serious crimes.

The death penalty has been administered throughout United States history without the U.S. Supreme Court holding that its use necessarily violates the Eighth Amendment's prohibition against cruel and unusual punishments. In the 1972 case of *Furman v. Georgia*,[50] the Court held that Georgia and Texas violated the Eighth Amendment by administering the death penalty in an arbitrary manner. In response states revised their procedures to require a separate sentencing phase at which specific criteria for the death penalty must be considered. The Court later held that the death penalty is cruel and unusual when administered to someone with diminished personal responsibility for the crime such as juveniles[51] and severely mentally impaired persons.[52] In recent cases a majority of the Court has agreed that the death penalty can be constitutionally sustained only if its imposition is consistent with "evolving standards of decency."[53] Based on a review of the consensus of state laws and experiences the Court held that the death penalty could not be imposed for child rape.[54]

Habeas Corpus

Habeas corpus means "have the body." In English law a writ of habeas corpus was issued to bring before the court someone alleging to have been imprisoned unlawfully. The U.S. Constitution acknowledged the availability of this procedure with the Suspension Clause in Article I, which provides, "The privilege of the writ of habeas corpus shall not be suspended, unless when in cases of rebellion or invasion the public safety may require it." The Judiciary Act of 1789 authorized the federal courts to grant the writ to prisoners held in federal custody "for the purpose of an inquiry into the cause of commitment."[55] As the U.S. Supreme Court explained, the writ's purpose "is to test by way of an original civil proceeding, independent of the normal channels of review of criminal judgments, the very gravest allegations."[56] If a petition is successful, the court may order the prisoner's release, reduce the sentence, or more likely remand the case to a trial court for retrial or resentencing.

Federal judges may grant writs of habeas corpus to prisoners in federal or state prisons who are being incarcerated in violation of the U.S. Constitution or federal law. A state prisoner must first exhaust remedies available in the state courts unless circumstances exist that make an available procedure ineffective to protect the prisoner's rights. Those who plead guilty and thereby waive, as a matter of state law, any constitutional claims, may not use federal habeas to revive them. State constitutions and statutes also provide for habeas corpus petitions to be brought in state courts by state prisoners.

Most petitions for habeas corpus are filed by prisoners convicted of violent offenses and the most common claim is ineffective assistance of counsel. Habeas petitions are commonly used to challenge the death penalty. Every year about 4,000 habeas corpus petitions are filed by inmates in federal prisons and over 20,000 by inmates in state prisons.[57]

The historic focus of the writ of habeas corpus was to protect individuals from being detained by executive authorities who did not comply with statutorily authorized procedures. The constitutional provision allowing suspension of the writ when necessary for public safety is set forth in Article I of the U.S. Constitution, which addresses the powers of Congress; the Constitution does not state that the president has any authority to suspend the writ. Nonetheless, during the Civil War President Abraham Lincoln suspended availability of the writ to allow detention of war opponents whom he feared would interfere with conscription and military movements, and he ignored a U.S. Supreme Court writ of habeas corpus issued for suspected rebel John Merryman who was imprisoned at Fort McHenry. More recently the president's power to restrict the availability of judicial review of imprisonment became an issue as President George W. Bush established military commissions and detention centers for noncitizens who were designated as enemy combatants, and the statute defining the federal courts' power to grant writs of habeas corpus was amended to exclude detained enemy combatants.[58]

Review Questions

1. How are elements used to define crimes?
2. What are the four levels of culpability based on mental states under the Model Penal Code?
3. How does the Eighth Amendment restrict the government's authority to make something a crime?
4. What is the "*M'Naghten* Rule," and why has it been criticized?

5. What is the diminished capacity defense, and under what kinds of circumstances has it been applied?

6. When is a warrant for a search required, and what are the principal exceptions?

7. What does *Miranda* require, and what are the principal exceptions?

8. What are a prosecutor's basic obligations to disclose known evidence against a criminal defendant?

9. What are sentencing guidelines, and to what extent are they mandatory?

10. What is a writ of habeas corpus, and to whom does it apply?

Notes

1. U.S. Department of Justice, Bureau of Justice Statistics, Courts and Sentencing Statistics (*available* at http://www.ojp.usdoj.gov/bjs/stssent.htm (last visited Feb. 20, 2009)).

2. *Id*. Correction Statistics (*available* at http://www.ojp.usdoj.gov/bjs/correct.htm (last visited Feb. 20, 2009)).

3. United States v. Hudson & Goodwin, 11 U.S. (7 Cranch) 32, 34 (1812).

4. American Law Institute, Model Penal Code art. 210 (1981).

5. Powell v. Texas, 392 U.S. 514, 533 (1968).

6. 370 U.S. 660 (1962).

7. *Id*. at 665–66.

8. M'Naghten's Case, 8 Eng. Rep. 718 (H.L. 1843).

9. *Id*. at 722.

10. 214 F.2d 862 (D.C. Cir. 1954).

11. *Id*. at 874–75.

12. Pub. L. 98-473, § 402(a) (codified at 18 U.S.C. § 17 (2006)).

13. Cal. Penal Code § 25 (West 1999).

14. 392 U.S. 514 (1968).

15. *Id*. at 535–36.

16. 18 U.S.C. § 371 (2006).

17. 389 U.S. 347 (1967).

18. New Jersey v. T.L.O., 469 U.S. 325 (1985).

19. Illinois v. Gates, 462 U.S. 213, 230–39 (1983).

20. Terry v. Ohio, 392 U.S. 1 (1968).

21. Malloy v. Hogan, 378 U.S. 1, 8 (1964).

22. 384 U.S. 436 (1966).

23. United States v. Leon, 468 U.S. 897 (1984).

24. New York v. Quarles, 467 U.S. 649, 655–59 (1984).

25. Hudson v. Michigan, 547 U.S. 586, 589–602 (2006).

26. 425 U.S. 957 (1976).

27. Bordenkircher v. Hayes, 434 U.S. 357, 364 (1978).

28. Wayte v. United States, 470 U.S. 598, 607 (1985).

29. Oyler v. Boles, 368 U.S. 448, 456 (1962).

30. County of Riverside v. McLaughlin, 500 U.S. 44, 57 (1991).

31. Berger v. United States, 295 U.S. 78, 88 (1935).

32. 18 U.S.C. § 3500 (2006).

33. 373 U.S. 83 (1963).

34. Crawford v. Washington, 541 U.S. 36, 50–59 (2004).

35. 372 U.S. 335 (1963).

36. Strickland v. Washington, 466 U.S. 668, 684–87 (1984).

37. Baldwin v. New York, 399 U.S. 66, 73–74 (1970).

38. United States v. Ewell, 383 U.S. 116, 120 (1966).

39. Beavers v. Haubert, 198 U.S. 77, 87 (1905).

40. Barker v. Wingo, 407 U.S. 514, 530 (1972).

41. 18 U.S.C. § 3161(c)(1) (2006).

42. *In re* Winship, 397 U.S. 358, 364 (1970).

43. *Id.* at 363–64.

44. Victor v. Nebraska, 511 U.S. 1 (1993).

45. Blockburger v. United States, 284 U.S. 299, 304 (1932).

46. Abbate v. United States, 359 U.S. 187, 195 (1959).

47. Blakely v. Washington, 542 U.S. 296, 301–02 (2004).

48. United States v. Booker, 543 U.S. 220, 245 (2005).

49. U.S. Dep't of Justice, Bureau of Justice Statistics (Capital Punishment—2007, Statistics).

50. 408 U.S. 238 (1972).

51. Roper v. Simmons, 543 U.S. 551, 571–75 (2005).

52. Atkins v. Virginia, 536 U.S. 304, 317–21 (2001).

53. Kennedy v. Louisiana, 128 S. Ct. 2641, 2649–50 (2008).

54. *Id.* at 2651–65.

55. Judiciary Act of 1789, ch. 20, § 14, 1 Stat. 73, 81–82 (1789).

56. Townsend v. Sain, 372 U.S. 293, 311–12 (1963).

57. Administrative Office of the U.S. Courts, Judicial Business of the United States Courts, table C-2 (2007).

58. Pub. L. 109-366, § 7(a), 120 Stat. 2635 (2006).

Chapter 11

Administrative Law and Procedure

A government is like fire, a handy servant, but a dangerous master.
George Washington

CHAPTER OBJECTIVES

After studying this chapter you should better understand:

- The governmental functions for which administrative agencies were designed
- The basic requirements of the federal Administrative Procedure Act and its state counterparts
- The constitutional limits on the delegation of legislative authority to administrative agencies
- The scope of judicial review of administrative actions
- The basic requirements for challenging administrative actions

Administrative agencies act in the most and least democratic ways. They act democratically when their decisions emerge from a broadly participatory process. They act undemocratically when they issue decisions about important rights based on rules they made themselves. This paradox puts administrative law in its own category for understanding basic legal principles and practical realities.

Legislators and judges accommodated the expansion of administrative agency power in response to urgent appeals for governmental action. Agency authority over the details of economic and social affairs emerged as a blend of powers that the U.S. Constitution had carefully allocated to separate branches expected to constrain each other's tendency toward the concentration of power. This accommodation occurred without any change to the constitutional framework.

While modern administrative law has taken shape only in recent decades, its influence on individual rights has been profound. Today administrative bodies at the federal, state, and local levels are involved in every major aspect of economic and social life. Several decades ago U.S. Supreme Court Justice Robert Jackson already had seen enough to make this observation:

> *The rise of administrative bodies probably has been the most significant legal trend of the last century, and perhaps more values today are affected by their decisions than by those of all the courts, review of administrative decisions apart. They also have begun to have important consequences on personal rights. They have become a veritable fourth branch of the Government, which has deranged our three-branch legal theories much as the concept of a fourth dimension unsettles our three-dimensional thinking.*[1]

The scope and detail of administrative rules now overlay the statutes and common law that once covered the legal canvas. Despite this proliferation of rules, most people, including many public officials, have little understanding of administrative law. Many of the rules affect only a few and therefore do not attract sufficient public attention to spur opposition. This combination—expansion of government authority without incentives for widespread public involvement—makes it possible for groups to gain previously impossible advantages with government requirements and restrictions. Such opportunities tend to divert productive resources toward efforts to influence self-interested government action, behavior that economists call "rent seeking."[2] Consequently, the legitimacy of administrative authority within a rule of law depends on whether public officials understand their roles and use the legal authority with which they are entrusted to achieve legitimate government goals and promote justice.

This chapter provides an introduction to the nature of administrative power, the basic procedures for its exercise, and the limits that have been retained to protect against arbitrary or unfair decisions. Administrative law is a bewildering array of rules of all sorts, some that prominently affect fundamental rights and others that almost silently address trivia. Entire law school courses are spent studying a single agency's rules. This chapter necessarily focuses on the unifying themes, most central of which is how administrative bodies have been enabled to make rules and apply them in ways not envisioned when the Constitution was ratified.

Development of Administrative Law

Administrative rules have always been part of governance in the United States. The U.S. Constitution authorizes the president to appoint federal department heads and other executive officers. Congress has always conferred power upon these administrative officers to issue rules to "fill up the details" of the legislative policies "the violation of which could be punished by fine or imprisonment fixed by Congress, or by penalties fixed by Congress or measured by the injury done."[3] But before industrialization executive departments carried out the president's policies without much involvement in the details of private economic and social affairs. Courts did not have to confront fundamental questions about how broad agency power could be reconciled with the traditional view of a three-branch government. As agency power rapidly expanded during the twentieth century, legislatures and courts facilitated that expansion but also defined some limits.

Growth of Agencies

Governments expand their role in economic and social matters in response to demands for a solution to a perceived crisis. Historically this occurs during times of war or severe economic contraction. Expanded government authority then becomes permanent as the public accepts what previously would have seen as an unwarranted intrusion on individual liberty.[4] In the twentieth century, government's role expanded beyond the administrative capacity of legislatures or established executive departments. Detailed regulatory programs require expertise in the field of governance and sufficient institutional capacity to generate and apply complex rules. New agencies were created, and existing departments expanded, most rapidly in response to the Great Depression of the 1930s as the federal government intervened in the economy and created permanent national social welfare programs. Later initiatives such as environmental protection resulted in further agency growth at the federal, state, and local levels. As U.S. Supreme Court Justice David Souter recently said, "The proliferation of Government, State and Federal, would amaze the Framers, and the administrative state with its reams of regulations would leave them rubbing their eyes."[5]

No fewer than 13 federal agencies have more than 10,000 employees. Many federal agencies are part of executive departments, such as the Immigration and Customs Enforcement within the Department of Homeland Security, the Bureau of Land Management within the Department of the Interior, the Occupational Safety and Health Administration within the Department of Labor, the Federal Aviation Administration within the Department of Transportation, and the Federal Energy Regulatory Commission within the Department of Energy. The Internal Revenue Service in the Department of the Treasury has about 100,000 employees. Many other agencies are considered independent because they are not part of an executive department. Examples of powerful independent federal agencies include the Securities and Exchange Commission, the Environmental Protection Agency, the Federal Communications Commission, the Federal Reserve Board, the National Labor Relations Board, and the Federal Trade Commission. The independent Social Security Administration has about 62,000 employees. The U.S. Postal Service, which in many respects is a federal agency, is one of the nation's largest employers with about 800,000 employees.

States have agencies with functions similar to federal agencies as well as some that regulate activities that state law entirely or principally governs. Examples of large state agencies include administrative bodies with responsibilities for taxation, environmental protection, labor conditions, education, law enforcement, public safety and transportation, corrections, health and human services, and veterans' affairs.

Administrative Procedure Acts

As agencies expanded in the 1930s, administrative law and procedure became the subject of much scholarly, professional, and governmental attention. As new agencies were created lawmakers tried to balance what they saw as a need for efficient administration with constitutionally required protection of individual rights. In 1946, after 10 years of deliberation, Congress enacted the Administrative Procedure Act (APA) to provide minimum standards for federal agencies. The APA addresses the fundamental aspects of agency rulemaking and adjudication and the availability of judicial review.

The APA authorizes two basic forms of administrative action: rulemaking and adjudication. As described in more detail later in this chapter, rulemaking is similar to legislation. The APA outlines basic rulemaking procedures the essence of which requires agencies to give interested parties an opportunity to study proposed rules and offer comments for the agency's consideration before the rules take effect. The APA also outlines minimum requirements for an adjudication process for agency determinations about particular cases. These requirements include prior notice of a hearing, an opportunity to submit facts and argument, and issuance of preliminary and final decisions. The APA also describes general rules for judicial review of agency actions.

Not all administrative authorities are subject to the APA. Also, many rulemaking and adjudicatory procedures involve additional requirements that lawmakers have imposed or that agencies require according to their rules. But these are variations built on the APA framework.

Most states have administrative procedure statutes that follow the Model State Administrative Procedure Act introduced in 1946 by the National Conference of Commissioners on Uniform State Laws. The state-law model was based on the federal APA. Some states closely follow the model with a single statute setting minimum requirements for administrative rulemaking, adjudication, and judicial review. In other states these subjects are addressed in different parts of the statutes. States also have continually adopted various procedural reforms that apply to administrative procedures generally as well as to particular agencies.

Typically, state administrative procedure statutes apply only to state-level agencies, boards, and commissions, and not to local government boards. As with the federal system, not all state administrative bodies are necessarily subject to the general administrative procedure act. State agency rulemaking and adjudication procedures tend to be similar to those of the federal system, including required publication of proposed rules in a periodical register. The availability and scope of judicial review of state agency action also are similar to the federal approach.

Administrative Powers

The notion that the people consent to be bound by the actions of the government authorized in the Constitution is fundamental to the rule of law. The U.S. Constitution establishes exactly three branches of government: the legislative to make law, the executive to enforce the law, and the judicial to resolve disputes and, as construed by the U.S. Supreme Court, to interpret the law. The Constitution separates these branches into spheres that are intended to restrain each other's authoritarian tendencies. The Constitution does not grant any legal authority directly to administrative agencies. The authority for agency actions is derived from the legislature's delegation of a part of its constitutional authority. This legal construct requires reconciliation of administrative power with the boundaries of the three constitutional branches of government.

Nature of Agency Power

Administrative law does not honor a pristine view of the separation of powers. Agencies make, interpret, and enforce rules. The nature of agency power can best be illustrated with an example of a commonly encountered federal regulatory regime: social security disability benefits.

Congress created the Social Security Administration (SSA) and gave it authority to regulate disability benefits. The nature of the SSA's power is described in the statute as follows:

> *The Commissioner of Social Security shall have full power and authority to make rules and regulations and to establish procedures, not inconsistent with the provisions of [the statutes governing disability insurance], which are necessary or appropriate to carry out such provisions, and shall adopt reasonable and proper rules and regulations to regulate and provide for the nature and extent of the proofs and evidence and the method of taking and furnishing the same in order to establish the right to benefits hereunder.*[6]

Congress set basic guidelines for the SSA to follow in making disability determinations, including a requirement that if the administration disapproves a claim it must provide "a statement of the case, in understandable language, setting forth a discussion of the evidence, and stating the Commissioner's determination and the reason or reasons upon which it is based."[7] But many of the procedural details are left to the SSA to define.

Congress defined a disability that could qualify someone for benefits as an "inability to engage in any substantial gainful activity by reason of any medically determinable physical or mental impairment which can be expected to result in death or which has lasted or can be expected to last for a continuous period of not less than 12 months."[8] A physical or mental impairment under the statute "is an impairment that results from anatomical, physiological, or psychological abnormalities which are demonstrable by medically acceptable clinical and laboratory diagnostic techniques."[9] Additionally, a disability exists under the statute only if the claimant's "impairments are of such severity that he is not only unable to do his previous work but cannot, considering his age, education, and work experience, engage in any other kind of substantial gainful work which exists in the national economy."[10] For most of the details, Congress directed the SSA, through its regulations, to prescribe specific criteria for determining whether these various conditions are met, including whether someone has a "medically determinable physical or mental impairment" or is able to "to engage in substantial gainful activity."[11]

The SSA has promulgated extensive regulations with detailed criteria used to determine whether someone meets the general conditions set in the statute. It publishes a list of recognized impairments.[12] The regulations also provide "medical-vocational guidelines" in the form of a grid of major functional and vocational patterns for determining whether someone who is over age 50 is considered disabled based on the claimant's age, education, and work experience in combination with the maximum sustained work capability.[13] The SSA applies these regulations to specific applications for benefits.

Someone who is denied disability benefits first requests a review within the SSA. If the denial is sustained, the claimant may ask to appear before an administrative law judge, who is an SSA employee. An appeal from the judge's decision goes to the Social Security Appeals Council, also part of the SSA. After exhausting this process the claimant may file an appeal in federal district court. By statute the reviewing court must affirm the SSA if the decision is supported by substantial evidence in the record as a whole and is consistent with the law.[14] The review normally consists of an examination of the record to confirm that the administration followed the regulations and that there was some evidence to support the conclusions. The court will defer to the SSA's resolution of conflicting evidence provided the ruling is at all reasonable.

This example can be replicated for many other exercises of agency authority within the federal and state systems. With many such programs, which sometimes involve millions of claims every year, the rules largely are made, interpreted, and applied by the agencies. Courts are very deferential to the agency action and regularly note the practical impossibility of judicial intervention in the details.

Limits of Delegated Authority

Although the courts have approved of broad legislative delegations of authority to agencies, they also have identified constitutional constraints. The U.S. Supreme Court has noted "that 'the integrity and maintenance of the system of government ordained by the Constitution' mandate that Congress generally cannot delegate its legislative power to another Branch."[15] The Court also has instructed, however, that Congress may delegate authority to executive agencies "according to common sense and the inherent necessities of the government co-ordination."[16] The Court requires that Congress provide "an intelligible principle" for direction in the exercise of delegated authority.[17] The court set this low threshold in 1935 when it struck down two extremely ambitious economic regulatory programs during the Great Depression.[18] Since then the Court has not intervened in regulatory initiatives even when Congress provided only very broad standards. The Court explained that its decisions have "been driven by a practical understanding that in our increasingly complex society, replete with ever changing and more technical problems, Congress simply cannot do its job absent an ability to delegate power under broad general directives."[19]

State courts have followed a similarly deferential approach, requiring only that legislatures provide general guidelines with delegations of authority to agencies. For example, as the Michigan Supreme Court explained its approach, "There is no doubt that a legislative body may not delegate to another its lawmaking powers. It must promulgate, not abdicate. This is not to say, however, that a subordinate body or official may not be clothed with the authority to say when the law shall operate, or as to whom, or upon what occasion, provided, however, that the standards prescribed for guidance are as reasonably precise as the subject matter requires or permits."[20]

The source of an agency's power is the enabling statute that grants it authority. An agency's actions must then be consistent with this mandate and expressed policy directives, but courts will "uphold reasonable and defensible constructions of an agency's enabling act."[21] Enabling acts tend to be very broad. For example, regulators commonly are statutorily authorized to set rates for public utility services that are "just and reasonable" based on cost and such rates may include a "reasonable profit." The regulators then develop complex formulas for calculating permissible rates based on this broad guidance, to which the courts generally defer.

The development of regulatory regimes from general statutory origins can be illustrated with a few examples. At the federal level, consider the Federal Communications Commission (FCC), which regulates radio and television broadcasts. The FCC's regulations became a notorious news item in 2004 after the FCC fined a network $555,000 for performer Janet Jackson's surprise partial nudity—for nine-sixteenths of one second—during the Super Bowl Halftime Show. The FCC's authority to impose the fine begins with a statute that requires a broadcaster to get an FCC license based on the FCC's finding "that public interest, convenience, and necessity would be served."[22] Another federal statute prohibits public broadcast of "any obscene, indecent, or profane language."[23] As part of its licensing authority the FCC promulgates regulations, one of which prohibits broadcast of something that is "obscene" at any time and something that is "indecent" between 6 a.m. and 10 p.m.[24] To enforce its prohibitions the FCC may impose administrative sanctions, including revocation of a license for a willful or repeated failure to comply with the rules.[25] Congress authorized the FCC to impose substantial forfeiture penalties for violations of the statute prohibiting indecent or obscene broadcasts.[26]

The FCC has not specifically defined "obscene" or "indecent" with regulations. It considers material to be impermissibly obscene according to the U.S. Supreme Court's cases that allow regulation of material deemed patently offensive according to community standards. Material that is not obscene cannot be restricted, consistent with the Court's first Amendment cases, unless the government identifies a compelling interest and uses the least restrictive means to achieve it. As a compelling interest to restrict indecent material, the FCC focuses on protecting children from unpredictable depictions of sexually explicit or graphic material, which the FCC says by community standards would be deemed patently offensive.[27] The FCC has imposed penalties in many indecency cases without judicial disapproval. But in a rare instance of judicial invalidation of agency action, a federal court of appeals overturned the FCC's imposition of the $550,000 fine for the Janet Jackson episode. The court held that the FCC had "arbitrarily and capriciously" departed from its policy of tolerating "fleeting broadcast material from the scope of actionable indecency" and that the fine was unsupported by any evidence of a willful or repeated violation for which the statute authorized such a penalty, a view that was later subjected to reconsideration by direction of the U.S. Supreme Court.[28]

Land-use regulations are an example of regulatory programs at the local level. As in most states the New Hampshire statutes empower local municipal boards to regulate land development.[29] Local boards are authorized to adopt regulations addressing a long list of matters pertaining to proposed development.[30] Courts presume land-use regulations to be a lawful exercise of the police power and will sustain them against challenge if the court can discern any "rational tendency to promote the safety and general welfare of the community or to conserve property values throughout the municipality."[31] The statutes set only basic requirements for procedure, such as prior public notice of a hearing.[32] An owner or neighbor can challenge a board's decision in court, but board findings are assumed to be lawful and reasonable, and the person challenging them must prove that there is no reasonable basis for the decision or that a law was misinterpreted. If the court finds that a local board applied the wrong legal rule, the matter will be sent back to the board with instructions about the proper rule to be applied, leaving the applicant to continue with a process before the board whose actions were challenged.

These examples give some insight into common features of regulatory regimes. Consistent with the purpose of administrative authority—empowerment of bodies with the expertise and resources to make decisions at a level of detail the legislature itself could not administer—agencies usually are given wide latitude for making, interpreting, and applying rules. But legislatures still hold the reins and may limit agencies' discretion by narrowing permissible areas of regulation or by defining the details about how it will be exercised.

Standards and Safeguards: *Bring v. North Carolina State Bar*

Administrative law regulates many details of modern life. Some of the most conspicuous regulated activities include home construction, charges for electricity and media services, terms for banking and credit, health-care facility operations, school programs, and qualifications for business and professional licenses. Some rules result from elaborate and conspicuous federal or state regulatory proceedings in which different interests vigorously pursue competing agendas. Other rules are promulgated with little attention.

In the following case the North Carolina Supreme Court considered its state's approach to setting the educational requirements for becoming a lawyer. With an enabling statute the state's legislature delegated rulemaking authority to a Board of Bar Examiners, which adopted a rule that required applicants to be graduates of programs approved by the American Bar Association. The petitioner was an experienced lawyer but did not graduate from a law school that was on the American Bar Association's approved list. The North Carolina State Bar denied her permission to take the bar admission exam.

Bring v. North Carolina State Bar
501 S.E.2d 907 (N.C. 1998)

Justice Webb, writing for the North Carolina Supreme Court.

The petitioner challenges the refusal of the Bar Council to approve New College so that she can sit for the bar examination. She contends that the scheme with which she must comply to take the examination violates the North Carolina Constitution. She also says the refusal of the Council to allow her to take the examination was arbitrary and capricious. We disagree.

The Board of Law Examiners was created by N.C.G.S. § 84-24. This section states in part:

> *The Board of Law Examiners, subject to the approval of the Council shall by majority vote, from time to time, make, alter and amend such rules and regulations for admission to the Bar as in their judgment shall promote the welfare of the State and the profession: Provided, that any change in the educational requirements for admission to the Bar shall not become effective within two years from the date of the adoption of the change.*

Pursuant to this section, the Board of Law Examiners adopted the Rules Governing Admission to Practice of Law. Rule .0702 provides:

> *Every applicant applying for admission to practice law in the State of North Carolina, before being granted a license to practice law, shall prove to the satisfaction of the board that said applicant has graduated from a law school approved by the Council of the North Carolina State Bar or that said applicant will graduate within thirty (30) days after the date of the written bar examination from a law school approved by the Council of the North Carolina State Bar.*

The Bar Council refused to approve New College, and the petitioner was not allowed to sit for the examination.

In determining whether legislation violates the rule that the General Assembly cannot delegate its power to legislate, we are guided by *Adams v. N.C. Dep't of Natural & Economic Resources*, 249 S.E.2d 402 (N.C. 1978), in which we upheld the constitutionality of the Coastal Area Management Act. In that case, we said:

> *In the search for adequate guiding standards the primary sources of legislative guidance are declarations by the General Assembly of the legislative goals and policies which an agency is to apply when exercising its delegated powers. We have noted that such declarations need be only "as specific as the circumstances permit."* N.C. Turnpike Auth. v. Pine Island, Inc., *143 S.E.2d 319, 323 (N.C. 1965). When there is an obvious need for expertise in the achievement of legislative goals the General Assembly is not required to lay down a detailed agenda covering every conceivable problem which might arise in the implementation of the legislation. It is enough if general policies and standards have been articulated which are sufficient to provide direction to an administrative body possessing the expertise to adapt the legislative goals to varying circumstances.*
>
> *Additionally, in determining whether a particular delegation of authority is supported by adequate guiding standards it is permissible to consider whether the authority vested in the agency is subject to procedural safeguards. Procedural safeguards tend to encourage adherence to legislative standards by the agency to which power has been delegated. We thus join the growing trend of authority which recognizes that the presence or absence of procedural safeguards is relevant to the broader question of whether a delegation of authority is accompanied by adequate guiding standards.*

We hold that the legislative goals and policies as set forth in N.C.G.S. § 84-24 combined with procedural requirements in regard to adopting rules and regulations are sufficient to withstand a constitutional challenge. There is a need for expertise in the achievement of the legislative policy. The Board, with its sixty years of experience, can apply its expertise to the issue in a manner which the General Assembly cannot. It is not practical for the General Assembly to micromanage the making of rules for the Board such as what law schools are to be approved. The directions given by the legislature are as specific as the circumstances require. We believe the statutory direction of N.C.G.S. § 84-24 that the Board shall make such rules governing the admission to the bar which will "promote the welfare of the State and the profession," when considered with the other provisions of the statute, means that the Board must make rules governing the admission to the bar which are intended to produce attorneys with the learning and character to serve the public well. Furthermore, we find that there are adequate procedural safeguards in the statute to assure adherence to the legislative standards. N.C.G.S. § 84-24 and N.C.G.S. § 84-21 require that the Bar Council and this Court must approve rules made by the Board. Thus, there is a sufficient standard to guide the Board so that N.C.G.S. § 84-24 does not create an unconstitutional delegation of legislative power.

The petitioner next argues that the policy of the Council in allowing only graduates of ABA-approved law schools to sit for the bar examination was not promulgated as a rule under the Administrative Procedure Act (APA), chapter 150B of the General Statutes, or under N.C.G.S. § 84-21. Because this rule was not promulgated properly, says the petitioner, it was arbitrary and capricious for the Council to rely solely on this rule in excluding her from the bar examination. However, the petitioner concedes that if the rule had been properly promulgated, it would not be arbitrary and capricious to enforce it.

We believe the rule was properly adopted. It was not necessary to adopt the rule in accordance with the requirements of the APA. N.C.G.S. § 84-21 gives specific directions as to how the Board shall adopt rules. These directions must govern over the general rule-making provision of the APA.

The Board's rules, including Rule .0702, were submitted to this Court as required by N.C.G.S. § 84-21 and published at volume 326, page 810 of the North Carolina Reports. This complies with the statutory requirement. Rule .0702 was properly adopted.

Justice Orr, dissenting.

In the case before us, the only guidance given in N.C.G.S. § 84-24 to the Board of Law Examiners is that the Board "make, alter and amend such rules and regulations for admission to the Bar as in their judgment shall promote the welfare of the State and the profession." N.C.G.S. § 84-24 para. 6 (1995). I find this guidance to be totally inadequate in that it is a sweeping delegation of legislative power to the Board of Law Examiners with no guidance or standards being set forth. This broad delegation allows the Board to make policy, rather than follow the policy set by the legislature.

Rule .0702, adopted by the Board of Law Examiners, provides that an applicant "shall prove to the satisfaction of the board that said applicant has graduated from a law school approved by the Council of the North Carolina Bar." The Council's recent practice is to accept only schools that have been accredited by the ABA. The Council's and through it the Board's reliance on ABA accreditation to determine what law schools are satisfactory is essentially a further improper delegation of the original unlawful delegation of authority.

Ms. Bring submitted information to the Board that New College School of Law enrolled its first class in 1973. The law school has a unique mission of preparing students to practice public interest law. Students are required to participate in a formal apprenticeship program and receive on-the-job training as a condition of graduation. The school also has a complete law library and requires similar classes as other law schools. There are over five hundred graduates of New College currently practicing law. New College has been fully accredited since 1982 by the State Bar of California. New College has never sought ABA accreditation and has no plans to do so.

In this case, we have a graduate from a California law school that has been fully accredited by the California State Bar. In addition, Ms. Bring practiced law in good standing in the State of California for fifteen years. She sought an opportunity, not to be automatically admitted to the North Carolina Bar, but to merely sit for the Bar Examination to show her proficiency and ability to practice law in this state. Without even considering the merits of her educational and professional background, but instead relying on an accreditation process by an outside organization, the Board of Law Examiners summarily refused her right to even attempt to obtain a license to practice law by prohibiting her from taking the Bar Exam. Such a decision is arbitrary and capricious and is based solely upon an unlawful delegation of legislative power without benefit of acceptable standards, and a further delegation or abdication by the Board of Law Examiners and the State Bar Council.

Bring v. North Carolina State Bar illustrates how little courts usually require of legislatures to satisfy the requirement that agencies be given a directive "intelligible principle," or as the North Carolina Supreme Court put it, "adequate guiding standards." The incorporation of another association's standards meant that there was no administrative procedure in North Carolina for public participation in decisions about the sufficiency of particular law schools for bar qualification. The majority of the court approved of the legislature's decision to leave such matters to the Board of Law Examiners, a group of North Carolina lawyers appointed by the state bar's governing council. The majority of the court also was satisfied that the board could further delegate the determination about adequate educational qualifications to the American Bar Association's law school accreditation committee. The American Bar Association is a voluntary national association of lawyers headquartered in Chicago. Some law schools have objected to its accreditation process as emphasizing such things as library facilities and faculty publications in traditional law journals and failing to recognize the value of working faculty with practical professional experience and nonconventional students. *Bring* demonstrates that administrative law and procedure can result in governance by rules generated a great distance away from the representative lawmaking process.

Executive Orders

Legislatures delegate legal authority, but they retain some control over agency actions with the purse strings, the power of approval of some appointments, the ability to conduct hearings, and ultimately the power of further legislation to alter the delegated authority. But agencies are part of the executive branch, and the executive also may influence their actions. A common method for exercising such influence is an executive order or other policy directive.

Each recent president has issued hundreds of executive orders, proclamations, memoranda, and other directives. Some state governors and local government executives also have used orders to wield significant influence over state and local administrative bodies. At the federal level executive orders are used to address routine matters such as federal holidays or authority within agencies, but they also can have a profound impact on national policy. One notorious example is President Franklin Roosevelt's executive order resulting in the internment of 120,000 Japanese-Americans. Executive orders also have been used to fulfill presidential political platforms. For example, the "global gag rule," alternatively imposed and withdrawn by Republican and Democratic administrations, denied use of federal funds for overseas health centers that provide abortion counseling.

On a few rare occasions courts have struck down executive orders because they encroached too far on legislative powers. In *Youngstown Sheet & Tube Co. v. Sawyer*,[33] the U.S. Supreme Court declared invalid an executive order directing the Secretary of Commerce to take possession of the country's steel mills in the face of a threatened strike. The Court made the following distinction between the executive's policy discretion and improper attempts at lawmaking: "The President's order does not direct that a congressional policy be executed in a manner prescribed by Congress—it directs that a presidential policy be executed in a manner prescribed by the President."[34] An order that is plainly contrary to a statute or promulgated regulation also is subject to challenge. A federal court of appeals struck down President Bill Clinton's executive order that directed agencies not to enter into contracts with employers who hire strike replacements. The court held that the order contravened a statute that assured employers the right to permanently replace strikers.[35]

Rulemaking

Federal, state, and local administrative bodies issue rules to carry out the authority that legislatures have delegated to them. In common usage "regulations" refer to the rules that have been promulgated to guide the activity of those subject to the agency's authority. Sometimes "regulations" and "rules" are used synonymously. Rules can be categorized as substantive, which prescribe requirement or implement policy, procedural, which guide practices by and before the agency, and interpretive, which explain an agency's understanding of the law or its regulations.

Rules can be aimed at millions of people, such as income tax regulations, or a single enterprise, such as a power-plant license. There are a myriad of federal, state, and local rules, and they are constantly undergoing revision and expansion. The Federal Register, which is the daily publication of federal rules, proposed rules, notices, and executive orders and other presidential documents, now exceeds 80,000 pages annually. The Code of Federal Regulations, which contains the federal rules in effect, has 50 titles and now requires more than 200 printed volumes. State rules are not as numerous but can also be voluminous. For example, California, which has more than 200 state agencies that issue regulations, has an administrative code of 28 titles the printed version of which requires 38 binders.

Obviously not many people regularly scour the federal and state administrative periodicals for proposed rules of interest. In reality most important rules are no surprise to those with a direct interest in them. Rules usually result from an ongoing discussion between agencies and interest groups.

The following section generally describes the procedures for promulgating rules under the federal Administrative Procedure Act. As described above, states have administrative procedure acts that are similar to the federal act and, accordingly, state rulemaking procedures mirror the basic procedures that federal agencies use.

Formal Rulemaking

Formal rulemaking begins with publication of the proposed rule in the Federal Register, followed by an opportunity for public comment through written or electronic submission of information and arguments. Pursuant to sections 556 and 557 of the federal Administrative Procedure Act, with a formal procedure a hearing on the proposed rule is conducted before one or more members of the agency or an administrative law judge. Some proceedings are similar to courtroom trials, involving witnesses, evidence, and opportunities for cross-examination, and rulings by a decision maker.[36] With formal rulemaking, the presiding authority issues an initial decision of which review may be sought from a higher authority within the agency.[37]

Formal rulemaking involves a lengthy and expensive process. An example of use of the formal rulemaking procedure is the Food and Drug Administration's determination about appropriate labeling of foods represented for special dietary use, which is initiated with a petition for an order followed by a 30-day opportunity for objection. If an objection is filed that raises genuine and substantial factual issues, the Secretary of Health and Human Services, after providing further notice in the Federal Register, must conduct a public hearing. The Secretary must then rule on the objections and provide detailed findings of fact. Except in emergencies, the regulation may not take effect until 90 days after the decision, which gives interested parties an opportunity to challenge it with the agency or in court.[38]

Informal and Hybrid Rulemaking

Informal rulemaking does not require the elaborate hearing process involved with formal rulemaking. Under section 553 of the Administrative Procedure Act, with the informal procedure agencies must publish information about proposed rules and afford the public with an opportunity to comment. In most cases the proposed rule must be published at least 30 days before its effective date. The Administrative Procedure Act requires that "[a]fter consideration of the relevant matter presented, the agency shall incorporate in the rules adopted a concise general statement of their basis and purpose."[39] Some actions are expressly exempt from even these minimal requirements, including "a matter relating to agency management or personnel or to public property, loans, grants, benefits, or contracts."[40]

An example of an informal rulemaking is the procedure for setting the maximum driving time allowed for truck drivers. A federal statute authorizes the U.S. Secretary of Transportation to prescribe the "maximum hours of service of employees of, and safety of operation and equipment of, a motor carrier."[41] Maximum service hours are adopted by the Federal Motor Carrier

Safety Administration through a notice and comment procedure in which maximum driving time is specified for a time span.[42] Although informal rulemaking provides the trucking industry with an opportunity to submit arguments about limits that are safe yet allow cost-effective operations, the agency decides the weight to be given to the information. Drivers must restrict their driving time to the limits in the regulations, or they can be stopped on the road, and they and their companies can be subjected to fines.

Informal rulemaking allows public participation in rule adoption and requires that the agency provide a statement of a rule's basis and purpose. It does not require that the agency produce a detailed record tracking the information considered or showing the details of the methodology employed. Some statutes craft a hybrid rulemaking procedure that does not require formal rulemaking hearings but affords interested parties or experts more of an opportunity to participate than informal rulemaking. An example of hybrid rulemaking is the procedure for promulgating air emission standards under the Clean Air Act.[43] The procedure involves many steps not required with informal rulemaking. For example, a statute requires that the Environmental Protection Agency include in its proposed air emission rules a summary of supporting factual data and methodologies and the underlying legal and policy interpretations. The agency must maintain a docket for public submissions and afford interested persons an opportunity to make oral presentations of which a transcript must be made. The promulgated rule must include a response to significant comments and new data that were submitted and may not be based on information or data that were not in the docket. These additional requirements enable industry and environmental experts to submit scientific data and analysis to attempt to persuade the agency in its rulemaking and to later challenge rules as capricious.

Negotiated Rulemaking

Administrative rules often are the product of extended discussions among administrative agency staff and affected industry representatives or other directly interested groups. While the notice-and-comment rulemaking requirements are intended to provide interested parties with an opportunity to express their views to an agency before the rules are adopted, even the most informal process can become adversarial as goals diverge and positions become entrenched. To encourage agencies and those significantly affected by regulations to cooperate in rulemaking, the federal Administrative Procedure Act authorizes "negotiated rulemaking,"[44] and some states have a similar procedure. With negotiated rulemaking the agency asks a neutral party to convene an advisory committee of agency personnel and public interest groups to develop a proposed rule to be subjected to public comment. A typical committee consists of a dozen or more members. A neutral facilitator leads the meetings. If a committee cannot reach a consensus, the agency follows the normal rulemaking procedure. But when a committee is able to reach a consensus, the rule is less likely to be subjected to legal challenges, and the rule is therefore more apt to be implemented without significant delays common for other procedures. Use of committees may also result in better cooperative relationships between agencies and those whom they regulate.

Public Petitions for Rulemaking

Administrative procedure acts afford the public with the opportunity to petition agencies to make new rules or to change old ones. Some agency rulemaking procedures are designed to accommodate external requests for rulemaking, such as for approval of a new food additive or drug. For other situations in which the agency normally initiates rulemaking, the federal Administrative Procedure Act provides, "Each agency shall give an interested person the right to petition for the issuance, amendment, or repeal of a rule."[45] State administrative procedure statutes contain similar provisions.

Public petitions for rulemaking are most commonly submitted by organizations representing industries, consumer groups, and environmental protection groups. The agency to which a petition is submitted has wide discretion to reject it or to grant it and to commence a rulemaking procedure. The U.S. Supreme Court explained that agencies must have discretion to manage their limited resources, and, as the Court said, court review of agency responses to public requests for rulemaking are to be "extremely limited" and "highly deferential."[46] Not surprisingly, few rulemaking procedures are begun with a request from the public.

Administrative Adjudication

Legislatures create agencies to address a perceived need to regulate a particular activity, and agencies promulgate rules to govern those activities in the future. Some rules have widespread application, but others are directed at a single activity, such as approval of a new drug or a license for a new nuclear power plant. The absence of a general rule does not mean that an agency is without power to deal with specialized problems that arise. As the U.S. Supreme Court explained,

> *Not every principle essential to the effective administration of a statute can or should be cast immediately into the mold of a general rule. Some principles must await their own development, while others must be adjusted to meet particular, unforeseeable situations. In performing its important functions in these respects, therefore, an administrative agency must be equipped to act either by general rule or by individual order. To insist upon one form of action to the exclusion of the other is to exalt form over necessity.*[47]

The Court further explained that "the choice made between proceeding by general rule or by individual, *ad hoc* litigation is one that lies primarily in the informed discretion of the administrative agency."[48]

Some agencies make very specific decisions about how statutes and regulations apply to particular cases. Agencies grant licenses, award benefits, and order compliance with regulations. Many of these decisions are made in the context of a fact-finding process similar to a trial, which in administrative law is called an "adjudication." Adjudications are also sometimes called "quasi-judicial" to reflect their similarity to court procedure. As described in Chapter 3, procedures that determine rights must satisfy due process, and the analysis of a procedure's sufficiency depends on three considerations: the importance of the interest at stake to the individual, the extent to which additional procedures are likely to result in a more reliable determination, and the burdens additional procedures would impose on the government.

Decision Makers

In an administrative procedure the decision maker can be the agency's presiding authority, such as a board or commission, or an individual official acting in the name of the agency. Commission or board members commonly preside over hearings before state agencies and local boards. Some decisions are initially made by one authority and reviewed by another within the same agency.

Many federal agencies employ administrative law judges. The position of administrative law judge, formerly called "hearing examiner," was created by the Administrative Procedure Act of 1946. Although the concept was to create a neutral arbiter, administrative law judges are employees of the agency for which they apply regulations. Nonetheless they conduct proceedings in a judicial manner. As the U.S. Supreme Court said, "There can be little doubt that the role of the modern federal hearing examiner or administrative law judge within this framework is 'functionally comparable' to that of a judge."[49] To create some distance from agency influence in the federal system, all federal administrative law judges' compensation and promotion are determined by a single federal Office of Personnel Management.

Procedure

Procedures for adjudications vary widely among the federal, state, and local agencies and other bodies that conduct them. At one extreme the procedure resembles a judicial trial with a judge, rules of evidence, and witnesses placed under oath and subjected to cross-examination. At the other extreme the process looks more like a meeting in which a proposal is discussed.

The federal Administrative Procedure Act gives only general guidance about adjudication procedure.[50] It requires that the subject of a proceeding be given timely notice of a hearing and the factual and legal matters involved and be afforded an opportunity to submit facts and arguments. Agencies may define their rules for taking evidence and for conducting the hearing. Large federal agencies adopt rules of practice and procedure that are similar to federal rules of civil procedure and evidence. Hearings at the state and local levels tend to follow less formal strictures. Hearings at the local level commonly are conducted according to basic parliamentary rules. For example, a hearing on an application may begin with an introduction by board members or employees, an opportunity for the applicant to describe the request, an opportunity for public comment, and board deliberations. The absence of strict rules and the inclination to be informal and tolerant of opinions at local hearings can result in lengthy and occasionally unruly sessions.

Investigation

Many individuals and institutions are required to provide information to administrative bodies in connection with regulatory requirements. To give just a few examples, individuals and businesses must file income tax returns with the Internal Revenue Service in connection with tax obligations; many workplaces must file reports with the Occupational Safety and Health Administration in connection with safety rules; and publicly traded companies must file disclosures about stock ownership and financial affairs with the Securities and Exchange Commission. Massive amounts of information are collected and maintained by agencies at the federal, state, and local levels. It can be used for serious adverse decisions, including compliance orders and monetary penalties. Agencies may also refer matters to justice departments for criminal prosecution.

Legislatures sometimes give investigatory powers to agencies to collect information needed to enforce their regulations, including subpoena powers to compel production of documents and witness testimony. For example, the U.S. Securities and Exchange Commission is statutorily authorized to investigate suspected violations of the federal securities laws and for that purpose may issue subpoenas for witnesses and for the production of any records that "the Commission deems relevant or material to the inquiry."[51] Many other federal and state agencies have similar subpoena powers. If a subpoena recipient does not comply, the agency may file an action in court for an order to compel a response. To object to a subpoena the recipient may ask a court to quash it. The courts impose a low threshold for administrative subpoenas. An agency need not show probable cause as with a search in a criminal investigation. The U.S. Supreme Court has instructed that administrative subpoenas are to be enforced unless they seek information "plainly incompetent or irrelevant to any lawful purpose" of the agencies' consideration.[52]

Agencies also collect information about regulatory compliance from sources other than the subjects of the investigation, such as bank records that reveal a subject's financial affairs. The U.S. Supreme Court held that the subjects of regulatory investigations do not have a constitutional right to prior notice of subpoenas on third-party record holders. The Court said that requiring prior notice "would be highly burdensome" for both the agency and the courts and that such notice would "increase the ability of persons who have something to hide to impede legitimate investigations."[53] Consequently, in collecting information, as in many other administrative actions, agencies have wide latitude to focus their efforts as they choose.

Judicial Review

As a practical matter agency legal interpretations, and the decisions made based on those interpretations, cannot be made contingent on a court's determination that it would reach the same interpretation or make the same decision. But giving agencies unlimited discretion to interpret laws and determine rights would give them authority not entrusted to any single entity in the U.S. Constitution, and it would be contrary to the fundamental nature of a rule of law. Courts have therefore tried to strike a balance between appropriate deference to agency expertise and protection of individual rights against abuses of discretion.

Scope of Review

The likelihood that a court will overturn an agency decision depends on the court's scope of review. The scope is limited in several ways. It is limited with respect to what can be presented to the court for its review. With few exceptions courts will consider only facts that were presented and arguments that were made to the agency whose decision is under review. Courts regularly note that allowing parties to introduce new material upon judicial review is inefficient and unfair to the agency and to other parties. The scope of judicial review also is limited with respect to the deference accorded agency decisions. Courts will not substitute their own views about conflicting but plausible facts, and they will not overrule reasonable agency legal interpretations. Courts will intervene only when agency decisions fall outside these highly deferential boundaries.

When agencies promulgate rules they must abide by any parameters set in the statute that delegated rulemaking authority to them. Within those parameters agencies have discretion to make rules that will accomplish the legislative directive. The U.S. Supreme Court explained in *Chevron U.S.A., Inc. v. Natural Resources Defense Council, Inc.*,[54] that an unclear legislative directive does not empower the courts to impose their own interpretation. The Court said, "Rather, if the statute is silent or ambiguous with respect to the specific issue, the question for the court is whether the agency's answer is based on a permissible construction of the statute."[55] In a later case, the Court further explained that the appropriate degree of deference depends on "the circumstances, and courts have looked to the degree of the agency's care, its consistency, formality, and relative expertness, and to the persuasiveness of the agency's position."[56]

In most cases the standard of review for an agency action is a deferential default standard set in the federal Administrative Procedure Act[57] and in similar state administrative procedure statutes. According to this standard a court will overturn an action if it is unconstitutional, exceeds statutory authority, or materially violates statutorily required procedure. Otherwise actions are overturned only if they are "arbitrary," "capricious," an "abuse of discretion," or "unsupported by substantial evidence."[58] As the U.S. Supreme Court explained, the review is "narrow and a court is not to substitute its judgment for that of the agency."[59] The court looks for "a satisfactory explanation for [the agency's] action including a 'rational connection between the facts found and the choice made.'"[60] As the Court also explained, "Normally, an agency rule would be arbitrary and capricious if the agency has relied on factors which Congress has not intended it to consider, entirely failed to consider an important aspect of the problem, offered an explanation for its decision that runs counter to the evidence before the agency, or is so implausible that it could not be ascribed to a difference in view or the product of agency expertise."[61] Such circumstances are rarely found to exist.

The Record: *Frankel v. Board of County Commissioners of Teton County*

The meaningfulness of any court review of an administrative action depends on the availability of a record that shows the information on which the challenged action was based and the rationale given for it. Without a record a court has no way to determine that an action was anything other than arbitrary. To address this necessity federal and state statutes often prescribe recordkeeping requirements, and some agencies have very well-developed procedures for keeping a thorough record of submissions and agency deliberations. Records of local administrative body proceedings and decisions are more apt to be sketchy. Often local board members are volunteers who meet in the evenings and listen to many hours of presentations. The board's record keepers may not see the need for extensive documentation of seemingly routine matters, and they may encounter understandable practical difficulties keeping track of all that occurs.

The following is part of a Wyoming Supreme Court opinion reviewing a local land-use board decision that rejected a grading permit for a driveway that would lead to a huge new home on a ridge line. As is often the case in such matters, the board's focus was on the impact of the ultimate proposal rather on than the precise lines of legal authority for approval of a driveway grading permit. As the court struggles to determine whether there was a reasonable basis for the board's denial of the application, the court discusses the importance of the record to judicial review.

Frankel v. Board of County Commissioners of Teton County
39 P.3d 420 (Wyo. 2002)

Justice Hill, writing for the Wyoming Supreme Court.

Appellant, Sheldon Frankel (Frankel), asks that we review a decision of the Appellee, Board of County Commissioners of Teton County (Board), which denied his application for a grading and erosion control permit. Frankel contends that, in denying his application, the Board erred in considering regulations pertaining to land development, rather than just those pertaining to a grading and erosion control permit. The Board considered its skylining regulations, apparently because the grading and erosion control permit was an application to build a driveway to a proposed home site. The skylining regulations limit construction along a ridgeline that is visible from certain roadways in Teton County, *i.e.*, the home may not be built into the skyline. The Board determined that there was an "alternative site" on Frankel's property where a home could be built without invading the skyline.

Frankel contends there is not substantial evidence to support that finding. Frankel also contends that the Board inappropriately relied upon opinion testimony from interested parties and factors unrelated to the decision at hand, and that these errors render the Board's decision arbitrary and capricious, as well as a violation of his rights to due process of law. Frankel asserts that the Board has made exceptions to the skylining regulations in other cases and that he is the victim of unequal or disparate treatment. Continuing, Frankel contends the skylining regulation is void for vagueness, and that the Board violated his due process rights by not affording the full protections required under his right to have a contested case hearing.

We agree that the Board failed to follow required procedures in resolving this matter and, therefore, we will reverse.

We will provide only a brief overview of the facts because our disposition does not rely on what little factual material is contained in the record available for judicial review. In October of 1999, Frankel purchased the property at issue in this case with the intent that he would build a 10,000 square foot home on the ridge that ran through the lot. That location would have allowed Frankel to maximize the size of the home to be built, whereas other locations on the lot may have permitted only the construction of a home of considerably smaller size (only 6,000–8,000 square feet). Frankel had made informal inquiries of Teton County Planning personnel to determine if he could build a house on the ridgeline, and the preliminary inquiries led him to believe that he could build just such a home. Of perhaps greater importance, the location on the ridgeline provided spectacular views of the Tetons, including the Grand Teton. Other locations on the lot did not afford Frankel that same view. Of course, an important factor with respect to the view is that it was "a million dollar view," both figuratively and literally.

In March 2000, Frankel submitted an application for a grading and erosion control permit to the Teton County Planning Department. The purpose of that permit would have been to allow Frankel to build a driveway beginning at the cul-de-sac at the lower elevation of the lot and ascending to the ridgeline of the lot. Based on the record extant, the purpose of the driveway obviously was to gain access to a home site where Frankel wanted to build a home on the ridgeline location. On March 24, 2000, the Teton County Planning Department denied Frankel's application for the permit, basing their denial on a matter seemingly unrelated to the matter of grading and erosion control, to-wit:

> *Development shall not penetrate the Skyline on buttes and hillsides, as viewed from any public road, except in the case of an existing lot where there is no other siting alternative that complies with the standards of these Land Development Regulations.*

Further regulations set out mitigation efforts required where skyline penetration is necessary. Frankel considered that the rejection of his application for a grading and erosion control permit on that basis to be improper because he had not submitted plans to build a home. On the other hand, some of the materials submitted by Frankel made it clear that the building of the driveway was the first step in his plans to build just such a home. Frankel appealed that decision to the Board and by order signed on August 15, 2000, the Board upheld the planning department's denial of his permit application.

What we are able to glean from the record is that Frankel submitted an application for a grading and erosion control permit, and the application was denied because the Board determined that Frankel's proposed home would violate the skylining regulations, and he had an alternative building site on his lot. Frankel argued that the skylining regulations should not have been applied to his grading permit. Irrespective of the fact that Frankel himself sought approval of the ultimate building site through the submittal of the grading permit, the only logical conclusion that can be reached after a review of the Land Development Regulations is: It is appropriate and sensible to determine at the earliest stage possible whether a building site is acceptable before substantial time and effort are expended designing a residence in a particular location, so later that location will not be deemed unacceptable because the residence violates the skylining prohibition. The skylining regulation applies to all "development," and the grading permit is a "development permit" within the meaning of the regulations. On remand, the county commission must determine whether the requirements of the skylining regulation can be met if the residence intended to be accessed by the proposed driveway is constructed at the location proposed.

It also seems clear that Frankel acquiesced in the proceedings that the Board conducted and sought review only once the result was contrary to his hopes. Nonetheless, in conducting a contested case hearing, it is the Board which must conform its proceedings to the governing law. All involved agreed that this matter constituted a contested case. Yet, the hearing was conducted as a legislative hearing without sworn testimony or examination and cross examination and even included consideration of random comments from the public. In addition, the record is incomplete and sketchy and even devoid of such essential facts as evidence of proper notice as required by statute, consideration and disposition of an alleged request for rehearing, and identification of some of the witnesses providing "testimony." The record contains only limited excerpts from the county's regulations. Apparently, § 5120 constitutes the county's rules of practice and procedure governing contested cases as required by Wyo. Stat. Ann. § 16-3-102(a). The confusion inherent in this case likely stems from the failure of these regulations to clarify that participants in contested cases, such as the appeal of the planning director's denial of a development permit, are entitled to discovery, cross-examination, and other procedures appropriate to a trial-type hearing. Failure to follow such procedures resulted in a record, which is so inadequate that this Court is unable to conduct any meaningful review. In matters as important as the approval or disapproval of the use of a person's property, it is critical that all parties know the procedures in advance and that those procedures insure a fair and careful consideration of all the evidence.

Likewise deficient is the final order, which fails to contain a "concise and explicit statement of the underlying facts supporting the findings," as required by Wyo. Stat. Ann. § 16-3-110. In fact, the final order contains only one finding of fact related to the matter in controversy, which states simply that the County Engineering Department "determined that other siting alternatives exist for the location of a residence on Appellant's lot that will not result in the residence penetrating the skyline on the West Gros Ventre Butte." Leaving aside the question of whether substantial evidence existed in the record to support such a finding, it fails to provide such obvious underlying facts as where this site is located, what size house could reasonably be constructed on such site, and whether such a house could in fact be built there in light of other requirements of the Land Development Regulations. In addition, no findings are made by the county commission with regard to these facts. We are left with no option but to remand this matter back to the county commission with the direction that an appropriate, trial-type hearing be conducted in this contested case, and that full and complete findings of fact be made which may be reviewed by this Court.

Here, the record is so deficient and in such a state of confusion that we are unable to perform our duty in passing on errors raised and in reviewing the order issued by the Board. For this reason, the matter is remanded to the district court with directions that it be further remanded to the Board for further proceedings, which shall begin anew.

In *Frankel* the court acknowledged the well-developed body of law allowing administrative bodies broad discretion to make decisions regarding matters statutorily delegated to them. As the court said, it will only look to "insure a fair and careful consideration of all the evidence." For the most part, court review of administrative decisions is limited to insuring that the administrative bodies follow the statutes and their own rules and not make seemingly arbitrary decisions. But without a record of the facts on which the body relied and the rationale for its decision, the court is unable to determine whether even these minimum constraints were honored. *Frankel* demonstrates that court review of local regulatory decisions sometimes gets stalled because of problems with the record. Failure to keep an adequate record not only subjects actions to being overruled but also results in unnecessary costs for the parties and the public.

Protected Interests

Someone who is the object of an agency regulation or adjudication normally will have a right to judicial review. More difficult questions arise when someone who is not the object of agency action wishes to challenge it. Courts could not manage legal challenges to agency actions from every quarter. This problem is addressed with the concept of "standing," which refers to the right of someone with a sufficient interest in an action to ask a court to review it.

The federal Administrative Procedure Act embodies a broad view of standing. It states, "A person suffering legal wrong because of agency action, or adversely affected or aggrieved by agency action within the meaning of a relevant statute, is entitled to judicial review thereof."[62] Such a broad definition is not constitutionally required. The U.S. Supreme Court has delineated a constitutional minimum to determine whether someone has standing to seek relief in federal court. Constitutionally, a federal court only has jurisdiction over cases or controversies involving the parties before it. According to the Court someone seeking to challenge government action must satisfy three conditions to have standing. First, the person must have suffered an "injury in fact" that is "concrete and particularized" and "actual or imminent," not conjectural or hypothetical. Second, this injury must be connected to the action being challenged. Third, standing exists only if this injury "likely" will be "redressed by a favorable decision."[63] Application of these standing requirements does not always reveal neat distinctions. For example, the Court held that visits to an affected wildlife habitat was an insufficient basis to challenge a regulation affecting endangered species,[64] but later held in a different case that regular use of an area affected by a wastewater treatment plant was sufficient for standing to challenge a water discharge permit.[65]

Individuals usually do not have sufficient personal interest or resources to challenge agency regulations. Industry groups or other associations may seek to challenge regulations in behalf of their members or as part of their policy agendas. An association may have standing in its own right if its interests as an association are involved. The U.S. Supreme Court has instructed that association may sue as a representative of its individual members only if three conditions are met. First, when an association sues in behalf of its members, the members must individually satisfy the standing requirements. Second, the interests affected by the challenged action must be germane to the association's purpose. Third, there must be no requirement that the individuals participate directly, as could be the case if members had differing interests.[66]

Exhaustion of Remedies

In most cases of requests for judicial review, the party seeking it must first have exhausted all opportunities for relief within the agency whose action is being contested. This "doctrine of exhaustion of administrative remedies" insures that agencies have the opportunity to consider the matters that the legislature entrusted to them rather than allow piecemeal court intervention. Requiring completion of the administrative procedure also provides an opportunity for agencies to assemble an appropriate record for judicial consideration.

Exhaustion of remedies is sometimes required by the statute governing the administrative authority. Even without such an express requirement courts usually require exhaustion of administrative remedies as a matter of efficiency and fairness to the agency. In an unusual situation involving potential prejudice, courts will not require exhaustion of all avenues for administrative relief, such as if rights would be irretrievably lost before the administrative process could run its course. Similarly, further administrative proceedings may not be required if the agency has no power to grant the requested relief, such as if the appeal is to challenge a statute's constitutionality. Courts also have made rare exceptions when an administrative body expressed an agency-wide position that left no question about disposition of the administrative procedure. But in the usual case an attempt to circumvent any part of the administrative process will be unsuccessful.

Review Questions

1. What caused the growth of administrative agencies?
2. What are the constitutional limits on the delegation of legislative authority to administrative agencies?
3. What are the basic requirements for formal rulemaking under the federal Administrative Procedure Act?
4. What are the basic requirements for informal rulemaking under the federal Administrative Procedure Act?
5. What is hybrid rulemaking?
6. What is negotiated rulemaking?

7. What are the basic requirements for administrative adjudication under the federal Administrative Procedure Act?

8. What kinds of investigatory powers do administrative agencies have, and by what authority do they acquire them?

9. What is the basic scope of judicial review of administrative action?

10. What are the basic requirements for standing to contest an agency's action?

Notes

1. F.T.C. v. Ruberoid, 343 U.S. 470, 487 (1952) (Jackson, J., dissenting).

2. "Rent seeking" was first employed in this context by Anne Krueger and later developed by Gordon Tullock with whom the term is commonly associated. Gordon Tullock, *Rent Seeking*, in vol. 5 The Selected Works of Gordon Tullock, The Rent-Seeking Society 11, 11, 25 (Charles K. Rowley Ed., 2005).

3. United States v. Grimaud, 220 U.S. 506, 517 (1911).

4. *See* Robert Higgs, Crisis and Leviathan (1987) (describing the "ratcheting" of government power over economic and social affairs in response to national emergencies).

5. Alden v. Maine, 527 U.S. 706, 807 (1999) (Souter, J., dissenting).

6. 42 U.S.C. § 405(a) (2000).

7. *Id*. § 405(b)(1).

8. *Id*. § 423(d)(1)(A).

9. *Id*. § 423(d)(3).

10. *Id*. § 423(d)(2)(A).

11. *Id*. § 423(d).

12. 20 C.F.R. pt. 404, subpt. P, app. 1 (2008).

13. *Id*. app. 2.

14. 42 U.S.C. § 405(g) (Supp. 2005).

15. Mistretta v. United States, 488 U.S. 361, 371–72 (1989) (quoting field v. Clark, 143 U.S. 649, 692 (1892)).

16. J. W. Hampton, Jr., & Co. v. United States, 276 U.S. 394, 406 (1928).

17. *Id*. at 409.

18. A.L.A. Schechter Poultry Corp. v. United States, 295 U.S. 495 (1935); Panama Refining Co. v. Ryan, 293 U.S. 388 (1935).

19. Mistretta v. United States, 488 U.S. 361, 372 (1989).

20. Osius v. City of St. Clair Shores, 75 N.W.2d 25, 27 (Mich. 1956).

21. Bureau of Alcohol, Tobacco & Firearms v. Federal Labor Relations Auth., 464 U.S. 89, 97 (1983).

22. 47 U.S.C. § 309(a) (2000).
23. 18 U.S.C. § 1464 (2006).
24. 47 C.F.R. § 73.3999 (2008).
25. 47 U.S.C. § 312 (2000).
26. *Id*. § 503(b).
27. F.C.C. v. Pacifica Found., 438 U.S. 726, 732 (1978).
28. CBS Corp. v. F.C.C., 535 F.3d 167 (3rd Cir. 2008), *vacated and remanded*, 129 S. Ct. 2176 (2009).
29. N.H. Rev. Stat. Ann. § 674:35 (2007).
30. *Id*. §§ 674:36, :44.
31. Rockingham Hotel Company v. North Hampton, 146 A.2d 253, 255 (1958).
32. N.H. Rev. Stat. Ann. § 676:1–7 (2007).
33. 343 U.S. 579 (1952).
34. *Id*. at 588.
35. Chamber of Commerce of the U.S. v. Reich, 74 F.3d 1322 (D.C. Cir. 1996).
36. 5 U.S.C. § 556 (2006).
37. *Id*. § 557.
38. 21 U.S.C. §§ 343 (j), 371(e) (2006).
39. 5 U.S.C. § 553(c) (2006).
40. *Id*. § 553(a).
41. 49 U.S.C. § 31502(b)(1) (2000).
42. 49 C.F.R. pt. 395 (2008).
43. 42 U.S.C. § 7607(d) (2008).
44. 5 U.S.C. §§ 561–570a (2006).
45. *Id*. § 553(e).
46. Massachusetts v. E.P.A., 549 U.S. 497, 527–28 (2007).
47. S.E.C. v. Chenery Corp., 332 U.S. 194, 202 (1947).
48. *Id*. at 203.
49. Butz v. Economou, 438 U.S. 478, 513 (1978).
50. 5 U.S.C. §§ 554, 556 (2006).
51. 15 U.S.C. § 78u(b) (2006).
52. Endicott Johnson Corp. v. Perkins, 317 U.S. 501, 509 (1943).
53. S.E.C. v. O'Brien, 467 U.S. 735, 749–50 (1984).
54. 467 U.S. 837 (1984).
55. *Id*. at 842–43.
56. United States v. Mead, 533 U.S. 218, 228 (2001).
57. 5 U.S.C. § 706 (2006).

58. *Id.*

59. Motor Vehicle Mfrs. Ass'n v. State Farm Mutual Auto. Ins. Co., 463 U.S. 29, 43 (1983).

60. *Id.* (quoting Burlington Truck Lines, Inc. v. United States, 371 U.S. 156, 168 (1962)).

61. *Id.*

62. 5 U.S.C. § 702 (2006).

63. Lujan v. Defenders of Wildlife, 504 U.S. 555, 560–61 (1992).

64. *Id.* at 562–67.

65. Friends of Earth, Inc. v. Laidlaw Environmental Services, Inc., 528 U.S. 167, 180–83 (2000).

66. Hunt v. Washington State Apple Advertising Comm'n, 432 U.S. 333, 343 (1977).

Chapter 12

Public Ethics Law

The essence of immorality is the tendency to make an exception of myself.

Jane Addams

CHAPTER OBJECTIVES

After studying this chapter you should better understand:

- Possible criminal sanctions for abuse of public authority
- Public officials' accountability for violations of constitutional requirements
- The nature of public ethics laws and their limitations on participation in public deliberations and receipt of outside rewards
- The basic nature of federal and state ethics authorities and their responsibilities
- The basic nature of laws restricting third-party dealings with the government

A rule of law depends on the perceived legitimacy of the actions of those who enact and administer the formal laws. The prerequisite culture of integrity is built on the everyday choices of public leaders and the many others employed by federal, state, and local governments. Formal rules cannot create an ethical culture, but they are a means to reinforce the public's commitment to it and for removing from responsibility those who threaten to undermine it.

The public's perception of their leaders' ethics suffers from notorious examples of individuals who were entrusted with power and abused it. There is a widespread sense that decisions are made by bureaucrats who are shaded from public scrutiny. But most of those who carry out the routine business of government are part of the nation's social fabric, working in government offices and volunteering for service. To an extraordinary extent most honor the public's trust by carrying out their responsibilities faithfully. Unfortunately the temptation of personal gain causes some to forsake the public's interest.

Federal, state, and local governments enact ethics laws and standards as guideposts away from such conduct. These laws also provide authority for disciplinary action, removal, and punishment when necessary. In 2005 a special commission convened by the New Jersey Governor, comprised of judges, attorneys, scholars, and other political and public leaders, identified these three necessary conditions for integrity in government: "First, public officials must know and understand the governing ethics strictures and permissible parameters of conduct. Second, their financial affairs must be subject to routine, independent audits, and must be shielded, to the greatest extent possible, from the specter of undue influence. Third, it must be made plain that their official conduct is subject to transparency, scrutiny and accountability."[1] The following provides an overview of the laws intended to promote these conditions, including the criminal laws that punish egregious conduct and the public ethics laws aimed at insuring that public officials and employees honor the public's trust. As the discussion makes clear, the details vary widely among the various government settings but the rules embody two core principles:

- Public officials and employees are not to use their official positions for the purpose of private gain
- Public officials and employees must be impartial in carrying out their official duties

Public Authority and Criminal Law

Control over public resources offers many opportunities for criminal acts. Among the most commonly implicated criminal laws are those addressing misappropriation of property, bribery, perjury, and conspiracy.

Embezzlement occurs when someone who controls public property improperly converts it to personal use. Larceny occurs when someone steals or gives away someone else's property. Fraud and a number of related crimes, such as forgery and false pretenses, involve false communications intended to take something of value or deprive someone of a right. Voter-fraud laws, for example, address such circumstances as changing someone's ballot or corruptly influencing a vote. Fraudulent schemes also can be prosecuted under the federal mail- and wire-fraud statutes, which authorize substantial fines and lengthy sentences. Federal prosecutors commonly invoke these sweeping criminal statutes when prosecuting public officials and employees involved in fraudulent schemes.

Bribery occurs when someone demands or accepts something of value in return for being influenced in an official act or for being induced to violate a lawful duty. There are criminal laws specifically prohibiting public officials and employees from improperly accepting anything of value in return for an official act.

Perjury is an intentionally false material statement given under oath. Subordination or perjury is inducing someone else to commit perjury. Public officials and employees commonly participate in hearings, investigations, and other proceedings involving sworn testimony that could become the subject of a perjury prosecution.

As discussed in Chapter 10, conspiracy is an agreement with someone to commit a crime. The conspirator need not directly carry out the crime nor need the crime actually be completed. A public official or employee who enables others to defraud the public may be prosecuted for conspiracy under federal or state law. Also, the federal Racketeer Influenced and Corrupt Organizations Act[2] (RICO) provides for enhanced penalties for the operation or management of a criminal enterprise that engages in a pattern of racketeering. Schemes that involve a series of acts, such as receipt of kickbacks in return for the award of contracts, can be grounds for a RICO prosecution.

Public officials and employees also are subject to many laws specifically aimed at ethical conduct in public service. Violation of a public ethics statute may be designated as a crime. For example, the Arizona conflict-of-interest laws for state and local government make an intentional or knowing violation of the ethics laws a felony and a reckless or negligent violation of them a misdemeanor.[3] Statutes also may broadly authorize criminal sanctions for violations of an oath of office to carry out duties according to the law. Georgia law, for example, provides for imprisonment of between 1 and 5 years for "[a]ny public officer who willfully and intentionally violates the terms of his oath as prescribed by law."[4]

These and other criminal laws provide ample basis for prosecutors to punish abuses of the public's trust. Public officials are held to a higher standard than those who do not assume the responsibilities that go along with this trust. Criminal laws are aimed not only at punishing acts of corruption but also at deterring conduct that tends to lead to corruption. As the U.S. Supreme Court explained, lawmakers should understand that even the most well-meaning individuals face temptation when they act in behalf of the government, and criminal statutes therefore may appropriately be "more concerned with what might have happened in a given situation than with what actually happened" and prohibit "relationships which are fraught with temptation."[5]

Constitutions and Misconduct: *People v. Howard*

A public official's authority is derived from the constitutional foundations that empower the government for whom the official acts. Federal and state laws usually require public officials to take an oath of office that they will discharge their duties faithfully according to the constitution and the law. Taking the oath is usually a ceremonial event. But it is not a legally empty exercise.

Many types of official misconduct are very specifically addressed by the criminal laws, such as embezzlement and bribery. Other types of conduct are not the subject of a specific prohibition, but they are inconsistent with a commitment to honor the law and the official's oath to act according to it. In the following Illinois case, a mayor had used city credit to finance personal gambling at a legal casino. The mayor was charged with actions contrary to the state constitution's imperative that public funds be used only for public purposes. The Illinois Supreme Court considered whether the prosecution could be sustained.

People v. Howard
888 N.E.2d 85 (Ill. 2008)

Justice Garman, writing for the Illinois Supreme Court.

In 2005, defendant, Lyndell W. Howard, was indicted for nine counts of official misconduct related to his use of a City of Pekin credit card. Six of the counts alleged that defendant violated section 33E-16 of the Criminal Code of 1961, while three counts alleged that defendant acted contrary to article VIII, section 1(a), of the Illinois Constitution of 1970. Based upon the above, the indictment alleged that defendant violated section 33-3(c) of the Criminal Code, the official misconduct statute.

Defendant moved to dismiss all of the counts against him. The circuit court of Tazewell County dismissed the six counts predicated on section 33E-16 of the Criminal Code. Defendant's motion to dismiss was not granted, however, with regard to the three counts of official misconduct predicated on article VIII, section 1(a), of the Illinois Constitution, which provides that "[p]ublic funds, property or credit shall be used only for public purposes." A jury found defendant guilty of all three counts. Defendant was sentenced to 30 months' probation, required to perform community service, and ordered to pay costs.

Defendant was elected mayor of the City of Pekin in 2003. Several years earlier, the city council of Pekin obtained a credit card (the City's card) from the Herget National Bank. Pursuant to council resolution, the heads of city departments were allowed to use the City's card to confirm hotel reservations, pay in advance for training sessions, order educational materials, and pay expenses while engaged in city business. After his election as mayor, defendant received and completed a "Business Card Application" from Herget National Bank and became an authorized user of the City's card.

On three separate occasions in 2004, defendant used the City's card to obtain over $1,400 in cash advances to play video poker at the Par-A-Dice Casino in Peoria, Illinois. Defendant used the City's card only after he exhausted the funds available to him through his personal debit and credit cards. In its brief the State asserts, and defendant does not dispute, that defendant obtained two benefits from this use of the City's card: (1) additional funds with which to continue gambling; and (2) "player points," which could be used either to pay for meals or to receive cash back. At oral argument and in the trial court, the State asserted that defendant obtained a third benefit from his use of the City's card, that being what the State termed "the float." According to the State, "the float" was essentially an interest-free loan, whereby defendant used the City's credit to access money and continue gambling without paying the expense of that gambling until the City card's monthly bill came due.

While the City of Pekin was the sole obligor with respect to the City's card, defendant would pay the bills from his own assets when they came due. Defendant conceded, however, that at least one of his checks for payment bounced. Defendant asserts, though, that he quickly remedied the problem and made the payment in full. If defendant had not paid the credit card bills, the City of Pekin would have been liable for them.

Defendant was indicted for three counts of official misconduct based upon the conduct discussed above, one count for each occasion he used the City's card to obtain a cash advance. The indictment alleged the following:

> That the said defendant, a public official, the Mayor of the City of Pekin, while acting in his official capacity and with the intent to obtain a personal advantage for himself, knowingly performed an act in excess of his lawful authority in that he used credit of the City of Pekin to receive cash to gamble at the Paradice Casino contrary to Article 8, Section 1 of the Constitution of the State of Illinois which provides that public funds, property or credit shall be used only for public purposes.

While the three counts of the indictment were predicated on the Illinois Constitution, each count alleged violation of section 33-3(c), and defendant was ultimately convicted of violating that statute.

Defendant asserts that the above-described indictment was insufficient because the law it identified—article VIII, section 1(a), of the Illinois Constitution—cannot serve as a predicate unlawful act for the offense of official misconduct.

As indicated, this court has stated that the Illinois Constitution is the "supreme law" of this state. In recognizing that "[t]he constitution is the supreme law" in the past, we have also stated that "every citizen is bound to obey it and every court is bound to enforce its provisions." *People ex rel. Miller v. Hotz*, 158 N.E. 743, 745 (Ill. 1927).

Section 1-3 does not alter our analysis. Section 1-3 provides that "[n]o conduct constitutes an offense unless it is described as an offense in this Code or in another statute of this State." Defendant was convicted of violating section 33-3(c) of the Criminal Code, and thus his conduct is described as an offense in the Code.

Likewise, our ultimate finding in this case is not altered by defendant's suggestion that allowing a constitutional violation to suffice as a predicate unlawful act for purposes of the official misconduct statute will result in the overzealous prosecution of undeserving defendants. Such a charge could be leveled against almost any prosecution for the violations that this court recognized in *People v. Grever*, 856 N.E.2d 378 (2006), as cognizable predicate unlawful acts under the official misconduct statute. Moreover, the plain language of the official misconduct statute provides no basis for the imposition of a *de minimis* exception.

While the specter of overzealous prosecution does not alter the outcome in this case, we are not unsympathetic to defendant's argument. Moreover, we think it important to note that even the State would acknowledge that winning a conviction under the official misconduct statute is not a simple matter, particularly if a prosecutor should attempt to utilize the statute without considering that its reach is not limitless. At oral argument, the State pointed out that one of the elements of official misconduct is that a defendant must have acted with the intent to obtain a personal advantage. Accordingly, if a defendant has otherwise violated the official misconduct statute, but only unintentionally obtained a personal advantage, a conviction will not stand.

Defendant's overzealous-prosecutor argument essentially constitutes an assertion that the official misconduct statute would be improved by the addition of a *de minimis* exception. This is a policy argument and it could be asserted against a great many criminal statutes. As we have stated in the past, "'few, if any, laws are ever enacted which are not subject to some criticism or capable of some improvement. The question as to whether or not a better law might have been enacted is for the legislature and not for the courts, and criticisms against the wisdom, policy or practicability of a law are subjects for legislative consideration and not for the courts.'" *People ex rel. Armstrong v. Huggins*, 94 N.E.2d 863, 871 (Ill. 1950) (quoting *Perkins v. Board of County Commissioners*, 111 N.E. 580, 589 (Ill. 1916)).

As we noted above, then, it is not that we are unsympathetic to defendant's argument regarding overzealous prosecution; rather, we believe that it is the legislature that must decide whether the official misconduct statute would benefit from a *de minimis* exception. Finding no support for such an exception in the plain language of the statute, we will not carve it out on our own initiative. We do believe, however, that the proper scope of the official misconduct statute is an issue ripe for legislative review, and we strongly suggest that the parameters of the statute be addressed in that forum.

We hold that a violation of the constitution can serve as a predicate unlawful act for the purposes of the official misconduct statute. Accordingly, the indictment against defendant in this case, alleging a violation of article VIII, section 1(a), of the Illinois Constitution, was sufficient.

To most observers use of an employer's credit card to finance gambling would seem improper. In this case the defendant explained that the government did not suffer a monetary loss because he paid the credit card bills personally. The trial court dismissed six charges for willful misapplication of funds, and the state supreme court seemed to sympathize with the contention that the prosecutor was making too much of the impropriety. Those charged with setting ethical standards commonly cite the enforcement difficulties encountered when the ethics laws on the books seem inconsistent with common sympathies. The New Jersey commission that proposed ethics reform found that "ethics lapses, when they occurred, were sometimes attributable to good faith ignorance of the governing ethics rules."[6] To promote more ethical conduct reformers recommended, among other things, clearer and simpler ethical codes and more training to educate public officials and employees about them.[7]

Ethics Laws

Public officials and employees have always been subject to prosecution under the criminal laws for dishonesty and corruption. But faithful public service is more than avoidance of criminal prosecution. For most of the country's history a culture of ethics in government depended mostly on public opinion and self-enforcement. As a result of the alarming revelations from the Watergate scandal in the 1970s, Congress enacted the Ethics in Government Act of 1978,[8] for the first time subjecting federal executive officials and employees to detailed conflict of interest rules, requiring disclosures of financial interests, and creating an Office of Government Ethics to provide ethics guidance and monitor compliance. Since then most states have adopted similar ethics laws governing officials in state government, and some have applied the laws to local governments.

Ethics codes vary in applicability. Generally they apply to "public officials" or "public officers," which include those elected or appointed to an office. Many apply also, in whole or in part, to some "public employees" as well, which includes those who work in government but who are not within the definition of public officials. In general, the federal ethics laws apply broadly to both officials and employees.

The federal executive branch is now subject to many ethics laws. They include rules about potential conflicts of interest,[9] procurement and contracting,[10] gifts and travel,[11] outside employment,[12] hiring of relatives,[13] use of government property and information,[14] political activities,[15] and financial disclosures,[16] among other things. The Office of Government Ethics promulgates supplemental regulations.[17] Presidential Executive Orders 12674 and 12731 further supplement the ethics statutes and regulations and stress the need for public officials and employees to be aware of the rules and to comply with their letter and spirit.

States' ethics laws vary in their application to local governments. Some apply only to some state officials.[18] Some apply to both state and local officials.[19] Some have provisions tailored to particular government units and positions.[20] Some states encourage local governments to adopt their own ethics rules according to minimum standards and subject those who do not to the state standards.[21] Some state laws make a further distinction based on whether the public official or employee is compensated or a volunteer.

Legislators usually are not governed by the same ethics laws as other public officials and employees. They are subject to statutes specifically aimed at legislative activity. Typical among such statutes are prohibitions against voting on matters in which legislators have a direct interest, campaign-finance restrictions, financial disclosure requirements, and restrictions on dealing with lobbyists. Enforcement is largely retained by the legislative bodies themselves, usually a committee of legislators.

Restrictions on state and local legislators vary widely but tend not to be restrictive for those who receive little public compensation. The Executive Director of the Center of Public Integrity made the following observation:

> *There are some 7400 elected stated lawmakers, the majority of whom spend a fraction of their time working for the people. These men and women pass laws influencing everything from the education of children to the hospice care of the elderly; they set environmental policy and determine the manner in which citizens vote in federal elections. All of them have private financial interests, and few have any restrictions over whom they can work for or how much money they can earn while holding office.*[22]

As a practical matter legislative ethics depend on personal integrity and an institutional ethical culture.

Judges are sometimes subject to the same ethics codes as other public officials, but more commonly they are subject to special judicial codes of ethics. Judicial branches have investigatory and enforcement bodies, some of which are staffed with members drawn from the public.

Other professionals working for the government, such as attorneys, are subject to rules of conduct for their professions. They also may be subject to conduct rules that specifically address government employment or representation.

The following are some generalizations about the nature of the ethics codes to which federal, state, and local officials are subject. As the discussion points out, very different rules may apply depending on the individual's role and the jurisdiction.

Misuse of Government Property and Information

Ethics laws commonly prohibit use of public property "for private gain." Clearly public officials and employees may not use public resources for purely personal enjoyment, such as use of a government vehicle for a vacation trip, nor may they conduct private businesses with public resources. In less-clear circumstances, restrictions on use of government property can be a subject of interpretive dispute. For example, issues arise about whether public officials and employees may use computers and telephones for incidental nonwork purposes. Most rules try to balance the need to prevent abuse with modern workplace realities. Governments or their ethics authorities develop and publish guidelines to avoid confusion and to forestall abuse.

Ethics laws also prohibit public officials and employees from improperly using information obtained in their official capacities. Federal law authorizes discharge from employment, fines, and imprisonment for unauthorized disclosure of classified information, trade secrets, confidential statistical data, proprietary business data, and other information that is legally protected from disclosure.[23] States have similar provisions. These prohibitions against misuse of information continue to apply after an official leaves public employment.

Limitations on Participation

Many public officials have discretionary authority that could be used to promote personal relationships or further business interests. Even the appearance of impropriety threatens to undermine the perceived legitimacy of the actions in which the official is involved. Ethics laws restrict participation in questionable circumstances while the official has government authority and to some degree after the official departs government service.

During Service

A public official's direct involvement in matters affecting personal and business relationships threatens to undermine perceptions of legitimacy by suggesting that the outcome was due to favoritism or prejudice rather than merit. To protect the process, federal and state ethics laws require impartiality in performing official duties.

Conflict laws prohibit public officials from being substantially involved in decisions involving their personal and financial interests. Ethics laws take various approaches to defining the nature of actions in which officials should not be involved if a disqualifying relationship exists. The federal executive branch prohibits participating "personally and substantially as a Government officer or employee, through decision, approval, disapproval, recommendation, the rendering of advice, investigation, or otherwise, in a judicial or other proceeding, application, request for a ruling or other determination, contract, claim, controversy, charge, accusation, arrest, or other particular matter."[24] Other ethics laws may be more specific in describing prohibited actions, or more general such as prohibiting involvement in "any action" or "any decision or recommendation." Ethics laws commonly require that the matter involve a discretionary act. This requirement reflects that conflict of interest concerns likely are not implicated with nondiscretionary actions carried out by many in public service, especially in local government, for their friends, families, and others with whom they have a personal or business connection.

Ethics laws also vary in how close of a connection is required for disqualification to apply. The federal executive branch prohibitions apply to matters involving an official's spouse, minor child, general partner, organization in which the official is an officer, director, trustee, general partner, or employee, and a person or organization with whom the official has prospective employment.[25] There are narrow exceptions. One exception applies if the official makes full disclosure to the official's appointing supervisor and the supervisor determines in writing that the interest "is not so substantial as to be deemed likely to affect the integrity of the services which the Government may expect from such officer or employee."[26] Among those whom other laws sometimes include within the sphere of disqualification are these: the official's relatives' employers and organizations; siblings and step-siblings; parents, grandparents, and grandchildren; other members of a household including domestic partners; customers and clients; and significant debtors and creditors. The definition of a disqualifying financial stake in a business is also variously defined, sometimes requiring a minimum threshold of investment in order not to trigger disqualification based solely on very minor stock ownership.

Public officials need to review the particular laws and guidelines that apply to them. The safe course is to disclose any connection and to decline any involvement or influence whenever there might be an appearance of favoritism or prejudice.

Local Officials and Conflicts: Van Itallie v. Franklin Lakes

Many citizens serve in government positions in their neighborhoods. They are likely to know many of those with whom they work. They also may have personal and business interests that depend on the activities of the offices in which they work. Lawmakers and judges have recognized that the conflict of interest rules must be realistic and consistent with promoting good government. Those willing to serve should not unrealistically be expected to be completely dissociated from the matters they encounter.

The following excerpt from a New Jersey Supreme Court decision addresses allegations that two borough council members' indirect connections to a zoning matter should have disqualified them from participation. The opinion illustrates the balance that the courts attempt to strike between protecting the integrity of local proceedings and being sensitive to the nature of citizen government.

Van Itallie v. Franklin Lakes
146 A.2d 111 (N.J. 1958)

Justice Proctor, writing for the New Jersey Supreme Court.

Plaintiff, a taxpayer, filed a complaint in lieu of prerogative writ in the Superior Court, Law Division, challenging the validity of two ordinances of the Borough of Franklin Lakes, principally on the ground that a conflict of interest existed on the part of two of the borough councilmen, Birrer and Bender.

Franklin Lakes is a rural community in Bergen County encompassing about ten square miles. It has a population of about 2,700 persons and approximately 750 homes. An area of 1,250 acres, about one-fifth of the borough, is owned by the Archdiocese of Newark.

In 1955 the Archdiocese entered into a contract with Urban Farms, Inc., for the sale and development of [a portion of its] land. The contract was contingent upon a change in the zoning ordinance because it was felt that development would not be possible under the then existing zoning ordinance. The Archdiocese also retained Urban Planning Associates to draft an appropriate re-zoning plan. Through these representatives the Archdiocese submitted to the planning board a request for re-zoning. This request contained numerous proposals including a reduction of the two-acre requirement in portions of the residential area to one-acre lots, re-zoning of 50 acres for a memorial park cemetery, a cultural area, a church and a parochial school. The proposed plan became the center of controversy and a citizens' committee, of which the plaintiff was a member, was formed to oppose it. The principal opposition was to the proposed reduction of the area comprising the two-acre zone established by the 1953 ordinance.

On this appeal plaintiff first contends that Councilman Birrer was disqualified from participating either as a member of the planning board or as a member of the council because of his conflicting interests. Plaintiff also challenges Bender's participation as a member of the council for the same reason. The defendant borough denies that either councilman had a conflicting interest. In addition, the borough argues that in the enactment of the ordinances the councilmen were acting in a legislative capacity and thus a showing of actual bad faith or improper motivation is necessary to vitiate their actions.

The citizens of a community have a right to expect that a public official in the performance of his duty will exercise his best judgment unaffected by anything which will inure to his personal advantage. In order to secure complete impartiality in matters coming before a municipal planning board, the Legislature has prescribed that a member of such a board shall not be permitted to "act on any matter in which he has either directly or indirectly any personal or financial interest." N.J.S.A. 40:55-1.4. Members of the governing body, in their consideration of recommendations by the planning board, should not be permitted to act where a similar interest is present.

The interest which it is alleged conflicts with Councilman Birrer's duty to impartially act on the ordinances in question arises from the following circumstances: (1) Councilman Birrer's younger brother, Robert Birrer, has since 1952 been employed as an accountant-bookkeeper by the Frank A. McBride Company. J. Nevins McBride is the executive vice-president of the Frank A. McBride Company and is also the president of Urban Farms, Inc., which held the contract to purchase part of the Archdiocese's property and intended to develop it. He is also a principal officer in Urban Planning Associates, which prepared and submitted the proposals, many of which culminated in the ordinances. He appeared several times before the planning board and borough council to urge the adoption of the Archdiocese's request. There is sufficient proof that Frank A. McBride Company, Urban Farms, Inc., and Urban Planning Associates were controlled by substantially the same persons and were affiliated at least to the extent of having a common interest in the proposal of the Archdiocese. We agree with the plaintiff that Councilman Birrer's brother was employed by a corporation which was interested in obtaining the passage of the challenged ordinances. Councilman Birrer did not attempt to hide the fact that his brother was a McBride employee. Indeed, he volunteered this information at a meeting of the planning board in August 1955. (2) In 1954 or 1955 Councilman Birrer engaged in a conversation with J. Nevins McBride concerning the possibility of locating a golf course in the borough. It was indicated that among the possible locations for the course one might encompass the Birrer lands. During the August 1955 meeting of the planning board, Birrer voluntarily informed the members of the board of this conversation. (3) Councilman Birrer owns a 40-acre plot in the borough. It has a 210-foot frontage on Summit Avenue. A portion of the rear of the land is contiguous with a 300-acre quadrant owned by the Archdiocese. Somewhere within this quadrant the proposed cemetery is to be located. Plaintiff contends that the cemetery could be so located that a permitted street on the periphery of the buffer zone would materially benefit Birrer's land, in that it would provide a means of access to the rear portion of his property.

Does any one of the above allegations or all three in concert establish the personal interest requisite for the demanded disqualification?

The decision as to whether a particular interest is sufficient to disqualify is necessarily a factual one and depends upon the circumstances of the particular case. No definitive test can be devised. The question will always be whether the circumstances could reasonably be interpreted to show that they had the likely capacity to tempt the official to depart from his sworn public duty.

Local governments would be seriously handicapped if every possible interest, no matter how remote and speculative, would serve as a disqualification of an official. If this were so, it would discourage capable men and women from holding public office. Of course, courts should scrutinize the circumstances with great care and should condemn anything which indicates the likelihood of corruption or favoritism. But in doing so they must also be mindful that to abrogate a municipal action at the suggestion that some remote and nebulous interest is present, would be to unjustifiably deprive a municipality in many important instances of the services of its duly elected or appointed officials. The determinations of municipal officials should not be approached with a general feeling of suspicion, for as Justice Holmes has said, "Universal distrust creates universal incompetency." *Graham v. United States*, 231 U.S. 474, 480 (1913). We recognize that certain circumstances, such as the existence of a substantial association, financial or otherwise, of an official's relative with an interested organization might constitute grounds for disqualification. And there may be other factors which would call for the official's withdrawal, e.g., promotion of a relative in the event of favorable municipal action, or the relative's participation in the request for favorable municipal action. But none of these factors appears in the present case. Nothing more is shown than the bare fact that Councilman Birrer's brother was a subordinate employee of a corporation of the McBride enterprises. This circumstance is entirely too remote to be considered as tending improperly to influence the councilman's official judgment.

Plaintiff's contention that a conflicting interest arose because of the conversation between Councilman Birrer and J. Nevins McBride concerning a golf course is without merit. The conversation was most vague and contained no definite proposals. Birrer had merely been asked if he would be interested in a golf course. We find nothing in this conversation that had in any fashion the slightest possibility of influencing Birrer's action.

We are also of the opinion that Councilman Birrer's ownership of property in the vicinity of the quadrant in which the Archdiocese tentatively proposes to establish a cemetery is not sufficient to warrant his disqualification. In relation to cemeteries, Ordinance 140 does no more than make them a permitted use in residential areas. Ordinance 139 regulates the manner in which cemeteries may be located and established. All applications for the location and establishment of a cemetery must be submitted to the governing body for approval. Neither ordinance fixes a

particular location for a cemetery within a residential area. The location of the proposed cemetery of the Archdiocese has not been determined. The only indication respecting a location for
the proposed cemetery is found in the plan submitted by Urban Planning Associates on behalf of
the Archdiocese in its request for re-zoning. If we assume that the Archdiocese will locate its
cemetery in the manner shown by its proposal, that in itself would be of no benefit to Councilman
Birrer. The only benefit which he could derive from the establishment of a cemetery would be the
creation of a public road on the periphery of the required buffer zone which would touch upon his
property. The Archdiocese's proposal indicates no such road and Ordinance 139 merely permits
and does not require the construction of a road upon the buffer area. Moreover, our study of the
maps accompanying the Archdiocese's proposal discloses that the Birrer property is several hundred feet beyond the minimum of 250 feet required as the buffer area round the cemetery. That
a cemetery will be established by the Archdiocese in such a location as to be of any benefit to
Councilman Birrer is entirely too speculative and remote.

Plaintiff contends that Councilman Bender had a personal interest in the passage of the ordinances on the following grounds: (1) Bender's father under the will of John MacKenzie, his
long-time employer, was given a life estate in a house, a mill and four acres of land, which
property is situated in the new BB historical and cultural zone. This zone encompasses an area
of about 15 acres. The senior Bender is 84 years old and has lived on the property for 60 years.
He operates the mill to sharpen tools and to make cider for about two and a half months each
year. The cider mill is about 55 years old and contains a wood lathe, unique because it is water-
powered. Ordinance 140 provides that historical sites shall be preserved in the zone. Plaintiff
contends that the ordinance contemplates that the cider mill as a historical site will be the
nucleus of new business enterprises, with the result that the value of the life estate held by
Councilman Bender's father will be enhanced. (2) A brother of Councilman Bender is a tenant
on the Archdiocese's property. This tenancy commenced 30 years ago, long before the Archdiocese acquired the property.

We think that the interests of Councilman Bender's father and brother are too insubstantial to
warrant his disqualification. The 84-year-old father has only a life estate in the property. On his
death the remainder does not go to Councilman Bender or any member of his family. Any increase
in the value of this life estate is highly speculative, at the most of slight worth, and unlikely of
realization. The father's interest in the passage of these ordinances is too insignificant to warrant
an assumption that it would in any manner influence Councilman Bender's vote. And the same is
true as to the brother who has tenanted a house for 30 years on the Archdiocese's property.

We are of the opinion that the trial court properly found there was no evidence from which
it could fairly be concluded that either Councilman Birrer or Bender had any interest in the
passage of the ordinances which would conflict with their official duties.

The New Jersey Supreme Court noted that a council member accused of an impermissible
conflict volunteered information about his connection to the matter at a public meeting. This
disclosure enabled participants to be alert to signs of favoritism. Those who consider allegations of impermissible conflicts are more likely to be sympathetic to questionable judgment
than to apparent deceit.

The court interpreted the connections to be too distant to warrant serious concern. Still, the attention that even these distant links were able to garner at the state's highest court illustrates that even a tangential personal connection can result in claims of impropriety. Public officials must be scrupulous about their participation in decisions to avoid providing fodder for later challenges by citizens who feel aggrieved by the outcome.

Van Itallie was decided in 1958, before modern ethics codes were enacted. The connections described in the opinion may be treated differently under later-enacted codes. While some jurisdictions press for application of state codes to local governments, local governments tend to have ethics codes that proclaim only very general aspirational principles rather than provide detailed rules. This approach illustrates the continued vitality of the New Jersey Supreme Court's warning that we "must also be mindful that to abrogate a municipal action at the suggestion that some remote and nebulous interest is present, would be to unjustifiably deprive a municipality in many important instances of the services of its duly elected or appointed officials."

After Departure

Public officials develop relationships with other decision makers within their offices and connections with members of the public who interact with their offices. While in their government positions public officials are expected to serve the public's interest and not devote their energies to leveraging their positions for development of private interests to be pursued in a later endeavor. A possibility of favoritism arises when officials who have departed government represent private interests in dealings with their former offices. But the ability to use government experience in later employment is an incentive to attract well-qualified individuals to public office. Consequently ethics laws restrict—but do not entirely prohibit—former public officials from representing private interests in matters involving their former offices. These restrictions are sometimes called "revolving door" rules, reflecting the goal of discouraging short-term entry into a public position for the purpose of developing contacts for pursuit of private outside interests.

In general, the public ethics laws, including federal law, prohibit former public officials from any communication with their former offices in behalf of someone in connection with a matter in which the official had direct and substantial involvement while in office.[27] Ethics laws typically also temporarily prohibit former public officials from representing anyone who had a matter pending before their former offices regardless of any direct involvement while in office. Federal law, for example, contains a two-year restriction against representation of anyone who had a matter pending within one year prior to the official's departure.[28] Additionally, high-level officials may be strictly prohibited from communicating with their former offices with intent to influence action in behalf of anyone for a defined period. Federal law contains a one-year restriction of this sort.[29]

Gifts

Public officials and employees are often able to help others and they may be offered gifts out of honest gratitude. Or they may be offered gifts with the expectation of special treatment, or out of fear that good-faith cooperation will be withheld. Even if a public official would not act differently as a result of a gift, someone who learns of its acceptance could reasonably wonder about the official's impartiality. To protect against such implications, ethics laws narrowly restrict the gifts that public officials and employees may accept.

Gifts include not only tangible objects—such as money, event tickets, and gift certificates—but also discounts and accommodations for which others would have to pay. Gift restrictions typically do not apply to personal gifts within the context of family and personal relationships, although there may be restrictions or disclosure obligations when the giver also has business involving the recipient's office. Restrictions typically also allow acceptance of meals, refreshment, and entertainment at conferences and social functions, as well as very small gifts. The restrictions on federal executive officials and employees, for example, allow acceptance of gifts valued at $20 or less provided that the total from the same person does not exceed $50 per year, and of such things as coffee and donuts, greeting cards, plaques, and other items of little intrinsic value.[30]

Outside Income and Honoraria

In general, ethics laws do not prohibit public officials and employees from outside employment and activities that do not conflict with official duties. Prior approval from a supervisor may be required before such employment or activity is undertaken. Approval may be denied based on an identifiable conflict potential or based on restrictions that apply to the particular position. In general, public officials and employees have a First Amendment right to accept honoraria for speaking, but they are prohibited from teaching, speaking, and publishing for outside compensation if it relates to official duties except in connection with specified educational programs.

Financial Disclosure

To discourage public officials with significant responsibility from using their public offices to pursue personal business, some ethics laws require them to disclose their personal income sources, business interests, investments, real estate interests, agreements for future employment, and certain other financial information. In some jurisdictions, including in the federal executive branch, the information is filed confidentially with an ethics review body that looks for potential conflicts and provides counseling.[31] Some jurisdictions make the information public.[32] The reach of the disclosure requirements vary but typically extends at least to executives and agency and department heads and candidates for such offices.

Ethics Authorities

The head of the federal executive branch's Office of Government Ethics is appointed by the president with the Senate's advice and consent. The office is responsible for ethics rules and regulations, monitoring and ordering compliance, and recommending disciplinary action for violations.[33] Most states have bipartisan monitoring entities with similar duties and powers. Commission members typically are appointed by leaders of executive agencies or by a combination of leaders of executive and legislative bodies. The members must not be among those currently or recently subject to the rules. In addition to the power to recommend disciplinary action, some ethics authorities have the power to impose fines and to bring legal action against former officials. They typically are responsible for ethics educational programs and may have the power to conduct ethics audits.

Ethics Training

Public ethics laws will not accomplish their intended effect unless those whom they govern know and understand them. Ethics offices use various methods to educate public officials and employees, and the public, about the rules. For example, they publish rules and guidelines and provide orientation and periodic review sessions. Agencies and departments covered by the rules may be required to designate ethics liaisons who are responsible for developing in-house ethics programs. Some ethics offices provide advisory opinions upon request about questionable situations.

Laws Governing Third Parties Dealing with the Government

The criminal and ethics laws discussed in this chapter are aimed at public officials and employees. But as the old saying goes, "it takes two to tango," and most ethical issues that arise involve a third party dealing with the government. Third parties are subject to prosecution under general criminal laws and may also be subject to laws specifically aimed at interactions with the government. Two areas in particular have been the subject of such laws: lobbying and public contracting.

Lobbyists are in the business of influencing public officials. Many jurisdictions have lobbying laws to protect against use of improper incentives in pursuit of such influence. The laws typically require individuals to register as lobbyists if they are compensated for communicating with government officials for the purpose of influencing legislative or administrative action. The laws require the lobbyists to file periodic disclosures about their activities, including lists of expenditures. The laws typically prohibit attempts to deceive legislators and other state officials either in lobbying activities or in filing required disclosures.

Statutes require public contractors to follow prescribed procedures before entering into contracts to pay public funds to private companies. Recipients of such funds also are subject to statutory ethics requirements. For example, bidders are prohibited from making misrepresentations and may not offer payments or kickbacks to government representatives in exchange for contract awards. Penalties for violations include suspension or disqualification from future work, and criminal prosecution.

Review Questions

1. What two core principles are embodied in the public ethics laws?

2. What are the principal criminal laws likely to be implicated with abuse of public authority?

3. On what basis might courts allow prosecution of public officials based on conduct inconsistent with constitutional requirements?

4. What are the typical subjects addressed by government ethics laws?

5. In what basic way are federal and state conflict of interest laws different?

6. What are the typical kinds of restrictions on a public official's participation in deliberations and receipt of outside income and other rewards?

7. What are the typical kinds of restrictions on a public official's or public employee's receipt of gifts?

8. What is the basic nature of federal and state ethics authorities and their responsibilities?

9. What are the basic kinds of restrictions that apply to lobbyists?

10. What are the basic kinds of restrictions that apply to public contractors?

Notes

1. Paula A. Franzese & Daniel J. O'Hern, Sr., *Restoring the Public Trust: An Agenda for Ethics Reform of State Government and a Proposed Model for New Jersey*, 57 Rutgers L. Rev. 1175, 1178 (2005).

2. 18 U.S.C. §§ 1961–1968 (2006).

3. Ariz. Rev. Stat. Ann. §§ 38-503–38-505, 38-510 (2001).

4. Ga. Code Ann. § 16-10-1 (2007).

5. United States v. Mississippi Valley Generating Co., 364 U.S. 520, 549–50 (1961).

6. Franzese & O'Hern, *supra* note 1, at 1180.

7. *Id.*

8. Pub. L. No. 95-521, 92 Stat. 1824 (1978) (codified as amended at 5 U.S.C. app. (2006)).

9. 18 U.S.C. §§ 201–219 (2006).

10. 41 U.S.C. §§ 423–433 (2000 & Supp. 2006).

11. 5 U.S.C. §§ 4111 (2006) (contributions, awards, and other payments); 5 U.S.C. § 7342 (2006) (foreign gifts and decorations); 5 U.S.C. §§ 7351–7353 (2006) (gifts to other officers and employees); 22 U.S.C. § 2458a (2000) (cultural exchange programs); 31 U.S.C. 1353 (2000 & Supp. 2006) (travel and related expenses).

12. 5 U.S.C. § 5533 (2006) (dual pay); 5 U.S.C. app. §§ 501–505 (2006) (outside income and activities).

13. 5 U.S.C. § 3110 (2006).

14. 18 U.S.C. § 641 (2006) (public money, property, or records); 18 U.S.C. § 1719 (2006) (franking privilege); 18 U.S.C. § 1913 (2006); 31 U.S.C. § 1344 (2000 & Supp. 2006);

18 U.S.C. §§ 798, 1905 (2000) classified information); 50 U.S.C. § 783(a) (2000) (classified information).

15. 5 U.S.C. §§ 7321–7326 (2006) (administrative); 18 U.S.C. §§ 601–610 (2006) (criminal).

16. 5 U.S.C. App. §§ 101–111 (2006).

17. 8 C.F.R. ch. XVI (2008).

18. *E.g.*, N.C. Gen. Stat. Ann. § 138A-3(30) (2007).

19. *E.g.*, Ala. Code §§ 36-25-1(23), (24) (2001).

20. *E.g.*, Mass. Ann. Laws ch. 268A (1992 & Supp. 2008).

21. *E.g.*, Del. Code Ann. tit. 29, § 5802(4) (Supp. 2006).

22. Roberta Baskin, *The State of State Legislative Ethics: Watching the Watchdogs*, 39 Ind. L. Rev. 487, 488 (2005–2006).

23. 18 U.S.C. §§ 798, 1905 (2006).

24. *Id.*

25. 18 U.S.C. § 208 (2006).

26. *Id.*

27. 18 U.S.C. § 207(a)(1) (2006).

28. *Id.* § 207(a)(2).

29. *Id.* § 207(c).

30. 5 C.F.R. 2635.204 (2008).

31. 5 C.F.R. pt. 2634 (2008).

32. *E.g.*, Alaska Stat. § 39.50.020(b) (2006).

33. 5 U.S.C. app. § 402 (2006).

Chapter 13

Civil Litigation and Alternative Dispute Resolution

Those disputing, contradicting, and confuting people are generally unfortunate in their affairs. They get victory, sometimes, but they never get good will, which would be of more use to them.

Benjamin Franklin

CHAPTER OBJECTIVES

After studying this chapter you should better understand:

- The nature of legal disputes and the limitations of using litigation to resolve them
- Basic features of the litigation pretrial and trial procedures
- The basic features of the appeals process
- The basic considerations involving collection of judgments
- The benefits and limitations of mediation and arbitration

Some trials get a lot of public attention. Courtroom drama is a favorite topic for news reports and in theatre, film, and literature. The drama can be real and the stakes can be high—important rights and substantial wealth may depend on the outcome of a trial. But most civil litigation results from petty disputes or stubbornness. It unfolds awkwardly and leaves everyone dissatisfied, except perhaps the lawyers who are paid for their time. False impressions about the process and what it can really accomplish cause many reasonable people to become embroiled in unproductive litigation. If in the beginning they had a more realistic view, they may have worked harder to find a compromise that in the long run would have saved time and other resources. But sometimes litigation is unavoidable. The parties may have irreconcilable views about each other's obligations, or they may have real need to clarify uncertain legal rights.

This chapter provides an overview of civil dispute resolution procedures, including the court-enforced litigation process and the most commonly employed consensual alternatives.

A better understanding of the realities of the litigation process and its alternatives should be helpful for managing disputes.

Disputes and Uncertainty

Some things in litigation are predictable: time and money will be spent, and reasonable people will become contentious. Most likely the outcome will be somewhere between the parties' competing positions, and it will be based on something that neither party thought was most important. Even if a party achieves the desired judgment after a trial, the ultimate ending will be unsatisfying. In most cases success also requires collection, which usually is more difficult than the litigants first assumed.

Organizations learn that they can best achieve their objectives if they routinely consider litigation-avoidance strategies. They learn from experience that litigation usually is an unproductive way to resolve a problem. Rather than quickly becoming entrenched in litigation, they look for ways to move past disputes that arise, not necessarily in ways that vindicate their positions, but in ways that make the best of a potentially worse situation. In their bestselling book *Getting to Yes: Negotiating Agreement without Giving In*, Roger Fisher, William Ury, and Bruce Patton discuss how problems are more likely to be solved if participants consider whether they have shared interests rather than pursue staked-out positions. In litigation the parties tend to become entrenched in positions and to attribute negative motives to opponents, making a workable resolution even less likely to be achieved. As they invest their resources in lawyers' fees and other litigation costs, and as they are confronted with adversarial behaviors, the dispute takes on life of its own. Everyone involved probably would have been much better off if they had made every reasonable effort to explore common interests before confrontational dynamics took control.

This chapter discusses two common alternative procedures for resolving disputes without litigation in court: mediation and arbitration. In most circumstances these procedures offer significant opportunities for resolving disputes more quickly and less expensively than with litigation. But they also involve their own costs and risks. Before invoking any dispute resolution process involving a third party the participants would be wise to consider whether there is a way to resolve the disagreement with reasonable compromises. Open-mindedness, self-reflection, realism, and a willingness to be fair are powerful antidotes to the forces that cause reasonable individuals and effective organizations to become embroiled in disruptive disputes with uncertain outcomes.

Remedies

With civil litigation parties seek court judgments to compel someone to do or not to do something. There always is a cost involved in invoking a governmental process, in time and in diversion of resources, and also potentially in financial loss and reputational harm. Before pursuing any dispute resolution process, those involved should realistically assess the likelihood of obtaining the remedies they seek.

Types of Relief

At the outset parties to litigation make a request for relief. If the goal is an award of money, usually in the form of damages, in most jurisdictions a request is made in approximate terms with the specific amount to be determined by the court or jury. The general request must satisfy any jurisdictional minimum or maximum amount for the particular court. For example, in a diversity case in federal district court between citizens of different states, the dispute must involve at least $75,000 not including interest and costs. State courts typically have maximum amounts that can be sought in local courts, and claims for more than that amount must be brought in the county court. Although a party to litigation may be able to amend a request for relief, especially if new evidence comes to light, courts usually will not allow a party to add claims at the last minute that are a surprise to an opposing party. Ultimately the finder of fact—the judge or jury—will decide the amount of damages to be awarded, if any, based on the evidence presented and the law governing the claims that have been made. The finder of fact usually is not bound by the amounts that the parties request.

Another remedy that is commonly sought in litigation is injunctive relief. An injunction is a court order that someone do or not do something. For example, an employer seeking to protect trade secrets may seek an injunction to prevent a former employee from divulging information in a new job with the former employer's competitor. Someone who violates an injunction will be liable for resulting damages and could face penalties for contempt of court. If the need for injunctive relief is immediate, court process allows for a temporary injunction to be issued at the beginning of the litigation, with a later determination about whether the temporary injunction should become permanent or be dissolved.

In some contract cases, a court may also order specific performance, by which the court orders one party to carry out a promise, such as to convey property that is the subject of a contract found to be enforceable. Specific performance is awarded only when the subject of the promise is unique. It is uncommon because an award of money almost always is considered to be a sufficient remedy.

Another basic type of litigation remedy is a declaration of rights. This may be the case, for example, if the parties disagree about the interpretation of a contract and want the court to resolve the disagreement.

Whatever the relief may be, the parties also need to consider the cost of obtaining it. Court rules usually require a losing party to reimburse a prevailing party for certain court costs. The recoverable costs may include such things as filing fees, transcript fees, and witness appearance fees. There are good reasons to require some litigants also to pay a prevailing party's lawyers' fees, especially when claims have been brought or opposed with no reasonable basis. The outcome of litigation is heavily influenced by the cost of lawyers' services. Parties who were forced to bring litigation to obtain what clearly was their entitlement should not be forced to suffer from the other party's intransigence. But lawyers' fees are usually not among the damages that are recoverable from opposing parties. This approach is known as the "American Rule" to distinguish it from the rule in many other countries that requires losing parties to pay at least some of the prevailing party's lawyers' fees. There are exceptions to the American Rule. Some statutes, such as civil rights laws, require a losing party to reimburse the successful claimant for reasonable lawyers' fees. Also, a party may be compelled to pay the other party's lawyers' fees if the parties agreed to do so in a contract. Another basis on which lawyers' fees are occasionally awarded is a judicially created exception applied when claims or defenses are deemed to have been frivolous or indefensible. Courts tend not to see cases in such stark terms, however, so application of the entirely frivolous claim rule is rare despite the litigants' sense that it should be applied.

The American Rule: *Alyeska Pipeline Service Co. v. Wilderness Society*

Leaving the parties to absorb their litigation lawyers' fees can fundamentally alter a party's assessment of the value of litigation. Many worthy lawsuits are foregone because parties understand that fees can easily consume or exceed any possible recovery. Someone who otherwise should bear the loss—for causing a personal injury, contract breach, or other harm for which the law is supposed to provide a remedy—thereby escapes accountability even though litigation costs were just as foreseeable a loss as the recoverable damages. On rare occasions courts have attempted to address the unfairness of such an outcome by fashioning new exceptions to the rule. In the following 1975 case, the U.S. Supreme Court considered a court of appeals' effort to award lawyers' fees to a conservation group that opposed the Alaska oil pipeline.

Alyeska Pipeline Service Co. v. Wilderness Society

421 U.S. 240 (1975)

Justice White, writing for the Court

This litigation was initiated by respondents Wilderness Society, Environmental Defense Fund, Inc., and Friends of the Earth in an attempt to prevent the issuance of permits by the Secretary of the Interior which were required for the construction of the trans-Alaska oil pipeline. The Court of Appeals awarded attorneys' fees to respondents against petitioner Alyeska Pipeline Service Co. based upon the court's equitable powers and the theory that respondents were entitled to fees because they were performing the services of a "private attorney general." We reverse.

A major oil field was discovered in the North Slope of Alaska in 1968. In June 1969, the oil companies constituting the consortium owning Alyeska submitted an application to the Department of the Interior for rights-of-way for a pipeline that would transport oil from the North Slope across land in Alaska owned by the United States, a major part of the transport system which would carry the oil to its ultimate markets in the lower 48 States. A special interdepartmental task force studied the proposal and reported to the President. An amended application was submitted in December 1969, which requested a 54-foot right-of-way, along with applications for "special land use permits" asking for additional space alongside the right-of-way and for the construction of a road along one segment of the pipeline.

Respondents brought this suit in March 1970, and sought declaratory and injunctive relief against the Secretary of the Interior on the grounds that he intended to issue the right-of-way and special land-use permits in violation of § 28 of the Mineral Leasing Act of 1920, and without compliance with the National Environmental Policy Act of 1969 (NEPA). On the basis of both the Mineral Leasing Act and the NEPA, the District Court granted a preliminary injunction against issuance of the right-of-way and permits.

Subsequently the State of Alaska and petitioner Alyeska were allowed to intervene. On March 20, 1972, the Interior Department released a six-volume Environmental Impact Statement and a three-volume Economic and Security Analysis. After a period of time set aside for public comment, the Secretary announced that the requested permits would be granted to Alyeska. Both the Mineral Leasing Act and the NEPA issues were at that point fully briefed and argued before the District Court. That court then decided to dissolve the preliminary injunction, to deny the permanent injunction, and to dismiss the complaint.

Upon appeal, the Court of Appeals for the District of Columbia Circuit reversed, basing its decision solely on the Mineral Leasing Act. Finding that the NEPA issues were very complex and important, that deciding them was not necessary at that time since pipeline construction would be enjoined as a result of the violation of the Mineral Leasing Act, that they involved issues of fact still in dispute, and that it was desirable to expedite its decision as much as possible, the Court of Appeals declined to decide the merits of respondents' NEPA contentions which had been rejected by the District Court.

Congress then enacted legislation which amended the Mineral Leasing Act to allow the granting of the permits sought by Alyeska and declared that no further action under the NEPA was necessary before construction of the pipeline could proceed.

With the merits of the litigation effectively terminated by this legislation, the Court of Appeals turned to the questions involved in respondents' request for an award of attorneys' fees. Since there was no applicable statutory authorization for such an award, the court proceeded to consider whether the requested fee award fell within any of the exceptions to the general "American rule" that the prevailing party may not recover attorneys' fees as costs or otherwise. The Court of Appeals . . . held that respondents had acted to vindicate "important statutory rights of all citizens . . . "; had ensured that the governmental system functioned properly; and were entitled to attorneys' fees lest the great cost of litigation of this kind, particularly against well-financed defendants such as Alyeska, deter private parties desiring to see the laws protecting the environment properly enforced. Title 28 U.S.C. § 2412 was thought to bar taxing any attorneys' fees against the United States, and it was also deemed inappropriate to burden the State of Alaska with any part of the award. But Alyeska, the Court of Appeals held, could fairly be required to pay one-half of the full award to which respondents were entitled for having performed the functions of a private attorney general.

In the United States, the prevailing litigant is ordinarily not entitled to collect a reasonable attorneys' fee from the loser. We are asked to fashion a far-reaching exception to this "American Rule"; but having considered its origin and development, we are convinced that it would be inappropriate for the Judiciary, without legislative guidance, to reallocate the burdens of litigation in the manner and to the extent urged by respondents and approved by the Court of Appeals.

At common law, costs were not allowed; but for centuries in England there has been statutory authorization to award costs, including attorneys' fees. Although the matter is in the discretion of the court, counsel fees are regularly allowed to the prevailing party.

During the first years of the federal-court system, Congress provided through legislation that the federal courts were to follow the practice with respect to awarding attorneys' fees of the courts of the States in which the federal courts were located, with the exception of district courts under admiralty and maritime jurisdiction which were to follow a specific fee schedule. Those statutes, by 1800, had either expired or been repealed.

In 1796, this Court appears to have ruled that the Judiciary itself would not create a general rule, independent of any statute, allowing awards of attorneys' fees in federal courts. In *Arcambel v. Wiseman*, 3 U.S. (3 Dall.) 306 (1796), the inclusion of attorneys' fees as damages was overturned on the ground that "[t]he general practice of the United States is in opposition [sic] to it; and even if that practice were not strictly correct in principle, it is entitled to the respect of the court, till it is changed, or modified, by statute." This Court has consistently adhered to that early holding.

In 1853, Congress undertook to standardize the costs allowable in federal litigation. In support of the proposed legislation, it was asserted that there was great diversity in practice among the courts and that losing litigants were being unfairly saddled with exorbitant fees for the victor's attorney. The result was a far-reaching Act specifying in detail the nature and amount of the taxable items of cost in the federal courts.

Although, as will be seen, Congress has made specific provision for attorneys' fees under certain federal statutes, it has not changed the general statutory rule that allowances for counsel fees are limited to the sums specified by the costs statute. Under § 1920, a court may tax as costs the various items specified, including the "docket fees" under § 1923(a). That section provides that "[a]ttorney's and proctor's docket fees in courts of the United States may be taxed as costs as follows. . . . " Against this background, this Court understandably declared in 1967 that with the exception of the small amounts allowed by § 1923, the rule "has long been that attorney's fees are not ordinarily recoverable. . . . " *Fleischmann Distilling Corp.*, 386 U.S. 714, 717 (1967). Other recent cases have also reaffirmed the general rule that, absent statute or enforceable contract, litigants pay their own attorneys' fees.

To be sure, the fee statutes have been construed to allow, in limited circumstances, a reasonable attorneys' fee to the prevailing party in excess of the small sums permitted by § 1923. In *Trustees v. Greenough*, 105 U.S. 527 (1882), the 1853 Act was read as not interfering with the historic power of equity to permit the trustee of a fund or property, or a party preserving or recovering a fund for the benefit of others in addition to himself, to recover his costs, including his attorneys' fees, from the fund or property itself or directly from the other parties enjoying the benefit. That rule has been consistently followed. Also, a court may assess attorneys' fees for the "willful disobedience of a court order . . . as part of the fine to be levied on the defendant, *Toledo Scale Co. v. Computing Scale Co.*, 261 U.S. 399, 426–28 (1923)," *Fleischmann Distilling Corp. v. Maier Brewing Co.*, 386 U.S. at 718; or when the losing party has "acted in bad faith, vexatiously, wantonly, or for oppressive reasons. . . . " *F. D. Rich Co. v. Industrial Lumber Co.*, 417 U.S. 116, 129 (1974). These exceptions are unquestionably assertions of inherent power in the courts to allow attorneys' fees in particular situations, unless forbidden by Congress, but none of the exceptions is involved here. The Court of Appeals expressly disclaimed reliance on any of them.

Congress has not repudiated the judicially fashioned exceptions to the general rule against allowing substantial attorneys' fees; but neither has it retracted, repealed, or modified the limitations on taxable fees contained in the 1853 statute and its successors. Nor has it extended any roving authority to the Judiciary to allow counsel fees as costs or otherwise whenever the courts might deem them warranted. What Congress has done, however, while fully recognizing and accepting the general rule, is to make specific and explicit provisions for the allowance of attorneys' fees under selected statutes granting or protecting various federal rights. These statutory allowances are now available in a variety of circumstances, but they also differ considerably among themselves. Under the antitrust laws, for instance, allowance of attorneys' fees to a plaintiff awarded treble damages is mandatory. In patent litigation, in contrast, "[t]he court in *exceptional* cases *may* award reasonable attorney fees to the prevailing party." 35 U.S.C. § 285 (emphasis added by Court). Under Title II of the Civil Rights Act of 1964, 42 U.S.C. § 2000a-3(b), the prevailing party is entitled to attorneys' fees, at the discretion of the court, but we have held that Congress intended that the award should be made to the successful plaintiff absent exceptional circumstances. Under this scheme of things, it is apparent that the circumstances under which attorneys' fees are to be awarded and the range of discretion of the courts in making those awards are matters for Congress to determine.

Congress itself presumably has the power and judgment to pick and choose among its statutes and to allow attorneys' fees under some, but not others. But it would be difficult, indeed, for the courts, without legislative guidance, to consider some statutes important and others unimportant and to allow attorneys' fees only in connection with the former. If the statutory limitation of right-of-way widths involved in this case is a matter of the gravest importance, it would appear that a wide range of statutes would arguably satisfy the criterion of public importance and justify an award of attorneys' fees to the private litigant. And, if *any* statutory policy is deemed so important that its enforcement must be encouraged by awards of attorneys' fees, how could a court deny attorneys' fees to private litigants in actions under 42 U.S.C. § 1983 seeking to vindicate *constitutional* rights? Moreover, should courts, if they were to embark on the course urged by respondents, opt for awards to the prevailing party, whether plaintiff or defendant, or only to the prevailing plaintiff? Should awards be discretionary or mandatory? Would there be a presumption operating for or against them in the ordinary case?

As exemplified by this case itself, it is also evident that the rational application of the private-attorney-general rule would immediately collide with the express provision of 28 U.S.C. § 2412. Except as otherwise provided by statute, that section permits costs to be taxed against the United States, "but not including the fees and expenses of attorneys," in any civil action brought by or against the United States or any agency or official of the United States acting in an official capacity. If, as respondents argue, one of the main functions of a private attorney general is to call public officials to account and to insist that they enforce the law, it would follow in such cases that attorneys' fees should be awarded against the Government or the officials themselves. Indeed, that very claim was asserted in this case. But § 2412 on its face, and in light of its legislative history, generally bars such awards, which, if allowable at all, must be expressly provided for by statute, as, for example, under Title II of the Civil Rights Act of 1964, 42 U.S.C. § 2000a–3(b).

We do not purport to assess the merits or demerits of the "American Rule" with respect to the allowance of attorneys' fees. It has been criticized in recent years, and courts have been urged to find exceptions to it. It is also apparent from our national experience that the encouragement of private action to implement public policy has been viewed as desirable in a variety of circumstances. But the rule followed in our courts with respect to attorneys' fees has survived. It is deeply rooted in our history and in congressional policy; and it is not for us to invade the legislature's province by redistributing litigation costs in the manner suggested by respondents and followed by the Court of Appeals.

Justice Marshall, dissenting.

In reversing the award of attorneys' fees to the respondent environmentalist groups, the Court today disavows the well-established power of federal equity courts to award attorneys' fees when the interests of justice so require. While under the traditional American Rule the courts ordinarily refrain from allowing attorneys' fees, we have recognized several judicial exceptions to that rule for classes of cases in which equity seemed to favor fee shifting. By imposing an absolute bar on the use of the "private attorney general" rationale as a basis for awarding attorneys' fees, the Court today takes an extremely narrow view of the independent power of the courts in this area—a view that flies squarely in the face of our prior cases.

I see no basis in precedent or policy for holding that the courts cannot award attorneys' fees where the interests of justice require recovery, simply because the claim does not fit comfortably within one of the previously sanctioned judicial exceptions to the American Rule. The Court has not in the past regarded the award of attorneys' fees as a matter reserved for the Legislature, and it has certainly not read the docketing-fees statute as a general bar to judicial fee shifting. The Court's concern with the difficulty of applying meaningful standards in awarding attorneys' fees to successful "public benefit" litigants is a legitimate one, but in my view it overstates the novelty of the "private attorney general" theory. The guidelines developed in closely analogous statutory and nonstatutory attorneys' fee cases could readily be applied in cases such as the one at bar. I therefore disagree with the Court's flat rejection of the private-attorney-general rationale for fee shifting. Moreover, in my view the equities in this case support an award of attorneys' fees against Alyeska.

In Alyeska the Court rejected a judicially created "private attorney general" exception to the long-standing general rule requiring parties to bear their own lawyers' fees. The recognized exceptions for judicial imposition of fee awards, mentioned in the case, are based on extreme conduct—disobedience of a court order or oppressive litigation—that courts are unlikely to attribute to parties in civil litigation. As the Court also made clear, legislatures have the power to expand the availability of fee awards, and they have done so for particular kinds of litigation such as for civil rights claims. Neither Congress nor the state legislatures have moved significantly to shift toward the approach long followed in many other less litigious countries that requires unsuccessful parties to bear the burdens of unsuccessful litigation they instigated. Various alternatives are possible, including a system that would correlate a fee award to the extent to which a party recovers what was sought, allowing a party who recovers only a small portion of what was demanded to recover only a proportionately small amount of lawyers' fees. Some powerful lawyer organizations, especially those comprised of lawyers whose practice focuses on filing personal injury lawsuits, have vigorously opposed liberalizing fee awards. They offer a number of reasons, including the typical plaintiff's limited resources compared to commercial defendants and insurance companies, and the disincentive fee shifting would create for those who seek justice but cannot be assured of success in an imprecise litigation system.

Litigation Process

Litigation in the federal and state courts is begun when at least one party, a plaintiff, files a claim in a court asking for relief to be granted against at least one defendant. Defendants may file counterclaims that are directly related to the plaintiff's claims and under some circumstances even if they are not. Although no one should file litigation without expecting to see it through to the end, most cases settle at some point and many others are decided on legal grounds before trial. Only a small percentage of the cases for which litigation is begun are decided by a trial.

Depending on the nature of the dispute and the parties' residences, some cases must be brought in a particular federal or state court. When there is a choice, the considerations can be complex. The time it takes for a case to get to trial varies depending on the court. Cases involving juries consume more of the courts' resources and consequently usually take longer to schedule. Courts set a schedule for the trial and deadlines by which certain actions must be completed. Although extensions are granted for good cause, the courts will hold a party accountable for failing to meet a deadline and could even dismiss the case or award a judgment. This means that lawyers and their clients must begin to address the pretrial requirements early enough to meet the deadlines.

Depending on the dispute's complexity, the need for the parties to gather information, and the court's docket, the case will be scheduled for trial within months or years. Courts schedule overlapping civil trials because many cases settle, and if the court scheduled only one case at a time, then courtrooms would usually be idle. The scheduling process can lead to frustration. Parties to litigation commonly find out the day before a trial is set to begin, or even the very day they appear in the courthouse, that the trial has to be rescheduled due to court scheduling conflicts.

Pretrial

The public hears a lot about trials but very little about the pretrial process. In fact more cases are resolved during the pretrial process than as a result of a trial. Before the parties get to attempt to persuade a judge or jury of the righteousness of their causes, they must address the legal merits of their claims and defenses, disclose and collect information, and deal with a number of procedures, many of which could dispose of the case.

Pleadings

Pleadings are the documents that the parties file with the court. They are important for several reasons. The statutes and common law set prerequisites for commencing and continuing litigation. Failure to comply with these requirements could result in delay, wasted expense, and even dismissal of the action. Pleadings form part of the litigation record. Trial judges and appeals courts rely on pleadings for a glimpse of the nature of the dispute. Claims, counterclaims, offsets, and many other matters must appropriately appear in the pleadings or they may be deemed to have been waived on an appeal and therefore ultimately lost.

A case is normally begun with a complaint, sometimes called a "petition" or a "writ." In the complaint the plaintiff will allege entitlement to relief in a cause of action based on a statute or a common law principle. The defendant being sued then has a time limit within which to appear in the case and file an answer or other response, usually within 20 days. To appear or file an appearance does not mean what it literally suggests; it means to file a document with the court with required information, not so show up in person. The defendant's answer usually will respond to the allegations in the case by either admitting them, denying that they are true, or stating that the defendant has insufficient information on which to admit or deny the allegation. Sometimes the defendant may instead respond with a motion to dismiss the case without responding to the particular allegations. Additionally, defendants may be able to make counterclaims or may be required to make them if they are ever to be made.

Motions to Decide the Case

Most cases involve potentially dispositive motions filed with the court. The two most common are a motion to dismiss and a motion for summary judgment. With a motion to dismiss a party contends that the law does not recognize the claim or that the party filing it has no right to be in that particular court. A motion for summary judgment contends that there is no need to resolve disagreements about what happened because the law requires only one result regardless of how differing versions of the facts would be resolved. Judges review the submissions and often do their own research or have their law clerks do it for them. In many courts the judges also will hear arguments from the lawyers before reaching a decision. The judge's decision may be given at the hearing, a few days later, months later, or not until the trial, depending on the nature of the motion and the judge's inclinations.

Discovery from Other Parties in the Case

Discovery is the process by which the parties learn about each other's cases and prepare for trial. Discovery can involve production of documents, written answers to questions, testimony under oath, and other methods. Discovery typically has two purposes. One is to find out information. The other is to create a record of a party's or witness's version of the facts, which can be used to prevent surprises at the trial and to contradict a witness who might later become creative with new recollections.

A party is entitled to review all documents in another party's possession that might have something to do with the case unless they are subject to a privilege. Documents do not have to be relevant to be subject to discovery. Someone receiving a request for production must collect and make available the documents identified in the request if they are within the person's control, unless they are subject to one of the narrow exceptions, such as for client–lawyer communications. Discoverable material includes paper files as well as information stored in electronic format including e-mails, databases, and electronic archives. Document production can be onerous especially for organizations without thoughtful record-retention practices.

Interrogatories are another common form of discovery. They are written questions from one party to another. Lawyers are usually involved in drafting interrogatories and in preparing answers, but the parties should be thorough and careful with responses because they will be held accountable for them at trial.

Also common are depositions at which a deponent, or witness, while under oath to tell the truth, answers a lawyer's questions and the exchange is recorded in a transcript and sometimes on video. To preserve the testimony of someone who might be unavailable for trial, lawyers sometimes take depositions of their own clients or of their own cooperative witnesses. Depositions are taken to learn information and to commit witnesses to testimony. If the trial testimony differs, the deposition transcript can be used to show inconsistencies.

There is no judge at a deposition, and questions do not have to be relevant. Deponents who have never before been subjected to the experience are usually surprised about how wide-ranging the questions can be. Work histories, educational background, and relationships to the parties are typical lines of questioning. Lawyers may not coach their clients during a deposition. Even though there are few limits on the questions that can be asked at a deposition, lawyers will interject an objection to the form of the question as confusing or otherwise inappropriate. Although the inquiring lawyer might agree to rephrase a question after hearing such an objection, the witness may still be compelled to answer, and any continuing disagreement about the form of the question is left for the judge's ruling at trial if the testimony is offered.

Depositions can get very expensive. The stenographer's fees alone can cost thousands of dollars. This affords some lawyers the opportunity to take depositions not for a proper purpose but instead to try to exhaust their opponents' resources or willingness to continue. Nonetheless, depositions are often important for proper trial preparation, and an effective or disastrous deposition can change the entire course of the litigation.

Discovery from Third Parties

Those who are parties to litigation have an obligation to produce documents and to provide deposition testimony to the other side upon request. Documents and testimony can also be obtained from others who are not parties to the case by agreement or by use of a subpoena. Lawyers have the power to subpoena documents and witnesses. Receipt of a subpoena can raise tricky issues, especially when the request involves confidential or private information such as personnel files or proprietary secrets. Sometimes there is a legal basis for not giving the demanded information. If the requesting lawyer will not agree to withdraw the subpoena, a motion to quash it can be filed with the court in which the case is pending. Subpoenas should never be ignored, however, because they have the effect of a court order and the court could hold someone in contempt simply for refusing to cooperate rather than asking the court to intervene.

Pretrial Conduct: *Dondi Properties Corp. v. Commerce Savings & Loan Ass'n*

Much of the pretrial process is intended to unfold without court involvement. Court rules require lawyers to attempt to agree before filing a contested motion. Court rules also usually require the parties' lawyers to meet—in person or telephonically—to work out a pretrial schedule and other procedural matters. The agreement is submitted to the court for approval, which normally is routinely granted, and becomes compulsory. Unfortunately, many lawyers, and many clients, see the litigation process as a battleground for making things difficult and inflicting costs on adversaries. Judges must deal with unproductive litigation tactics regularly. Lawyers commonly accuse each other of improper or abusive tactics and ask judges to intervene. Judges usually deflect such efforts, but occasionally they become fed up and react. In the following opinion the several judges of a federal district took the unusual step of issuing an opinion en banc—meaning "all together"—to crack down on what they saw as out-of-control behavior. The case involved claims of insurance and consumer-protection law violations and the lawyers filed numerous motions accusing each other of improper conduct *during* the litigation. The unusual opinion provides insight into judges' perception of counterproductive tactics.

Dondi Properties Corp. v. Commerce Savings & Loan Ass'n,
121 F.R.D. 284 (N.D. Tex. 1988)

We sit en banc to adopt standards of litigation conduct for attorneys appearing in civil actions in the Northern District of Texas.

Dondi Properties is a suit for recovery based upon civil RICO, common law and statutory fraud, the Texas Fraudulent Transfer Act, federal regulations prohibiting affiliate transactions, civil conspiracy, negligent misrepresentation, and usury, arising in connection with activities related to the failed Vernon Savings and Loan Association. *Knight* is an action for violations of the Texas Insurance Code and Texas Deceptive Trade Practices—Consumer Protection Act, and for breach of duty of good faith and breach of contract, arising from defendant's refusal to pay plaintiff the proceeds of a life insurance policy.

In *Dondi Properties*, the following motions have been referred to the magistrate pursuant to 28 U.S.C. § 636(b) and N.D. Tex. Misc. Order No. 6, Rule 2(c): the Stool defendants' third motion for sanctions or, in the alternative, to compel (and supplement to the motion); the third motion for sanctions of defendant, Commerce Savings Association (and supplement to the motion); defendant, W. Deryl Comer's, first motion for sanctions or, in the alternative, motion to compel (and supplement to the motion); the Stool defendants' motion for sanctions against plaintiffs' attorney; defendant, Jack Franks', first motion for sanctions or, in the alternative, motion to compel; defendant, R. H. Westmoreland's, motion for sanctions and, in the alternative, to compel; and various submissions containing additional authorities in support of the motions and briefs already filed. Plaintiffs have responded to the motions, and the Stool defendants have filed a motion for leave to file reply to plaintiffs' response.

The sanction motions complain of plaintiffs' failure to answer interrogatories, failure to comply with prior orders of the court pertaining to discovery, misrepresenting facts to the court, and improperly withholding documents.

In *Knight*, there is pending before a judge of this court plaintiff's motion to strike a reply brief that defendant filed without leave of court. On April 8, 1988, defendant filed four motions, including motions for separate trials and to join another party. On April 27, 1988, plaintiff filed her response to the motions. Thereafter, without leave of court, defendant, on May 26, 1988, filed a reply to plaintiff's response. On June 3, 1988, plaintiff filed a motion to strike the reply, to which motion defendant has filed a response. Plaintiff contends the reply brief should be stricken because defendant did not, as required by Local Rule 5.1(f), obtain leave to file a reply, because defendant failed to seek permission immediately upon receipt of plaintiff's response, and, alternatively, because defendant's reply was filed in excess of 20 days after plaintiff filed her response. In the event the court does not strike the reply, plaintiff requests leave to file an additional response.

The judicial branch of the United States government is charged with responsibility for deciding cases and controversies and for administering justice. We attempt to carry out our responsibilities in the most prompt and efficient manner, recognizing that justice delayed, and justice obtained at excessive cost, is often justice denied.

We address today a problem that, though of relatively recent origin, is so pernicious that it threatens to delay the administration of justice and to place litigation beyond the financial reach of litigants. With alarming frequency, we find that valuable judicial and attorney time is consumed in resolving unnecessary contention and sharp practices between lawyers. Judges and magistrates of this court are required to devote substantial attention to refereeing abusive litigation tactics that range from benign incivility to outright obstruction. Our system of justice can ill-afford to devote scarce resources to supervising matters that do not advance the resolution of the merits of a case; nor can justice long remain available to deserving litigants if the costs of litigation are fueled unnecessarily to the point of being prohibitive.

As judges and former practitioners from varied backgrounds and levels of experience, we judicially know that litigation is conducted today in a manner far different from years past. Whether the increased size of the bar has decreased collegiality, or the legal profession has become only a business, or experienced lawyers have ceased to teach new lawyers the standards to be observed, or because of other factors not readily categorized, we observe patterns of behavior that forebode ill for our system of justice. We now adopt standards designed to end such conduct.

We begin by recognizing our power to adopt standards for attorney conduct in civil actions and by determining, as a matter of prudence, that we, rather than the circuit court, should adopt such standards in the first instance.

By means of the Rules Enabling Act of 1934, now codified as 28 U.S.C. § 2072, Congress has authorized the Supreme Court to adopt rules of civil procedure. The Court has promulgated rules that empower district courts to manage all aspects of a civil action, including pretrial scheduling and planning (Rule 16) and discovery (Rule 26(f)). We are authorized to protect attorneys and litigants from practices that may increase their expenses and burdens (Rules 26(b)(1) and 26(c)) or may cause them annoyance, embarrassment, or oppression (Rule 26(c)), and to impose sanctions upon parties or attorneys who violate the rules and orders of the court (Rules 16(f) and 37). We likewise have the power by statute to tax costs, expenses, and attorney's fees to attorneys who unreasonably and vexatiously multiply the proceedings in any case. 28 U.S.C. § 1927. We are also granted the authority to punish, as contempt of court, the misbehavior of court officers. 18 U.S.C. § 401. In addition to the authority granted us by statute or by rule, we possess the inherent power to regulate the administration of justice.

The Dallas Bar Association recently adopted "Guidelines of Professional Courtesy" and a "Lawyer's Creed" that are both sensible and pertinent to the problems we address here. From them we adopt the following as standards of practice to be observed by attorneys appearing in civil actions in this district:

(A) In fulfilling his or her primary duty to the client, a lawyer must be ever conscious of the broader duty to the judicial system that serves both attorney and client.

(B) A lawyer owes, to the judiciary, candor, diligence and utmost respect.

(C) A lawyer owes, to opposing counsel, a duty of courtesy and cooperation, the observance of which is necessary for the efficient administration of our system of justice and the respect of the public it serves.

(D) A lawyer unquestionably owes, to the administration of justice, the fundamental duties of personal dignity and professional integrity.

(E) Lawyers should treat each other, the opposing party, the court, and members of the court staff with courtesy and civility and conduct themselves in a professional manner at all times.

(F) A client has no right to demand that counsel abuse the opposite party or indulge in offensive conduct. A lawyer shall always treat adverse witnesses and suitors with fairness and due consideration.

(G) In adversary proceedings, clients are litigants and though ill feeling may exist between clients, such ill feeling should not influence a lawyer's conduct, attitude, or demeanor towards opposing lawyers.

(H) A lawyer should not use any form of discovery, or the scheduling of discovery, as a means of harassing opposing counsel or counsel's client.

(I) Lawyers will be punctual in communications with others and in honoring scheduled appearances, and will recognize that neglect and tardiness are demeaning to the lawyer and to the judicial system.

(J) If a fellow member of the Bar makes a just request for cooperation, or seeks scheduling accommodation, a lawyer will not arbitrarily or unreasonably withhold consent.

(K) Effective advocacy does not require antagonistic or obnoxious behavior and members of the Bar will adhere to the higher standard of conduct which judges, lawyers, clients, and the public may rightfully expect.

Attorneys who abide faithfully by the standards we adopt should have little difficulty conducting themselves as members of a learned profession whose unswerving duty is to the public they serve and to the system of justice in which they practice. Those litigators who persist in viewing themselves solely as combatants, or who perceive that they are retained to win at all costs without regard to fundamental principles of justice, will find that their conduct does not square with the practices we expect of them. Malfeasant counsel can expect instead that their conduct will prompt an appropriate response from the court, including the range of sanctions the Fifth Circuit suggests in the Rule 11 context: "a warm friendly discussion on the record, a hard-nosed reprimand in open court, compulsory legal education, monetary sanctions, or other measures appropriate to the circumstances." *Thomas v. Capital Security Services, Inc.*, 836 F.2d 866, 878 (5th Cir. 1988).

We do not, by adopting these standards, invite satellite litigation of the kind we now see in the context of Fed. R. Civ. P. 11 motions [in which lawyers accuse each other of violating pleadings requirements]. To do so would defeat the fundamental premise which motivates our action. We do intend, however, to take the steps necessary to ensure that justice is not removed from the reach of litigants either because improper litigation tactics interpose unnecessary delay or because such actions increase the cost of litigation beyond the litigant's financial grasp.

Similarly, we do not imply by prescribing these standards that counsel are excused from conducting themselves in any manner otherwise required by law or by court rule. We think the standards we now adopt are a necessary corollary to existing law, and are appropriately established to signal our strong disapproval of practices that have no place in our system of justice and to emphasize that a lawyer's conduct, both with respect to the court and to other lawyers, should at all times be characterized by honesty and fair play.

Although in excess of 20 pleadings and letters from counsel have been presented to the court involving various defendants' motions for sanctions, the common denominator of all is whether or not plaintiffs have complied with the previous discovery orders of the magistrate.

In seeking dismissal of plaintiffs' case, the moving defendants have categorized plaintiffs' conduct and that of their counsel as being in "bad faith" and "in defiance" of the court's prior orders. Such characterization of a party opponent's conduct should be sparingly employed by counsel and should be reserved for only those instances in which there is a sound basis in fact demonstrating a party's deliberate and intentional disregard of an order of the court or of obligations imposed under applicable Federal Rules of Civil Procedure. Such allegations, when inappropriately made, add much heat but little light to the court's task of deciding discovery disputes.

Although there are conceded instances of neglect on the part of plaintiffs and their counsel and instances of lack of communication or miscommunication among counsel for the parties in the present discovery disputes, there is no showing of intentional or willful conduct on the part of plaintiffs or their counsel which warrants dismissal under Rule 37(b), Federal Rules of Civil

Procedure. However, the disputes which exist amply demonstrate an inadequate utilization of Local Rule 5.1(a).

Local Rule 5.1(a) implicitly recognizes that in general the rules dealing with discovery in federal cases are to be self-executing. The purpose of the conference requirement is to promote a frank exchange between counsel to resolve issues by agreement or to at least narrow and focus the matters in controversy before judicial resolution is sought. Regrettably over the years, in many instances the conference requirement seems to have evolved into a pro forma matter. If disputes can be resolved after motions have been filed, it follows that in all but the most extraordinary circumstances, they could have been resolved in the course of Rule 5.1(a) conferences.

The manner in which the conference is held and the length of the conference will be dictated by the complexity of the issues and the sound judgment of attorneys in their capacities as advocates as well as officers of the court, with the objective of maximizing the resolution of disputes without court intervention. Properly utilized Rule 5.1(a) promotes judicial economy while at the same time reducing litigants' expenses incurred for attorneys' time in briefing issues and in preparing and presenting pleadings.

Because the present controversies may well be resolved, or appreciably narrowed, following further communications among counsel and because the court is not presented with circumstances which warrant dismissal under Rule 37, the movant defendants' motions will be denied at this time.

Insuring that members of the legal profession comply with ethical standards should be a matter of concern to all attorneys, and alleged breaches should be brought to the attention of the grievance committee by an attorney without charge to a client, which is appropriate only when resolution by a court is warranted. By the same token, absent a motion to disqualify, which if granted would adversely affect his client's interests, an attorney whose conduct is called into question must himself bear the cost of defending his actions before a grievance committee.

It is undisputed that defendant did not obtain court permission to reply to plaintiff's response to defendant's motions for separate trials and to join a party. Defendant explains in its response to the motion to strike that "because of the flurry of activity in this case, it failed to secure permission from the Presiding Judge to file the reply." Although defendant clearly violated a Local Rule of this court, the court concludes that the error did not warrant plaintiff's filing a motion to strike.

In the present case, the parties have presumably incurred the expense of preparing, and the court has expended time considering, pleadings that go not to a question that will advance the merits of this case but instead to a collateral determination whether the court should consider a particular pleading. In isolation, such expenditures may appear inconsequential. Considered in the proper context of numerous civil actions and frequent disputes, it is apparent that cooperation between opposing counsel is essential to the efficient operation of our justice system.

Turning to the merits of the motion to strike, the court concludes that the reply brief should not be stricken and that plaintiff should not be permitted to file a further response. Although defendant did not immediately seek permission to file a reply, the court has yet to consider the underlying substantive motions; it thus will not interfere with the court's decisional process to consider the reply. The court declines to permit plaintiff to file a further response because the burden on the motions is upon the defendant, who should thus be given the opportunity to open and close the argument.

Presumably the parties in the cases involved in *Dondi Properties* had real disputes to resolve, but instead they devoted resources to fighting about discovery procedures and about whether certain documents could be filed with the court. Some clients who become involved with such tactics do so unwittingly, but the reality is that others want to use slash-and-burn litigation tactics to punish their opponents, and they select lawyers who have reputations for using them. As the judges in *Dondi Properties* make clear, the litigation process is intended to facilitate resolution of disputes and not to provide fertile ground for new disagreements and unproductive consumption of the parties' and the courts' resources. In the judges' collective words, "justice delayed, and justice obtained at excessive cost, is often justice denied."

Experts

Expert witnesses are common in cases involving medical or other professional standards of care, faulty design or construction, and damage claims based on valuations or projections. Individuals with scientific, technical, or other specialized knowledge are allowed to give their opinions to help the judge or jury understand the evidence or decide a disputed fact. The court determines whether a proposed expert is sufficiently qualified to testify based on knowledge, skill, experience, training, or education, and whether the testimony is based on sufficiently reliable principles and methods applied to facts.

An effective expert becomes a teacher in the case and is perceived as giving honest opinions based on a neutral evaluation. There also are "professional experts," who make a handsome living working for lawyers in litigation. Some seem to reach "opinions" that coincidentally always support the lawyer hiring them. Finding experts can be very important, if not absolutely necessary, for success in a case. Experts can be expensive. As with other professions, those who give expert testimony usually charge for their time and some have high rates. The cost involves more than the expert's time required for the actual trial. Experts also charge for time spent reviewing the facts, doing research, meeting with the lawyer, giving a deposition, and then appearing at the trial. It adds up quickly.

Trials

Trial procedure varies somewhat depending on the court and the nature of the claims and counterclaims. All federal trials follow the same basic sequence of events due to the Federal Rules of Procedure and the Federal Rules of Evidence, with minor variations due to local rules and customs. Most state courts now have rules of procedure and evidence that are very similar to the federal rules. Notwithstanding basically similar rules, the scope and tenor of trials vary substantially. Some involve straightforward legal issues and only a couple of witnesses. Others involve the testimony of many witnesses and contentious arguments about legal issues.

Judges and Juries

For some cases there is no right to a jury. When juries are an option, the parties choose whether they want the case decided by a judge or jury. If either party wants a jury, both get it. A request for a jury trial must be made at the beginning of the case. The choice between judge and jury depends on complex considerations. Jury cases generally take longer to be brought to trial, and the trial itself usually takes longer and is more expensive. The main reason for choosing a jury is an expectation that a group of ordinary citizens will view a cause more favorably than a judge. But the common assumption that juries are likely to be more generous with damage awards than judges is not clearly established statistically. Some lawyers prefer judge-only cases because the trial probably will progress more quickly and be less expensive. Some opt for judges because they are convinced that their cases are legally sound and believe that judges tend to be swayed more by legal reasoning than by sympathy or other influences unrelated to the merits.

In cases with a jury the selection process is intended to form a panel of open-minded individuals. The parties and the court all have some say about who will be on the jury. The usual reason for excusing a potential juror from service for cause is a personal connection to the dispute or to a party, lawyer, or key witness in the case. The parties usually also have preemptory challenges to remove individuals from the jury pool without having to give a reason, which they exercise for potential jurors whose background suggests an unfavorable predisposition.

Trial Procedure

Trial procedure depends on formal rules of procedure and evidence, rulings made by the judge in each particular case, and custom. The course of a trial can take sudden turns and can sometimes come to a surprising end, but most cases follow a similar pattern.

In a case with a jury the lawyers will make opening statements that introduce the dispute to the jury and attempt to set a tone for the trial that favors the lawyers' clients. If a jury is not involved, the practice varies. Some judges prefer to hear brief introductory statements from the lawyers, and others want to get right to the testimony.

After the opening statements plaintiffs present their cases. Witnesses are called and placed under oath. The lawyers calling the witnesses conduct direct examinations by asking non-leading questions such as "who," "what," "when," "where," and "how." If the other side objects to a question or response, the judge will decide whether the question should be answered. After direct examination, the opposing lawyer has the opportunity for cross-examination. This may be to get more information from the witness, but is more likely to be to contradict or discredit the testimony already given. Lawyers conducting cross-examination are allowed to ask leading questions, such as "would you agree that"? The judge will only intervene if the questioning becomes overly abrasive, repetitive, or otherwise violates the lenient rules and standards for cross examination.

Documents must be entered into evidence for them to be submitted to the judge or jury for consideration. Documents and other items sought to be used as exhibits are first marked "for identification." If the other side has no objection, it is marked as an exhibit and can be used in the case as evidence. If there is an objection, the lawyer seeking to use the item first attempts to establish that it meets the requirements for being an exhibit, through witness testimony and perhaps through legal argument. The other side then makes its objections, and the judge rules on admissibility.

Some cases involve views, where the judge, the jury if there is one, the parties, and the lawyers travel to a site to see something involved in the dispute. For example, in real-estate boundary disputes a view often is taken to give a first-hand sense of the property configuration.

After the evidence has been heard, in a jury case the lawyers have an opportunity for closing argument. They recap the testimony and attempt to put it into a context that will persuade the jury of the correctness of their position. In a judge case, the lawyers usually have a brief opportunity to summarize.

After the closing argument, if there is a jury, the judge instructs its members about the law and defines the questions to be answered. Each side submits its version of proposed instructions to the judge, who reviews and revises them. After the instructions are given, the jury goes into a private room and deliberates. Usually, unless the parties agree otherwise, juries must be unanimous in their verdict. They sometimes reach a decision in a few hours; sometimes it takes days. The result is reported to the judge and then read to the parties and their lawyers in the courtroom.

In a case without a jury the parties submit requests for rulings of law and findings of fact. The judge considers the requests, reviews the evidence, and issues an opinion. The opinion may be quickly reached—sometimes immediately at the end of the case. Or it may take days or weeks for the judge to work through the issues and to prepare a written opinion.

A few trials are finished within a day. Some take several weeks or months. The typical trial is a few days. It is an intense and exhausting experience for anyone directly involved. The lawyers must shift rapidly from one task, such as giving an opening statement or arguing a point of law, to another, such as cross-examining an expert. Most people who have been parties to a trial have found it to be interesting, frustrating, and bewildering—at various points in its course.

Appeals

Most decisions of judges and juries can be appealed to a higher court. There are strict deadlines for filing an appeal and very narrow exceptions for extensions. Appeals are not retrials. For the most part appellate courts review the legal principles and address errors made by trial judges in interpreting the law. If the error was important enough, the result may be overturned, or a new trial may be ordered. Although there are grounds to overturn jury verdicts, including for insufficient evidence to support the verdict, appellate courts defer to the juries' interpretation of the facts if it is at all plausible.

To support their appellate requests the lawyers submit briefs discussing the law and summarizing the facts as presented at the trial. In some cases appellate courts make a decision based only on the written submissions. In many cases they offer the lawyers an opportunity to orally present their appeals. Appellate courts usually assign a panel of judges to hear several cases on a day on which they "sit." The panel usually has three or five judges; the U.S. Supreme Court has nine. The panel will allow the lawyers from each side a few minutes to argue the legal issues, but usually the judges do not wait for long to start probing the lawyers about their positions. Even when the judges already are nearly certain about their decision, they usually will test their own convictions by challenging the parties' arguments. Appellate courts usually release decisions within weeks or months after the oral argument. The outcome can be an affirmation of the trial-court result, a reversal with a new result, or a remand to the trial court for a new trial or other proceedings.

Collecting Judgment

Regardless of a party's success in litigation, recovery of the awarded relief usually is not a simple matter. Appellate courts frequently overturn or alter trial decisions, or send the case back for another trial, extending the process. In many state courts the judgment cannot be collected as long as any appeal is pending in the case. The reason for this is obvious: if a judgment is paid and the outcome is later reversed, the party that paid may not be able to get the money back. Even when a party is not entitled to delay collection pending appeal, courts usually have the authority to postpone collection by issuing a stay of the judgment. Sometimes courts will require the losing party to post a bond or other security for payment in exchange for the stay, but this likely will not be required if the party held liable has more than adequate assets to pay the eventual judgment. Federal courts will stay enforcement of the judgment if a sufficient bond is posted, but federal courts generally have interpreted the rule as allowing them sufficient discretion to postpone collection even without requiring a bond.

These realities require that those seeking a desirable result in litigation assess the likelihood of collecting before beginning the litigation. Procedures are available for plaintiffs in some circumstances to obtain liens on the defendant's property at the start of litigation as security for a judgment. Once a judgment is obtained there are civil procedures at that time for seizing bank accounts and arranging for a sale of the liable party's property. Courts also may order defendants to pay the judgment over time. These procedures are by no means a guaranty of collection. Established enterprises may have sufficient assets and longevity to pay sizeable judgments, and many enterprises and individuals have insurance to pay damage awards. But many of the kinds of companies that are most often involved in litigation use organizational forms that have limited liquid assets and that insulate owners from personal liability. Many individuals who are inclined to be involved in litigation have sheltered their assets by putting them in trusts or by keeping them where they are difficult to find. State laws also afford judgment debtors exemptions from seizure of their homesteads and certain other property. Additionally, collection usually can be halted with a federal bankruptcy filing in which debts can be discharged. The sum of these realities is that collection often requires a relentless and costly effort with unpredictable results.

Alternative Dispute Resolution

Before and after a lawsuit has begun the parties should explore alternative methods of resolving their dispute. There are several possibilities for resolving a dispute without the delay, expense, and uncertainty of a trial. The two most common forms are mediation and arbitration. With mediation someone who is not involved in the dispute, usually a lawyer or retired judge trained in mediation, leads the parties and their lawyers through a discussion intended to identify common ground and narrow differences. With arbitration the parties submit the resolution of their dispute to a decision maker—a person or a panel—as with litigation.

Mediation

Courts sometimes require or encourage mediation, but in any event it is usually worthwhile. Mediators do not issue decisions. They invite the parties to exchange information, discuss their interests, and work toward an agreement acceptable to all concerned. If the parties can see that those on the other side are really people with a problem just like them, they sometimes become more willing to compromise. Experienced mediators will say that the opportunity to vent is a key to success. Parties want to be heard, and this impulse sometimes drives them to litigation. Once a party has had the chance to express a point of view, compromise may be easier to achieve.

In mediation the parties are free to address all issues of concern to them, not just legal causes of action. They retain control over the outcome because they must agree to the resolution. They do not relinquish that control to a judge or jury. Mediation can save everyone considerable expense and enable the parties to devote their time and energy to things more productive than litigation. Parties also are more likely to honor agreements they reach in mediation than they are to readily satisfy litigation judgments.

In a typical mediation session, the mediator begins with an opening statement that explains the goals and sets the session ground rules. Next a joint session, or caucus, is held in which the parties take turns expressing their perspectives to the mediator and, more importantly, to each other. Sometimes the lawyers speak or the parties may choose to speak for themselves. The next steps differ among mediators and types of mediations. Usually the process entails a series of joint and separate discussions in which the mediator explores the parties' interests and possible resolutions. If an agreement is reached, the parties will jointly document its essential terms. If no agreement is reached, the mediator may review with the parties whatever progress was made and discuss possibilities for continuing the discussion about a resolution.

Generally the rules of evidence prohibit use of statements made in compromise negotiations to prove liability or the amount of a claim in litigation. In addition, parties to the mediation typically agree, at the mediator's urging, to confidentiality of all information obtained in the mediation unless they later agree to its disclosure. Sharing information with the mediator and each other facilitates settlement. To insure that everyone understands these rules, the common practice is for the mediator to have a joint discussion at the beginning of the session with all parties about confidentiality.

In recent years the courts and many lawyers have promoted use of mediation vigorously. Many lawyers and others have seized on this trend to attempt to develop mediation practices or to enhance their reputations within their professional communities. The ability to be an effective mediator does not necessarily follow from being a judge or lawyer. Good mediators are able to grasp contentious issues quickly. This ability can come from a legal or judicial background, or simply from a knack for figuring out what is truly important. A good mediator exudes confidence about solutions, is tenacious about finding them, and has infectious energy. In most disputes the things that really separate the parties are not as big or as complicated as they first seem. A good mediator knows this and can focus on the real barriers to compromise. But the parties ultimately are responsible for a successful mediation and can ruin the possibilities of a mutually acceptable resolution with a combative or begrudging attitude.

Arbitration

As mentioned above, in arbitration the parties submit their dispute to a decision maker. Parties use arbitration if required to do so by contract or if they jointly wish to do so after the dispute arises. An advantage of arbitration is the opportunity to submit the disagreement to someone with expertise in the subject area of the dispute. For this reason arbitration is common in construction and labor disputes. Some arbitrations use a panel of arbitrators, but most are submitted to a single arbitrator. Regardless of whom the parties choose as an arbitrator, the starting point is usually an agreement in writing about the details of the process to be followed and responsibility for paying the arbitrator's fees.

Parties can structure arbitration as they wish and confine the process or narrow the differences to be resolved. For example, they could agree to a maximum and minimum award amount, or require the arbitrator to choose between two amounts. Usually the process loosely follows trial procedure. The parties or their lawyers make opening statements, file documentary evidence, present witnesses, and cross-examine the opposing party's witnesses. They may request arbitrators to make legal interpretations and to exclude claims or defenses before or during the session. At the end arbitrators usually ask for written summaries and issue their decisions weeks or months after considering parties' the submissions and their own notes and research.

With arbitration the parties should have more control over scheduling than with a court trial. In theory the arbitration process will be less costly than litigation because there is likely to be less pretrial discovery and procedural wrangling and more control over scheduling. But arbitrators tend to be less strict with deadlines and procedure, and the process can be prolonged and diverted in ways that most judges would not tolerate. Arbitration hearings also can become just as personally contentious as trials, especially if the arbitrator gives free rein at the hearing.

State and federal laws generally provide that arbitration decisions are entitled to be enforced in the same ways as court judgments. Arbitration decisions may be challenged in a court only under rare circumstances, such as if the arbitrator's award involved fraud, a party was substantially prejudiced by not being given notice required by an arbitration agreement, or the arbitrator exceeded powers given in the agreement. The absence of appellate review of the arbitrator's legal interpretations is a reason that many lawyers prefer the court process even if it is slower and more expensive.

Review Questions

1. In dispute resolution what is the difference between staking out a position and considering shared interests?
2. What are the principal types of remedies that can be sought in litigation?
3. What is the "American Rule" for recovery of attorneys' fees in litigation, and what are its recognized exceptions?
4. What are a "motion for summary judgment" and a "motion to dismiss"?
5. What are the principal forms of pretrial discovery available to the parties to litigation?
6. What kinds of attorney conduct have been the subject of judicial objections?
7. What function do experts perform in litigation?
8. What do appeals courts consider?
9. At what point in litigation should parties consider the possibilities of collecting judgment, and why?
10. What are the advantages and disadvantages of mediation and arbitration?

Chapter 14

Managing the Lawyer Relationship

An eminent lawyer cannot be a dishonest man. Tell me a man is dishonest, and I will answer
he is no lawyer. He cannot be, because he is careless and reckless of justice;
the law is not in his heart, is not the standard and rule of his conduct.

Daniel Webster

CHAPTER OBJECTIVES

After studying this chapter you should better understand:

- The dynamics of law practice and important considerations for choosing a lawyer
- The nature of a lawyer's obligations of loyalty and confidentiality
- Professional and other considerations for determining lawyer compensation and the consequences of insurance coverage for retaining lawyers
- The nature of a lawyer's professional obligations to the court, opposing lawyers and parties, and the public
- The basic remedies for lawyer misconduct and negligence

This book is intended to help readers better inform themselves about the law and the legal system. Such knowledge is useful for avoiding legal entanglements and for resolving problems in ways that might avoid costly legal fees and other diversions of time and resources. There are circumstances, however, in which getting a lawyer's expert advice or advocacy is the reasonable thing to do, such as when making important decisions that involve complex legal issues or when involved in litigation. This chapter is intended to be useful to those who are considering hiring lawyers and to those who are managing ongoing legal representation. It examines the nature of the client–lawyer relationship, including lawyers' obligations to their clients, the legal system, and other parties. It also describes some important considerations for selecting a lawyer and for making good decisions as a client.

The Lawyer's Role

Many people see lawyers as untrustworthy opportunists who look to profit from others' problems. There are lawyers who deserve such a bad reputation. Other people see at least some lawyers as avengers or protectors who will champion a righteous cause. There are lawyers who have earned this esteem. But lawyers should not be regarded entirely apart from the individuals whose interests and causes they represent. Lawyers' actions, for good or bad, usually reflect their clients' interests. Those who empower lawyers bear some responsibility for the impact of positions taken and causes pursued, and the resulting costs to individuals and society. Clients are a necessary part of the equation that defines lawyers' role in society, both with respect to whom clients choose to empower and with respect to clients' influence on lawyers' goals and methods.

Clients decide to engage lawyers for many different reasons. The need for legal representation is easy to see for those who find themselves involved in a legal proceeding. The need is less obvious for matters that do not necessarily require a lawyer's expertise or skill, such as contract negotiations, making controversial decisions, or responding to threatened claims. But the law is complex, and the ways in which it can be interpreted are subject to many variations. Someone without legal training may be unaware of this complexity and variability and therefore not fully appreciate the potential value of expert advice. Lawyers who have experience with the law that affects the rights of those involved may be able to provide useful advice about the approaches that are most likely to avoid or resolve disputes.

Most people have occasional need in their lives for a lawyer's assistance with a common legal matter such as a will, divorce, or real estate conveyance. There are many lawyers who regularly handle such matters as the staple of their practices. A good way to find a competent lawyer to handle a common legal matter is by referral from someone else who has had a positive experience with a lawyer handling a similar matter. Referral is also a good way to identify a lawyer who specializes in a particular area of the law. Good referrals can come from other clients, or from other lawyers. Lawyers who practice in firms may have colleagues within their firms with other specialized expertise. Lawyers also may have had positive experiences with other lawyers who have relevant expertise or at least be able to find out about someone who does.

Many organizations can benefit from an ongoing relationship with a legal advisor for assistance with making important decisions and preventing problems from arising. The role of such an advisor may extend beyond what is strictly a legal matter. A lawyer may be someone with the kind of sound judgment and broad knowledge that is useful for working through difficult problems generally—that is, a trusted advisor. According to management experts David H. Maister, Charles H. Green, and Robert M. Galford, as described in their book *The Trusted Advisor*, lawyers to whom clients can turn in times of difficulty tend to have common characteristics. The following are derived from the trusted-advisor characteristics described throughout their book:

- A focus on the client's interests rather than the lawyer's
- A focus on the client as an individual with unique needs, rather than as someone filling the role of client

- A focus on solving the client's problem rather than proving technical or content mastery
- A drive to be of service to the client rather than to claim victory or defeat a competitor
- A focus on doing the next right thing rather than aiming at specific outcomes or rewards
- A desire to develop and maintain a long-term relationship, including a willingness to take a personal risk with a particular matter
- An appreciation that dealing effectively with people is a good business practice

These are not skills that are taught effectively in law schools, and not all lawyers have the experience and outlook to make them suitable trusted advisors. Lawyers who have these characteristics can be a valuable resource for a broad range of helpful advice when it is most needed.

Clients and the Dynamics of Law Practice

While lawyers may seem to be able to make their own rules, in reality lawyer conduct is scrutinized far more than much of the public realizes. Applicants to become lawyers are subjected to background investigations and character fitness inquiries. Lawyers are subject to professional conduct rules, which, among other things, prohibit dishonesty and other violations of trust. Lawyers who violate these rules are subject to inquiries conducted by professional boards and courts, and those who are found to have engaged in prohibited conduct could face loss of their privilege to practice law. Lawyers also may have liability for harm they cause to clients by failing to meet professional standards. Of course the system does not always prevent wrongdoing, and there are many shades of gray in the rules and law of which lawyers seek to take advantage, as the judges clearly pointed out in *Dondi Properties Corp. v. Commerce Savings & Loan Ass'n*, discussed in Chapter 13 of this book. The reality, however, is that most lawyers do actively consider ethical questions in a more serious way than many others who have positions of influence in our society.

Lawyers' ethical and professional characteristics occupy a wide spectrum. Some lawyers are among the brightest, most thoughtful, and most noble people in society. Some are dull witted, self-absorbed, and treacherous. While individuals should not be stereotyped, the incentives, pressure, and other dynamics of the legal profession naturally affect its members' behavior. Understanding these dynamics is helpful for managing a relationship with a lawyer in a way that best achieves the client's legitimate goals. The following are among the dynamics of practicing law that may be helpful to consider:

The Practice of Law Is Fiercely Competitive   Lawyers know that there are other lawyers who want to take away clients. Lawyers therefore have an incentive to tell their clients what they want to hear, rather than tell them such things as a positive outcome is unlikely or there is nothing the legal system really can do to make things better. Lawyers also have an incentive to make a positive impression on other potential clients.

Lawyers Benefit Financially from Dispute and Complication   For practical reasons lawyers commonly are paid based on how much time is spent for a client. This creates a perverse incentive to prolong problems. Individuals may be able to rise above this pressure, preferring to earn a reputation for solving problems quickly and at minimum expense, and hoping that this reputation will attract reasonable clients. Lawyers who are not so inclined may seek the financial rewards offered by clients who continually get into unreasonable disputes, or who are always looking to prove a point or demonstrate their combativeness. Clients who are looking for solutions without wasting resources or becoming embroiled in unnecessary disagreements are best served by clearly communicating these interests to their lawyers.

Insincerity Seemingly Is Rewarded in the Adversarial System   Lawyers learn to advocate positions in which they may not personally believe. They are immersed in an adversarial environment in which someone else is trying to prove them wrong. This obviously applies to trial lawyers who have to convince judges and juries of their clients' cause. It also applies to lawyers in other contexts, such as when negotiating a contract. Lawyers face a challenge separating adversarial tendencies from their obligation to be straightforward with their clients and to be willing to see things from their clients' perspective.

Lawyers Face Temptations for Self-Interested Behavior   One reason that lawyers are subject to rules of professional conduct is obvious: their clients are vulnerable to violations of trust. Unscrupulous lawyers have opportunities to take advantage of their clients in obviously fraudulent ways, such as by exploiting confidential information or by using their clients' money for personal reasons. Fortunately, few lawyers engage in blatantly unethical conduct. Lawyers face more subtle temptations, however, such as competing demands for their time or opportunities for self-promotion that do not advance their clients' interests. Honorable lawyers are conscious of these influences and strive to overcome them when necessary to meet their clients' reasonable expectations.

Lawyers Have Specialized Knowledge and Expertise that Often Cannot Be Easily Communicated   Many areas of the law require highly specialized knowledge such as tax law and pension-plan regulations. Other fields of practice that many lawyers share—such as trial practice—involve the development of specialized skills and nuanced capacity for judgment. But being a good lawyer often means not only being a substantive expert but also being an effective communicator who is able to simplify and explain difficult concepts.

With an appreciation for these dynamics, and an otherwise realistic perspective, a client is better equipped to avoid problems in lawyer relationships that stem from misunderstanding. Regardless of any lawyer's professionalism, clients can protect their interests and contribute to a productive client–lawyer relationship by actively participating in management of the representation. Effective management includes a client's consideration of the following:

- Keeping lawyers well informed about concerns, new information, and other developments that may affect decision making and representation

- Asking questions about progress in the representation, about developments that are not well understood, and about budgets for ongoing representation
- Devoting the resources necessary for the representation, including making individuals available for consultation, interview, and testimony, and providing access to records needed for research
- Being reasonable and prepared to adjust expectations to achieve the best possible result under the circumstances, even when it does not feel like a "win"

In sum, an effective client–lawyer relationship is a reciprocal endeavor in which both parties focus on the same objective and openly share information and concerns with each other.

Choosing a Lawyer

One of the main considerations when choosing a lawyer is the nature of the representation. For example, for matters that involve preparation of common legal documents that any competent generalist lawyer should be able to handle, cost may be an important factor. In other kinds of matters involving complicated issues or high stakes, characteristics such as experience, expertise, and access to support may be important. Many organizations use different lawyers for different tasks, perhaps using a local practitioner for routine matters, but for high stakes matters using large firms with a variety of highly specialized lawyers and extensive staff support. The following general guidance may be useful when considering whether a lawyer is suitable for a particular matter.

Qualifications and Practices

Most lawyers, particularly those who practice outside urban areas, are generalists who provide services in the areas of law most commonly encountered by individuals, such as basic estate planning, real estate transactions, and minor criminal matters. Some lawyers specialize, either in a particular area requiring in-depth subject mastery, such as patents, taxation, or pension plans, or in an area requiring particular skills, such as family law or trial advocacy. Many state bar authorities accredit state or national organizations to certify lawyers as specialists. The specialties vary among the states and include such areas as estate planning, elder law, family law, bankruptcy, civil and criminal trial practice, real estate, and taxation. Such certification indicates that the lawyer has satisfied the accrediting organization's requirements for experience and examination. The absence of certification is not an indication that a lawyer cannot be expert in the field. Some states do not have certification programs, and many lawyers do not apply for the certification.

Organizations with ongoing need for legal representation may have one or more lawyers who are employees, commonly referred to as in-house counsel. They may also engage outside counsel with needed expertise. Governments also have in-house and outside counsel. The U.S. Department of Justice, which calls itself "the world's largest law office" and "the nation's litigator," has many lawyers to support federal government offices and programs, including U.S. Attorney offices in every state. Many federal departments and agencies have their own legal staff. States similarly have departments of justice as well as lawyers who work for particular agencies. Large municipalities and many other local governments have law departments with civil and criminal responsibilities.

Lawyers rarely work without the support of other people. Complex or high-stakes litigation may require more than one lawyer to be involved. Many lawyers involve paralegals, who are also sometimes called legal assistants. A paralegal has usually not been to law school but often has completed a formal paralegal educational program about law and the legal process. They typically do such things as interview witnesses, collect and manage documents, and prepare exhibits for trial. The charge for paralegal time is usually far less than for lawyers' time. Paralegals have the added advantage of being very skilled at a task that does not require, but otherwise might be done by, a lawyer.

Some Questions to Consider

Someone without much experience hiring and working with lawyers may wonder about appropriate questions to ask to explore whether any particular lawyer is suitable for the kind of representation being considered. Lawyers tend to be adept conversationalists even in stressful situations, and they are likely to be perceived as authorities not only about law but also about the nature of an appropriate client–lawyer relationship. These dynamics should not cause clients to engage a lawyer on blind faith. Instead, potential clients should ask relevant direct questions and lawyers should give informative straightforward answers. Although there can be no generic list of questions to fit all circumstances, some of the following may be worth asking to assess whether a lawyer would be a good fit:

What is your experience with this type of issue or problem?   Experience can be helpful to a lawyer not only for subject mastery but also for communicating with opposing lawyers, navigating the system, and avoiding pitfalls. The specific nature of a lawyer's experience matters. Lawyers who are experienced generalists may be effective at providing representation for common legal issues. For specialized matters more specific experience may be important.

What is the nature of the clients whom you have represented in connection with this type of issue or problem?   In some fields a lawyer's experience may be with particular kinds of clients. For example, lawyers who have previously represented government units may come to the relationship with a better understanding of the nature of government decision making and billing management. Experience with certain kinds of clients may contribute to a smoothly functioning client–lawyer relationship.

What rates will be charged by those who might work on this matter?   As described in the section on compensation, legal fees vary widely and the total fees for many legal matters are unpredictable. Hourly rates are only one factor in the calculation of expected cost, but they should be discussed.

Based on your experience with similar issues or problems, what do you anticipate to be the likely range of total fees and costs? For most kinds of representation there are too many variables for a lawyer to be able to predict total fees confidently, but experienced lawyers should be willing to discuss the range of fees and costs that other clients have incurred in similar situations. The answer to this question may be more important than hourly rates as a gauge of cost effectiveness. The aggregate fees incurred can vary among lawyers to a surprising degree.

How much of the work will you do yourself and will you check with me before you assign work to others for which I will be charged? Some experienced lawyers are valued by their firms mostly as "rainmakers" who bring in work for assignment to others. Clients should want to know about the capabilities and experience of those who will actually be doing their work. If a client's decision about representation is based on the capabilities and experience of a particular lawyer, the client probably wants this particular lawyer to handle the matter or at least be directly involved with it. On the other hand, some tasks can be handled just as well, or better, by a junior lawyer, paralegal, or other specialist whose billing rate is lower. For example, research, depositions, and analysis may be more cost-efficiently performed by someone who regularly handles such tasks. A lawyer who seeks to develop a trusting relationship with a client should welcome client involvement in decisions about who will be working on the matter.

Will you provide a written estimate of expected fees and costs and contact me before I incur charges that vary significantly from that estimate? In most lawyer engagements there is no requirement for a fee agreement to be put in writing. For some kinds of representation the rules of professional conduct or other rules do require a written agreement, as may be the case for a fee that is contingent on the outcome of the case. Even when not required the best practice usually is for lawyers to provide at least an "engagement letter" to outline the scope of the representation and any specific client goals, especially for new client–lawyer relationships. The letter will indicate the responsible lawyer's fee structure and billing procedures, the identity of other lawyers and specialists who may work on the file and their rates, and any requirements for client approval before other individuals work on the file. Some clients, including government units subject to public finance constraints, require a budget of anticipated expenses and specify the billing format and schedule.

Client–Lawyer Relationship

The nature of the relationship between client and lawyer is shaped not only by their agreement but also by rules and expectations for professional conduct. Although there are many considerations that affect any particular professional relationship, the following aspects are likely to be prominent in the course of legal representation.

Loyalty

An important feature of the client–lawyer relationship is the client's ability to expect that the lawyer's judgment will be exercised in the client's best interest, not in the best interest of the lawyer or the lawyer's other clients. Rules of professional conduct, and common sense, prohibit lawyers from engaging in obvious conflicts of interest. For example, a lawyer may not simultaneously represent a government unit and its employee against a claim if they seek to hold each other solely responsible. Conflicts of interest are not always so obvious, however, and the rules for avoiding them are full of subtleties. Two overarching considerations may help prevent problems. First, lawyers should talk to clients not only about actual direct conflicts but also about what could reasonably be perceived as potential conflicts. Second, a client should not hire or continue to engage a lawyer unless the client is comfortable that the lawyer will faithfully represent the client's best interests.

According to the rules of professional conduct, lawyers may not represent multiple clients if there is significant risk that the lawyer's responsibilities will be materially limited by other loyalties, unless the lawyer reasonably believes competent and diligent representation can be provided to each client.[1] Even when a lawyer has such a reasonable belief, the lawyer cannot proceed without informing each client of the situation and getting written consent.[2] A lawyer may not represent someone as an adversary against a former client in the same or a substantially related matter unless the former client gives written informed consent, and a lawyer generally is prohibited from using information obtained in former representation to the disadvantage of the former client.[3] With few exceptions, lawyers practicing together in a firm may not be on both sides of matter, and there are restrictions on a firm's involvement even after a lawyer leaves the firm.[4]

There are special professional conduct rules that govern lawyers who are government officials or employees. For example, lawyers are prohibited from representing private clients in matters in which the lawyer was directly involved in behalf of the government.[5] There also are notice requirements and other steps that a law firm must take if it represents the government on a matter as to which a member of the firm would be disqualified by prior government service.[6]

Lawyers' duties of loyalty extend to handling client property. They have strict duties to segregate and safeguard client funds entrusted to them.[7] Misappropriation of client funds usually leads to disbarment and sometimes criminal prosecution. Generally, clients also are entitled to have access to documents in the lawyer's possession that were collected during representation. Upon termination of representation the lawyer is obliged to turn over the file to the client or, at the client's direction, to the client's new lawyer. State law may provide a lawyer with some right to payment of fees owed in connection with turning over files.

Confidentiality

The "attorney–client privilege" enables clients to communicate with their lawyers confidentially. The privilege is intended to allow clients to be candid with their lawyers to obtain the best possible advice. Confidentiality also allows lawyers to share frank advice with their clients.

Confidentiality in the client–lawyer relationship is a privilege that belongs to the client. Lawyers must honor the privilege—only the client has the power to agree to disclose information that is otherwise confidential. There are a few narrow exceptions to this obligation, including a lawyer's professional duty to comply with a law or court order and to disclose information reasonably believed necessary to prevent death or substantial bodily harm or fraud that could result in substantial financial harm to another.[8] When the client is an organization the confidentiality privilege applies to anyone who is required to speak for the organization for the facts involved in the situation that is the subject of legal advice. It does not necessarily apply to individuals within the organization who are witnesses to an event if the witnesses do not speak for the organization as a client.

When the client is a government unit, public-records laws may affect the discoverability of information. As discussed in Chapter 5, with few exceptions, such as for client–lawyer communications, public record laws allow anyone to obtain copies of documents that were produced or received in connection with public business. Government bodies usually have the ability to meet in closed session to discuss a pending legal matter with a lawyer. States typically apply this exception very narrowly, sometimes only to lawyer statements to clients, and the duration of confidentiality may be limited to a few years, after which records of the discussion become public.

In general the fact that a communication occurred—rather than the content of the communication—is not subject to the confidentiality privilege. Merely providing a document to a lawyer, or having a lawyer attend a meeting, does not make the content of the document or meeting confidential, unless the information is otherwise privileged legal advice. If the lawyer's involvement in a communication is in an administrative or business role rather than in the role of legal advisor, the communication will not be subject to the privilege.

To prevent inadvertent disclosure of confidential material, clients and lawyers should safeguard it by invariably adhering to common sense practices. They should consider whether information is expected to be kept confidential before communicating rather than after when it may have already been disseminated. Confidential documents should be marked as such and should be stored away from information that is not protected. The information should be shared only with those who are directly involved with handling the legal matter for the organization. Sharing otherwise confidential information with a third party could be a waiver of the privilege unless the third party's involvement is necessary in connection with legal advice. Although there are rules that may prevent use of confidential information that has been inadvertently disclosed, those rules are subject to exceptions and may be of only pyrrhic value once the information is known by someone with an adverse interest.

Decision-Making Authority

Lawyers often speak for their clients, but they do not have unfettered authority to do so. Clients are entitled to make fundamental decisions about objectives of representation—such as whether to settle a civil case or plead guilty to a criminal charge. Lawyers give advice about the merits and risks of these objectives and the ways in which they can be accomplished.

According to the lawyers' rules of professional conduct they have discretion to make decisions about the means for pursuing their clients' objectives, such as what motions to file and what witnesses to call in a case, but lawyers must consult with their clients about significant decisions and keep them informed about details.[9]

A lawyer may have authority to bind a client to an agreement if, under the circumstances, a reasonable person would believe that the client authorized the lawyer to act in the client's behalf, even if the client did not actually give the lawyer that authority. This is known as "apparent authority." The rules vary among jurisdictions, but in general apparent authority exists when the client has said or done something that gives others the impression of authority. To avoid misunderstandings about authority, those who represent the government should be clear about any approvals that are needed before an agreement can bind the government, such as the need for a vote of an elected body. Some courts have held that those who deal with the government have an obligation to determine approval requirements for themselves regardless of whether the government's representative is aware of them. Accordingly, those who deal with the government should be clear in their own minds about any approval contingencies.

Compensation

Legal fees are a cost of doing business for most organizations, especially when operations involve significant risks of dispute and liability. Most government units have a limited budget for routine legal representation. Unexpected developments can result in substantial fees that divert resources from other more productive uses. Regardless of whether legal fees are anticipated or extraordinary, an understanding of the basic nature of compensation arrangements can be helpful for effective planning and management.

For many routine legal matters, such as preparation of a straightforward deed or a simple will, lawyers charge a flat fee that is likely to be comparable with fees that other lawyers in the same community charge for the same service. For representation that requires more than preparation of a fairly standard document, most lawyers charge on an hourly basis for their time and for the time of other lawyers and legal assistants to whom they delegate work on the matter. They usually charge for all the time they spend in a client's behalf, whether it is drafting a document, cross-examining a witness, doing legal research, or returning a phone call. Compensation agreements usually also require the client to pay actual expenses. Some expenses, such as photocopying costs and filing fees, may be relatively small; more substantial expenses include such things as transcripts and expert fees, which can cost thousands of dollars each.

The fees charged by lawyers and other legal professionals vary widely. They depend on locale, experience, and expertise, among other things. Rates for experienced lawyers can be less than $100 per hour, often are $100–$200 per hour, and can be more than $1,000 per hour for specialists in large firms. Hourly rates for paralegals can be $50–$200 per hour or more. Government units and other organizations with ongoing needs for legal services may be able to reach agreement with lawyers for fees that are below rates charged to other kinds of clients, based on the lawyer's expectation of reliable payment and a continuing relationship. These agreements usually apply to routine matters and not when highly specialized experience is required.

Under most circumstances lawyers are not required by law or the rules of professional conduct to provide a written statement of their fees, but the rules of professional conduct encourage them to communicate about the fees within a reasonable time after beginning the representation, and to communicate about any changes in rate or fee.[10] The rules of professional conduct prohibit lawyers from charging an "unreasonable fee," but the rules allow consideration of a number of factors in determining what is reasonable, including the nature of the work, the lawyer's experience, the amount involved and results obtained, and the effect of the representation on the lawyer's ability to work for other clients.[11] A client and lawyer can agree to adjust the fee based on the results obtained. A contingent fee based on a percentage of damages obtained in a case is common in personal injury cases but unusual in other kinds of representation. Many jurisdictions require contingent fees agreements to be in writing, and even if not required a written agreement is appropriate to make sure the parties understand the terms of their agreement, such as how the percentage is calculated, the extent of services to be provided for the fee including whether representation on appeal is included, and whether expenses are deducted before or after the fee is calculated. The rules of professional conduct prohibit contingent fee agreements for obtaining a divorce, alimony, or domestic relations property settlement, or for representing a defendant in a criminal matter.[12]

Compensation arrangements can be creative. For example, some lawyers will agree to a fixed amount as a fee when they know from experience what to expect. Fee agreements can also involve incentives. For example, a lawyer may agree to a guaranteed rate or fee if there is the possibility of a bonus based on the outcome. These are matters for discussion when the lawyer is hired.

Of course a lawyer's livelihood depends on receipt of fees earned. Compensation agreements usually involve monthly billing and payment within a similar time frame. Often lawyers will request that clients deposit an amount at the start of significant representation, especially in new relationships, to be held as security for payment until the end or to be applied to periodic bills. If a client fails to pay, a lawyer may be entitled to terminate the representation, and in some states a lawyer may retain possession of the client's papers, money, and property held by the lawyer in the course of representation as security for payment of fees. This "attorney's lien" may also allow retention of amounts that the lawyer recovered for the client as a judgment.

Fee disputes between clients and their lawyers are not uncommon, especially when the client is unsatisfied with the results of the representation. Legal costs can mount quickly, and paying them can be especially unwelcome when the matter for which the representation was provided generated financial loss. Disagreements over fees sometimes result from unreasonable client expectations, and often disagreement could have been avoided with better communication. Sometimes the problem is a lawyer's lack of attention to reasonable cost controls. The following are among the expenses that most commonly raise concerns:

- Billing for one lawyer's consultation with another lawyer in the same firm when the additional lawyer adds no expertise or other value for the client
- Billing for time spent researching law of which the lawyer should already be familiar as part of the lawyer's reasonably anticipated expertise

- Billing for time spent working on drafting standard documents when the drafting adds nothing of substance or of value to the client
- Billing for housekeeping matters, such as for printing a cover letter that adds nothing to the enclosure
- Billing for routine administrative expenses, such as word processing or filing
- Marking up out-of-pocket costs, such as photocopying or mail
- Conducting expensive discovery in litigation that can lead only to irrelevant or already known or easily obtained information
- Billing for time spent in litigation fighting over discovery or procedural matters that are of no real importance in the case
- Billing for time spent quibbling with opposing counsel over inconsequential details

Concerns about billing issues are best addressed as they first arise before the relationship has soured.

Lawyers and Insurance Coverage

Circumstances that result in legal entanglements often involve insurance. Most people are aware that automobile policies cover liabilities associated with traffic accidents and homeowners' policies cover property losses. They may be less aware that many kinds of public, organizational, and commercial disputes are covered by liability insurance that may provide resources not only to pay claims but also to engage a lawyer to defend against those claims. The availability of such benefits depends, however, on compliance with the actual terms of any applicable policies.

Insurance policies are contracts, and their coverage is defined by the policies' terms and conditions. Policies define who is covered, the acts and period for which coverage exists, the maximum amount of coverage, the obligations of those covered by the insurance to give notice and to cooperate in defense of claims, and the parties' other rights and obligations.

When insurance coverage is available, policies typically require the insurer to defend against the claim and to pay for a lawyer if one is necessary. Policies typically authorize the insurance company to select the lawyer when a defense is provided. Policies may also give the insurer the option of paying the claim, or settling it, rather than defending against it. Insurance policies also usually give the insurer the right to negotiate directly with someone suing the insured for a covered claim, and the right to settle the claim. Typical policies prohibit an insured from admitting liability or settling a claim without the insurance company's prior agreement. Doing so could be a basis for denying coverage.

When lawyers are involved with insurance coverage, the insured person or organization should be clear about whom the lawyer represents. Insurers sometimes engage lawyers to represent their own interests, such as when there is likely to be a dispute about the policy's coverage. In that case the insured should not expect the lawyer also to represent the insured's interest or to keep shared information secret. When the lawyer has been engaged to represent the insured, however, the lawyer's primary loyalty is to the insured as the client, even though the insurer pays the fees and the bills are sent directly to the insurer. In that relationship the lawyer maintains the same confidentiality with the client as would apply without the insurer's involvement, and the client's consent is required for disclosure of confidential information to the insurance company. The nature of these relationships can get complicated, and the allegiances can become confusing. A client with concerns about whom a lawyer truly represents may wish to consult an independent lawyer.

Lawyer Obligations to Others

Lawyers are advocates. They are expected to act in their clients' best interests and to achieve results advantageous to their clients. They have a professional interest in achieving their clients' objectives even when it works to others' disadvantage. Lawyers also have obligations to others. They are officers of the legal system with a special responsibility for "the quality of justice."[13] They are members of a profession that requires candor toward judges and fairness in dealing with opposing parties and lawyers.[14] The kinds of things that may be expected among business competitors could draw scorn or discipline for a lawyer. Lawyers can be penalized if they engage in dishonest conduct, bring frivolous claims, or pursue entirely baseless defenses. They may have a professional obligation to decline a baseless or frivolous course of action that their clients might wish to pursue and for which they are willing to pay fees. This is not to say that lawyers always play by the rules—of course some do not. But experienced, honorable lawyers know that crossing over the line is not only a violation of the rules of professional conduct but also can hurt their clients' interests in the long run.

Each state has rules of professional conduct that govern lawyers that set boundaries on acceptable conduct toward others. For example, lawyers may not offer evidence to a court that the lawyer knows is false, and under certain circumstances may have to notify the court about false evidence or about a client's criminal or fraudulent conduct.[15] Lawyers are obliged to inform a judge about controlling authority not disclosed by opposing counsel.[16] When a lawyer appears before a court and the opposing party is not present or represented, the lawyer may be required to inform the court about known material facts to enable the court to make an informed decision, even facts that hurt the client's cause.[17] As discussed in Chapter 10, prosecutors have additional disclosure obligations in criminal matters, including a duty to disclose to the defense evidence that shows the defendant was not guilty or that affects the punishment the defendant would receive.[18]

Federal and state court rules impose additional obligations on lawyers with respect to the representations they make in court filings. For example, Rule 11 of the Federal Rules of Civil Procedure holds a lawyer responsible for filing documents with a court that the lawyer knows to be false or that are submitted merely to harass. The rule provides that a lawyer filing a document is presumed to be making a representation to the best of the lawyer's information and belief, after reasonable inquiry under the circumstances, that the factual allegations have support or are likely to have support after reasonable opportunity for investigation. Lawyers are deemed to pledge that their court-filed arguments are not frivolous or merely intended to harass a party or increase litigation costs.

Lawyers' professional obligations also restrict their communications with others. A lawyer may not communicate directly with someone whom the lawyer knows to be represented by another lawyer in the matter, unless the other lawyer gives consent or a court order authorizes the communication.[19] There is no rule prohibiting parties from communicating directly with each other, although of course a party may choose not to do so.

While representing their clients, lawyers are not supposed to speak in proceedings about having personal knowledge of facts or offer a personal opinion about a witness's credibility, a party's liability or guilt, or the justness of a cause. This rule protects the lawyers' ability to be an advocate without having to personally believe in clients' causes. Lawyers must argue about how cases should be decided based on the facts and law, and judges and juries should rely on the facts and law without having to assess whether lawyers as individuals deserve to succeed. It is, of course, a blurry line between a personal opinion and an argument.

Lawyers who violate rules of conduct face disciplinary actions administered by courts and bar associations. They also face loss of credibility. From the clients' perspective, although there may be a combative allure to engaging lawyers known for bending rules or stretching the truth, being associated with such a reputation may ultimately harm the clients' interests. In a particular matter, opposing counsel, judges, and juries may become skeptical about a lawyer's contentions, and this doubt can be extended to the client. A meritorious position may be discounted when conveyed through a voice known for distortion. Disingenuousness also can have a long-term effect. A reputation earned in one matter can affect others' willingness to do business in the future.

Lawyer Termination of Client Relationship

In most lines of work an employee may terminate the relationship subject only to potential liability for damages if a contract is breached. The issue of withdrawal can be more complicated when a client–lawyer relationship is involved due to a lawyer's duty to protect a client's interests.

A client has the right to discharge a lawyer although a court may have the authority to postpone termination to prevent undue delay in a pending proceeding. In some circumstances a lawyer is required to terminate a relationship with a client. A lawyer must withdraw regardless of the client's instructions if the lawyer knows that continued representation will violate a rule of professional conduct or law or if the lawyer's condition materially impairs the lawyer's ability to provide representation.[20] The rules of professional conduct also enable a lawyer to terminate a relationship regardless of a client's wishes for a number of reasons, including if a lawyer reasonably believes that a client is persisting in criminal or fraudulent conduct, if a lawyer believes a client's actions are repugnant or imprudent, or if a client fails substantially to fulfill an obligation in connection with a lawyer's services, such as payment of fees.[21] A lawyer may have an obligation to take reasonable steps to protect a client's interests upon termination, such as by giving the client notice and a reasonable opportunity to find a substitute.[22]

Lawyer Misconduct and Liability

A lawyer's violation of a rule of professional conduct can result in disciplinary proceedings, reprimand, and suspension or disbarment from the practice of law. Clear violations of lawyer responsibilities should be reported to state disciplinary authorities, if for no other reason than to minimize the likelihood of harm to other prospective clients. Each state has a lawyer disciplinary office that investigates allegations of lawyer misconduct and has the authority to prosecute violations. These offices may be part of the bar association or the court system.

A lawyer's violation of a rule of professional conduct does not mean that the lawyer is liable to the client. Sometimes disciplinary proceedings result in a lawyer's promise to reimburse a client, or the disciplinary authority makes such reimbursement a condition of the lawyer's punishment. But professional conduct rules are ethical standards that do not necessarily equate to liability.

A lawyer who breaches a duty to a client by failing to use the skill and diligence lawyers ordinarily possess could be liable for actual damages to the client caused by the negligence. For example, a lawyer may have liability for advising a client that title to property is entirely clear when in fact there was an easily found recorded easement that will prevent the development that the lawyer knew the client intended for the property. Or a lawyer could be liable for missing a deadline for filing a pleading in a case without good cause when the client would have recovered a judgment if the pleading had been filed. In these examples the lawyer failed to do something a competent lawyer is expected to do. Lawyers are not assumed to be guarantors of favorable trial outcomes or advantageous contracts, nor is a lawyer liable for mere error of judgment or for making tactical decisions that ultimately prove to be unsuccessful.

Lawyers usually have malpractice insurance coverage to pay for losses suffered by clients as a result of the lawyers' negligence. Some state bar associations have indemnity funds to protect clients who cannot recover from lawyers.

Review Questions

1. What are some basic questions to ask of a lawyer in connection with possible representation?
2. What are a lawyer's basic loyalty obligations according to the rules of professional conduct?
3. What are a lawyer's basic confidentiality obligations according to the rules of professional conduct?
4. What is the basic allocation of decision-making authority between a client and lawyer according to the rules of professional conduct?
5. When is a contingency fee allowed in lawyer representation?
6. What in general are the professional constraints on a lawyer's compensation?

7. What are some common expenses charged by lawyers that cause clients to be concerned?

8. When an insurance company pays for a lawyer to represent an insured, whom does the lawyer represent and how does this affect the relationship among the insurance company, insured, and lawyer?

9. What is the basic nature of a lawyer's professional obligations to the court, opposing lawyers and parties, and the public?

10. What kinds of remedies are available to a client for lawyer misconduct and negligence?

Notes

1. American Bar Association, Model Rules of Prof'l Conduct R. 1.7.
2. *Id.* 1.7(b).
3. *Id.* 1.9.
4. *Id.* 1.10.
5. *Id.* 1.11 (a).
6. *Id.* 1.11(b).
7. *Id.* 1.15.
8. *Id.* 1.6.
9. *Id.* 1.2(a).
10. *Id.* 1.5(b).
11. *Id.* 1.5(a).
12. *Id.* 1.5(c)–(d).
13. *Id.* Preamble.
14. *Id.* 3.3–3.4.
15. *Id.* 3.3.
16. *Id.* 3.3(a)(2).
17. *Id.* 3.3(d).
18. *Id.* 3.8.
19. *Id.* 4.2.
20. *Id.* 1.16(a).
21. *Id.* 1.16(b).
22. *Id.* 1.16(d).

Chapter 15

Educating Yourself About the Law

It is error only, and not truth, that shrinks from inquiry.
Thomas Paine

CHAPTER OBJECTIVES

After studying this chapter you should better understand:

- The nature of legal research and how to approach it
- The nature of legal reference material and the tools for finding it
- The benefits and the limits of relying on Internet research
- The basic components of legal citations
- Basic approaches to researching legislation, cases, and administrative regulations and decisions

The law should not seem like a cryptology that only lawyers can decipher. Some legal issues are so subtle, or so complex, that their exploration is exceedingly difficult without in-depth legal education and experience. But everyone is affected by the law and can benefit from being better able to inform themselves about it. This chapter describes the basic nature of legal research, offers some general guidance about where to begin, and provides an introduction to widely available print and Internet resources. The last section contains a few exercises designed to give some exposure to common legal reference material.

The Nature of Legal Research

Legal research is rarely about finding a clear answer to a simple question. Productive legal research depends on a good sense that a formal rule might exist and should be consulted. This capacity is developed through experience and education and begins with an appreciation for the nature of legal research.

A threshold consideration with any legal research is the distinction between "primary authority" that governs an issue and "secondary material" that interprets or analyzes primary authority. Primary authority, which is sometimes referred to as "the law," includes:

- *Constitutions*, ratified by citizens or their representatives
- *Statutes*, enacted by federal and state government representatives, often referred to as "laws"
- *Ordinances*, adopted by local government representatives or citizens
- *Regulations*, adopted by federal and state agencies through exercise of powers conferred upon them by federal or state legislatures
- *Court opinions*, also referred to as cases, written by judges to decide disputes; to interpret constitutions, statutes, ordinances, and regulations; and to provide common law rules in the absence of such legislation

Secondary material includes a wide range of research tools, books, articles, and other material on which researchers rely to find primary authority, to understand what it means, and to argue about what it should be.

Sometimes a single source provides all the essential information. Often the law is not so clear, and the potential relevance of various authority must be assessed. Research also might merely confirm that there is no clear answer to a question. Then the challenge is to reason by analogy and from basic principles. Someone without a law school education is likely to be confused about when potentially productive research has been exhausted. Even experts who have completed exhaustive research usually wonder, at least a bit, whether they have missed something important. Regardless of these limitations, educating oneself about the law is worthwhile for the obvious reason that more knowledge about the law is better than less.

How to Approach Legal Research

This chapter should not give anyone a sense of total comfort about finding reliable answers to legal questions. It is intended only to help responsible leaders and managers help themselves better understand law. No one undertaking legal research should expect quick results, especially someone without extensive legal training.

There is no such thing as a generic decision tree or checklist for legal research. Formal legal training and experience may be necessary to research many legal issues. But reasonably literate, intelligent, and diligent individuals should be able to work their way through most issues in order to become more informed and to make better decisions. The following general considerations may make use of research time most productive:

What is the research purpose?   The appropriate scope of research may be different depending on its purpose. Reading secondary material may be enough if the purpose is merely is to learn some basics about a subject. If the legal issue is relevant to an important policy choice or a looming legal claim, more careful and exhaustive research may be necessary and more appropriately performed by a lawyer.

What facts are known about the situation in which the legal issue has arisen? Researchers should gather as much information about the issue as possible before beginning the research. The importance of this information may not become apparent until the law is better understood.

Is there a published guide aimed at the issue? Many subjects have been comprehensively covered in a treatise or other book, including books addressing a particular state's laws. Checking for such on-point resources can save considerable time.

What authority potentially governs? Success with legal research means finding the most relevant authority, and making this determination requires an understanding of the nature of law and legal process. If this were not the case there would not be so many lawyers, courts, and judges, nor would there be so much legal reference material. Sometimes a particular issue is addressed by a single authority, but often the nature of the potential governing authority is unclear until several possibilities are examined. Sometimes the laws of more than one jurisdiction may be potentially applicable. Is it something likely to be addressed by an ordinance, statute, or administrative regulation? If so, local, state, or federal, and which jurisdiction? These are a few of the recurring guiding questions.

These considerations help frame the research. They need to be revisited as the research progresses and the strategy can be fine-tuned based on what has been learned and what has been eliminated.

Where to Begin

A visit to a law library, and especially speaking with a law librarian, can be time very well spent. Law librarians can point researchers to relevant materials. Many are lawyers, or at least have substantial experience with legal issues, and can help frame research questions and suggest efficient ways to look for answers.

One of the challenges to overcome with legal research is unfamiliar terminology. Even basic legal terms may seem foreign. A good legal dictionary is therefore often the best starting point for legal research. Law dictionaries provide brief substantive discussions of areas of the law, and sometimes supply references to cases. *Black's Law Dictionary* is the most common, but there are other excellent legal dictionaries.

A logical further step toward gaining basic familiarity with a law topic may be use of a legal encyclopedia such as *Corpus Juris Secundum* or *American Jurisprudence*. As described in more depth in the section on legal encyclopedias, such resources provide broad coverage of almost every legal topic. Specialized secondary sources, such as treatises, also discussed below, provide a deeper introduction to a specific law subject. Many other resources are available for an overview of the law.

Annotated statutory compilations also can be very helpful research tools. They have collections of cases appearing after particular statutes. For statutes involving many cases, the collection will be subdivided into topics tracking subparts of the statute or arranged by subject. Each of the states has an annotated set of statutes, and there are two sets of federal statutes with annotations: the blue-colored volumes of the LexisNexis *United States Code Service* and the burgundy-colored volumes of West Publishing's *United States Code Annotated*.

A recent court opinion can be an excellent resource for understanding an issue. Most courts provide background for the issues they are addressing including a summary of other important cases. The U.S. Supreme Court's cases often include a very thorough discussion of prior relevant opinions. The extent to which state appellate courts provide such background varies among jurisdictions.

The researcher's task is to use available resources to become as informed as possible about all potentially applicable authority. At some point the research must end, and getting a sense of an appropriate level of comfort (or discomfort) is a matter of experience and savvy. Legal research tends to be disconcerting to those who are just beginning to learn how to do it, and to many who have done it for a long time. Feeling lost at first is common when using legal resources, but usually the process begins to make some sense as time is invested.

Internet Research

Today researchers can use the Internet and its search engines to access an amazing and bewildering array of resources. Researchers with access to these tools have advantages over their predecessors who had to travel to libraries and learn how to use indexes, card catalogs, and microfilm. But today's researchers face new challenges. The ready abundance of resources includes much that is confusing, unreliable, and potentially misleading. The likelihood of finding an Internet resource may depend as much on a Web master's tagging strategy as on any real indication of reliability.

A persistent theme in this chapter is that there is an important difference between finding some information about a legal topic and finding the most relevant authority. No single resource is likely to appear in an Internet search that will be sufficient. Researchers must follow trails of authority, continually assessing relevance and considering other routes that should be investigated. The Internet should be viewed as a door to more potentially helpful information, not as a shortcut to an easy answer.

Commercial Subscription Services

The Internet's promise for legal research became apparent early in its deployment with subscription service databases, in particular the two major competitors Lexis and Westlaw. Other databases also are now available for a fee. For example, Casemaker is an Internet law database made available by subscription to about half of the state bar associations, and VersusLaw has Internet law databases available to subscribers. The kinds of resources made accessible to users depend on the agreement between the service and the subscriber. Various university and public libraries, and organizations, have made arrangements for access to various subscription online libraries. As described below, some of the resources available through subscription services are also available elsewhere on the Internet, and most are available in print form in major law libraries.

Internet legal databases are a convenient way to retrieve cases, statutes, and other primary material merely by entering the citation into a search field. Lexis and Westlaw also allow a researcher to check to see whether a case has been further appealed or overruled, as well as to check for cases that have cited the case in question as can be done with Shepard's as described later. Other legal databases may allow for a search of subsequent cases affecting a prior decision by entering the name of the prior decision in the search field.

With Internet databases, resources can be searched for use of terminology associated with an issue. The search terms can be modified to expand or narrow the search, enabling a researcher to engage in a kind of 20-question conversation with courts and legislators. The researcher begins by choosing a database to be searched, such as court opinions in a particular jurisdiction. The search can be refined by designating other variables, such as the dates of the opinion. The search is then conducted for terms used in the sources, either by constructing Boolean logic connectors or with plain language. To construct a Boolean search, the researcher uses connector characters to specify how the desired search terms will appear in the source, in a manner similar to advanced searches with Internet search engines such as Google. The following are commonly used connectors:

AND, and, or &: Used to specify that terms will be in the same document. For example, to search for cases involving the free speech protections for public employees, "free speech" AND "public employees" will result in cases using both phrases in the same case.

OR: Used to find discussions using either of the connected words. For example, a search for "free speech OR First Amendment" would result in cases in which either free speech or the First Amendment is mentioned. Here is an example of why the user must be familiar with the connectors in the particular service being used: in Westlaw a space between words is the equivalent of OR, but in Lexis it returns cases in which the words appear together in that sequence. To specify that multiple words appear together in sequence in Westlaw the words are put within quotations marks.

/: Used together with other letters or numbers to require that words appear in the same paragraph, sentence, or within a certain number of words. In Lexis w/p requires the words to be in the same paragraph; /p is the same in Westlaw. For example, to find cases in which the word "grossly" is used within five words of "negligent," in Lexis it would be "grossly w/5 negligent," and in Westlaw it would be "grossly /5 negligent."

Use of proximity connectors can be a particularly productive search technique because legal terms frequently are associated together in a particular way. Of course successful construction of such a search depends on a prior or quickly learned appreciation for the appropriate terminology.

Services also use expanders and characters to enable researchers to locate cases using terms that have the same meaning but appear in different spelling variations. The most commonly used are these:

!: When preceded by a portion of a word used to locate terms with the same root but different endings. For example, a search for "negligen!" will locate uses of both negligence and negligent.

* When used together with letters functions as a "wild card" for the place in which it appears. For example, a search for "wom*n" will locate uses of both women and woman.

With "natural language" searches the researcher enters a phrase without regard to how it is structured. The search engine uses algorithms to ignore words that appear too frequently to be helpful and returns results based on the frequency with which keywords appear. Experienced researchers may be better able to target their searches using connectors, whereas the natural language search may be easier for those who are not skilled at using connectors.

Effectively using law research databases depends on familiarity with how searches work and the ability to construct searches that lead to reliable material. Search queries commonly return too many hits or surprising results. While access to research databases can be efficient and helpful, researchers should not assume that searches done based on preconceived notions of relevant terms will lead to the most relevant authority. As described above, legal research is not just about finding an answer. It usually requires ongoing refinement of the question. Despite all of the previously unimaginable wealth of resources that the Internet has made available, search programs still are no substitute for human learning and reasoning.

Other Internet Resources

The Internet has many sites devoted to law resources. For example, most federal appellate courts and many state courts maintain Web pages with their rules and recent opinions. Specific opinions can be found with a term search or by browsing collections. U.S. Supreme Court cases are available on several Web sites. The federal Administrative Office of the Courts' Public Access to Court Electronic Records (PACER) Internet service has case and docket information for the federal appellate, district, and bankruptcy courts. Access is for a fee based on the number of pages accessed and is available to those who register online. PACER allows access to much case material and information that is not otherwise available except by visiting the courthouse, such as unpublished decisions and court pleadings.

Law Internet sites continue to evolve. Many libraries provide links to collections of law-related resources. Among the sites available at the time of publication of this book are the following:

FindLaw (http://www.findlaw.com) is a portal that organizes law-related material on the Internet. It has an annotated U.S. Constitution with commentary and citations to U.S. Supreme Court cases addressing particular constitutional provisions. The "For Legal

Professionals" section contains links to a broad range of primary material, including state and federal codes and court opinions available on the Internet, as well as encyclopedic and other secondary material. It also has sections with news about the law, and information about lawyers and the legal profession.

Hieros Gamos (http://www.hg.org) calls itself a "worldwide legal directory" and has links to resources about law and the legal profession in the United States and other countries. Most links are accompanied by brief descriptions of the resource to which they are connected.

Internet Legal Resource Guide (http://www.ilrg.com) has an index to thousands of Web sites internationally.

Jurist (http://www.jurist.law.pitt.edu), maintained by the University of Pittsburgh School of Law, has news articles and commentaries about current legal topics.

Legal Information Institute (http://www.law.cornell.edu) is maintained by Cornell Law School. It has a searchable database with the U.S. Code and U.S. Supreme Court opinions, as well as extensive links to federal and state codes and opinions, and other federal, state, and international primary material. It also has articles about many basic law topics, a guide to legal citation, and links to directories about lawyers, libraries, and reference material.

Library of Congress (http://www.loc.gov) maintains a number of databases and links to international, federal, and state law. Its "Guide to Law Online" (http://www.loc.gov/law/help/guide.html) provides topically organized descriptive links to online information about government and law. The site also provides commentary on current issues, with recommended resources.

U.S. Government Reference Center and General Government (http://www.usa.gov/Topics/Reference_Shelf/Laws.shtml) provides general information about federal laws and regulations and links to laws and regulations.

Zimmerman's Research Guide (http://www.lexisnexis.com/infopro/zimmerman), composed by a law librarian, is an encyclopedia of law-research topics, including brief descriptions of law terms and links to reference material.

Being Current

The law is always changing, but publications are revised only occasionally. Internet databases may be updated more quickly than print, but there still is delay between a change in the law and its incorporation into a database. The status of any legal resource should be checked before concluding that it reflects current law.

Supplements, Pocket Parts, and Other Updates

Law publishers use various methods to update their information. Some volumes, such as statutory compilations, are reprinted in their entirety as frequently as annually. Publications in looseleaf binders similarly are frequently updated, with page substitutions as well as inserts. Many books are periodically updated with supplements. When supplements are inserted into the inside of the back cover of a book they are called "pocket parts," and when they are printed separately they usually are just called "supplements." Publishers of statutes and case reporters also issue "advance sheets," which are periodic paper supplements to bound volumes. Researchers must be careful to check publication dates and to look for updated supplementary material. When using Internet databases, researchers should check for information about the last date on which the database was revised.

Shepard's Citations and Internet Search Service Updates

The burgundy-colored volumes known as *Shepard's Citations* are a valuable resource for linking a particular case or statute to other cases or statutes addressing the same issue. Lawyers still commonly refer to the process of checking to see whether a case has been affected by a later-decided case as "Shepardizing." The Westlaw electronic search service has a similar feature called "KeyCite," which provides cross-references using the West key number system, which is discussed below. Both Lexis and Westlaw have a feature that checks for cases that overrule or question the case been viewed ("AutoCite" in Lexis, "InstaCite" in Westlaw).

Sherpardizing serves two main important functions. It is a means of checking to see whether a particular case remains binding authority. It also is a way to identify other authority that addresses the same issue.

There are more than 200 different Shepard's series covering cases, statutes, and other resources. To use the print version, a researcher looks up a case or statute in the appropriate volumes using basic citation information—volume and page for a case, statute number for a statute. Shepard's will have a list of the citations for other cases, and other resources such as law review articles, that have mentioned the subject of the inquiry. For example, if a New Jersey case cites an Idaho case for some proposition, the Shepard's list for the Idaho case will provide a cross-reference to the New Jersey case. Often headnote numbers (discussed in the section on the key number system below) are shown to identify particular issues that are discussed in the cross-reference. Shepard's does this by including a number corresponding to the head-noted issue to which the case is referring.

Shepard's uses single-letter abbreviations to note whether a cross-reference appears to have some bearing on the continued validity of the case being looked up in Shepard's. For example, an "r" will appear if the opinion was reversed on appeal or a "c" if the other case disagrees with the subject case's reasoning. A list of abbreviations appears in each volume. The following is an example of a hypothetical listing for a case that is reported at the Atlantic Reporter 2d Series, volume 200, page 12:

Vol. 200

- 12 -

(125NH102)

202A2d[1]450

d 210A2d812d

o 212A2d16

The parenthetical "(125NH102)" refers to where the same opinion appears in another reporter, in this case the New Hampshire Supreme Court's official reporter. Shepard's is therefore useful for finding opinions when the citation in hand is to a reporter other than what is available. The next item (202A2d¹450) identifies a case addressing the same issue summarized in the first headnote of the subject case being Shepardized. The third item (d 210A2d812d) is a citation to a case that makes a distinction between the linked cases—thus the abbreviation "d." The final item (o212A2d16) is a reference to a case that overrules the case being examined—thus the abbreviation "o." This is obviously an important development that fundamentally affects the persuasive value of the subject case.

To check for all potentially relevant and related authority, the researcher must check all volumes and supplements published since the case or legislation being Shepardized was decided or enacted. This usually involves at least one bound volume, a cumulative annual supplement, and cumulative monthly supplements. Supplements have a "What Your Library Should Contain" statement that lists the parts of a complete set.

Legal Citations Generally

A citation is a reference to a resource. Citations are important to enable readers to go directly to the cited resource to confirm the reference and, if desired, to follow a trail toward further research. The nature of some citations is readily apparent, such as a book cited with an author's name, title, and date of publication. In essence a citation to a legal resource should give a reader enough information to see the resource's relevance and significance. But many law references are in a form that, to be understood, requires some familiarity with legal citation conventions. Law students toil with learning the intricacies of legal citation and become intimately familiar with *The Bluebook, A Uniform System of Citation*, which is compiled by the editors of four law reviews and has long generally been considered the "bible" of citation form. Those who are writing to communicate basic information about the law, rather than for publication in a law journal, need not be concerned that form matches what is prescribed in any manual. But they should be concerned about sufficiently identifying sources to enable a reader to recognize a source and to locate it easily for examination. The safe approach is that whenever in doubt give more information rather than less.

Shortened forms of citation are used when a full citation to an authority has already been provided. Conventions have changed over time and are not uniformly followed. Typically, once a case citation has been provided in full later citations to the same case provide only a shortened version of the case name, volume, and page number. Cross-references sometimes are made using the following directions:

> *Supra* to refer to material previously cited in full in the document.
> *Infra* to refer to material later cited in the document.
> *Id.* to refer to material cited in an immediately preceding citation or footnote.

Researching Legislation

In legal terminology a "statute" is an enactment of the U.S. Congress or a state legislature currently in effect. An individual legislative enactment is usually called a "law" or a "session law." Laws can be new statutes or revisions to or repeals of previously enacted statutes. Municipal and other local government legislative acts are generally referred to as "ordinances."

How to Read Legislation

A good starting point when reading a statute is to consider it as a whole. What is the point of this statute, and how does it fit with other statutes? The statute's structure may be informative. Does it have independent parts, or are the subparts interrelated? If other statutes are incorporated by reference (for example, "except as provided in section 100 of this title"), the cross-referenced statutes should be read. A common mistake made when reading a statute is to focus on a section that seems to provide a rule to answer the question at hand, ignoring another section that contains a qualification to the rule.

Researchers should not assume that sections within a statute are necessarily entirely consistent with each other or with other statutes. Statutes are sometimes compromises of competing approaches, and the result may be ambiguity or even contradiction. Legislation drafters do not always take a comprehensive approach to enacting or amending laws, and a new provision or newly revised provision may be inconsistent with other statutes. There are many litigated cases involving attempts to resolve statutory ambiguities and contradictions, and when the meaning of the statute is important lawyers and courts invoke complex interpretive rules with more than one plausible conclusion.

The rules for determining the retroactive effect of changes in the law are complex. Sometimes questions about applicability can be clarified by consulting a statutory provision's "effective date." Sometimes this is specified within the statute, or it may appear in the notes that a publisher attaches to the statute.

An important consideration whenever reviewing a statute is the date of publication of the version being reviewed. Print volumes are at most published annually, and a statute appearing in any print volume may have been affected by later legislation. Publishers provide various forms of print updates, but they can become dated. To determine whether a statute may have been revised after the printed supplements, the most likely useful resource is the particular state legislature's Web site, which will contain lists of enacted bills and hopefully some additional reference material that connects the bills to the affected statutes. An understanding of when a legislature is in session can be helpful because no changes will occur while it is in recess. Most state legislatures meet for only a few months in any given year.

How to Find Legislation

A researcher must first assess whether an issue is likely to be addressed by a statute. Assessing whether a matter is likely to be addressed by federal or state law depends on a basic understanding of the federalist system, a general sense of matters that have been addressed by Congress and the states, and what is learned during the research. These topics are introduced in Chapter 1 of this book.

Statutory compilations are organized topically, and the table of contents may be useful for identifying potentially applicable provisions. Topics tend to be very general, however, and their coverage may not match the researcher's expectation. Potentially relevant provisions may appear under more than one topic. Statutes are enacted at various times, and the collection rarely undergoes a comprehensive logical reorganization. Researchers typically find that they must use other methods to identify potentially relevant statutes.

Internet database collections of the statutes allow keyword searches. Effective searches depend on the researcher's ability to identify the appropriate keywords and to recognize relevant results. Even experienced legal researchers often are frustrated with keyword searches of statutes because the results are too numerous or seemingly unrelated.

Statutory print and Internet databases also have topical indexes. Successful use of indexes depends on the researcher's ability to identify the relevant keywords. Topical indexes tend to be a more effective tool for finding statutes than electronic keyword searches. Editors provide cross-references to related topics, and by looking at statutes together with the indexes researchers usually can navigate their way to relevant provisions. Of course the researcher still must be able to identify the relevant index terms, which may require creative thought as well as adaptation during the research.

Federal Statutes

The Government Printing Office publishes all laws enacted by Congress in the United States Statutes at Large. The legislative acts are published in chronological order.

The U.S. House of Representatives publishes a consolidation of the federal statutes in effect at the time of publication in the United States Code (U.S.C.). It is considered to be the official reporter and is cited in formal court pleadings. A citation in the form of "18 U.S.C. § 1001" would be to section 1001 of title 18. The federal statutes are organized in 50 titles. The code is published every 6 years, with cumulative annual supplements. An electronic version is available on the GPO Access site (http://www.gpoaccess.gov/legislative.html). Federal statutes also are published with annotations by LexisNexis in the *United States Code Service* (U.S.C.S.), and in West Publishing's *United States Code Annotated* (U.S.C.A.), both of which are updated with an annual insert or pamphlet supplement. Researchers generally prefer to use the unofficial versions because they have annotations and supplements that are easier to use than the U.S.C.

State Statutes

Most states' statutory compilations have a series of volumes organized by topic with sequentially numbered sections. A few states, including California, Maryland, New York, and Texas, organize their statutes into separate codes, or subjects, each of which separately contains sequentially numbered sections. To make matters even more confusing, some states change their systems, and different approaches may appear in print at the same time. Consequently, a researcher who is not familiar with a particular compilation will first have to spend some time becoming familiar with the contents' organization and indexing.

The statutes of every state are compiled and published in at least one print collection, and many states have more than one published statutory compilation. The statutes are organized by topic and usually by subtopics. A typical approach is to have a few dozen first-level parts, called such things as "titles," "chapters," or "articles," with broad titles such as "transportation," "criminal law," and "real property." These parts are further subdivided into subparts and numbered sections. The methodology of a state code's section numbering system may not be readily apparent. It can involve dashes, periods, and slashes in a wide variety of progressions. A common form of reference has two elements, such as "§ 1–25," which would indicate a twenty-fifth section within the first major part.

As a matter of practice, the abbreviation of state codes within a particular state can be idiosyncratic. For example, Alaska cites its statutes as "AS," for Alaska Statutes, North Carolina as "G.S." for General Statutes of North Carolina, and New Hampshire as "RSA," for the New Hampshire Revised Statutes Annotated. Note that the last two abbreviations do not indicate the state, which is a common practice for citations within a state to the home statutes.

Local Government Ordinances and Regulations

Local government units—municipalities and counties—adopt ordinances addressing powers entrusted to them. As discussed in Chapter 1, typical areas of local ordinance attention include land use, business licenses, housing, and local traffic and police matters. Rules adopted by local authorities, such as planning and zoning boards, have the effect of ordinances but usually are called "regulations." Local governments typically make print or electronic disk copies of their ordinances and regulations available and state and local public libraries usually have collections of them. Most local governments also maintain Internet sites and post their ordinances and regulations on them, which affords the added advantage of most likely being up to date. The Municipal Code Corporation (http://www.municode.com) hosts ordinances posted by many cities and counties, with no charge for access to a particular jurisdiction and the capability of searching across jurisdictions for a fee.

Legislative History

Sometimes a current statute remains in exactly the form in which it was originally enacted. More commonly a current statute is a compilation of several legislative acts, including an original statute and later revisions or supplements. The way in which statutory language was revised or supplemented may be revealing about what the lawmakers meant to say or not to say.

Statutory compilations provide a chronological history of the various enactments that comprise each section. Sometimes but not often the list indicates how the enactment changed the statute. This history of enactments that comprise a current statute is "legislative history" in one sense, but this term can be used to refer to other kinds of potentially illuminating information.

Usually a researcher needs to look deeper into the archives of legislative material. Potentially useful legislative material includes committee reports, hearings testimony, and committee studies. Such material is more prolific in the federal legislative process than in the states.

Published federal legislative materials usually link to the public law number of the statutory enactment, which consists of a sequential number for the particular act, the abbreviation "Pub. L.," and the number of the Congress and session. For example, the seventh law of the 110th Congress is "Pub. L. 110-7." In some forms the session also is indicated. For example, because the 7th law was enacted in the first session (each Congress has two sessions), it could be "7 Pub. L. 110-1."

The U.S. Code and Congressional and Administrative News (USCCAN) publishes several volumes each year with federal public laws, legislative material, and executive orders. Tables provide cross-references to the U.S. Code. The Congressional Information Service Index (CIS/Index), with print and online versions, contains abstracts of hearings and reports. The GPO Access Web site (http://www.gpoaccess.gov/legislative.html) has links to bill histories, the Congressional Record, and conference reports, among other things. The Library of Congress' Web site THOMAS (http://thomas.loc.gov) has information about bill histories, Congressional Record digests, and committee reports as far back as 1973 for some material. Lexis and Westlaw also have legislative history databases.

Researching the history of state legislation is more difficult than researching federal law. Some state legislatures, state libraries, and law schools have posted on their Web sites guides to researching the history of their states' legislation. State legislatures do not commonly produce reports in connection with bills, nor do they publish much of their legislative material. Diaries and summaries may provide nothing more than a few words about a bill or its status.

Researching Cases

Federal and state appellate courts publish most of their opinions. The federal district courts also publish some trial rulings and decisions, usually only if the judge considers the opinion to be especially important or to contain a useful discussion of legal issues. State courts sometimes selectively publish trial court opinions on the Internet or in other collections.

How to Read Cases

Publishers add preliminary and editorial information to the cases they publish. The case excerpts in this book retain only the heart of the published decisions and omit much material that would be encountered in legal research. Usually a case begins with a caption and provides the following information:

> *Parties' names*: The first name in a case citation will be the name of the party who started the lawsuit (plaintiff) or appeal (appellant), depending on court convention. The name of the opposing party (defendant or appellee) will appear after a "v." If there is more than one party on the same side of the case, usually all of the names are listed, but it is

customary when citing cases to identify only the first name on each side, and if it is a human name only the last name is stated. For example, for a case brought by John Adams and Abigail Adams against George Washington and Martha Washington, the case name would be cited as *Adams v. Washington*. The case caption will list all of the parties' names.

Docket number: The opinion will indicate the case number assigned by the court issuing the opinion.

Court: The opinion will identify the court issuing the opinion.

Date of argument and date opinion: The opinion will show specific dates, usually both for when the case was argued and when the court issued the opinion. A citation to a case refers only to the year in which the opinion was issued because that is when it became authoritative. A more specific date is given only for ease of identification if the case does not yet appear in a reporter.

Disposition: Most introductions to opinions indicate the outcome of the lower court opinion, such as affirmed or reversed, as well as the identity of the lower court that issued the opinion or ruling being addressed.

Syllabus, background, or other summary: Most reported cases have the publisher's brief description of the nature of the case, its procedural history, and the court's holdings. This information may be helpful for understanding the court's opinion, but it is not primary legal authority, and it should not be misunderstood to be the court's voice.

Headnotes: The publisher usually lists points of law drawn from the opinion, in "headnotes." The numbers preceding headnotes link them to points in the opinion where the court discusses the issue. The headnotes may also have reference numbers, known as key numbers, that link the headnotes to other cases discussing the same issue. Key numbers are explained below. Headnotes are a publisher's interpretation and should not be misunderstood to be part of the opinion.

Counsel: The opinion usually identifies the lawyers who submitted briefs or argued the case.

Judges: The case will identify the judge who wrote the deciding opinion for the court. It also will identify, before or after the opinion, the judges who were on the appellate panel that heard the case, and whether they join in the opinion, join in the result but have a concurring opinion, or dissent or take no part in the decision. A judge may decline to participate due to a conflict as a result of personal involvement with the case, the parties, or their counsel.

Result: The outcome of an appeal usually also appears at the end of the opinion. A mistake commonly made by new law researchers is to read segments of a case out of context with the rest of the opinion and the result. It is possible, for example, to read a passage that seems to be standing for a particular rule, when in the end the court qualifies the rule based on other considerations. The court's entire opinion, and the result, must be read before the researcher can conclude that any part of the case stands for any given proposition.

Opinion: The first part of the case usually describes what happened in the trial court or the lower appellate court. Most courts will then identify and summarize the issues being considered in the opinion. A decision will address only issues that have been properly appealed by a party. Issues that arose in the case but that do not figure in the outcome, or that no party wishes to contest, may not even be mentioned. Most courts will then summarize the facts. Some give a relatively complete summary of the case; others will only mention facts relevant to the issues being decided

The next part of the opinion is the analysis of the issues, usually one issue at a time. The court will describe the issue, indicate the relevant facts, and describe the law as the court understands it. Some courts will provide a full description of authority and precedent: potentially applicable statutes, cases, or other authority, and how they apply or are distinguishable. If there is no authority that is sufficient to decide the issue, the court is likely to explain what the law will be and why.

Analysis in an opinion is considered to be binding precedent only when it is necessary to the result. Remarks about the law that are not essential to the decision—such as those made by way of analogy, or explanation of possible implications—are called *dictum*. This distinction becomes important to a court's consideration of whether it is bound by a prior decision. By the principle of *stare decisis*, custom binds a court not to depart from its prior decisions unless the court is convinced that developments in the law or society demand it. The extent to which judges may legitimately depart from precedent based on perceived changes in society is a fundamental jurisprudential debate, as discussed in other chapters of this book.

A judge on an appellate panel who disagrees with the result as decided by a majority may issue a dissenting opinion. Dissenting opinions are not the law. They can be helpful for understanding the complexity of an issue and may provide insight into how the court collectively might decide another case under different circumstances. Sometimes a dissent indicates a trend that will later become the majority view. If a judge agrees with the outcome but wishes to express disagreement with some aspect of the majority's opinion, the judge can issue a concurring opinion. U.S. Supreme Court justices now commonly issue concurring opinions. Federal courts of appeals judges and state court judges are less likely to do so. A plurality opinion expresses the rationale of most justices in support of the court's ruling when less than a numerical majority of the justices join in it.

Case Citations

A case citation begins with the surname or nonhuman name of the first party listed on each side separated by a "v," for versus. Next follows information about the reporter: volume, abbreviated reporter title, and the first page in the reporter at which the opinion begins. Finally, in a parenthetical, the year is given and, if the reporter name does not sufficiently identify the court, the court is identified by its abbreviation. To give the simplest example, a citation for a U.S. Supreme Court case commonly would be in this form:

Griswold v. Connecticut, 381 U.S. 479 (1965)
Parties-Volume-Reporter-First Page-Year–of Decision

The name of the judge writing the opinion is included in a parenthetical at the end only when the citation is to an opinion that is not clearly a holding of a majority of a court. For example, the judge would be identified if the citation is to a concurring or dissenting opinion.

Citations to other federal court cases will contain the information necessary for identifying the court, the reporter, and the date. For example, an opinion in a case brought by Joseph Slovinec against American University, at the U.S. District Court for the District of Columbia, appearing at volume 520 of the Federal Supplement, 2nd series, beginning at page 107, would be cited as follows:

> Slovinec v. American Univ., 520 F. Supp.2d 107 (D.D.C. 2007)
> Parties-Volume–Reporter-First Page–District–Year of Decision

Citations to state cases also identify the court, the reporter, and the date. For example, the citation to a case brought by Gonzalo Cotto against United Technologies Corporation in the Connecticut Supreme Court would be cited as follows:

> Cotto v. United Technologies Corp., 783 A.2d 623 (Conn. 1999)
> Parties–Volume–Reporter-First Page–Court–Year of Decision

Mention of the state name alone ("Conn." above) indicates an opinion of the state's highest court. Additional information is provided if the opinion was issued by an intermediate appellate court or by a trial court.

Courts decide whether they are going to publish any particular decision. Cases that do not yet appear, or will never appear, in printed reports are called "unpublished." The court may warn against relying on its unpublished decisions as authority. Cases appear in electronic databases before they are published in a print reporter. Citations to such sources include the case name and docket number, a citation to the database and the service at which it can be found, the record-specific identifier assigned by the service, a "star" page number if the reference is to a specific page identifier provided by the service, the court, and the full date of the opinion. A hypothetical example of such a citation is as follows:

> Adams v. Jefferson, No. 08-107, 2008 LEXIS 55555, at *10, (1st Cir. Apr. 1, 2008)

If the information for finding an unpublished opinion in an electronic source is not known or is not yet available, the opinion might be available on the court's Web site or from the court clerk's office as a printed "slip opinion." A citation to a slip opinion includes the case name and docket number, a reference to "slip op.," a page of the slip opinion if the reference is to a specific page, the court, and the full date of the opinion. A hypothetical example of such a citation is as follows:

> Adams v. Jefferson, No. 08-107, slip op. at 10 (1st Cir. Apr. 1, 2008)

Citations will mention later proceedings that affect the significance of the case being cited. For example, if a case has been reversed on appeal, the reversed court's opinion may still be relevant to the discussion, but it is misleading to cite the case without mentioning that it was reversed. A common note about subsequent history is "cert. denied" to indicate that the U.S. Supreme Court declined to take up an appeal. "Cert." is an abbreviation of "certiorari," which is Latin for "to be informed."

How to Find Cases

Fortunately for the law researcher, there are many tools for finding cases. What follows is a description of the most useful tools for general research. A description of any tool is only useful for deciding whether or not it might serve a purpose; the ability to use it requires actual practice.

Digests

Law digests collect and topically arrange summaries of how various courts address particular issues. The most widely used digest system is West's. It uses the West keynote system discussed in the next section of this chapter. The most comprehensive digest is the West General Digest, which includes cases from all states issued during a given time period, formerly 10 years and now 5. Other digests cover particular states or regions. Digests have a descriptive word index that can be used to attempt to identify the topics and key numbers that may be relevant to the research. Digests are usually an effective means of getting the sense of the law for a given topic. They attempt to cover a lot of ground and should not be assumed to include all relevant cases or fully capture their analysis.

Key Number System   West Publishing uses a key number system that topically links legal issues among cases. The key numbers are organized into 400 major topics, and the major topics are divided into subtopics and subsections, each with a key number, for a total of approximately 100,000 points of law. The West editors assign key numbers to issues raised within the reported opinions and place headnotes for each in the order in which they appear. For example, a court's discussion of breach of contract by acting in bad faith was assigned the key number "95 – 312(1)(k)." This corresponds to the major topic "Contracts," which is topic number "95," the subtopic "Performance or Breach in General," which is "312(1)," and the issue k, which is "in General."

A common method for using key numbers is to start with any case that discusses the issue to identify appropriate topics. Then by looking in a digest and reading through summaries under the same key number, other potentially relevant topics and key numbers can be identified. Another method for identifying key numbers is to use the descriptive word index. This involves the same techniques used with indexes in general, but law's complexity and special language can make topical word association difficult. Often a researcher must experiment with possibly relevant topics before finding a promising direction.

Annotated Statutes

As noted in the "Where to Begin" section on page 309, when researching cases related to legislation, annotated statutory compilations provide a type of digest of cases that have decided issues related to particular statutes. The annotations appear after the relevant constitutional provision or statute and are organized according to the subparts of the statute or according to topics and subtopics. Finding links to potentially relevant cases is a matter of identifying statutory provisions that address the same or related issues, then reading the cases for references to other cases more directly related to the issue. Every state has an annotated compilation of statutes, and federal statutory annotations are contained in the LexisNexis United States Code Service and West Publishing's United States Code Annotated.

Federal Cases

As discussed in Chapter 1 of this book, federal courts interpret the U.S. Constitution and federal law, and they decide cases involving state law. The U.S. Supreme Court's opinions address fundamental rights and other important federal law issues. The opinions of the courts of appeals cover a much broader range of federal law issues, sometimes inconsistently among circuits. The district courts resolve disputes and regularly issue opinions that interpret federal and state law.

U.S. Supreme Court opinions are published officially in the more than 500 volumes of the tan-colored U. S. Reports. The opinions also are freely available on a number of Internet Web sites, some of which are described in the section on page 312 titled "Other Internet Resources." The Court's opinions also are also published in several commercial print collections. Unofficial reporters of Supreme Court cases include the *United States Supreme Court Reports Lawyers' Edition, the Supreme Court Reporter*, and *U.S. Law Week*. The *Supreme Court Reporter* uses West headnotes and key numbers.

The decisions of the federal courts of appeals are published in the Federal Reporter, a West publication that adds headnotes and keynotes. It is abbreviated "F." The Federal Reporter is now in its third series or "F.3d." Publishers begin a new series after a series exceeds approximately 1,000 volumes. Cases are published in the order in which the courts release them for publication. Front matter contains a list of the cases organized by jurisdiction. Opinions of all federal circuits are published in the same Federal Reporter. The citation will indicate the circuit. The *Federal Appendix* is a reporter series with some opinions not authorized for publication in the *Federal Reporter*.

All states have at least one federal district court, which is the federal trial court. Several states have more than one district. California, New York, and Texas each have four. Published district court opinions appear in the *Federal Supplement* reporter, abbreviated "F. Supp.," now in its second series or "F.Supp.2d." Not all district court opinions are published—the court makes that determination. Opinions that are not published usually can be obtained directly from the court, or through the Internet database Public Access to Court Electronic Records (PACER) maintained by the Administrative Office of the Courts. The citation to a district court case will indicate the district.

State Cases

The opinions of state appellate courts usually are published in two print resources. The most common citation form is by reference to the regional West reporters, of which there are seven. Most states also have "official reporters." When citations are given to more than one citation they are referred to as "parallel cites." The West regions are arranged as follows:

- *Atlantic (A.)*: Connecticut, Delaware, District of Columbia, Maine, Maryland, New Hampshire, New Jersey, Pennsylvania, Rhode Island, and Vermont
- *North Eastern (N.E.)*: Illinois, Indiana, Massachusetts, New York, and Ohio
- *South Eastern (S.E.)*: Georgia, North Carolina, South Carolina, Virginia, and West Virginia
- *Southern (S.)*: Alabama, Florida, Louisiana, and Mississippi
- *North Western (N.W.)*: Iowa, Michigan, Minnesota, Nebraska, North Dakota, South Dakota, and Wisconsin
- *South Western (S.W.)*: Arkansas, Kentucky, Missouri, Tennessee, and Texas
- *Pacific (P.)*: Alaska, Arizona, California, Colorado, Hawaii, Idaho, Kansas, Montana, Nevada, New Mexico, Oklahoma, Oregon, Utah, Washington, and Wyoming

Researching Regulations

As discussed in Chapter 11, federal and state executive agencies issue regulations about the matters under their jurisdiction and about their procedures. The simultaneously possible breadth and specificity of regulations make researching them a challenge. Federal agencies have well-developed mechanisms for publishing their regulations and the records of their proceedings, many of which are readily available on the Internet. The availability of state regulations and records of state agency proceedings varies among the states. A good beginning point often is the agency's Internet site, which may describe the scope of its activities and have search tools for the agency's regulations. The following are general guidelines about locating regulations.

Federal Regulations

The print collection of federal regulations is the *Code of Federal Regulations*, or C.F.R., with scores of paperback volumes. The regulations are organized into 50 titles that correspond to the titles in the *United States Statutes*. Without a citation finding regulations in the C.F.R. can be bewildering. The C.F.R. *Index and Finding Aids* contain a topical index. The Congressional Information Service also publishes an Index to the Code of Federal Regulations. Each C.F.R. volume is updated annually, in a quarterly rotation. The GPO Access Web site (http://www.gpoaccess.gov/cfr/index.html) is maintained by the National Archives and Records Administration and has the C.F.R. with browse and search features. Westlaw and Lexis also have the C.F.R.

Federal agencies publish their proposed and promulgated rules chronologically in the *Federal Register*, which is printed every weekday except holidays. Each issue contains lists of agencies that have published rules in that issue, lists of C.F.R. sections affected, and the notices or rules being published. The *Federal Register* also publishes weekly and monthly cumulative tables. Westlaw and Lexis have the *Federal Register* for recent years. Shepard's has a volume devoted to federal regulations, which provides references to cases and other reference material. The *List of CFR Sections Affected* is published monthly as a supplement to the C.F.R. print version. This list indicates whether a section has changed since the volume was published and provides a reference to the *Federal Register* in which changes appear.

State Regulations

State agencies issue proposed regulations in a publication similar to the *Federal Register*. Their regulations typically are available on the agency's Web site. States also have state administrative codes, published in print in a series of volumes, which are available at state law libraries and some public and law school libraries. A few states have annotated code publications. Some states also have administrative codes available on a state-government Web site, and Lexis and Westlaw have administrative code databases.

Finding a state administrative regulation is similar to finding a federal regulation. Annotated statutes often provide links to regulations. The administrative code index may be helpful, as well as a search of the table of contents for the regulations issued by agencies likely to have authority over the issue.

Researching Administrative Decisions

Some federal agencies publish administrative decisions in official reporters, or on their Internet sites. For example, the Interstate Commerce Commission and Securities and Exchange Commission publish reporters. Internal Revenue Service rulings are published in bulletins that are then collected in its *Cumulative Bulletin*. Looseleaf services also collect agency rules, as well as regulations and interpretative material. Some administrative decisions also can be found on Lexis and Westlaw. Shepard's publishes a volume covering many administrative citations.

Secondary Reference Material

Law libraries and the Internet are packed with secondary reference material in which authors and editors describe and analyze statutes, cases, and other legal authority. The following are among the potentially useful resources for an introduction to a subject or as part of an in-depth study.

Encyclopedias

West Publishing's *Corpus Juris Secundum*, commonly just called "C.J.S.," is a legal encyclopedia with more than 80 volumes addressing several hundred general topics. The topics appear alphabetically, and each is subdivided into logically arranged subtopics. The same publisher produces a similar encyclopedia, *American Jurisprudence* 2d edition, commonly just called "Am. Jur.," which also has more than 80 volumes with topics and scope very similar to C.J.S. Am. Jur. is available online through Lexis and Westlaw. There also are some state-specific legal encyclopedias.

Legal encyclopedia articles summarize the law and provide footnote references to relevant cases. C.J.S. and Am. Jur. provide citations to both state and federal cases from throughout the United States. Legal encyclopedias are useful for beginning to understand broad principles of the law, and for finding some cases on a given subject. They should not be assumed to be a complete statement of the law in general or an accurate indication of the law in any given jurisdiction.

Treatises

A law "treatise" is a book or a series of books containing an in-depth discussion of a legal subject. "Hornbooks" are condensed treatises aimed at law students. Treatises are published on basic law subjects, specialized topics, and the law of particular jurisdictions, such as real estate law in a particular state. Treatises can be an excellent source for learning about a subject generally, and for learning about particular issues that arise within that subject. The following is a sampling of some of the most well-recognized national treatises, some of which are available on Internet services. Researchers should check to be sure that the available edition is the latest edition.

Administrative:
   Charles H. Koch, *Administrative Law and Practice*

Bankruptcy:
   Asa S. Herzog & Lawrence P. King, *Collier on Bankruptcy*

Contracts and Commercial:
   Arthur L. Corbin, *Corbin on Contracts*
   E. Allan Farnsworth, *Farnsworth on Contracts*
   James J. White & Robert S. Summers, *Handbook of the Law under the Uniform Commercial Code*
   Samuel Williston, *A Treatise on the Law of Contracts*

Constitutional:
   John E. Nowak & Ronald D. Rotunda, *Treatise on Constitutional Law: Substance and Procedure*
   Laurence H. Tribe, *American Constitutional Law*

Criminal:

Ronald A. Anderson, *Wharton's Criminal Law and Procedure*

Wayne R. LaFave, *Substantive Criminal Law*

Education:

James A. Rapp, *Education Law*

Employment:

Mark W. Bennett, Donald J. Polden & Howard J. Rubin, *Employment Relationships: Law & Practice*

Charles B. Craver, Mark A. Rothstein, Elinor P. Schroeder, & Elaine W. Shoben, *Employment Law*

Lex K. Larson, *Employment Discrimination*

N. Peter Lareau, *Labor and Employment Law*

Environmental:

Sheldon M. Novick, Donold W. Stever, & Margaret G. Mellon, *Law of Environmental Protection*

William H. Rodgers Jr., *Environmental Law*

Immigration:

Charles Gordon & Stanley Mailman, *Immigration Law and Procedure*

Insurance:

John A. Appleman, *Insurance Law and Practice*

Lee R. Russ, *Couch on Insurance*

Property:

Richard R. Powell, *Powell on Real Property*

David A. Thomas, *Thompson on Real Property*

State and Local Government:

Thomas A. Matthews & Byron S. Matthews, *Municipal Ordinances: Text and Forms*

Eugene McQuillin, *The Law of Municipal Corporations*

C. Dallas Sands & Michael E. Libonati, *Local Government Law*

Torts:

Dan B. Dobbs, *The Law of Torts*

Fowler B. Harper, Fleming James Jr., & Oscar S. Gray, *The Law of Torts*

William L. Prosser & Page Keeton, *Handbook of the Law of Torts*

Zoning and Planning:
Kenneth H. Young, *Anderson's American Law of Zoning*

American Law Reports

The American Law Reports, commonly referred to as "A.L.R.s," contain articles, called "annotations," that summarize and organize federal and state case law on particular topics. Articles contain cross-references to other articles on related topics. The author lists cases discussing the issue, organized by jurisdiction, and provides brief descriptions of them. When there is disagreement in approach among the courts the article organizes the cases according to similarities or differences. An A.L.R. annotation can be a very helpful introduction to the law, especially if the article was recently written or updated. There are six general law series and two federal law series in print. Early series have their own index, and later series are covered in a single topical index. The collection and an index are available on Lexis and Westlaw, and these databases allow key word searches. Pocket parts and a later case service provide supplements with information about cases decided since publication of the print volume.

Law Journals

Law professors, practitioners, and other scholars publish analytical articles about legal topics in law reviews, most of which are edited and published by law school student organizations. Almost every law school has a law review devoted to general law topics, and many have specialized law journals. Usually the intended audience is other scholars and legal experts. Although practitioners do not commonly refer to law journals in practice, and courts rarely cite law journals in their opinions, some authors and articles have been influential. A law journal article on a subject of interest can provide extensive background and analysis as well as references to relevant cases and other legal authority.

Law schools and public libraries have print versions of many law journals. The Internet database HeinOnline, which can be accessed through many libraries, contains the full text of many journals. Lexis and Westlaw also contain journal databases. These Internet databases allow keyword searches.

The two most common indexes to law journals are the Index to Legal Periodicals and the Current Law Index, which include subject indexes. The Current Law Index has an Internet index resource, LegalTrac, which can be accessed through libraries, and the Legal Resource Index is available on Lexis and Westlaw.

Restatements

"Restatements of law" are published by the American Law Institute, which is an organization of experienced judges, law professors, and lawyers. Restatements are a consensus view on common law subjects, which is derived from cases and not statutes. Most have been reissued in a second or third series. Among the most commonly cited restatements are those covering agency, conflict of laws, contracts, judgments, law governing lawyers, a range of property topics, torts, and trusts. Restatements are not binding legal authority in any jurisdiction, but the rules contained within them often are adopted by courts or incorporated into statutes by state legislatures. The comments and annotations can be very helpful for understanding prevailing approaches to common law issues. They are not useful for a general introduction to a subject.

Researching International Law

International law is a specialty field within the legal profession. It involves treaties, the rules and decisions of international organizations and tribunals, and other sources of authority governing relationships among countries and citizens of different countries. Researching international law involves an understanding of the nature of international law as well as methods for identifying potentially applicable sources of law. The scope of this book permits only brief mention of some of the most commonly encountered international law sources.

Some international organizations, such as the United Nations, provide Internet access to treaties that have been registered with them. Internet legal databases including Lexis and Westlaw have treaty collections. Until 1948, all U.S.-approved treaties were published in U.S. Statutes at Large. Currently, the U.S. Department of State maintains the United States Treaties and Other International Agreements publication available on the State Department's Web site. The Department also issues Treaties in Force, which lists international agreements to which the United States has become a party. The Library of Congress' Thomas Web site also has a page for treaties (http://thomas.loc.gov/home/treaties/treaties.html).

Learning by Doing

Those who are seriously trying to research law for the first time probably will feel confused by the seemingly limitless resources. Searches that were assumed to be simple lead nowhere or to an indistinguishable multitude of possibilities. But with some perseverance the process usually begins to make some sense. As with many challenges in life, legal research must be learned by doing. Toward that end, the following exercises are designed to give some exposure to common legal reference material. Trying to use both print and Internet resources to find this authority will be a good start toward making sense of the research process.

Locate each of the following using library or Internet resources. Provide a full citation for each:

1. Your state's statute that defines what is considered to be a public record that must be made available to the public upon request.
2. The pre-World War I opinion by the U.S. Supreme Court holding, on re-argument, that a federal income tax was unconstitutional.

3. The federal statute authorizing the U.S. Secretary of Transportation to make payments to states for the value of materials stockpiled near federal highway construction projects in conformity with the project specifications.

4. The federal joint regulation of the U.S. Fish & Wildlife Service, Department of the Interior, National Oceanic and Atmospheric Administration, and Department of Commerce, identifying the factors for listing, delisting, or reclassifying endangered species.

5. Your state's administrative regulations specifying the licensure process for real estate agents.

6. The local ordinance in your municipality governing noise.

7. The most recent opinion of your state's highest appeals court describing the extent to which the state constitution requires that the power of eminent domain be exercised only for a public use.

8. A recent federal trial court decision in your federal district describing the standard for summary judgment in federal court.

9. A law-review article published within the past few years about libel law and political campaign advertisements.

Review Questions

1. What useful references are provided by annotated statutory compilations?

2. Why is an Internet keyword search not necessarily a complete or reliable method of doing legal research?

3. What is the function of Shepard's Citations and other search service updates?

4. What are the three print versions of the U.S. Code, and how do they fundamentally differ?

5. What are the most common methods for finding potentially applicable statutes?

6. What are the most common methods for finding potentially applicable cases?

7. How does the key number system work for legal research?

8. In what resources can federal regulations be found?

9. What are the two most common legal encyclopedias?

10. What is contained in the "American Law Reports"?

Index